LIBERTY CALL...
PORT OF SPAIN

AZREAY'L

Gotham Books

30 N Gould St.
Ste. 20820, Sheridan, WY 82801
https://gothambooksinc.com/

Phone: 1 (307) 464-7800

© 2023 Azreay'l. All rights reserved.

No part of this book may be reproduced, stored in a retrieval system, or transmitted by any means without the written permission of the author.

Published by Gotham Books (September 06, 2023)

ISBN: 979-8-88775-525-0 (H)
ISBN: 979-8-88775-523-6 (P)
ISBN: 979-8-88775-524-3 (E)

Because of the dynamic nature of the Internet, any web addresses or links contained in this book may have changed since publication and may no longer be valid.

The views expressed in this work are solely those of the author and do not necessarily reflect the views of the publisher, and the publisher hereby disclaims any responsibility for them.

TABLE OF CONTENTS

Dedication	vii
Special Acknowledgment And Commitment	viii
Meet The Author	x
Plan of Action And Milestones (POA&M)	xii
Disclaimer	xiii
Prologue	1
Chapter One	30
Chapter Two	58
Chapter Three	92
Chapter Four	120
Chapter Five	151
Chapter Six	181
Chapter Seven	212
Chapter Eight	243
Chapter Nine	280
Chapter Ten	310

DEDICATION

    This novel is in loving commemoration of my great grandmother, Laura A. Pelham, who was 99 years young when she went with the Lord! She was spiritual, fun, loving, strong, and the cornerstone of our family. While writing this novel, I knew that she would have approved of the comedy without the profanity.

    As a kid, she always would remind me that 'time waits for no man.' Well…, let me tell you…, as of today, I'm living the truth because time surely does not wait!

SPECIAL ACKNOWLEDGMENT AND COMMITMENT

Above all things, I give thanks and praise wholeheartedly to Almighty GOD and my LORD, JESUS CHRIST, who laid down HIS life for us all. I realize I'm nothing without the ALMIGHTY ONE! HE gives me every breath I breathe, so I'm continually grateful.

God has blessed me with the ability to explore my talents in; inventing, songwriting, literary writing, business planning, and business development. HE has enabled me to dream dreams and live them. HE is my LORD, HEALER, SAVIOR, and DELIVERER, at my best or worst.

There is one thing consistent in my trials and tribulations: HE has been, is, and will always be; according to HIS Word, on which I stand. GOD First! HE is GOD alone!

A momentous toast to my developmental stage fans, who previously previewed Liberty Call in its rarest form through various online excerpts. Thanks to the generous strangers who pulled no punches in critiques. Your welcomed comments, appraisals, and constructive criticism have helped bring Liberty Call to where it is today.

Cover illustration: James Steidl

My hat goes off to my great cover illustrator, James Steidl, at jgroupstudios.com. For excellent illustrations for many occasions, view James and his team's marvelous works at www.jgroupstudios.com.

Liberty Call…, Port of Spain, now listed on Gotham Books website, leading bookseller sites, dynamicdimenzion.com (patent & copyrights) and other official sites!

Bravo Zulu to my adept editor! Thanks for your quality time and endless efforts in making Liberty Call a delightful read. With your help, Liberty Call… Port of Spain has received professional reviews, constructive criticism, and production polishing.

For new authors: You can never do it all with just spell and grammar check alone. ~smile~

My learning experience is that you write one way, proof another, and go to production another. Of course, it seems like there are a gazillion other little gadgets with which to contend…, LOL. Relax and just enjoy what you do and have fun doing it!

For future fans: Thanks in advance for your eager eyes, which first caught Liberty Call. . . Port of Spain's funny and beautiful cover, drawing you near and sparking your curiosity. Your excellent taste has not gone unnoticed, my dear friends.

MEET THE AUTHOR

Who is Azreay'l? He is a freelance, amateur author, inventor, poet, business developer, songwriter, business planner, and visionary. He lives in Newport News, Virginia, with his lovely wife, Mary. His greatest gifts are those revealed from the North, encompassed through extraordinarily vivid imaginations, dreams, daydreams, and nightmares. Spiritual interventions are the creative blessings for his talents.

He joined the U.S. Armed Forces in 1980, served in the Army & Navy, retiring from the Navy, June 2001. He served 20 years of faithful and honorable military service and retired as a highly decorated Chief Petty Officer/Enlisted Surface Warfare Specialist (ESWS).

Azreay'l concentrates his authoring on the success of being a mixed genre author. His first four novels are under copyright by the Library of Congress (LOC). He is ecstatic about the release of his three new patented inventions – GRID-LOCX (a new strategic board game), the Viral Shield (VS-2000), clear face, and Personal Protective Equipment (PPE) and CLICK! (a new, strategic board game). He works diligently on his mega-billion-dollar valuation business plans for his future global-enterprise venture(s): Dynamic Dimenzions, LLC, a mega job creator, which ties multiple LLCs together, i.e., STITCHUZ, and JVINCO, to name a few of over 50 business concepts and portfolios under the Dynamic Dimenzions, LLC's umbrella. Azreay'l's business plan aids new investors in increasing the return on investment (ROI) for these new start-up portfolios while assisting entrepreneurs in launching their businesses with low to no overheads.

Advice to new authors: Regardless of the world, which is full of critics, those jealous of your accomplishments, and those envious because they can never reach the goals you are achieving; so they try to discourage you. Forget about em', as my Old Italian buddy would say! Just go for it, and enjoy what you do, and have fun doing it! Nothing hurts a failure but a try…, some knowledgeable person once quoted.

As for Azreay'l, if he's not working the 9-5 IT Security or skylighting in intelligence operations; he's drafting that next new invention, detailing a prototype, detailing an intense plot for a future novel, or working on that subsequent inclusion or expansion for his enterprise business model.

Azreay'l's hobbies:
- Mixed-genre writing
- Inventing
- Drafting leading company business plans
- Developing strong business models

PLAN OF ACTION AND MILESTONES (POA&M)

NOVELS

Other novels by Azreay'l/Now Showing!!!
"MadUsoul's Crossing" – Spine-tingling and nail-biting, Horror,
"Tainted Obsessions" – Suspense, Erotica
"STITCHES" – Gut-bustlingly, hilariously, and outrageous, Comedy

Other novels by Azreay'l/in the makings!!!
"The Mirror in the Mirror" – Bone-chilling, Horror
"To…, Nowhere" – Suspense, Inspiration
"Forgotten Sorrows" – Heart and mind-melting, Inspiration
"Drugged" - Heart and mind-melting, Inspiration

GOALS

Short-term: To be an established, well-known mixed-genre author, inventor, invention-publisher financier, and chairman of the board of directors for my future businesses.

Long-term goals: Become a business planner and developer for several new Dynamic Dimenzions, LLC's companies, and portfolios. To develop into a thriving, generous venture capitalist and philanthropist focused on impacting the lives of those in needs while improving the lives of others through various owned-non-profit business portfolios.

DISCLAIMER

Liberty Call..., Port of Spain

What is *Liberty Call... Port of Spain*? It is merely a compilation of words pulled together from one's vision, the author, and simply thoughts that have crossed the minds of many generations before us, those with us, and those to come. They are words written yet playfully scripted to soothe the mind.

This novel is for relaxation, pleasurable reading, entertainment, laughter, and a remedy to heal the body and soul.

I spent two years in the Army and eighteen in the Navy. I love my fellow Soldiers and Sailors and other brotherly-sisterly branches that serve and protect this magnificent country.

In no way does the content of this novel reflect the distinguished men and women of our armed services. The locations, titles, positions, and the military setting is an outreach into my military past and the fun things I did or saw while serving as a U.S. citizen, foreign and domestic. Besides, our military only reflects our society, so you can't separate the two.

This novel does not reflect upon or target any group, but it's a compilation of various groups that make up our society.

God gives us free will in his love for us, but the things he despises, I'm growing to despise in my soul as I grow, mature, and wax old.

Note: This publisher has run this novel against quality plagiarism software. All perceived indications of plagiarism have been removed from this document, but if such plagiarism is noted later, I will add a citation in my next novel.

Please sit back, relax, and sip on your favorite glass of wine, a drink of class, or some bubbly while I present to you, Liberty Call... Port of Spain

~smile~

Freedom of speech..., there is nothing like it, so enjoy!

PROLOGUE

In 2016…, off the coast of Spain sits two beautiful islands, Port Copan Retaunas, to the north, and Port La Gaigiuana, on the southern tip.

Port Copan Retaunas is a beautiful paradise with miles of rolling hills melding into rich gardens and vineyards. Its' most elegant beauty and natural scent of the bewildered countryside is full of plentiful orchards. Its background drifts through pearly blue skies and slow-moving white clouds. Retaunas sits neatly nestled in the serene Leggy Valley and is in the heart of Spain's Horny Region. Its thick, tall forest leads through huge plantations and vineyards to breathtaking, lush landscapes beyond one's wildest imagination. Its mountainous coastline is over fifty kilometers, with a beautiful, floral landscape running along the back shores, rocky mountains, and deeply sloped hills.

The suburb is just outside Mount Tittius, where the fabulous country resort, Migrantanise, a place of restful and breathless relaxation and revitalization, sits. Migrantanise keeps the charming scenery of ancient-style angler villages, with one of its leading and most prosperous imports and exports being the United States. Not far from the city, which serves as a starting point for many one-day trips to nearby attractions, like the ruins of Duck Man Two or Pompeii of Gorrilius, is Mount of Sum Yung Guy, attached to Sum Yung Chik. The central city is not as rich as other cities in its beautiful mosaic sights but offers many unforgettable, majestic, and panoramic views.

At the most northern mountainous tip is one of the highest, top-secret, joint-forces intelligence bases, built in World War II-style barracks, with undisclosed, underground nuclear bunkers. It has a beautifully landscaped design, conveying a friendly little community to deflect from its robust military presence. The town employs over two-hundred un-uniformed officers from various nations to make up the Joint Air Force, Navy, Army, and Marine Corps Intelligence Gathering Command (JAFNAMCIGC), commanded by COMJAFNAMCIGC, which falls under Commander in Chief, CINCCOMJAFNAMCIGC. All complicated for sure, but. . ., hey…, well, you get it!

Lieutenant Barry Soliere, a chief intelligence officer, reported here for duty two years ago. He's six-foot-one, two-hundred-and-thirty pounds, slender build, and originally from Boringham, Utah. He's a brilliant, single, has no kids, is a mastermind for practical jokes, and is usually a good negotiator. Though never married, he has a live-in girlfriend, Erica, born and raised in Port Copan Retaunas.

Barry and Erica met at a nightclub on his first night of reporting to the island for his four-year tour, and from that night, sparks flew, and they have been inseparable.

Erica is a registered nurse and soon-to-turn doctor. She's the only woman on the island to capture Barry's attention. Erica's five-foot-eight and one-hundred-thirty pounds, of slender build, with a body out of this world. She's a spoiled military brat, and her relationship with Barry and his pampering has her in another little world.

Barry is extremely friendly and exceptionally skilled at attracting women with his sex appeal and delightful humor, though abundantly playful and childish. Honestly, Barry's so childish that he would be sitting back in the second grade if it were his way, and the only exception would be to be more creative, meddlesome, and conniving.

There are three misfits back in the States: one is Barry's friend, Ken, an old roommate when stationed in Charleston, South Carolina, years ago. The other two are close friends of Ken and are stationed aboard a ship together. These three are asinine and constantly run upper management into the ground daily.

Chief Warrant Officer Kenneth Nelton is stationed on board for a year. He's a prior-enlisted operations type who worked hard to earn his commission. He's the Combat Information Systems Officer (CICO), six-feet tall, two-hundred-and-sixty pounds, medium build, and originally from Spokewater, Idaho. He's single and the most daring, though most people consider him wild, crazy, and a party animal. Ken has been married, but due to his childish behavior, his wife moved into the arms of another, refusing to raise her three kids and a man who needed serious rearing.

Ensign Alfred Boltan has been stationed on board for a year as well. He is the Electronics Warfare Officer (EWO) for the Operations Department. Alfred is five-foot-eleven, two hundred pounds, of a slender build, and from Tupellio, Mississippi. He's single, has never been married, but has been engaged. Though quite yet witty, he's the most unpredictable jokester of them all and a spur-of-the-moment type.

Last but not least is Ensign Gregory Washington, the Communications Officer (COMMO). Greg is five-foot-nine, two-hundred-and-ten pounds, a medium build, and originally from Micponawau, Iowa. He's single and the funniest looking character of them all. Greg's well in touch with his feminine side, an "undercover sucka," but tries not to let it show, especially around his best friends. His demeanor around his closest friends is reciprocal with people he feels more comfortable around. Most people think he's naturally poised but question his nature after a short time. He's particularly outgoing and flirtatious with men and women. Regardless, it's hard for friends to pinpoint his sexuality because he's keen on role-playing, but they're inseparable.

The ship's Commanding Officer (CO) has had issues with these misfits for some time now, never able to tie them to incidents due to their clever misdeeds.

The three usually do things methodically with detailed plots, leaving no witnesses or stones unturned. They do their dirt with low-down tactics whenever an opportunity presents itself, sometimes earlier in the morning when most of the crew is fast asleep.

The CO is seriously contemplating splitting them up to improve senior management's morale. He knows they are parasites and could corrupt others, so he's keen on counseling other officers against them. He always uses them as examples of those lacking discipline and displaying conduct unbecoming of an officer. The CO spends countless hours adjusting their performance marks during fitness reporting, ensuring they are borderline to prevent promotions but straddles the fence on their performance appraisals should an opportunity come to offload them.

These three genuinely have been instrumental in their nonstop practical jokes. They have pulled pranks on the CO, XO, and most senior officers almost daily.

The CO dislikes the lack of leadership these men display and their low productivity in the officer's community.

However, they manage to keep morale high amongst the enlisted ranks, as shown in the Annual Command Assessment Team (CAT) Demographics Report to the CO.

Their last joint effort in a prank sent the CO and XO skyrocketing in anger when they managed to steal a stenciled pair of the visiting admiral's underwear from the laundry room. They intentionally skid marked his underwear with dark brown and black markers and fly them from the admiral's flagstaff while underway.

The CO knows his career is at its end from the admiral's remarks, 'I'll get you for this, you jackass!'" or something of that nature.

In the admiral's and CO's eyes, this indeed was so unbecoming.

In the wardroom (conference room) sits the admiral, CO, and XO discussing an upcoming exercise with NATO.

The conference doorknob begins turning slightly until the lock quietly clicks, with the mellow contemporary music lightly flooding into the passageway.

A beam of light shines outward and into the hallway creasing three fast-jerking heads in laughter.

Barry's foot eases into the door's kick-plate, inching it further open when three slingshots spring tight, a lighter shaking hand nervously trembling while quickly lighting three cherry bombs lunging forward, almost simultaneously when Barry screams out 'Fire in the damn hole!'

The three seniors officers in command follow the fast-moving red balls as they ping off several walls until almost in slow motion when dropping back, flat on their backs, and rolling, then low crawling fast.

They sit with feverish eyes scanning the room, watching each other fade into red smoke while remaining low and crawling to corners for safety, screaming all kinds of curse words. They finally hear the door squeak again with all eyes going back, not seeing a thing but hearing three distinct slaps against the far wall when tensing and screaming.

A loud pop comes, and then a barrage of fire sounds off like distant gunfire when the long string of 100 or more firecrackers sounds off mixed with another rack of a hundred when screaming in fearful voices when screaming even louder.

The door squeaks again, and all eyes go back, barely seeing the door when hearing one distinct slap against the far wall when jumping as the smoke somewhat clears.

The admiral's eyes wander feverishly, finding the makeshift end of what looks like a stick of dynamite when screaming at the top of his voice before taking cover. He flings a chair around quickly, taking cover behind it while pulling another close with the CO and XO coming up behind him and grabbing his fast-kicking foot.

"Kaboomaloomaloom!" The M80 explodes, vibrating the room with more screams.

"Get the hell off me, you idiots! You've got these clowns and demons running amok around here!" the admiral screams, kicking them away.

Barry quickly enters the galley, motioning and silencing the cook when peeking and finding the three still huddled with their backs to him when throwing a big Limburger Cheese marinated water balloon at them and slamming the door.

Their head simultaneously goes over their shoulders, spotting something inbound when instantly, no longer dressed in all whites but red and white uniforms when springing up quick, pissed and soaked with frowned faces. They frown even harder in unison when getting a whiff of the poop-smelling cheese.

From that day forward, the CO secretly put out transfer papers to various commands worldwide, and begins making calls in search of the most degrading jobs available.

Kenneth, Alfred, and Greg soon get wind of the captain's plan to ship them off to shit detail and try straightening up, but it's too late.

The CO is dead set and fueled by the admiral's plot to get rid of them.

One night, Kenneth, Alfred, and Greg chill out at the officers' club.

Reality sets in, and they are depressed about the grim thoughts of separation.

Ken receives a call from Barry Soliere, and put it on speakerphone when they begin having a grand old time, reminiscing on the past. They go through a list of unheard-of pranks conjured up and most in the name of 'good laughs.'

Ken soon grows excited as they stroll down memory lane until feeling as though Barry is in the same room when missing the good old days. A teardrop rolls down Ken's face out of nowhere before he can wipe it away unnoticeably.

Alfred notices the second tear and nudges Greg, who slyly points to Alfred, then dips his head toward the phone in the middle of the table.

Ken wipes quickly but not fast enough to stop it from splashing on the table.

"Man..., you got your boy over here crying those lonely tears." Greg bursts out laughing.

"Shut up, stupid! I was laughing at something Barry did a long time ago," Ken says, cutting a quick eye over at Alfred and frowning when looking at Greg.

Alfred looks off, smiling. "Oh yeah? Then share it!" Alfred responds sarcastically. His eyes wander over to Ken's shocked face, finding him deep in thought when his mind speeds up to a hundred mph in a twenty-five mph zone, trying to think of something funny but draws blank.

"Yeah, right!"

"Just as I thought, man..., your mind is as empty as this bottle!" Alfred blurts out, turning up the empty bottle and holding it over his wide mouth without a drop falling.

"Aw!" Greg whispers. "Barry and Ken, sitting in a tree. . .," he began to sing.

"Knock it off, you freakin' nut!" Ken jumps up in rage with a tight fist, easing the other fist onto the table, eye-to-eye with Greg, not blinking until Greg looks away.

Greg turns, leading into other pranks pulled on the ship while carefully watching Ken, then leads into his creativity until inquiring of available positions at Barry's base.

Barry thinks deeply about how bored he is with the high-strung people there, and then thinks longer, missing the great times with Ken when thinking harder.

There are seconds of silence with the three huddled closer, listening as Barry's lips slowly parted, spilling a devilishly clever initiation of a plan.

Two days later, Barry's plans are final when he pulls off the plan much more manageable than he thought. He calls Ken early that morning and asks him to procure and fax a copy of his CO's formal request for their transfers. He works diligently to doctor the official documents and makes them look authentic.

Later that night, Barry pops his XO's office lock, slips in, and places the illegal documents under a stack of papers in his in-box.

Two days later, Barry receives a call from his XO inquiring about immediate fills for three vacancies and asks Barry to schedule a conference call with both COs before lunch.

That morning, Kenneth, Alfred, and Greg work in their divisions, managing people and carrying out their daily routines.

The PA system keys up, requesting that the three report to the briefing room.

Alfred and Ken arrive in the passageway about five seconds apart.

Within seconds, the XO peeps out from alongside a doorframe. He quickly wobbles down the passageway with a slight limp, his worn-out, thick-hill, padded leather boots making squishy fart sounds with each timed step. He rushes up to Ken and Alfred, and with one last step, his shoes make a slight whistling sound. He instantly put them at parade rest and then turns upon hearing footsteps when bringing them to attention.

Out of nowhere, Greg loudly slams into the adjacent wall, bounces back, and then rushes over and slides next to Ken, quickly coming to attention.

The XO looks at the e-mail, stamped 11:30 a.m. for the conference call. He stares at his watch, which reads 09:30, when sticking out his chest and marching in front of them with a raised eyebrow. He performs various ridiculous-looking facing movements, with squeaky shoes, from Alfred to Ken, to Greg, though now not as loud.

Thirty minutes later, the XO finds them slouched or moving to get the blood flowing in their legs, and each time, he screams, 'Attention!' to get them adequately postured again, and then smiles, knowing they're deeply in pain.

Ken asks permission to speak after thirty more minutes, but the XO denies the request.

Ten more minutes pass when the XO smiles, seeing Greg buckle at his knees; seconds from passing out. He observes Alfred with beads of sweat on his forehead, and Ken with his eyes clenched tight. The XO keeps a straight face, but deep inside, the XO laughs. He turns, making a few more facing movements, putting them at parade rest, telling them they had five minutes for the bathroom and then getting back in ranks.

They drop and kick their legs to get the circulation flowing and then slowly stand.

The XO stares with a mean face and then leans forward, screaming to remind them that they now have only three-and-a-half minutes left.

The three rushes down the passageway, bursting through the bathroom door, then rush back into the passageway with seconds to spare and fall back into ranks. They stare at the mean XO, who's still pacing with eyes glued to his watch. They stay at parade rest until he screams, bringing them back to attention.

The XO stares them down and then looks over their uniforms as if in a full-scale dress inspection, and before long, he performs a left-face movement, patrolling before them again.

A PA system announcement comes for the XO to report to the CO's in-port cabin.

The XO stares even meaner; warning them to stay at attention, then threatens them by telling them that if he finds them any other way, they'll wish they never knew him. He quickly executes a flimsy about-face, falling into the wall, sliding down slowly until his feet move fast, slipping across the shiny floor to regain footing.

The three peeps then look up fast with teary eyes when the XO swiftly comes to his feet and sprints away in loud squishy shoes. They close their eyes tight in silent laughter, listening to his feet banging against the flimsy ladder well until the door below slams.

The ladder-well stays quiet for minutes until they fall forward, screaming in laughter until uncontrollably falling into each other, laughing even harder.

After some time, Ken cut his laugh short, easing his walkie-talkie out. He listens longer, then radios an enlisted First Class Petty Officer from his division and has him report to the briefing room to shadow and report the XO's position and movement.

Instantly, the distant ship's entertainment radio system turns on, switches channels, and blares in the room across from the briefing room, where a young Sailor begins cleaning until dancing, then waltzing with the broom.

Ken spots a female he's accustomed to flirting with approaching quickly.

She comes within inches from Ken and he shoves off the wall, playfully puckering up when her hand expressly comes to his chest, abruptly shoving him back into the wall.

Ken bounces back in a silly dance, acting crazy and performing made-up moves.

Alfred and Greg go into tears watching Ken dance and act silly.

The female turns giggling when Ken advances, circling her to get her to laugh harder when his hand goes over her head in a silly step dance.

Ken's wrist bumps her head, and his button becomes tangled in her hair.

"Oh man..., sorry!" He holds his arm high until he's on tiptoes.

"Ouch...! Ouch!" she moans with feet drawn back fast, kicking him in the shin.

"Oooouch!" Ken groans, and then dances on one leg with his arm still high.

Alfred and Greg go into profound tears watching Ken dance to balance while trying not to apply more pressure to strands of her hair.

Ken slowly eases down and calmly tries to remove the button.

Alfred and Greg laugh until bumping into each other, howling in laughter until a door slams, and they jump in fear, slamming into the wall.

Ken fearfully pulls his arm down fast, spins her out of control to the floor, and then flies backward into the wall.

Their heads come up fast, to attention almost as if precision.

The female rolls in pain until balanced on all four and slowly crawls to her feet with an evil look plastered over her face, gritting her teeth.

Alfred peeps around and then looks at the woman. "What's up, Little Rooster?" Alfred hollers, pointing to the stubby tail of hair where the long ponytail used to be.

Ken does not notice the extension still at his wrist until his eyes shoot to his wrist screaming with wide, excited eyes.

The woman's hand thrust forward. She grabs Ken by the back of the head, slamming him headfirst into the other wall, then watches him stagger and stumble to the floor. She reaches for his cuff, grabs her long ponytail, stands over him with a tightly balled fist, and stares him down with a mean look for seconds.

Ken grabs the wall, balancing. He graciously shakes his head, and before opening his big mouth, she knees his inseam, and he buckles to his knees.

The woman stares longer, then turns, stepping away but looks back, staring again.

Ken remains lightheaded but crawls until his foot goes forward to kneel when her shiny padded leather boot presses hard on his butt.

She raises high on one foot as he advances, then off the other foot, lunging him forward when he farts.

Ken's body springs forward in a fast-paced crawl until dropping on his belly and sliding over the shiny floor until his chin drops, and his arms fold at his side, still sliding a few feet on his chest and stomach. He stops at the far end of the non-skid, which grips his beard and shaves it bald. "Aii! Aii!" Ken screams at the top of his lungs. He shoots upward in a flash, high-stepping until his hands expressly rub the bruised and bald area.

The woman's face stays frowned until looking up, finding Ken with a split goatee. She points, falling into the wall in a burst of deep, possessed laughter, then laughs harder until Ken fades off to the side of Alfred as he falls back into ranks.

The XO finally arrives, knocking three times and entering, finding the CO smiling.

The CO stops swiveling his chair, leans forward, and flips open a document, briefing the XO on the transfer meeting and afterward, orders the XO to carry out the berthing inspection that minute and then meet him in the briefing room at 11:15 a.m.

Back in the hallway, the three misfits continue listening to the woman's uncontrollable, silly giggle while she proceeds further down the long corridor.

The woman closes a door and giggles until louder, and they hear her when they come off the wall, looking down each side of the passageway, listening for the XO.

Greg's stomach jumps up and down, and so does Alfred's. Greg falls forward in a loud burst of laughter, followed by Alfred, who is even louder.

The two-point and laugh at Ken's beard for minutes, and their laughter grows so outrageous that the man in the room across from them stops and looks back at the door.

Within minutes, they calm down.

Ken freezes, then looks up and down the hallway. "Cover for me," he says with hands, running over the bruised area faster until taking off in a stride. Ken burst through the bathroom door, running chilled water and splashing it on his chin. He fills the basin, dipping his chin in the cool water, and then takes scissors from the first-aid box, trimming hair so it's not so obvious.

Minutes later, Ken storms into the passageway, finding Alfred and Greg entertaining each other with jokes about his beard.

At the captain's cabin, the XO exits with the Master-at-Arms (police), guiding him on the berthing tour after greeting him in the passageway.

The junior petty officer, the recorder for the inspection, appears seconds later and the three get constant updates from the shadowing Sailor.

An hour or so later, the XO completes the quick run-through of the berthing areas and rushes to his office with the First-Class Petty Officer secretly following, unnoticed with the low-volume walkie-talkie in his grip.

The XO eases into his desk, completes his report, signs the document, springs from his office, and rushes into the passageway.

The First-Class Petty Officer hides and then turn to find a female officer waving him over to ask questions concerning her division's berthing inspection, and walks away. He turns, not seeing the XO, and runs feverishly to each door looking for him. He peeps around more corners, rushing through the upper decks, nervously continuing his search.

The XO swiftly moves toward the briefing deck via a secure passageway. He flings open the door leading to the ladder-well and tiptoes halfway up. He comes up five steps from the passageway when a junior Sailor in charge of cleaning the ladder well comes from behind him and speaks.

Instantly, Ken, Alfred, and Greg fly back to the wall. Their heads slam into the metal bulkhead (wall) but out of synchronization.

Ken quickly makes eye contact with Alfred and Greg, looking down and motioning for them to make their legs wobbly.

The XO listens for seconds while slowly creeping up the stairs, where he peeps out, quickly pulling his head back when peeping again.

The walkie-talkie blares and Ken's hand snaps, quickly adjusting the volume.

The XO listens to the loud, screaming voice of the First-Class Petty Officer when springing into the passageway with squashy shoes sounding like farts again and this time whistling when expressly wobbling and limping. He rushes for Ken, snatching the walkie-talkie from his waistband, and questioning the transmission, but Ken plays clueless.

The XO step back and turns up the volume when the First-Class Petty Officer screams again to warn them that he can't find the XO.

The XO stays eye-to-eye with Ken until his mouth drops open, and he screams in his face until the door to the lower-level stairwell flings open and bangs against the wall. The XO turns, listening to the screaming First-Class Petty Officer, and then his feet banging loudly against the ladder-well until the door flies open and his body flies up against the wall when overcompensating his turn.

The First-Class Petty Officer freezes and stares eye-to-eye with the XO until his eyes slowly drift down to the tightly gripped walkie-talkie in the XO's hand.

The XO stares, looking meaner, and before he can get a word out, Ken motions for the First-Class not to say a word with a quick finger crossing his lips then throat several times.

The XO closes in on the First-Class Petty Officer and holds the walkie-talkie to his face while drilling him on why he was looking for him.

The First-Class Petty Officer sweats bullets but keeps his eyes pierced over the XO's shoulder, trying to interpret Ken's motions and nervously getting it wrong several times.

The XO grows frustrated, and his finger comes to the First-Class Petty Officer's face, dismissing him when hearing a slight bang and turning to find Ken swaying back and forth from jumping to the wall fast. He rushes over, slamming the walkie-talkie into Ken's chest. He stares the three down for minutes before putting them at ease, then feverishly marches until stopping and telling them why he called them there.

Ten minutes pass when the CO appears.

A junior Sailor about to head down the ladder-well sees the CO and drops his mouth wide open. "Attention on deck!" He yells with everyone coming to attention.

The CO rushes toward the four, putting them at ease before throwing the briefing room door open and holding the door against his back with a devilish smile.

The XO rushes in and looks the room over.

Ken, Alfred, and Greg struggle inside, taking seats and smiling at each other, knowing they're not under observation.

The CO opens three manila service jackets, gazing over the folders as he and the XO begin re-reviewing them, with the room quietly growing to a whisper. The CO quietly sits reading and peeping at them from time to time, senselessly snickering at times. The room soon grows so quiet that one could have heard a rat pissing on cotton two blocks away. The CO pushes the papers forward and freezes until slightly swiveling, deep in thought. He slowly turns, facing them, until staring deep into their blushed faces, and then looks back down; plotting out his deceptive plan.

Ken, Alfred, and Greg begin acting sad, but every time the CO and XO step out for sidebar (private chat), they giggle or act crazy.

The CO looks at his watch and nods for the XO to dial in the shore command XO's conference number.

The XO leans forward, bringing up the bridge circuit for collaboration, and seconds later, the two commands have a successful connection.

The ship's CO briefs the shore commander and staff at Port Copan Retaunas on his three outstanding officers but continually fights, refraining from bursting into laughter, coughing and clearing his throat when discussing their outstanding contributions.

Both commands soon go quiet as they review the transfer documentation.

The CO of Port Copan Retaunas continues looking in silence and then turns to look over their fitness reports while the ship's CO nervously stares into the screen. He closes the last folder, looking up into the big screen, and gazing around at the three, then the ship's CO and XO, who shamefully looked away at intervals.

The ship's CO and XO stare back nervously but intentionally and continually, looking as if busy taking notes while refraining from laughter.

The ship's CO eases a hand over the telecommunications button, muting it. "Please don't let him ask us questions," the ship's CO mumbles under his breath.

"Ok, let's talk fitness reports," the Port Copan Retaunas CO says, looking at the documentation and then quickly back into the screen.

The ship's CO chokes for seconds. He nervously shuffles through papers and then scrambles for a glass of water. Seconds later, he compensates for the embarrassment and deflects questions by putting his misfits on the spot.

Each officer introduces himself and then presents a short biography but the CO and XO nervously watches when Ken stands.

The CO's fingernails anxiously tap against the mahogany tabletop but instantly slow and stop after the first few professional sentences. His mouth drops open in disbelief with eyes glued to his XO.

The biography alone baffles the ship's CO because it's totally out of character.

The three surprise him and don't act like the band of misfits he knows them to be.

After the last interview, the ship's CO is even more stun at their professional mannerisms. His mouth drops open, and his eyes stay on them as if in a deep trance.

The CO of Port Copan Retaunas asks two more questions, but the ship's CO doesn't hear them until the XO kicks him in the shin hard and smiles when the ship's CO lunges forward, in a fast lean with his face turning pink, then bright red. He leans even further with painful tears dropping when going forward, quickly rubbing his pained shin until a few more tears fall onto the fitness reports. He quickly shakes off the shock of the question that finally registers, then the pained shin when repositioning, sitting up, and coming with his A-game. He knows he can't afford to screw up this once-in-a-lifetime, long-awaited opportunity, so he becomes more alert.

After the conference call, the ship's CO dismisses the men. He talks to the XO about how much work is required to get the men processed, including bumping their fitness report up by thirty percent at a minimum.

Later that evening, the three young officers are back at the officers' club and celebrate with round after round of beers and mixed drinks.

Barry is on the third shift coordinating briefings for upcoming conferences but calls Ken when he finishes the preparations for the last briefing.

The four stay in tears, reenacting the classic call, and an hour later, they get out all of their laughter when Alfred inquiries about exciting things to do on the island.

Barry tells them a little about their new jobs, then the places they would go on assignments, four hours away. He gets sidetracked when Ken asks about women but tells them about the influx of beautiful island women. He pauses, and then tells Ken about the right female he has in mind, and then talks about other minor things. The conversations bring more discussions about their jobs when Barry mentions the temporary duty location again and then brings up a few more business items.

There soon become more questions than answers, but Barry deflects talking about Port Copan Retaunas more when transitioning into a slew of things to do at Port La Gaigiuana. He tells of the extravagant resort area four hours south of Port Copan Retaunas, then talks about the island's true beauty, a vision to behold. Barry takes them on a very descriptive tour of the various Chinese castles turned over to the Spanish government in the 1900s. Barry proceeds, naming a few castles, such as Sum Dum Chik, Wai Tu Dum, Tu Young Poo-poo, and Chok Sum Trik, to name a few. Barry discusses in detail the nineteenth-century villages constructed from ancient Chinese walls. He speaks of Spain's incredible atmosphere and classicalism, mixed with its modern elegance. Moreover, he talks about how the region is famous for its millennial culture.

Barry continues. "Port La Gaigiuana is diversified in its province and for the unique, ancient architectural wonders. It has about seventy-six kilometers of coastline and a Mediterranean climate, making its shores perfect for sun-bathing at least six months out of the year. Besides its delightful beaches and magnificent restaurants, it welcomes its unique family-owned boutiques, ceramics, flea markets, and surfing shops. This island offers the most popular summer destinations, amusement parks, and attractions. Along the Eastern Seaboard are breathtaking frogman and fisherman villages that form one of the most impressive marina reserves with many taverns. There are so many extraordinary things to see or sights for extravagant photos."

The three sit, looking at each other in excitement.

Barry gives them a short description of the naval base at Port La Gaigiuana. He explains the highways, roads, and city structure, including its main ocean-going fairway into the island. There is still total silence when Barry meditates on what he might have forgotten. "Oh yeah. . ., did I mention the base being located at the island's far end? Yeah, inside the base is encased, a secluded intelligence conference center, where most planning and coordination for fleet sea, land, and air take place with Joint Coalition Forces (JCFs)."

Ken, Alfred, and Greg's jaws instantly drop open, and their eyes widen.

"Dude..., silence on the line! Did you just disclose classified information like it's no big deal?" Ken nervously looks around. He shakes his head and then looks around to find an old, nosey commander staring with his mouth and eyes open wide in excitement.

"My friend. . .!" Alfred covers the speaker quick, whispering with his index finger to his lips. He stares at the commander, circling his ear to insinuate Barry is short a few screws. "Poor guy. . ., still thinks he's in Vietnam," Alfred shakes his head, and then turns up his bottle, making all kinds of drunken gestures concerning Barry's last comment.

A month later, they have orders and are ready to leave the ship. The three stop by the wardroom (dining room), dropping off the CO and XO fruit baskets with two decorative small mason jars inside, then rush to the quarterdeck (guarded entry area).

"Dinner for the crew!" The announcement blares out over the loud Public Announcement (PA) system.

The CO and XO walk inside the wardroom seconds apart. They take their seats at the head of the table, gazing over the menus placed before them.

The PA system keys up again, and bells ring, announcing Ken's departure, and then seconds later, more bells and the announcements for Alfred's and Greg's departure.

The CO and XO sit gazing at each other with gigantic smiles.

The junior officer, Ken had commandeered in his final departure prank, stands outside the wardroom with his back to the door. He slowly backs inside, turning with both arms full, walking up to the head of the table. He sits a basket in front of the CO, who looks up surprised, then walks to the other side and sits the other in front of the XO.

Immediately, over fifteen officers and cadets gathered around from the other side of the room, quietly watching the CO and XO stare nervously at the baskets for minutes until they slowly lean and slightly push away from the table.

"Go ahead, sir..., you first," the XO nervously says, swallowing hard when nodding.

"No..., you first..., age before beauty..., please, I demand it," the CO mischievously says with an assuring smile. He stares into the XO's eyes until he slightly raises one eyebrow, digging heels deep into the carpet and sliding back a few more feet.

"No..., together," the XO cleverly says, fumbling in his shirt pocket, pulling out a government-issued pen. He slightly slides his seat back, tilting the basket on one side as if he's about to dismantle a bomb.

The CO and XO jump back, knocking chairs backward upon hearing an officer pop the top of his soda bottle in the background.

A burst of zealous laughter explodes, but several officers look on in excitement.

Other officers reach for their turned-over chairs, honorably repositioning them.

The CO looks at his watch and then around at the small audience. He motions for the XO to hurry and then eases up on his basket.

The CO and XO show communicable hand signs, counting down when stepping forward and pulling on the plastic simultaneously, which they inspect, finding it secure.

"Enough of this nonsense!" the CO responds. "Let's get this over and eat some prime ribs." The CO smiles, looking around at smiling and laughing faces. "It can't be wrapped any tighter than this..., can it?" he asks, nervously looking over at the XO and nodding with beads of sweat forming over his face when peeling back the first layer of shrink wrap.

Seconds pass, and the CO and XO finally have the clear wrap off and strewn over the table. They mysteriously look at the entire basket and then lift the two mason-style decorative jars about the same time. They bring the jars high and turn them around, straining to make out the intricate print under the small-looking, glistening diamond.

The CO looks around as he twists the canister with all his strength.

The XO shakes his head and smiles. "You wimp…, let me show you how it's done!" He twists his canister with all his strength with veins at his temple.

The CO and XO twist a few more times and reach the pre-set release levels, simultaneously when the lids release and they thrust their boots into the carpet, pushing back. Their chairs flip backward as a deadly stench instantly rises.

The stench of deadly captured fart and rotten Limburger cheese fills the room when more chairs fall back-to-back, and the wardroom (dining room) goes into an uproar.

Everyone tramples over each other, fighting to clear the funk-filled room and are stuck at the bottleneck in the doorway, screaming.

The following morning, the three misfits sit in a restaurant eating and drinking.

A waiter walks over with more sugar and miniature caffeine tablets, placing them in their cups. She returns later, and Alfred asks for a half-cup of sugar and caffeine cubes to go, and she honors it; easing the large, half-full cup from another table onto the table.

The three are in deep conversation when a different female server comes over and refills their cups as they become distracted when breaking news comes on about expected crummy weather brewing in the Atlantic Ocean.

The server runs off at the mouth and does not pay attention when accidentally pouring coffee over the tall, half-full cup of sugar and caffeine tablets, easing down another cup with a lid when walking away.

The three finish breakfast, and before departing, Alfred asks the server if she can get him a larger cup to go and top it off. He slowly stirs for minutes and then puts the lid on, pressing hard to ensure a good seal. He looks over for the other cup he had been drinking from, and it's gone, and then sees that the sugar cubes and caffeine is gone so he asks for more cubes of sugar and caffeine.

The three catch a taxi to the airport and arrive thirty minutes later but quickly realize they have an hour before their flight departs.

Forty-five minutes later, the attendant announces their flight number for boarding. Still, they sit for another hour before they begin boarding the front passengers because the military flight is carrying precious cargo.

Ken nudges Greg when noticing Alfred acting fidgety, and they look over, finding Alfred pacing as if nervous. They watch for minutes, then giggle, getting a good laugh from his crazy actions. Before long, they watch him continually play with a trashcan flip-type lid, pushing it back and forth with fingertips, patiently waiting for the lid to retract so he can push again. Ken eventually gets Alfred's attention and makes him stop. "Look, man…, why are you acting like a basket case?" Ken asks, staring deep into Alfred's face. He looks away then back, finding Alfred's playful waving fingers inches from his face when slapping Alfred's hand and grabbing him by his collar, pushing him into a wall. "Look…, you better get it together, Jack! You're freakin' annoying, dude!" Ken looks over his shoulder, patting Alfred's clothes down fast, when seeing an old security guard approaching at a slow pace. He reaches up again; brushing his collar down, then mildly shoves him off, walking off and taking his seat.

Minutes later, Greg kicks Ken's feet to get his attention.

Ken looks up, instantly frowning when finding Alfred rushing through the seats with his laptop held tight and using it as a steering wheel as if playing bumper cars.

Out of nowhere, a loud burst of laughter comes from the boarding area when people get a good, long laugh, and kids laugh, with some falling to the floor, pointing.

The security officer finally rushes up to one side waving his stick to get Alfred's attention. He stops in frustration, coming around the other way, but Alfred turns his laptop type steering wheel, coming the other way in a game of cat and mouse.

Alfred continually circles the chairs with his loud, engine-simulated voice, outmaneuvering the security guard until the guard is almost out of breath.

The guard drops down in a chair seconds later wheezing.

Ken looks over at the security guard, who shakes his hand, motioning him to help when the guard stands and immediately drops into another seat, catching his breath.

Ken's hands cover his eyes in embarrassment, and he's outraged at Alfred's silly tantrum. His head falls in his hands again when he screams, motioning to Alfred, who he watches drive more then make a few sharp turns with the laptop around more chairs.

Alfred rushes toward Ken, and before he can reach him, Alfred makes another sharp turn when Ken leans forward, grabbing him by the collar, staggering to one side with Alfred's collar tight around his neck.

Ken tries talking to him but finds Alfred's eyes bulging as if stoned out of his mind.

Alfred looks sweaty, and his hands shake nervously. His responses are twice as fast and higher than his speaking voice; his conversation doesn't make sense.

Ken makes him sit and keeps an eye on him for several minutes.

The three soon enter the boarding ramp, and Alfred looks around, bug-eyed when taking off like a lunatic.

Alfred rushes down the ramp and knocks a couple of people into the walls while rushing to the plane's door and taking one step inside.

The copilot extends a hand, greeting Alfred when his hand goes forward, grasping the copilot's wing pendant, unpinning one side, and leaving it crooked. He looks down to reposition his wings when Alfred pulls him into a death-grip headlock.

Alfred's hand comes up to the copilot's forehead, and his knuckles quickly go back and forth hard, for seconds, until it turns red and he screams, backing off quick.

Ken and Greg jump high a few times, over people's heads to see if they can spot Alfred, then take off in a sprint, hugging the wall as they rush to the door, finding the copilot looking at the red spot with a female flight attendant's makeup mirror.

Ken and Greg rush onboard, finding Alfred seated in the VIP section. They stand in the aisle, motioning him up, and then pull him, forcing him forward, but he refuses to budge. They finally hear a commotion and look back, finding the line backed up, so they shove him back in the seat and move forward, taking seats in coach.

Seconds later, the aisle is somewhat clear.

Ken looks up, finding a senior ranking officer escorting Alfred out of his seat.

Alfred finally gets up, faces the senior officer's back, and takes a few comical boxing swings until the officer turns and sees the dancing shadow and jump. Alfred's hands come down fast, and he pretends to be dancing to the music when quickly turning and making his way to coach, where Ken and Greg are seated.

Within the hour, the plane taxis the runway.

The aircraft is airborne in no time to Port Copan Retaunas via a Military Airlift Command (MAC) flight with its oversized cargo area carrying a whole load of the heavy military; artillery, helicopters, tanks, and other gear, so it's quite a noisy flight.

An hour into the seven-hour flight, Ken shakes his head, nudging Greg when finding Alfred peeping in the VIP area until easing through the curtains and vanishing.

Ken goes into deep frustration but patiently waits to see if Alfred will pounce back out. After five minutes, Ken unbuckles, making his way up to the thick demarcation curtains. He steps into VIP, looks around, and doesn't see Alfred, so he assumes he's in the bathroom. He turns and catches something out of his peripheral vision, finding Alfred on his knees, behind and under the same senior officer's chair.

Ken's eyes bulge, nervously whispering to get Alfred's attention.

Alfred finally looks back, finding Ken, and giggles, slowly backing up.

Ken stares with curious eyes and shoves Alfred back through the curtains as he floods into the aisle. He turns, still in first Class, and walks past the senior officer while heading for the restroom, and his eyes drift to the floor, finding the senior officer's shoestrings tied together. Ken walks off, shaking his head, and minutes later, comes out, accidentally slamming the door and waking a few people.

He heads for the curtains, walks through, and turns to close the curtain when hearing something slam to the floor. He draws the curtains open quickly, finding the senior officer face down and helplessly kicking and screaming. Ken giggles and then rushes, closing the curtains.

Ken's eyes wander over the cargo area for Alfred, but he doesn't see him until Greg aggressively points to the rear. Ken takes a few steps toward the back with his head bobbing over and under the heavy gear until finally finding Alfred in a seat with his head leaning into the window with fingers quickly tapping along the window seal. Ken takes his seat somewhat relieved but keeps his eyes on Alfred until suddenly nodding off.

Hours into the flight, boots loudly slam into the metal deck plates as two flight crewmembers rush through the cargo bay, screaming seconds later when finding Alfred in one of the two-ton jeeps.

Alfred spots them coming and jumps like a cougar from the jeep, instantly hopping into the seat of the mini-helicopter.

The male attendant anxiously reaches for Alfred, who slips away and loses sight of him for seconds until hearing a helicopter's preheaters warming up. He rushes over, finding Alfred tinkering with knobs until managing to light off the LED missile sensors.

Alfred looks up in a flash, finding the huge male attendant's hand slamming into his chest when letting off a muffled scream over the loud plane's engines.

The male attendant snatches Alfred from the seat, raises him high, and slams him into the hard cargo seats, with his body bouncing a few times upward.

The female crewmember shakes her head, looking back at the other twenty passengers strapped in and lined up on the plane's wall with eyes dead set on Alfred. She walks back over, carefully flipping switches until de-energizing the weapons and equipment.

Four hours into the flight, the plane lights flickered in the passenger and cargo areas until one last flicker comes, leaving the plane in total darkness.

Immediately, the plane slowly and unnoticeably descends until alarms sound, and the senior pilot announces for everyone to buckle up for a rough ride.

The pilots continually scream, fighting with various levers and flipping several buttons while checking a few then several crazy registering or fast spinning gauges.

The attendants run to the rear with flashlights shining over passengers and then up and down panels. They come upon Alfred swiftly, finding him with his head straightforward with bulged eyes. Their flashlights quickly shine over his body, to his hand, onto the cord, and then up to his cell phone, plugged into the central backup battery unit, marked 'danger – do not use!' which smokes before sparking.

Alfred stares at the black, long fiery streak and jumps from his seat when another long spark shoots out with a long steady flame. "Aii!" Alfred screams, knocking the attendants back and onto the floor.

The plane's nose drops fast, and the flight crew repositions in a forty-five-degree nosedive, anticipating the worst.

The pilots continually scream, fighting to get their parachutes strapped on tight.

Passengers rise from their seats and look out the window into the Atlantic Ocean's white caps, which look like specks, when beginning to scream, one after the other.

The pilot quickly drops back down in his seat, pulling hard on the steering unit to get the nose up.

The attendants continually fight the mini-fire with fire bottles until its smoldering.

The male attendant quickly reconnects the battery and then backs up and screams, jumping around and shaking off the numbness from his shocked fingers.

Seconds later, the lights reactivate, and the plane's nose shoots up quickly with the cockpit crew cheering the attendants.

Ken looks back and sees the male attendant gets physical with Alfred, so he rushes to the back and gets involved, assuring the attendants that everything would be fine. He tells them how strange Alfred's been acting in the terminal and then calms them by ensuring them that he would watch Alfred until they landed.

Ken sits, keeping his eyes on Alfred until growing sleepy when he and Greg eventually take turns watching Alfred.

Greg's turn comes again, and his eyes grow heavy and dead set on Alfred in minutes.

Alfred stares Greg down, waving to him as Greg's eyes slowly shut. Instantly, Alfred stares at the attendant's air wings on his jacket and near his head, reaching for the pin and taking off the back, turning it upside-down, and re-pinning it to the arm.

Greg and Ken jump as the plane instantly dip when hitting turbulent weather. They looked at Alfred, who smiles back as if drunk.

The plane continues in turbulent winds for an hour of the two hours remaining.

Ken falls to sleep, and Greg is watchful until nodding, only to have Alfred wave. Ken awakens minutes later, finding Greg asleep when stomping.

Greg's mouth drops open, springing forward in the tightly-strapped seat belt, snatched back with a frown, and then stares into the empty seat and looks around fast.

Ken and Greg spring forward, looking for Alfred, when instantly, a loud engine roars as Alfred starts up a two-and-a-half-ton truck with black soot filling the cargo hold.

Alfred lays into the pedal and horn until the male attendant rushes up, body-slamming him, then slam him a few more times until wrestling over the deck.

The big male attendant jumps up, walking up to Ken with his finger in his face, confronting Ken, who's embarrassed. He snatches a safety harness from the wall, buckling Alfred in when rushing to the cockpit to have the pilot radios ahead for security.

Barry arrives earlier than expected and sits listening to music for a while until turning it down when a torrential downpour comes out of nowhere. He sits longer until the rain slacks when emerging from his decked-out, black-and-silver, chromed SUV.

The plane soon passes high overhead, making practice landings before taxiing off.

Rain begins pouring like cats and dogs as the plane turn, taxiing to the gate.

Suddenly, the plane stops, still pointed in the tower's direction.

The lead air traffic controller looks at the plane through binoculars and reports that the plane has blown out a tire.

Barry finally dashes inside and almost knocks over an old woman who had just walked through the door. He quickly stops, rendering assistance when reaching to grab her hat from the floor, and her cane rises high, quickly whacking him on top of his head. "Ouch!" he yelps, still holding the top of his head.

The woman stands wide-legged, with her hand drawn into a tight fist, and lets him have it again with a strong right to the forehead when he looks up with a big knot shining.

"Where in the hell is the freakin' fire? I want to know where?" she screams. She snatches her hat off and draws the cane even higher. "You need to watch where you are going, Sonny!" she screams with a mouth full of tobacco, which she spits between his eyes.

Barry's hands go to his face, screaming a death cry from the burning sensation and temporary blindness.

"Gone mess around and make me break my damn hip again!" she screams, watching him shoot up and scramble back and forth as if confused or crazy. She draws the cane back, replicating his zig-zag and then wobbly movement in the hopes of getting in another good whack.

Barry rushes outside, dropping to his knees and dipping his head in a puddle of water. Minutes later, he rushes inside the terminal with a mean stare, gazing over the terminal, looking for the woman. He reaches for the cleaning cart, grabbing a broom handle and snapping off the head with his feet. His tight fist grips the wood harder, thrusting it forward a few whacks, when tightening his grip more. He rushes around the first corner and doesn't pay attention, running into a bunch of empty refrigerator-sized boxes, which he tears through, fighting to stand.

The female ticket agent bend over in tears of laughter, watching him make a spectacle of himself as he struggles a little longer until finally gaining his balance.

Barry steps off and accidentally steps up on the corner of a raised box, stumbling into a row of boxes, which creates a long, domino effect when ten boxes collide.

A smile grows on the ticket agent's face. Her eyes wander to Barry's face, and she finds him with a mean stare and quickly turns as if she has not seen a thing.

The grim seating area grows darker, with clouds darkening and the lights flickering.

Barry quickly makes his way to the flight display, squinting when reading over the lighted panel.

There comes a loud crack of thunder and sharp lightning out of nowhere.

Barry runs to the huge picture window, placing his hands on the glass, barely able to make out the plane in the torrential downpour. He moves further down the corridor, peeling back curtains but still can't see the plane but watches even thicker and darker clouds roll in when a booming sound comes, followed by more bright flashes of lightning.

Minutes later, the storm appears to have drifted further away, but it's hard to tell, so he turns and walks back toward the ticket counter.

The lights flicker a few times and then go out for minutes.

Barry picks up speed, clumsily slamming his head into a metal marquis, bursting the filaments and bending the frame. He stands dizzy, moving when the lights blink and steady. Barry rushes up to the counter, bends over, and looks for the agent. His hand comes to his head, feeling a sting when lightheaded. Finally, he hears something rattling below on the other side of the counter when bending further, finding a pair of trembling legs.

Loud, crinkled bags rattle a few times as the woman's head, and then her face nervously appears. She releases her hair, shaking her head to unravel her hair, and then allows it to fall down her back. She stares at him until dimming her eyes. Her index finger slightly parts her perfectly-formed lips. She gently grasps her shoulder strap and pulls it to one side; when it slips then playfully pulls it back on her shoulder.

Barry carefully watches the woman who is decidedly below average in appearance.

"Excuse me. . ., the plane," he begins to say when turning, finding several people screaming and running.

More commotion arises as people scramble to clear a ramp as a runaway cart, on a steep decline, slams into the wall and shatters the large window.

The throbbing pain at Barry's bruised temple makes him dizzier. His hand comes up to his head, and Barry stumbles a little, bracing the countertop when looking away again. He turns to the agent again and finds her face neatly made up but she's not the same woman but looks like a million bucks.

Barry's mouth drops open, and his eyes bulge. His fast rubbing hand crosses the bruise slower until his head is steadfast at his temple, and he's in a daze.

For sure, she has his undivided attention as he instantly falls into lust. She runs her fingers through her long, wavy hair, dropping her dress and standing with her hands on her hips, dressed in only panties and a bra. She turns to one side, sticks out one double-jointed, perfectly curved hip, and then the other. She twirls her hips and dance in a sexy Egyptian-style dance for seconds.

Suddenly, a thick, hairy hand waves in front of Barry's face as the heavyset security guard waves a few more times and then snaps his fingers twice.

Barry comes to, slightly shaking his head in disbelief when looking forward and up again, finding the short, stout attendant with thick bifocals, then down, to the left and the right, and then back over the counter and down to the floor. He looks to his left again, finding another security guard who looks the woman up and down and then gazes at Barry.

"Are you alright, lover boy?" the tall guard asks, giggling. "For a minute there, I thought you were getting sweet on ole' Betty, here," the heavyset guard says, smiling.

Betty blushes and covers her mouth with her hand. She finally shyly smiles again, bashfully putting her hands behind her back and arching her back in lust. She smiles with green, jacked-up, crooked teeth when Barry's eyes wander down at her again.

Barry's hand slams on the countertop, scrambling until turning with hands out, pretending to be blind when walking away, feeling over the wall and making his way to the window. Barry's cell phone rings when out of view, and he answers, hearing Ken mumbling something loud, nonstop, and very hysterical.

Barry manages to calm him to where Ken tells him that Alfred is about to be arrested by the authorities at the gate.

Ken briefly tells Barry what Alfred did during the flight and how he acted strangely and bounced off the walls.

Barry thinks longer, and then assures Ken that he has a plan and begins explaining. "Ok, look it. . ., be ready to run when you reach the gate." Barry hangs up and eases into a seat facing the large window. He drifts into a daze, trying to figure out what is happening with the plane. Barry is between breaths when a sudden, sharp lightning bolt and thunder cause him to jump surprisingly. He looks back, frozen, and remains quiet for seconds, listening closely until looking back, finding a different security officer barreling around the corner only to run smack dead into the same scattered boxes.

The officer tumbles over three of the eleven boxes, then loses his balance again and falls into another box.

Barry shakes his head, smiling, and then reclines in the chair with a confused look. His eyes roam over the plane, which becomes slightly visible when the rain slacks. He looks back, finding the security guard on his feet, until stumbling again. Barry fights his heavy laughter, putting his hand over his mouth with his belly, lightly giggling, and then heavily jumping up and down. He bursts out in silly but soft laughter and uncontrollably laughs until it tapers off to a smile. Barry shakes his head again and turns, refocusing on the plane and his plan. He sees a quick flash past the window and spots four men rushing out to the plane with long cylinders on the back of a motorized cart.

Barry looks back, finding the same two security guards as they vanish into the security hallway. He stands, walking over to the hallway, peeping through the glass window into the empty security hall when the PA system sounds off, requesting security's presence at the boarding gate.

Barry's hands go to his side, nervously scrambling back and forth until stopping with his head going from left to right. Barry quickly rushes, grabbing the flight number and exchanges numbers, hearing footsteps again and easing back in his seat, whistling.

Seconds pass, and Barry hears voices, finding an electronic side door opening.

A small crowd in military uniforms rush inside, looking for their flight number, and then rush over to the other side of the airport.

Like clockwork, the runway team quickly works on the tire, and thirty minutes later, the flagman stands in front of the plane, guiding it toward the gate.

Barry hears the security officers' footsteps behind the door as one security officer's voice grows louder.

The officers scream at each other until bellowing into the seating area. They stand wide-legged, checking stun guns and looking over at the empty seating area, scratching their heads when rushing to the desk and the door where the plane was to disembark.

One officer points to the number across the hall, and they quickly cross the wide walk area, coming up with guns drawn. They perform various unauthorized maneuvers, making the audience think a high-profile incident is going down. They take cover in prone positions behind chairs, trashcans, and posters while stirring up a commotion and watching people move fearfully away from the gate and closer to the aisle.

Five minutes later, Barry anxiously stands near the officers, pacing until finally taking a seat. He keeps his eyes on the plane, officers, and others while anxiously waiting for his plan to unfold.

The two guards stand patiently waiting for the PA system to report that the plane is at the gate and the PA system finally keys up, with a minimal squelch, reporting that the plane is at the gate. The security officers fling the door open.

The rear guard runs up on the heels of the other guard, tripping him, and they tumbled forward.

Spectators peep inside the ramp, laughing when rushing down the wrong ramp.

Barry patiently waits for the last man to enter and slams the door. He reaches back for the line of chairs, pulling over six connected seats and wedging them between the ticket stand and door. Barry rushes up to the security cart and grabs the passenger's security jacket. He tries to put it on but quickly realizes it's too small when throwing the bomber jacket over his shoulder but takes it down when hearing keys bang together. Barry reaches deep, nervously fumbling through a few keys and tries several before getting the right key. He hears a loud crash on the other side of the airport and jumps, seeing the pissed-off faces of the tall guard whose breath fogs the window and the short guard who jumps up and down in the window from time to time like a little dog.

Barry rushes down the ramp, finding the plane's door open, quickly flashing the badge and motioning the attendants to bring Alfred forward.

The big, mean attendant quickly shoves Alfred into Barry, causing Barry to fall a few feet backward and into the wall.

Barry rushes Alfred to a side door, shoving him through and down the steep ramp.

Their feet hit the pavement, and they sprint as fast as possible.

Ken and Greg rush outside, where they meet up with Barry and Alfred in the front parking lot. They jump into Barry's SUV and speed through the lot and out the exit.

Later on, after the security shift changes, Barry and Ken go back to the airport, break into the security office, and retrieve their luggage.

A month later, the three hook up and live with the women they are dating.

CHAPTER ONE

CURRENT DAY: Port Copan Retaunas, 7:30 p.m., Friday. A 2013 black and chromed-out 890 series four-door sports car sit in a crowded lot at the Arena stadium. The headlights go out, and the sleek parking lights energize. From time to time, the horn blows while tipsy females, Erica and friend Jenn, a six-foot, slim hottie, sit acting silly.

The women wink and wave at every passing hunk.

Jenn adjusts the radio to her favorite country station, but they can barely make out a song or artist due to the initial static.

The park lights and taillights flicker through the light mist and drizzle.

"Ahh! Come on, Girl! You have to get in a better mood because you're depressing the hell out of me!" Jenn says to Erica.

Jenn's pale, soft, intensely feminine hand turns up the half-empty, fist-gripped bottle of cognac, goose-necking a few swigs before passing it. Minutes later, she tunes the radio, lifting a cigarette from the ashtray. The volume slowly rises to a medium level when a song, not well-liked for Erica's taste, blares for seconds.

Erica stares at Jenn, shaking her head until turning down the volume. "Didn't you just mention depressing? Hell, Jenn..., what is downright depressing is this crazy-ass country song you're singing; that's what! Who in the hell is it, anyway? Up in here singing about picking up some hogs and getting up in some drawers!" Erica's face grows exceedingly serious when bursting into a senseless yet hilariously crazy laugh before taking another cognac hit. "Really, who is this damn weirdo?" Erica falls backward, bursting into another crazy and drunken laugh.

Erica meditates on the words, and then mellows into the rhythmic beat until she subconsciously moves her head. She freezes, listening closely while profoundly meditating on the lyrics, and freezes again. Erica tries making out something unclear, then thinks harder until she repeats his words and tries to make sense of it when bursting into deep laughter. "A whaaattt. . .? Girl, did he just say something about strapping down a damn hog?" Erica yells with eyes widening, and her mouth falling open as if surprised.

Erica rocks until reaching near the gearshift. She grabs the bottle and takes another swig. She overindulges, and her cheeks slightly poke out when freezing with eyes wide and in suspense, hearing the singer mention 'putting on some skins and not telling all his friends' when Erica sprays a heavy mist over the driver's side windshield.

"Ahh! Ha, ha, ha, ha, ha! Girl, look at you! You're pissy-ass drunk! Look at your ole' drunk ass!" Jenn yells, deep in laughter. "Up in here wasting my damn sixty-dollar bottle of cognac." Jenn cuts her laugh short, frowning.

Erica looks back, reaching for paper towels, peeling off several and quickly wiping from the top down. "I'm sorry!" She looks back for more tissues. "Girl, for real..., who is this damn weirdo? Talking about 'picking up some damn hogs and getting up in some drawers?' What is he, some kind of animal-loving man?" She looks over and finds Jenn's face torn up but in a fun-loving frown when her mouth drops wide open in a scream of laughter until quieting.

Jenn's shoulders slightly bounce, but nothing comes out until sounding like she's trying to catch her breath when her vocal cords sound off in great laughter.

Erica grabs her ears, holding her head tight, when bursting into a peal of laughter.

They laugh for minutes, and within seconds, they almost compose themselves until breaking out in another heap of laughter.

Patrons passing stop and stare at the car, which they find slightly rocking.

"Ole' girl, that's Lennie Western's new cd – 'Animal'. Why would you say something crazy like that about ole' Lennie?" Jenn leans toward the dash for her cigarette.

"Why? Why, Jenn? Did you not just hear him say he's going to pick up some hogs and get up in some damn drawers? Girl, he's talking about having sex with darn animals!" Erica screams when laughing so hard that tears flow down her cheeks.

"Girl, get for real! Damn..., you're hitting this damn Sekif Cognac too hard! Here, watch this," Jenn says, cautiously looking around with eyes anxiously wandering over and past a few people. She slightly rolls down the window, closely watching a few more people pass when leaning further, spotting two tall, heavy-set women approaching.

The women, heavily intoxicated, stumble by as if they're about to fall over in their oversized heels but then stop in the middle of the lane. They take a few more steps, turn face-to-face and take a pull on a joint, then blow each other a shotgun.

The tall woman digs in her purse, pulls out a lighter, and then cigarettes.

Lennie Western's lyrics cease, but an enjoyable beat continually plays with the guitar strumming and bass thumping.

Jenn holds the radio knob tight and then cranks up Lennie's song just when ole' Lennie is about to chime in with the chorus line again.

"Woohoo! Lennie! We love you, Lennie, babe!" The short, heavy-set chick screams, throwing her hands around like a bronco rider.

The two heavy-set chicks break out into more drunken cowgirl dances, getting down.

Jenn's mouth falls open in disbelief, immediately nudging Erica, taking another focused drunkenly hit of cognac when her jaws fill while sitting the bottle down.

Erica's eyes bulge, finally seeing the larger-than-life women spinning around like ballerinas. Her eyes wander up and down their front and backside, instantly spraying the windshield again when the tall chick's thick, white, pale cheeks pop out from under her high, tight dress. Erica blushes instantly with her hands, reaching for more paper towels.

The short chick's cheeks become quickly exposed as well as they continue dancing with more cheeks exposed when getting to one part where they look at each other; dip their heads forward, and bend over joyfully shaking their butts.

The tall chick has so much exposure that she looks like a bear's backside.

A little old woman and her male companion pass Erica's car, and the woman stops and looks up at the two towering dancing bears. She shakes her head and straightens her trifocals while shaking her head again.

The old man freezes with his mouth slowly dropping open, scratching his bald spot with tobacco juice dribbling to his chin, then overalls.

Jenn's laughter grows louder, and her second outburst causes the old couple to jump and stare at the car and then them before slowly turning and walking off.

"Now you see them..., do you? There are the big ole' hogs, and there are the big ole' drawers!" Jenn screams with her upper body continually falling forward and backward for seconds with laughter growing so loud that it sounds like a solid scream.

Erica sits in a river of tears. Her mouth drops and stays open, and her upper body continually falls forward and backward for seconds while watching the women go from dance to dance, non-stop.

The women perform only one familiar step in Erica's generation and messes that up. 'Woohoo! Lennie! Lennie!' the two women scream, dancing rodeo-style until the end.

Erica eases down the volume, endlessly giggling until she lays her head back on the headrest, almost catching her breath, and starts in on another tear-jerking laugh.

Jenn leans back into the door's corner, staring at Erica, smiling. Her shoulders jiggle a few more times and then finally settle. She stares at the roof, quickly lunging forward and flipping the sun visor's mirror down. Jenn runs fingers through her long, blonde, curly hair, staring at her beautiful blue eyes and winking at herself to look even sexier.

Erica wipes her eyes one last time, gazing over at the indigo dash lights until tapping the clock's face a few times to remove what she thinks is hair when she quickly realizes it's the design of the beautiful quartz face.

"We need to be out of here in thirty minutes if we plan to get a good seat." Jenn looks in the mirror at her pretty made-up face.

"Heck..., we can go now!" Erica says flipping the driver's-side sun visor down and staring at her lovely skin and free, department-store made-up face. "Girl, that young girl did an excellent job, huh?" She runs her hand over her slick, black eyebrows and then flips the visor up. Erica rolls down the window and sticks her hand out to see if it's still drizzling. "On second thought, why don't we wait a little longer? I'm not even trying to walk in the rain and look like I have a seventies-style Jerry or S-type curl." She laughs, gazing over at Jenn, still looking in the mirror and touching up her lips.

The car's interior lights brighten as Erica leans forward, putting on more eyeliner.

Jenn puts on more eyeliner, run her fingers through her hair, then fluffs it with the interior lights automatically, and slowly dimming. She becomes drunkenly numb.

Instantly, an unexpected loud crack of thunder roars from a distance, causing Jenn and Erica to jump. They quickly draw together in the middle and then draw even closer.

Severe, sharp flashes of lightning come with more thunderous claps that startle them and then fade off until the last roar of thunder claps loudly and directly overhead.

Erica nervously jumps, squirming while the soft-tip liner rides across her numb face several times until she pulls it away.

They fearfully look around for seconds, easing back when seeing lightning flashing.

"What the. . ., where did that come from?" Erica nervously asks.

Their heads move apart as they slowly lean toward the windows with another flash quickly bringing them back together. Their heads slowly turn until eye-to-eye when Jenn's eyes slowly scroll upward from Erica's shoulder.

"Ahh!" Jenn screams, staring into the black eyeliner deeply scribbled over Erica's now monstrous looking face.

Erica's mouth drops open, and she screams.

They continually scream until Erica nervously and vigorously shakes Jenn's hands.

Erica frowns, watching Jenn's face, which looks like she's seen a ghost.

Jenn drunkenly and aggressively fights, backing away from Erica, with hands flapping up and down like bat wings until Erica cannot touch her. Her hand clumsily feels around for the door handle until pulling and falling backward through the cracked-open door.

Erica lunges forward, grabbing Jenn's arm again, and fearfully shaking her. "What, Jenn? What is it?" Erica asks, leaning more than halfway over the passenger seat when Jenn takes another deep breath and screams again.

A few people walk past, backing up, and some fearfully run off in fear or excitement.

Jenn's body stretches from the car with her head turning from Erica when Erica's hand slips, and she catches Jenn at the thigh.

Jenn turns, looking back once more, finding light shining inside from the bright streetlight, and Erica's face instantly transforms, no longer looking horrifying but funny looking. Jenn freezes, staring a second longer, and then calms with her frown transforming into a radiant smile. Jenn's loud, drunken outburst of laughter follows when grabbing the door jam and easing inside. Her shoulders begin bouncing in deep laughter. "Girl, you 'bout scared the hell out of me! You got that eyeliner all over your face!" Jenn says, giggling. "Shiittt. . ., sitting up in here looking like damn the Chucky dolls' half-sister. Something about the light reflection had you looking like you were ready to star in a real damn horror flick. Girl, I'm not talking about just starring, but the damn main character…, damn! You done messed up my damn high, for real now!" Jenn takes a few more swigs, frowning.

They get another excellent laugh out while Erica looks in the mirror, cleaning her messy face. They sit a little longer in laughter until the rain slacks and then sit quietly a little longer listening to the light rain, which trickles along the window seal.

Erica looks at her watch again. She grabs her purse from behind the passenger seat, digging around for her cell phone to see if she had missed any calls.

Jenn looks out the window in deep thought, staring at a few people, and then goes into a daze, seeing a girl banging (wearing) the hell out of her outfit. She stares for seconds. "Ewe! Skank!" Jenn rolls her eyes, doing a double-take with eyes wandering over the pretty girl wearing the dress like no other. She slightly rises off her butt, balancing on her hands to see the girl again before she vanishes alongside a car.

Erica notices Jenn's erratic behavior, finally spotting the young girl when she and her friends pass between two cars. Erica cuts her eyes at Jenn, giggling. "Wow! Did you see that pretty young girl in your dress? Damn, she's rocking that like nobody's business!" Erica intentionally stares at her well-manicured nails, pretending to be playfully polishing them on her collar until lightly blowing them. Erica cuts her eyes over at Jenn and playfully rocks her head, acting like she's deep into the soft, low-playing music.

"Yeah, whateveeerrrrr!" Jenn puts her fully expanded and perfectly curved, open hand in Erica's face until lightly mushing her forehead.

Erica burst into a playfully loud laugh. "Your ass is straight up…, hattinnnggg!" she says in a high, drug-out pitch. "Hating to the Gluteus Maximus!" Erica says, creating some crazy slang off the top of her head.

"Yeah, whateveeerrrrr!" Jenn gives her the middle finger, playfully guiding it around Erica's face until slowly pointing downward and then upward again before withdrawing.

Minutes later, the rain subsides, and a mild, brisk wind kicks up.

Erica's door cracks open, and the interior lights brighten.

A few people walk by with heads leaning or peeping to look inside at the plush, expensive, light-tan leather interior and bold insignia design.

Erica and Jenn ease out and slip into thin sweaters and scarves.

Erica activates the electric locks and alarm, meeting Jenn on the passenger side, with their eyes wandering over the beautiful architecture of the enormous Arena. They make their way down one long corridor of vehicles, then more, until heading down the last long row, lined up at the main entrance and leading to the Arena's wall of doors.

Several cars stop or slow with windows down as several drunks or just excited men make it their business to make obscene or so-called sexy bird-callings or gestures. Some use old punch lines to get Jenn and Erica or other women to stop and talk.

An old battlewagon with fluorescent, bright colors pulls up alongside Jenn and Erica with an irritating horn plays some familiar Romper Room tune when sounding off.

"Hey, Mammi! Come over here and holla (holler) at your Pappi, Mamasita!" the stoned foreign-looking guy yells, motioning the driver to slow down. "Slow down and pull up on them, Homey!" He looks at the driver, pissed, yet quickly transforms his overly drunken face into a smile when leaning back out the window.

The war-torn car slowly rolls forward, pacing the girls, then stops altogether. The door flies open, and the foreigner's pink shoe ease out, shaking then ease down, staggering to the ground with his other foot shaking as it hits the pavement and stabilizes. He staggers a little more, until gaining his balance, and the car jerks forward when the driver's foot slips off the brake. The tall foreigner drunkenly hops on one leg a few steps, catching his balance, then leans against the car being drug a few feet until it stops.

One of the short foreign guys in the back turns up the mountainous liquor bottle, which undoubtedly is more significant than a gallon. He takes a hit from the corner that's left, throwing it over the backseat in a makeshift, pop-down back dash with glass breaking loudly against several other empty bottles.

The other foreign-looking guys sit, bobbing their drunken heads to the loud, muffled foreign music blaring from busted speakers.

"Say, Mammi! Closer!" the tall foreigner says, finally rebalancing when leaning heavily on the door and swaying. His hand comes up to his head with fingers slowly running through his long, dirty, greasy hair. His conditioner or whatever moisturizing gel is in his hair falls onto his shirt and pleather jacket, dripping as it forms into a milky-looking substance.

"Just ignore this slick-head clown, Erica!" Jenn screams, throwing up a middle finger and walking off faster until taking a few more steps and stopping. "Naw, uh..., uh! I can't let this one go! I'm fed up with these slick-head, illegal-ass cats who think they can say what they want to women. They always stare at us as if they done lost their puddle-jumping minds. What? Man gets for real with that tricked-out-ass perm!" Jenn screams.

Laughter rises from the small crowd that gathers.

"Look at you! Why are you even out here trying to pass for a Puerto Rican? Hell, everybody knows you're not Puerto Rican! You're nothing but a slick-head, greasy-head, musty-ass dude. Hell, I don't know what you are!" Jenn jerks her finger at him each time a word leaves her lips, with more laughter rising from the crowd.

The tall man stares long and hard and looks like he's about to nod. "Aw! Screw you, trick! You ain't all that!" He leans back, flipping her the bird (middle finger) then flips again with both heavy shaking fingers. The corners of his mouth floats downward as he tries to show off his 'don't give a damn' face.

More laughter rises from the crowd with screams in the background.

"Oh yeah! Well, if I'm not all that, you would not be standing here trying to holla! Ugh! You green shirt, yellow pants, pink-shoe-wearing clown!"

More laughter rises from the now medium-sized crowd.

"Look at you! Why are you sitting up here looking like a clown? Ugh! I can't even believe you are out here looking like this! Look! Obviously, you are at the wrong place; the auditions for Willie Fufu's Circus are on the corner of Fifth and Grandton Street!" She looks back, finally registering the loud laughter when looking over the growing audience when more loud laughter comes from the crowd.

"And what is all that white stuff dripping on your clothes and pleather jacket? Motor, or Johnson beater oil?" Jenn frowns, pointing in laughter. "Ewe! They call it getting a Jerry curl bag…, trust me…, get one, and you'll love me for it!"

The laughter increases from the crowd, and Jenn turns, walking away from the curb.

The tall man's face turns bright red, and fire appears in his overly drunken bloodshot eyes. He turns, kicking the car's frame, grasping the door again, slamming it, and causing the other seven men inside to jump, whispering.

The driver lights a joint and takes a long pull, passing it to the person next to him.

Erica stops and turns.

Jenn frantically rushes up to Erica with her hand easing into her purse. "Does he have a gun? Does he…, do he?" Jenn nervously whispers in a low but high-pitched voice, squinting with one eye open and peeping at Erica while drawing even closer and tensing with eyes shut tight while listening for a loud pop.

"Girl, no," Erica whispers with eyes dead-set on him.

"You tricks wanna play with ole' Pedro, 'ey? Pedro is gonna give you something you ain't never going to forget," he screams, grabbing and feeling his inseam for seconds until grabbing a handful of double-knit pants and staggers a few steps toward them.

Jenn grows pissed, and a serious frown comes when she spins around, stops, and then backs up a few feet with her hand searching even deeper in her purse.

Erica's hand comes up on Jenn's shoulder, trying to guide Jenn backward and closer to the sidewalk.

Jenn applies more pressure in her lean-to-tough look. "Girl, don't let me go," Jenn whispers, looking back before quickly staring at him.

Erika pulls on her more and even adds a fake frown to act as if she's exerting more energy to stop her than she's actually exerting.

"You have criticized ole' Pedro in front of his friends," he says, pointing back at the car with a slow, wide-opening hand. "So, now you force ole' Pedro to depart with something that will hurt but teach you a little some-some 'bout respect, hey?" He staggers back and forth, approaching slowly.

Jenn stands wide-legged, almost in a karate stance.

Erica pretends she has a heavy grip and lets off loud groans, adding more drama and gets more laughs for her role playing.

A couple more large groups walk by and stare at the tall man, then the car filled with red eyes. "Hey, are you ladies alright?" one young man asks.

The young man's friend comes up behind him and stops. "Hey, you two alright?" he asks, looking at Jenn's lovely figure and then Erica's, which is even hotter.

Erica calmly looks back, shaking her head to confirm they're fine, quickly refocusing and nervously staring back over Jenn's shoulder with more fake moans and groans. Erica grips Jenn's shoulder even tighter, and her other hand encompasses her mouth when pretending to nibble nervously at her fingernails to look even more comical.

The tall man draws closer but slower until a few feet away when briefly stopping. He staggers and strains, still digging deep but in both tight pockets. His fist balls in his right pocket, and his body shakes while trying for seconds to get either big hand free. He stops with a confused look and pulls again until finally brandishing a piece of metal which he slowly flips around a few times until it turns into a long, shiny switchblade.

"Oooh! Ahhh!" The medium size crowd mildly moans' with everyone backing up further with even greater interest.

A short body dashes past Erica and Jenn and comes up, off to the side, between them and the tall man. "Popcorn! Popcorn..., popcorn for sale!" the young lad, a drunk, and unpaid comic, says, bursting into laughter.

Laughter rises from the crowd.

The young kid springs forward further, finally seeing the long, shiny blade, jerking backward, screaming in a high-pitch yelp when running back onto the sidewalk and vanishing in the crowd.

The two concerned men stare at the knife, quickly turning and fading into the crowd and watching from afar.

Other patrons walk by and stare, but a few standoff a way, whispering.

The tall man takes a few steps, chanting something mean and vulgar in his native tongue, and though no one knows what, everyone knows it's downright nasty.

"Oooh! Ahhh!" the crowd grumbles staring at them alternatingly.

The tall man takes slower, staggering steps toward Jenn until his balled fist with the knife comes in a quick jab toward her face.

Jenn's head flies back and off to one side, accidentally head-butting Erica, who stumbles back into a few people who balance her and then pushes her back into Jenn.

Erica frowns, still staring back at the crowd, when slamming into Jenn's back, thrusting her a foot forward.

"Whoa, mama!" Jenn excitedly moans, ducking to the other side head-on with the sharp blade when her hand forces his blade-thrusting hand away at the wrist.

"Ooh! Ahh!" the crowd grumbles.

Erica's hand expressly goes forward, catching Jenn by the shoulder to compensate for her unbalanced stance, fighting hard to re-balance her.

Jenn looks over her shoulder with a mean stare. "What the hell are you doing? Girl, don't you see this clown has a knife? You trying to get me killed?" She regains her balance quickly and blocks the man's arm a second time when her hand finally draws from her purse, and a full blast of pepper spray shoots forward and in his face.

The man behind the driver's seat's eyes grows wide from the excitement, and he drops the joint between his legs, squirming to keep it from burning his light-orange pants.

Some of the solid, uncontrolled, yet continual stream of spray shoots over the tall man's shoulder and into the car.

Without warning, the other men in the car scream and move around quickly.

The car continually jerks, leans, and shifts as the seven bang into each other until the car looks like a full-scale riot.

The men fight for the door handles when two on the passenger side lean toward the open door and roll onto the asphalt.

The second man jumps up, rubbing his eyes while dancing as if barefoot on hot coals.

The man under him jumps up, shaking his hands and bloody, skinned knuckles while the other four bail out through the windows.

The driver stands, screaming when grabbing the frame, pulling and steering with one foot inside. He continually hops, trying to stop the car as it slowly rolls down a slight decline.

Jenn's finger presses even harder on the thin, tube-like canister, with an even steadier aim, but in the tall man's face until a mild hissing suddenly sounds. Her shoulder leans to one side from Erica's dead weight.

In a flash, Erica's foot shoots straight up like a stealth missile, kicking the tall man square in his inseam, causing him to fall back, spin out, and drop to the ground with legs accidentally sliding around and under the back tire of the slow-rolling car with the car lifting then dropping.

His head comes up quickly with a thick vein protruding at his temple. "Ahh…! Ahh…!" The man screams in a death cry when the car lifts high on the passenger side, from the back tire quickly dropping and picking up momentum. "Ahh. . . ! Ahh. . . !" he screams again, grabbing his leg and rolling over in agonizing pain with his longer-than-normal boot spurs bent all to hell.

A mild hiss grows loud and fast.

Suddenly, a light wind blows a light pepper mist against Jenn and Erica's faces. They shut their eyes tight, and their hands go up and out as they back up several feet.

The thin fog swiftly floats over the nosey bystanders, and everyone reaches for their faces and eyes with screams, scattering.

Folks pass in tears of laughter seeing the crowd running into one another.

The tall man screams one last time, echoing his voice over the humongous lot. He rolls over to his other side, grabbing his leg with his eyes shut tight, repeatedly fighting to open his eyes, finding his friend's car taillights smaller and smaller each time.

The bright taillights go up and down a few more times.

The driver blindly fights, still holding the frame, screaming. He hops alongside until jumping in but accidentally hits the gas with tires squealing and the car slamming into a parked car with him screaming and bursting into tears.

Jenn and Erica embrace for dear life, anxiously hopping around until they bump into an old man with a retired military cap on his head.

They scream a death-defying cry and blink a few times, realizing it's not the tall man when comforted.

"Shh...!" the old man whispers.

Jenn and Erica's hands embrace the man's face, and they relax when feeling his beard.

"Shh...! Shh...!" the old man whispers with his hand on their shoulders.

The girls fight to open their eyes, but the man's face fades in and out.

The old man turns them so the wind blows in their faces. He quickly twists the water bottle, dabbling water over their eyes, and soon their vision somewhat clears.

Seconds later, they graciously turn, thanking the man, but he's gone, so they look back, finding the crowd of pissed patrons, shaking their heads, cursing, and walking off. They look more, soon finding the old man entering the center arena entrance.

A muscle-bound man, one who knows Erica's boyfriend, Barry, rushes up, rendering assistance. He shields them from the mean-looking posse standing across the street, looking, pointing, and making slanderous remarks in their native language.

Erica and Jenn walk with the man and his friends, quickly fading into the vast crowd.

Jenn finds the tall man leaning on a friend's shoulders, hopping toward the car. She sees the driver with his head down on the headrest, slowly shaking his head in disbelief.

Erica and Jenn move with the fast-paced, heavy traffic, moving even faster when at the main entrance, where they are rushed in by security trying to keep the doors clear.

Out of nowhere, there comes a loud blast from behind them.

"Oooh! Ahhh!" The crowd moans in excitement when everyone hears a loud holler, and their heads instantly turn, finding the driver jumping from his flame-engulfed car.

"Oooh! Ahhh!" The crowd moans in even more excitement.

A distant siren soon rises.

Erica and Jenn thank the men, making their way to the shortest line, surrendering tickets. They rush to the concession stand, still cautiously looking for the thugs or authorities.

A louder explosion comes from outside, and people in the entrance stare outside.

Erica and Jenn hurriedly make their way inside and to the front looking for good seats. They quickly make their way, finding an empty table. "There! There! There's a closer table over there!" Erica shouts, pointing to a giant table when squeezing by people and coming upon the table that two other women are rushing up on.

Jenn eases her drink down, being the first.

The two women slow and shake their heads, disgusted.

The taller woman lifts her index finger, and her lips slowly part.

"Auutt! Auutt!" Jenn shouts over the loud voices, pointing for the woman to zip it. "Auutt!" Jenn says again. "Look. . ., didn't you see us beat down the tall man and those hopping around with their car on fire?" She jerks her chest forward. "Girl, you don't even want any of this hea (here) She pulls her hand from her purse, slipping a small jar of petroleum jelly on the table. She quickly greases her knuckles and without warning jumps at the woman who flinches, jumps back and bumps into others, spilling drinks.

"I didn't think so!" Jenn yells, staring until they fade quickly around the corner; the one pushing the other even faster.

Jenn and Erica ease into their seats, sipping.

They chill, listening to the mellow jazz, playing at a dull whisper over voices of over five thousand or more, filling the ten thousand-capacity Arena.

Erica looks in her purse, digging around until pulling out her phone, checking for incoming calls, and grows frustrated that she has no calls from Barry. "Jenn, check and see if you got a call from Ken?" Erica asks, staring at Jenn, who seems to be in a joyful mood.

Jenn's head cheerfully rocks back and forth and then left to right. "Nope, nope, nope, nope, nope!" she cheerfully sings when winking at a man passing and flirting with a couple of young men seconds later.

The jazz fades, and a beat rises high.

The crowd screams in a crazy uproar, and over a third begin dancing in seats or on their feet. The stands fill quicker as if someone had snapped their fingers when more people appear.

The beat continues with almost everyone dancing with a few seventy, maybe eighty-year-old women holding their clear or colored liquor glasses high while grooving.

An old grey head man wanders by Jenn and Erica's table, winking, and then starts in on some hilarious dance when playfully dancing around their table for seconds before moving on.

The beat fades into another new beat, which sounds even tighter.

The cheers grow louder, and even more people stand to dance.

"Alright now!" The DJ stands, pointing to chicks waving, blowing kisses, and screaming.

"How yawl (you all) feeling out there?" the producer screams, appearing from behind towering, plush, burgundy curtains. He stands proud, comically pulling his pants halfway up to his chest until high waters, breaking out in one of the latest dances and making the crowd go wild. He flicks his wrist, and the music stops, then starts at his command. "Welcome, friends, family, and colleagues! I want to extend a heartfelt welcome to everyone for coming out tonight! As you know, we have a fabulous show lined up, starting with Keyonton Worthington, Sherry Cartel, Keith Warbard, and last but not least, Jeff Tallento!"

The show starts out with the amateurs going before the pros and after the next to last comedian, the producer comes back out, announcing a break.

Everyone begins straggling back inside twenty minutes later when a dope beat blares out of the quality speakers.

"Now, for the main attraction!" the producer screams.

The crowd cheers louder than before, and people whistle, then clap harder.

The DJ cranks up the volume to the beat selected by the star comedian. "Up next, this fellow is out of Kinston, North Carolina, by way of Newport News, Virginia!" he says with the microphone shielded when pointing to the slow-rising curtains. "Give it up for my main man, Keyonton Worthingtoooonnn!" he screams, dragging Worthington's last name out as if he's at a world championship boxing match.

The crowd grows louder until their screams quickly taper off to a moderate roar.

"Damn that! Yawl better get up off your asses and show my man some real love!" the producer screams, turning, walking a few feet, and hugging the comedian before passing the microphone with three-fourths of the audience cheering even louder.

"Good evening, Port Copan Retaunas...! I said good..., evening, Port Copan Retaunas!" Keyonton yells, turning and pointing to the DJ.

Instantly, an out-of-sight new beat blares from the quality sound system.

Most hold their drinks up high over their heads or sit them down, dancing.

Keyonton starts in on some off-the-wall dance that has folks cracking up.

Jenn and Erica dance but find themselves tipsy as they laugh at the ridiculous dance Keyonton does with his wobbly legs until his arms go crazy. Jenn and Erica dance again and then stop and laugh so hard that they can hardly stand when tears of laughter drip.

The music plays for about thirty seconds until Keyonton signals the DJ to stop the track and then bursts into crazy laughter.

Everyone slowly settles into their seats with excited eyes.

Erica waits until Jenn turns away and then rechecks her phone.

"Man, I see some beautiful people out there! Hell! Some of you young folks ain't got anything on these old folks!" He makes more dance moves without music. "I just love dancing, it's something else. . .; you hear me? I mean, you can practically do any damn thing, and folks don't give a damn! Hell..., I can dance all night if you give me a sexy honey with a banging body. How many of yawl (you all) like to dance?" he asks, laughing while pointing to an old man who seems to be in his own world; the same old man who danced around Erica and Jenn's table, but by now, he's higher than a kite.

The old man sits, dancing some silly dance, and smiles to himself from time to time.

Keyonton points to the man again, giggling like crazy from watching him dancing to no music when motioning the camera and light men over to spotlight him.

Without warning, the man's head goes up like a shocked dog when easing up and walking toward a woman, trying to pull a young girl up to dance, and without success, he grows pissed, waving the young girl off, embarrassed.

Keyonton shakes his head in disbelief with laughter rising.

The old man walks back to his seat and flops down, even more pissed.

"Damn, speaking of straight gangster MAC! Now. . ., yawl (you all) know he gone pimp slap her before he leaves here tonight!" Keyonton giggles. "Hey, you alright, ole' dude?" Keyonton bends over to his knees, giggling as the camera zooms in on the man, until bringing him up on the main screen.

The old man pulls out a flask, hitting it again, and he's so high that he doesn't know he's the main attraction, even with folks pointing to the stage and big screen. He stares at the young girl, smiling while talking to himself, then frowns and smiles again with overly white teeth, looking like a possum.

Keyonton covers the microphone with both hands, deepening his voice. "Earth paging old man MAC! Earth to old man ma, ma, ma..., MAC!" Keyonton yells in a peal of deep laughter when great laughter breaks out. He senselessly runs around in circles, acting just like the old man, then makes more of the man's gestures and runs around some more, bringing people to tears.

The older man still is not receptive but endlessly stares at the young woman.

The young woman grows embarrassed and looks away when feeling uncomfortable with the man and under pressure from Keyonton's continual teasing.

Keyonton bursts out in a loud laugh each time the man smiles.

The old man smiles, cutting it short and looking like a sly fox this time, from the dark corner still showing his too-white teeth for his age. "And that, my dear people, is what we call a Charlie Sierra..., a Certified Stalker!" Keyonton shakes his head in disbelief. "I bet I'd get his attention if I cut on some music or horror sound effects." Keyonton comes back on his heels, making a full turn, then walking back to the front of the stage, giggling.

The people sound off with halfway applauses.

"Ok, let me do this because I still haven't forgotten that weak welcome!" Keyonton gives the audience a mean look to make them think he's pissed. He quickly paces until motioning the DJ to start the music, then quickly cuts it when seeing the old man ease up. "Aw, shit! We done got this idiot hype again! Yawl, settle on down!" He motions for the audience to take their seats, pacing longer until eagerly looking over a few females in the front rows. "You, stand up..., turn around, and sit down! You..., stand up..., turn around, and sit down! You..., stand up..., turn around, and sit down! Whoa! Yeah! You... yeah you! Girl, you better get your...; stand up! Now turn around again; yeah..., come on up here! I promise this ain't gone take but a hot sec," he says, stopping, staring, and then pretending to drool when playfully sliding his sleeve across his mouth.

Many folks burst into laughter.

The beautiful woman, who is extraordinarily shy, freezes as she looks back at the group of people at her table until her girlfriend motions for her to go on and get it over with.

"Woman, if you don't get your...!" he playfully yells again.

The crowd goes wild.

Keyonton rushes to the edge, pretending that he's about to jump off and go after her.

Out of nowhere come several bird calls.

The camera operator zooms in on the woman's perfect hourglass shape in her too-tight dress, and he keeps the camera on her plump bottom and extra-thin waistline.

"Alright, men, and many of you women! Calm your hormones!" Keyonton yells, staring at her sexy figure and well-rehearsed walk. "Damn, baby..., what's your name..., Annie May?..., Daisy Dukes?"

"Olivia," she shyly responds nervously approaching him at the top step.

"Oh, I see, one of those old, back-in-the-day, thick bottoms, country-ass names. No wonder you got one of those thick, round booties," Keyonton jokingly says when lifting her hand, twirling her, leaning into her, and whispering.

The Arena grows wild, whistling, chanting, and making the woman uneasy, though she manages to display a nervous smile.

A couple of people from her table call to her and make her blush.

Erica turns and looks over at Jenn, secretly rechecking her phone.

Keyonton pulls out a fake gun from his pocket, easing it to the woman's head to make her playfully flinch, and she plays along as agreed but playfully, yet as if frightened.

A man at the woman's table sits staring under-eyed and talking to himself until jumping up, nervously pacing and continually hitting himself in the head, as if he's going on stage. He stops as if in deep thought when talking to himself again, and then slowly turns from the stage without Keyonton noticing.

"Ok, we're going to try this applause stuff again!" Keyonton says, taking the gun and playfully yet lightly banging it against his head as if he's crazy when motioning for the producer to come back out and winking. "Now, when I come back out, yawl (you all) better get off your asses and show me some real love! You better show me love like you never showed anyone love before because if I come back out and I ain't feeling loved, I'm going to shoot this pretty mother…!" He points the gun, and Olivia playfully flinches when he makes a mean face. "And she better not even think about running because I'm an ex-Navy sharpshooter; I can pick a fly off a pencil point or anyone on that top row with nothing more than a head shot…, nothing less…, and I promise you!" he says, pointing high in the top rows and smiling. He slightly turns and walks toward the curtains, which slowly lowers, signaling the producer, who looks back and waits for his cue.

"Mr. DJ hit it!" the producer yells, watching Keyonton vanish.

The DJ cranks up the volume to Keyonton's original track.

"Up next, out of Kinston, North Carolina, by way of Newport News, Virginia," the producer yells, pointing to slow rising curtains with eyes constantly on the beautiful woman's backside. "Give it up for my man…, Keyonton Worthingtoooonnn!" The crowd jumps up with voices echoing from folks laughing hard and leaning into one another.

Keyonton walks by the producer and hands him the fake gun. He waves and then walks up behind the woman, whose half-bent over in laughter.

The beautiful woman turns when she feels him touch her lower back.

Keyonton turns, extending his arms out to embrace her for a few seconds when rocking her. "Hey, if your man ain't here, come backstage after the show," he whispers.

The woman's face transforms from a smile to a serious look and then a fake smile.

"If he's here, lose him and come by Mickey's place for the after-party. You can get my business card from the heavy-set dude, Ricky, in the red suit near the middle exit," he whispers.

The woman pulls away and turns to the audience, freezing, and tries to smile at their applauses but looks down, sadly exiting the stage.

Keyonton leans a few steps forward, patting her butt, then palms her right cheek, pulling on it for as long as possible until she pulls away, almost losing her balance.

Her date springs up in a rage, swinging as if shadowboxing. "That shit is not cool, man…not cool!" he screams when the DJ cuts the music.

The woman passes her date, rushing to her seat, pretending to be upset with a hand to her face.

Her date moves side to side in a fighting stance, freaking out and losing total control of Keyonton's disrespect. "Ahh!" He looks up at Keyonton, then quickly back at his date, then back at the stage. "That shit is not cool, man! The little gun thingy and touching her butt? Not cool, buddy!"

The camera operator finally gets Keyonton's attention, pointing to the man, Keyonton has not yet seen.

"Look! What's your name, sir?" Keyonton frowns, seeing the man shadowboxing heavily with fancy footwork until stumbling.

The man waves Keyonton off, disgusted when taking a few steps toward their table.

"Look! I'll come off this…!" Keyonton says in a mean frown, looking serious until bursting into laughter. He pretends to lean, puts the microphone down, and then fakes as if he's about to take his shirt off.

The man mumbles something unclear because of the loud crowd.

"Rufelus!" a woman at his table finally yells out when the loud crowd's voices mellow.

Rufelus jerks as if he wants to hit the woman and then freezes, staring and so embarrassed by his name which he too never liked. "Come off that damn stage; that's what I want!" he screams with fire in his eyes when thrusting for the stage, hoping to settle the score so folks know not to take him or his name lightly.

Security quickly closes in on the man, blocking him, and motioning him back to his seat.

"Ok, I get it now! No wonder you are one angry and evil little man…, geez! Hell, with a name like Rufelus Dufelus, I would be pissed at the world, too," Keyonton says, smiling.

"Oh, screw you!" the man yells, throwing up his right arm with his fist balled tight and stopping it in the crease with his left hand.

"Screw me? I'd rather screw that lovely Olivia. Hell! You need to go home and screw your mom and dad; they're the low-lives who gave you that silly-ass name! If it were my parents, they would be on the run after I dropped a hot ball (bullet) in their asses."

Folks crack up in laughter.

Everyone watches the man, throw another fit, and swing a few more times.

"Man, get your silly tail over there and sit down before. . . !" Keyonton pretends he's unbuttoning his shirt again. He points to his head as if he still has the gun, and grips the microphone, reenacting the man stomping and shadowboxing, but more hysterically.

The man makes a few more comments when a few people at his table motion him over and lean over the table in a semi-huddle.

One person, then all of them stand and grab their things.

Keyonton freezes in disbelief, with unbelieving eyes following them up the aisle.

"Look..., my apologies! It's all scripted! Look..., you saw me tell her what I was going to do. Heck, she could have left when I went behind the curtain." He looks at the woman faking her frustration even more until everyone is in front, and her date slowly pulls her into his arms walking slower and as if at a funeral.

The woman looks back once more, winking at Keyonton with a bright smile, and then frowns when her date turns to her.

A few of the girl's female friends boo Keyonton.

Another man with them throws his middle finger over his shoulder, waving it.

Keyonton thinks quickly and is at a loss as to how to pump the show back up when looking around and spotting the old man again. He points to the cameraman, finding the old man still not receptive.

The old man continually stares at the young woman who would not dance.

"Hey, security!" Keyonton yells, gigging.

Folks burst into great laughter.

"Ok, Port Copan Retaunas! Are yawl (you all) ready for some fun out there?"

Yells echo throughout the Arena.

Keyonton motions the DJ to get people back in the mood another track, and breaks out in another crazy dance. He turns and looks out into the audience, and when his eyes float up the main aisle, he cuts the music. He quietly watches a tall, older gentleman with his hair slicked back slowly make his way toward the stage. Keyonton does a double-take, noticing a pair of little feet in the old man's tow when pointing to the camera operator and light man who zoom across the floor and come upon the tall man.

"Excuse me, sir! Sir, excuse me! It's not right to sneak a little kid in here.

The old man stops and stares, then waves Keyonton off.

You see. . ., this here is an adult show; so that means what…, folks?"

"No kids allowed!" the crowd screams in laughter.

Keyonton looks seriously until excitedly dancing and pointing to the door.

The tall man ignores him, making his way to his row where he turns, stops, and then waves Keyonton off again.

One of the ushers directs the man when a dwarf finally steps out from behind him.

"Oh shit, naw. . ., and drinking liquor? Ushers…, please escort this kid out of here! You know we can't have this kind of publicity up in here; the media will eat us alive!"

The Arena grows full of laughter.

The dwarf throws up his middle finger, staggering forward.

Keyonton can no longer hold his laughter when bursting out in a crazy laugh. "Alright. . ., Alright, yawl (you all), I'm just messing! Those two is my people's right there! What's up, Pops?" He watches the tall man, his dad, wave back. "What's up, Unc (uncle)?" Keyonton says, throwing up a peace sign.

"Your girlfriend was up when I left your house," the uncle says, playfully grabbing his crotch. He humps his hand and then frowns with one eye shut tight, humping harder a few more times.

"See?" Keyonton shakes his head, forcing his chest forward and shoulders back. "Keep on!" He makes the meanest face. "You gone make me put these size twelves in your size one…, narrow ass! See? He plays too freakin' much! He knows good and damn well my girl is in the States. Now, since you want to play like that, go ask that sexy-ass Aunt Bettie, with that gigantic ole' bootie and luscious thighs!" He pulls his sleeve to his mouth, pretending he's wiping after a delicious meal, then turns to walk from the edge of the stage and toward the microphone stand. "Now, where was I?" he says in deep thought. "Shit! Come up in here with that silly-ass nonsense! He knows I'm strictly business, no-nonsense at all times. Hell, he done made me lose my train of thought!"

The crowd goes wild in laughter.

Keyonton pulls out his cell phone, pretending to call home but intentionally hits the send button, and giggles when hearing people burst into laughter.

The laughter grows uncontrollable with folks watching his uncle with one foot on stage, trying to climb up but can't.

Security is on the floor, laughing, knowing the dwarf can't get on stage without help.

"Ahh! I'm gonna kill you! You slick-ass son of a bitch!" the uncle screams.

The dad's eyes bulge in rage hearings his brother call his wife out her name.

"Don't use my wife's name in vain, damn it!" the dad yells, jumping to his feet, swaying with his fist tight while leaning forward, throwing jabs like a trained fighter.

"I knew you been up in my shit!" the uncle screams. His face frowns until it looks mean and even meaner as he continually strains, struggling to get on the stage.

"Ahh! Security! Security!" Keyonton screams, running around in circles, scared but trying to play tough at the same time, when seeing his uncle climbing up the camera operator's gear with his little foot inches from the stage.

The more serious security guard, who laughs but quickly maintains his composure, grabs the uncle just as his little pair of boots level out on the stage.

The crowd grows louder and crazier than ever in laughter.

Everyone laughs at the uncle as the tall guard carries him out on his shoulder.

The uncle fights with all that's in him and strains so hard that he busts a fart, which causes the security guard to stumble into the doorway.

A bigger security guard peeps through the window, flinging the door open. He grabs the dwarf, fans his face, and escorts him into the lobby and to the front door.

Erica turns and looks at Jenn, secretly rechecking her phone.

"Uh, uh, uh!" Jenn says, catches her again. "Girl, why do you worry about Barry's sorry ass?" Jenn turns up a stiff drink and downs it in two gulps.

Keyonton's phone rings again and he quickly answers in a continual furor of laughter until he jealously asks his girlfriend if she's back, then quickly hangs up. "Oh, that was my agent. How is he gone (going to) call me knowing I'm on stage?" Keyonton lets off a sigh.

"Yeah, whatever! That was your henpecked ass calling that woman of yours," his dad yells out, shaking his head when standing and heading for the aisle.

"Dad, please don't go, Dad..., Dad!" Keyonton playfully yells, trying to piss his dad off. "Tell Mother I'll be coming home soon, and tell old Blue, too!"

His dad makes his way up the aisle, and his hand comes up over his shoulder until his middle finger slowly extends outward.

Keyonton shakes his head in laughter. "Well, there goes the little family backyard gatherings and BBQs," he says, snickering. "All right, folks, sorry for that little crappy episode of family drama! You can bet your bottom dollar that is not part of the damn show! Alright! Let's get this thang started right!" Keyonton says, dancing without music.

"I love you, Keyonton!" a female screams.

"Aw! See..., that's what I'm talking about..., family! That's what a brotha needs..., real love, not this love-hate crap! Now..., can someone do ole' Key a favor and tell me how she looks?" He puts his hand over his eyebrows, blocking bright lights with eyes piercing through the semi-smoky room, finding a few pointing. "Hey, stand up for ole' Keyonton, Babes!" he says, finally able to see her when she's in front of another girl.

"She's a ten!" a man hollers.

"Yeah, I definitely need to get her number to have her tell me she loves me when my girl ain't acting right," he says, giggling. "Yeah, my number is seven, seven, seven, ninety-three, eleven," he playfully says, singing it like the old song from back in the day.

Most of the crowd burst into laughter, knowing it was a song.

The girl turns and starts to jot down the number.

Many others who did not get the joke take out pens and paper as well, but some put theirs back when they find folks pointing and laughing.

More laughter grows from people who see the girl and notice others as they look, shaking their heads, and laughing.

The girl turns around a few times in tight jeans with her hands on her hips and is so intoxicated that she trips over her feet and falls into an old couple's lap.

"Yeah, a ten, no doubt, but she has no damn brains!" the old woman shouts out loud, expressly rolling the girl to the floor and playfully dusting off her hands.

Mild laughter rises from those able to hear the comment or see the incident.

"On second thought, lose my damn number! I think I'll be better off telling myself I love me instead of getting it from a parakeet with no brain," he says. He goes into a deep laugh, bends over, and causes many to join in the laughter. He looks around at a few more people who wander inside and notices a small group in military uniforms when he points to the camera operator and then over to them. "Woohoo! Go Navy! Go Navy!"

Military folks scream, and a few drunken Sailors stand, waving hats. More male and female Sailors stand in other areas, shouting and waving glasses high overhead.

"Excuse me! Excuse me! How long have you been in, sir?" he asks a junior Sailor.

"Three months, fresh out of high school!" the young kid screams. The Sailor holds up his beer and excitedly flops down in his high chair.

"Wow, not long at all. So, in actuality, you just told on yourself before national television because you're not even old enough to drink..., now is that right, sir?"

"If I'm old enough to serve my country, then I'm old enough to splurge!" the young kid yells proudly in his drunken voice.

"Oookay..., waiter! Confiscate that beer, please! Ah..., ah..., ah..., thank yah, ah thank ya (you) very much!" Keyonton says in a perfect Elvis Presley impersonation. He walks away from that group and sees another group that catches his attention and stares until a hot female

Sailor sitting with a group of females catches his eyes. "You," he says, quickly pointing.

She points to herself, blushing.

"Yeah, you..., stand up!" Keyonton says.

Commotion brews at the young male Sailor's table when the waiter confronts him and tries to confiscate his drink.

Keyonton turns from her, redirecting his attention. "Wait! Excuse me, sir..., wait a minute! Excuse me! We have policies for underage drinking: You give up the juice and settle the score or run that trap and hit the door," Keyonton senselessly says, smiling with the crowd's laughter in an uproar.

"Screw you, you freakin' dick!" the young Sailor shouts, throwing his middle finger up when turning and half-mooning Keyonton.

"Really? Hmm..., screw Dick and me? Wow, that is the same exact thing your mother did to me and called me before I came to the show. What a coincidence! Trust me..., this is strictly ironic," he says, with one hand on his hip and staring as if in shock.

The crowd goes bonkers.

Keyonton turns, finding the hot female officer still talking to her friends.

The female Sailor moves in her seat as if dancing and the drinks have her going.

"My, you're mighty chipper!" Keyonton says, looking back over at the belligerent male Sailor who now has two security escorts at his service then back at the female. "Sorry for the interruption, ma'am, but can you dance that good, or is that all just seat, neck, and head work?"

"I can do a little something-something if you know what I mean," she screams, flinging her long blonde hair to one side when moving as if she's a terrific dancer.

"Hey there! What are you sipping on? I know they say you cannot outdrink a true Sailor, but damn, you must be one, because that's what..., one, two, three empty mix-drink glasses in front of you?" he asks, standing on his tiptoes, counting.

"Sekif's Delightful Passion!" she says, lifting her glass and sipping again.

"Great drink! You go, girl! Uh..., waiter, please get this beautiful young woman another, on me, and moreover, can you please take those other empty glasses away, so people don't misinterpret her as not being a classy woman?"

The hot blond takes one last sip and bursts into laughter.

"DJ, hit it…, track nine!" Keyonton shouts.

A hot beat begins playing.

The girl jumps from the high chair, stumbling but springs forward, quickly regaining balance when coordinating movement, but it definitely looks like she has two left feet.

The crowd goes wild.

"Cut, cut, cut!" Keyonton moves his hand, motioning the DJ, when falling forward in laughter. "Yeah, you sure can do a little some-some, but it damn sure as hell ain't dancing, boo-boo!" He shakes his head. "But hey, if you can handle four Sekif's Delightful Passion with one on the way, I'm really impressed that you can even stand!"

The crowd goes wild again.

Keyonton bends laughing when the Arena grows louder. He walks around, moving to the most serious-looking Sailor, an officer. "Excuse me, sir! Please sir! Sir! What is your name?" Keyonton asks in a proper professor's voice with eyes gazing over gold insignia bars.

The sophisticated junior officer stands, snapping as straight as a board and shouts in his deep-rooted country accent. "My name is Ensign Billy L. Blueknuckler, from Holley Hill, Utah!" The six-foot-three officer sways a little from the booze with his chest stuck out as if still at attention, breathing hard until looking ridiculous in a drunken smile.

"Ensign Billy Blueknuckler, from Holley Hill, Utah!" Keyonton playfully repeats, but faster and more country when standing like the dumbfounded, deep-country-looking officer.

The officer displays a proud smile, hearing his name echo throughout the Arena through the speakers when bursting into an even bigger smile.

"Ok, you can sit your big country-ass back down!" Keyonton says, still giggling.

The crowd immediately bursts into a peal of even louder laughter.

"I will be damn! Naw…, but on the real, sir. . ., you are a big-ass dude! What do you do in the Navy, workout or something for one of those Navy weightlifting teams?"

"No, sir, I'm an Assistant Operations Officer," he says, blushing.

"Then how do you stay so fit, with those big-ass arms and that massive-ass chest?"

"My secret? Well, there is none! It is remarkably simple. . ., if any, the only things I lift are biscuits and meat!"

Keyonton's mouth drops open, and he freezes with eyes bulging. He lowers the microphone at his inseam, allowing it to swing as if it's his manhood, and then lowers it to his kneecaps and eases it to the floor. He turns and runs around in circles like a laughing lunatic, dragging the microphone and creating a strange sound before lifting it.

Moderate laughs grow louder as more people catch on to the joke.

Keyonton staggers over and picks up the microphone. "Biscuits and meat? Biscuits and meat?" Keyonton screams in laughter.

"Yes, sir, I do not see a thing wrong with it, but if that is funny, I sometimes lift them taters (potatoes) too. I just love meat and taters!" the gullible officer says, smiling.

"Wooo! Wooo!" Keyonton screams, continually pulling his hand down like a train conductor pulling on the train's horn. "Boy! I hope your family isn't watching now or in the future because you just told the world, on national television, that you lift your butt up...," he says, laughing so hard that he can hardly talk. "And you take the meat! And," he screams, laughing harder, "and that you're particularly fond of tatters..., I mean testicles!"

The young officer drops in his seat in embarrassment, thinking long and hard when springing up fast, waving back and forth like a baseball coach calling a time out.

CHAPTER TWO

Keyonton tries to stop laughing, but it takes a few minutes. "It's alright, sir. . ., I hope we know what you meant. Look, the main reason why I chose you is because I saw how tall and big you were when you walked inside. Secondly, you reminded me of a dude I was stationed with while in the Navy. Glad to have you serve our country, sir; honestly, I am. Look…, you remind me of a friend of mine…, Carl. Now, my name for him was Crazy Carl," Keyonton says. "Sit down…, sit on down," he says, motioning the officer to sit.

The crowd goes into a burst of soft laughter.

"You see…, as a kid, Carl had acquired this habit of saying, 'Ah, uh huh!' and never broke it, even when joining the Navy. I mean, he could talk in a moderate tone and all…, oooh, yeah…he could hold one of the brightest conversations ever and was a formidable debater, but he was just crazy as heck. I tell you…, I avoided ole Carl like the plague."

The crowd goes into a burst of soft laughter.

"First off, let me briefly describe ole' Carl: built like you, sir, same height, weight, and everything. He had buck teeth, a Three Stooges Moe haircut, and a pale face with natural light, tinted raccoon ringed eyes. You see…, for some strange reason, ole' Carl had this dreadful habit of just blurting out, 'Ah, uh huh, uh huh' and for no apparent reason."

The crowd goes into a burst of soft laughter.

'Well, as time goes on, and from me hanging out with ole' Carl, I figured out that Carl would always yell out this nonsense when excited about something, hell. . ., that was almost anything…, a simple bastard!'

The crowd goes into a burst of soft laughter.

'Now, both of us were strikers, and I know you know what that is, but for those who don't, it's when you come into the Navy undesignated as an enlisted. That means you don't know your job yet, for you folks sitting with blank stares. In other words, you get to shop around, so to speak, for your career before selecting one. Now to me, it had an advantage because you get to see all of the Navy jobs that you are interested in, in action, and pick your career firsthand, hopefully, something you'll enjoy.

After boot camp, Carl and ten others received orders for the same ship. We had a tall captain, a little taller than yourself, sir, called Big John, and rightfully so because he was tall, stocky build, and a brilliant captain. Well..., Captain Big John had a special program for strikers, which consisted of a to team four Sailors. He would have them tour different divisions in a rotation in search of their new jobs. Now at the end of twelve months, you had to choose where you worked, providing the division felt you were an excellent candidate. Needless to say that I got teamed up with ole' Carl,' Keyonton says, smiling.

'Man. . ., I remember my first time out on the town with Carl; I mean..., it was so vivid that it feels like yesterday.'

The crowd goes into a burst of soft laughter.

'Well..., we ended up at the Military Circle Mall in Norfolk Virginia, and since this was our first time hanging out, we were full of excitement. Well..., we got off the bus and walked around a prestigious, name-brand store, and there we were..., just me and my new buddy, Carl. We must have window-shopped for hours before stopping at the pants rack. And there we stood; me on one side of the display and Carl on the other. From time to time, we would make eye contact until going about our business to other displays.

Suddenly, I see Carl flinch and look around like an Irish pointer when hearing him yell out, 'Ah, uh huh, uh huh.' Well, I looked down, and it had not registered until looking back up quickly, seeing Carl jumping into a huddle like a scrimmage and vanishing.'

The crowd bursts into soft laughter, with some folks louder than others.

'Carl comes back up quick, then fades until I hear another 'Ah, uh huh, uh huh,' when ole' Carl fades again. He comes up once more, then disappears quickly, but the last time we're eye-to-eye, and I find ole' Carl's face torn up. Immediately I know something is wrong, and before I can ask a thing, a big ole' fat, wet, slimy spitball hits Carl betwixt (between) his eyes and slowly roll down his cheek, hanging right at the lower cheek.'

The crowd goes into a burst of soft laughter.

'I call out to ole' Carl, and before I knew it, I heard, 'Ah, uh huh, uh huh.' Whew! I mean..., damn clothes start flying all over the damn place, and the damn men's clothing area looks like damn Jurassic Park.'

The crowd goes into a burst of soft laughter.

'Clothes continually sway until I hear Carl's thick body slam to the floor, low-crawling fast to find that smart-ass kid.'

The crowd goes into a burst of loud laughter.

'I take off in a sprint and as fast as possible, then even faster. From time to time, I would stick my head up and go low, following in the wake of slow-to-fast moving clothes, listening for the next, 'Ah, uh huh, uh huh.' Well…, I lost Carl's hot trail and came back up, then stopped, looking around until hearing him yell out, 'Ah, uh huh, uh huh' when gazing over at a blouse high in the air, in the women's department, where I find Carl tearing through women's clothes like nobody's business; and I mean he's hot on that kid's trail.

I stop, listening to the next call to the wild, but this time, I hear a loud slap and a little voice scream, 'Ma!' but should have said mama, which is cut short because ole' Carl has caught his prey.'

The crowd goes into a burst of louder laughter.

'Clothes in the girls' department begin falling like leaves, and the next thing I hear is, 'Ah, uh huh uh huh,' and after that, there is pure silence.

Man…, you talk about panicking! Let me tell you! Man…, I come up in stealth mode, ears growing more receptive to the faint screams that sound more like gags. I turn every corner I can find, even knocking a few women aside. Hell…, my main mission was to find this kid, and I do mean in a damn hurry because I know he's in grave danger.'

The crowd goes into a burst of loud laughter.

'When I turn down the bra aisle, I hear Carl yell, 'Ah, uh huh, uh huh,' but this time in a lower tone, which is uncommon. I turn and soon catch sight of those size-thirteens with the tops face down and beeline, coming up on ole Carl in a mad rush, pouncing at least twelve feet or more because I remember passing over them and seeing Carl's hands engulfed around the boy's neck so tight that it looks like the kid didn't even have a freakin' neck. Abruptly, something strange happens when my shoe clips ole' Carl at the hook in the back of his head because with eyes still looking back, I see Carl snatched, when tucking, and rolling.'

The crowd bursts into loud laughter, bringing many to tears.

'I lay mangled, trying to shake off my fast headache, then sit, unbending the metal rack wrapped around my head. I look over quick, finding ole' Carl climbing to his feet. I turn the other way, finding the kid limp, and look again, finding him kicking as if jerking, so I do a double-take, fearfully jumping up. I anxiously point to Carl, moving my hand fast as if holding a steering wheel, motioning for him to meet me at the bus stop, then peep at the kid, finally seeing his little fingers flinch, one at a time but slow.'

The crowd goes into a burst of soft laughter.

'My heart starts beating again, so I make it over to the kid and find his head a little wobbly, his mouth still wide open, but nothing coming out.'

The crowd goes into a burst of loud laughter.

'The kid's chest and stomach sink in, then sink deeper a second time. 'Mau, Mau, Maaaa!' the kid screams, continually for what sounded like all of two minutes straight. I mean…, he pauses a second, then sounds off, but this time it had to have been longer and more like five minutes.'

The crowd goes into a burst of soft laughter.

'I rush up on him and help him to his little feet, then release him, and the kid wobbles like he's drunker than Schooner Brown. I mean…, this kid is falling all into the damn clothes racks, mannequins, and wall until I grab him again steadying him.

The kid's mother rushes up out of nowhere, frantically looking down to find my hands on his shoulder.

I slightly shove him forward into her, staring into his bloodshot eyes and then over the generous handprint at his red, bruised neck.'

The crowd goes into a burst of loud laughter.

'I tried holding my laugh, but it filled me so quick that I bent down as if to pick something up but leaned around clothes, giggling like crazy.

'What! What is it, Timmy?' his mother asks, but the kid can't talk for some reason, but he cries an endless river.'

The crowd goes into a burst of soft laughter.

"You know…, I'm not sure, but I'm willing to bet a box of doughnuts that Ole' Carl crushed his damn Adam's apple all to smithereens."

The crowd goes into a burst of loud laughter.

'Well…, anyways, she asked what happened, and I told her I wasn't sure, but I heard him scream and rushed over, finding him lying there.'

The crowd grows wild, and Keyonton waits for them to calm down.

"But you know what? Since that incident, whenever I go anywhere with ole' Carl, I try telling folks he's a little off-balanced because I know that had they gotten into the mix with this clown, it would have been a high price to pay."

The crowd grows wild, and Keyonton waits for them to calm down again.

"Now…, for some reason, I feel they thought I did it to keep them from hurting Carl," Keyonton says, giggling.

'I remember when ole' Carl and I wanted to make a few extra bucks, so we take a shot at time-sharing, you know. . ., going door-to-door or using any tactic to get folks to seminars in exchange for a stay at a free hotel, cruise, money, or whatever promotions they're running that week. Well…, look a hea (here), we ended up wrapping up the day in a business park. I mean…, I had already made quota, and I was burned the hell out but still in a joking mood when teasing ole' Carl, getting majorly creative when counting my twenty sales versus Carl's one.'

The crowd burst out in laughter.

'I didn't want to sell anything else but wanted to give him a chance to catch up, seeing how he's looking down. Hell…, come to think of it; I think I had actually made about thirty sales to Carl's one. Well, come to think of it more, the one Carl made was from a man Carl knew from high school, or maybe even elementary…, you know, someone from back in Carl's bullying days because he sure looked nervous as hell, to me…, with all the stuttering, emptying of his wallet, and giving Carl all his goods when there was no cash to be exchanged for the timeshare.'

The crowd bursts into tears of laughter

'So, anyway, we come upon this doctor's office, stopping, backing, and looking inside. Now what I saw, and look…it may have just been me now, but what I saw was a tired, beat-down nurse wrapping up from a very, very, very long and intriguing day.'

The crowd laughs.

'Now, look hea (here), I tried talking ole' Carl out of going in, but he was determined to outdo me, and needed this sale. I mean…, honestly, I had a very, very, very bad feeling that it was an awful idea, seeing how the woman had not a smile at all left in her weary body. So, I peep in again, finding her walking around, talking to herself until snatching things off the counter, throwing things, and sometimes throwing her middle finger up to someone in the back office; more than likely her boss.'

The crowd laughs.

'I mean, this woman looked mad as hell, and if she had gotten into a fight, right then and there she would have torn somebody's tail up, yeah..., that kinda (kind of) mean and mad look.

So anyway, Carl quickly reaches over my shoulder, and I grab his hand, trying to fight ole' Carl and keep him from opening the door but what a waste of time.

Well..., instantly, the door flies wide open and we walk in, and I drop back, playfully shoving and coaching Carl on, you know..., a little morale booster, especially when I said, 'You go, champ.' I mean..., I'm his friend and all, so I have to pump him up..., you know, like at a little pep rally..., you know?

Well..., let me tell you, I stood back..., I mean way back and I do mean waaaayyyy..., way, way, way back, when moving hands around, and yeah, dancing and chanting a little bit louder. 'C.H.A.M.P., go, Carl, go Champ!' Keyonton says, playfully dancing like he's a cheerleader with a few moves to show off. 'Or something of that nature is what I said because I knew that either him or her was about to give a great end-of-day show.'

The crowd bursts into tears of laughter, watching closely.

'Well, ole' Carl sticks his chest out, approaching without hesitation.

The nurse looks up, and I mean..., she did not even crack a smile. Her eyes stay glued on ole' Carl like a strike Terrier! I mean..., she doesn't even attempt to roll the glass back but talks through it.'

The crowd bursts into tears, and Jenn almost falls off her seat from laughing so hard.

'Now, you see..., that there alone would have been my cue to ask for directions to the mall, location to a car wash, or even schedule to get a teeth extraction appointment, or anything except a darn sale. Heck, I would have even asked if they had a restroom, but there is no way in Hell that I would have taken a shot for a time-share sell, but nooooo..., not ole' Carl!

Carl proudly reaches for his back pocket, pulls out his pamphlet, and starts in on the first three words of his well-rehearsed pitch when the woman shakes her head no, not even hearing the last two of the three words, but ole' Carl's not having it.

The woman tells him no three times…, not once, but three…, that she's not interested.'

The crowd bursts into tears of laughter, watching closely.

'Well, the woman finally turns red and finally, she expressly rolls the window back, almost shattering it when asking him to leave not once but three times, and ole' Carl's still isn't having it. Out of nowhere, her last request comes loud and clear; but let me say this, well…, in my mind, there was no doubt when she tells him that if he doesn't leave that minute, he would be escorted off to jail for solicitation. Hell, she even points to the huge 'no solicitation' sign in the doors glass that both of us obviously missed.'

A peal of deep laughter arises from the crowd.

'Now, I don't know about you, Arena, but instantly the words cops and jail made my head hurt, and my butt cheeks tighten,' Keyonton says, pointing to folks in the front row who are bent over in tears. 'Well…, as for me…, I started high-stepping. I mean…, I didn't even look back once and sure as hell was not going to be looking back three times. Well…, I reached the glass door, shot through it, and was like ghost (gone). When I was far enough for her not to identify me, I finally look back, right when she slams the sliding glass closed, hard, and commences pointing at him then the door.'

The crowd bursts into tears of laughter, watching closely.

'Well, to me; I think she hurt ole' Carl's feelings because I've never seen him so sad.

Carl slowly walks out with his head low, and for a minute, I think he's just a bit embarrassed because his head stays low as he walks past, kicking a few rocks over the beautiful landscape. He finally turns when about ten feet away and walks back up to me, but I kept my back turned while watching his towering shadow swarm over me.

'Screw that trick! Let's get the hell out of here!' Carl says, still staring at the ground under-eyed.'

The crowd bursts into tears of laughter, watching closely.

'Well…, let me tell you…, I fight, covering my uncontrollable laugh that brews deep when Carl walks away a few feet, looking back at me. 'Come on, let's go!' Carl screams in anger, finding the back of my head and shoulders, uncontrollably jerking in silence.'

The crowd screams, bursting into tears of laughter, watching Keyonton's silent motions, with his back to them.

'I said come on!' Carl screams again but playfully pulls me by my collar when I turn, losing it when my mouth flies wide open. I mean…, I screamed so loud; you could have heard my laughter ten blocks away.'

The crowd bursts into tears of laughter, watching him closely.

'Carl stares, not cracking a smile. I mean…, instantly, he's three shades pinker and then as bright red as a fire engine, watching me lean hard until falling into the hood.

Let me tell you; I fall on my knees like the men in an old gun-slinging Western movie. I mean I'm in tears, and my eyes are so watery that I can't even see. I must have had my face down in the grass, screaming in tears for at least thirty minutes or so before getting it together and finding Carl's face still frowned.

Well, ole' Carl patiently waits until I get up and is somewhat quiet, immediately getting my undivided attention when hearing Ah, uh huh, uh huh, and let me tell you…, my face went from zero to sixty flat, from laughter to a serious face.

"Now about this time, Carl stares deep into my face and I will never forget what he said." 'He said, oh, you think that crap is funny? Well, it won't be that funny if I go in there and punch that trick in her damn face! Yeah, you'll be out here crying and screaming like a little sissy, saying…, Come on, Carl! Come on, man! Let's go before the cops get here!'

Now let me tell you…, before I know it, I hear Carl say, 'Ah, uh huh, uh huh.'

I look back quickly, finding him staring at the office door. Hell, I get very serious, very quick, and get up. Hell, the Jack in the box did not have shit on me! You see…, I already know that's my cue for when Carl's about to act a pure-T damn foot. Pure-T…, now that's some damn country slang for your ass!"

"Good ole' Carl," Keyonton says in deep thought when staring at the floor in even deeper thought. 'Oh yeah…, I have to tell you this one! Now, we had this one dude in our division whose family was rich, or so he claims. Well he was always loaded and got a new car every year, or so he claimed. Well, we were going to the beach, so back on the ship, I tried warning this dude about ole' Carl and how crazy he is when pissed.

The crow burst into a peal of laughter.

"Well, ole dude gone laugh, like, it was all fun and games."

"Well..., now that I think on it, most folks onboard thought this rich kid was a hothead and jokester."

'Well, anyway, we get to his car, and I do remember it being a candy-apple red sports car, fully decked out; I mean it was a head turner! Well, I rush to the front door to increase my chances of picking up the hotties, but how 'bout, this dude gone ask Carl to get upfront.'

The crowd bursts into tears of uncontrollable laughter, watching closely.

'I mean..., I was pissed that he played me like a fiddle, but something reminded me that I had already warned him, so I cheerfully get in the back with the other dude who's just as simple if not simpler that Carl; a bunk of damn basket cases they were.

Well..., the car exits onto the main highway and swerves around a few cars when the driver flips the nitrogen switch he's been bragging about.

Our heads drop back, and he comes up to sixty and then seventy miles per hour.

I mean..., this dude is driving like a bat..., out..., of..., Hell..., I mean a damn crazed maniac and speed demon!'

The crowd bursts into more tears of laughter, watching and listening.

'Well he begins swerves in and out of traffic as if we're the only ones on the damn highway, and not once does he look back to change lane but shouts, asking if the lane is clear after maneuvering, changing lanes.

The crowd burst into laughter.

'By now, my eyes are constantly glued behind us each time I feel the slightest tug at the steering wheel because I'm scared as heck. Each time I blurted out, I made damn sure it overpowered Carl's voice should he decide it was time to sound off.

The crowd burst into loud laughter.

Well, the rich kid comes up to eighty ten ninety and starts laughing and looking back like a crazy man.

Now ole Carl's eyes stay glued to the windshield or side mirror, but sometimes he looks back with nervous eyes. Carl's nervous body constantly rocks until I see almost all white, slightly pink, and red pupils each time I catch him in the sun visor or side mirror.

Anyway, out of nowhere, I catch a serious cramp in my neck and take a quick break, but catch a glimpse into Carl's bulged and nervous eyes again. I look back quickly, finding the tires on the white dotted line, which look solid from going so fast.

Suddenly, the car shifts into the lane, but I notice a blue car rolling up in a blur.

Out of nowhere, the driver opens his mouth, and before he can ask if the lane is clear, ole' nervous Carl yells out, 'Ah, uh huh, uh huh!'

The crowd bursts into tears of laughter, and many fall from their seats.

'Maaannnn…, let me tell you; that car swerves, and I scream like a girl screaming at the sight of a little spider.

We instantly slam into the blue car and force it headfirst into a guardrail. Everyone's mouths tear wide open as we go into slow motion spin out.

Now, I'm not sure if it is just my nerves or what, but for a minute, it looks like Carl's head turns a hundred-and-eighty degrees, and he's sitting there staring right at me.

Carl's mouth tears open so wide that I see that little thing, Now, I do not know the name of it, but it dangles down the back of his throat, like in the cartoons.'

The crowd bursts into tears of laughter, watching and listening.

'The driver stares back, screaming something as well, and I try reading his lips, and if I'm not mistaken, he says something like, 'You punk bitch!' but I'm not quite sure.'

The crowd bursts into tears of laughter, watching and listening closer.

'But let me tell you…, there is one thing for damn sure; the dude next to me called ole' Carl a freakin' idiot, and then there is this faint response; a whisper from Carl as I watch his death-gripped sharp nails sink deep into the dash, and that is, 'Ah, uh huh, uh huh.'

The crowd bursts into tears of laughter and many are bent over in deep laughter.

'Maaannnn! I think the only thing that saved us as we came down from the overpass even and almost aligning with the second highway is the high speed and the weight of the dude in the backseat's head when balanced out with Carl's; gargantuan head.'

The crowd bursts into tears of laughter, and a few screams of laughter follow.

'I mean, the drop seemed so long that it feels like we were taking a damn break from our screams until I see the ground draw closer when I scream like a little ole' girl again.'

The crowd bursts into tears of laughter, watching and listening.

'For sure, that car looked like a damn plane flying through the air. Maaannnn! We slam into the pavement…, whoooo! I see the tires roll past and veer off into a vacant field. We bounce a few times and then pass two state troopers, following each other with sparks flying like crazy on both sides, when we're looking like a transport steel mill.'

The crowd bursts into tears of laughter, watching and listening.

'All I can see is thick, sparkly arcs trailing down both sides until they die down when finally stopping at a red light.

The troopers roll up with guns drawn, and Ole' Carl screams at the top of his lungs as if he's in a damn Godzilla movie, pulling his fingers hard from the dashboard.

Everyone freezes with hands high overhead.

The trooper taps on the window, and the whole damn car falls apart at all the seams! There we sit, in nothing but the seat with just seat belts on. Now you talk about a damn Navy adventure! Well, that there is a real damn Navy adventure for my monkey ass!'

The Arena goes wild as Keyonton walks around, waiting for them to settle down.

"Oh, snap! I almost forget about the time when I was in revenge mode."

'Ole' Carl played me hard one day, tripping me in front of a group of hotties.

Well, I wanted to get ole' Carl back, and my main goal was humiliating him. I know my plot will take some time, and I can wait because he had to pay dearly. So…, there was this one night we had duty, and the duty officer ordered a main event boxing match. During the whole fight, Carl jumps up, making his fancy moves.'

Keyonton begins showing some ridiculous-looking moves and leaves the audience in an uproar of laughter.

'Carl was so into the fight that he pretends he's in the ring. Well..., when he finally calms down, I tell him my uncle and dad were professional boxers and that I used to coach boxing before the Navy. Yeah, I put it on thick, buddy, and sugarcoated that lie so sweet that ole' Carl almost forgot the fight was still on with thirty minutes left.

From that day forward, Carl begs me to coach him, but I constantly tell him that he's not ready, just to piss him off.'

The crowd bursts into tears of laughter, watching and listening.

'You know..., I would always have a new excuse for not teaching him. Well..., as time went on, I knew it was time for me to execute my plan or else Carl might lose interest, so I began taking ole' Carl to the gym so he could get in shape and get a feel for the ropes. Yes, you can say I had ole' Carl's mind warped because, for some reason, he thinks he's a skilled boxer from the way he always goes at it with the heavy and punching bags.'

The crowd bursts into tears of laughter, watching and listening.

'When we're at sea, I'd get him all pumped up on Rocky movies. Yeah, I'd tell him that I would continue being his coach if he ever got bold enough to get in the ring at the base gym, where they have professionals come in from different bases over the U.S., but he'd have to win his first fight.

Well back in port one day, we head out, picking up snacks. I get chips, and Carl gets a whopping bag of those red-hot pork rinds; some call them pork skins. After we get our drink on, I plan to go to the club and decide on taking a break from the gym because they had out-of-town folks from another base there for a championship fight. Now..., let me be honest; I didn't even tell Carl about the tournament because I knew he would get hurt trying to prove himself. I mean..., I want him to hurt, but not that particular kind of hurt because those out-of-town dudes are straight punishers..., kicking butt and taking names; no breaks and no holidays!'

The crowd bursts into tears of laughter, watching and listening.

'So anyway, we sit in the club's parking lot getting our drink and snacks on when one of our shipmates shows up, telling us he had just left the gym. Now, mind you that by this time, I had already knocked off two-thirds of the bottle of cognac, and ole' Carl had demolished two-fifths of. . ., I think it was Wild Spanish Rose that he was drinking.'

The crowd bursts into tears of laughter, watching and listening.

'Well, the dude keeps talking about the event, and instantly Carl gets excited. The next thing I know, the dude informs Carl that they still have five more fights left in the event. Well, what do you know…, we end up there. I mean…, we are higher than a freakin' kite and five sheets in the wind on a windy day. We are drunker than Joe Sucker Head and all his damn relatives.'

The crowd bursts into more tears of laughter, watching and listening.

'We float into the gym, staggering into the bleachers. Now, let me tell you…, this place is packed like sardines in a can, and I do mean…, packed.

I try hard to maintain my composure because they have some of the hottest women there. Come on now…, you know how men get when they get that liquid courage; thinking they can take on the whole world, so with women, it just adds fuel to the fire.'

The crowd bursts into tears of laughter, and a couple of guys in the front row exchange high-fives.

'Well, those champion fighters are in there, going to it…, do you hear me? I had to calm ole' Carl down on several occasions because he's too drunk and hyper to comprehend. He's fuller than a tick on a fat woman's ass and so excited that he just sits there punishing that jumbo bag of extra hot pork rinds in record time.'

The crowd bursts into more tears of laughter, watching and listening.

'Ole' Carl soon balls up the big bag and stares at the boxers on the sideline like a bull in heat. Instantly, I know Carl can taste blood; well you know…, that's just how he looked.'

The crowd bursts into tears of laughter, watching and listening.

'I just look at him from the side, shaking my head because I feel we're in trouble.

Well, the evening seemed like it was about to end.

People begin shuffling out, but lo and behold, they get down to the last fight, and the kid that is supposed to fight chickens out.'

The crowd bursts into uncontrollable tears of laughter, watching and listening.

'I mean…, his coach pulls and pushes this dude to the ring, but he doesn't want any parts of this iron-looking muscle-bound little dude in the ring.'

A loud uproar arises, and more of the crowd burst into tears of laughter.

'Well, look here..., immediately, there's a discussion not too far from us amongst trainers and referees.

Well, ole' Carl finally gets wind that they're looking to match up the dude when he has an out-of-body experience, intervening, then volunteering to fight.

The trainers and referee come together, standing off in the corner, talking for about two minutes, when one trainer points to the height difference, but the dude that is the fight's trainer secretly slips the other coach a wad of money; and they agreed.

My heart drops, and though I feel great about Carl's size and reach advantage, that all diminishes when I look back over at that little feller. I mean..., this little dude looks like he just came off a damn steel robot assembly line, and he's mad at the world.'

The crowd bursts into tears of non-stop laughter, watching and listening.

'Well..., let me tell you..., he looks meaner than the damn red, scaly devil himself.'

The crowd bursts into tears of laughter, watching and listening.

'Now, come to think of it; I guess there is something in that Wild Spanish Rose that made the man of steel look friendly to ole Carl, for some reason. I mean..., this man just looks evil for no darn reason. I know good and damn well that Carl is talking out of his head because it is definitely Mr. Rose doing all the darn foolish negotiating.'

The crowd bursts into tears of laughter, watching and listening.

'Well..., a minute or so later, the trainers walk over and tell Carl to go suit up.

Instantly, my smooth high leaves and common sense step in because I have to do something quick. Well. . ., I go into the dressing room and come up with all kinds of reasoning why Carl shouldn't fight this little, mean man, but ole' Carl is too pumped, full up, backed up, and hyped off the juice to listen to reasoning. So, I got serious. . ., I pull Carl to the side and put on my trainer's face, looking Carl straight in his bloodshot, red eyes. 'Now I said, Carl, now you listen to me..., this man is a trained professional; he's well-conditioned and trains year-round. He does this here for a living.' I tell Carl that the man lives, sleeps, and eats boxing, but obviously, ole' Carl turns a deaf ear because I blink, and he rushes for the door like he's about to win millions if he beats the man.'

The crowd bursts into more tears of laughter, watching and listening.

'Well…, I tell you…, I stand there dumbfounded, looking around, then rush off in the corner, pull out a bucket, and mop for mopping up ole' Carl off that mat.'

The crowd bursts into tears of laughter, watching and listening.

'Before I know it, a trainer and referee meet Carl in the hallway, rushing him to the ring.

I stagger back out and come up next to the ring, giving ole' Carl some moral support, and before I can talk him out of the fight, out of nowhere, the bell rings.

Carl comes out instantly with fancy footwork, and for a quick second, a very, very, very, very quick second, I'm proud of ole' Carl, but only for a second. . ., ok, half a second, and even that was short-lived.

I'm impressed with his short-lived moves until the little man finally comes out, throwing jabs so swift that I hear wind behind them. This dude walks straight forward, never taking a single step back but marching straight through Carl.'

The crowd bursts into tears with several new outbursts coming as everyone laughs.

'Well…, Carl takes more devastating, near-death-looking blows, stunned, and is so busted that he can't even scream, but I scream for him, bobbing and weaving as if I'm in the darn ring.'

The crowd bursts into tears of laughter, watching and listening.

'Well…, let me tell you…, with all, that's in me…, I scream for Carl to duck, stick and move, repeatedly until tongue tired, I tell yah (you). And sure enough, Carl finally spins out, looking like he's in one hundred percent slow mode for sure, and I know this because every time Carl ducks, that little mad man hits him before and after the duck, then before and after the stick and sure as hell before and after the damn move…, damn!'

The crowd bursts into more tears of laughter, watching and listening.

'I mean…, this little dude has opened a fresh can of whoop-ass on ole' Carl with about twelve rounds remaining. The little man comes continually with high jumps and steel-power drivers to Carl's head, and

I soon hear him scream, 'You want some more of me, punk!' and each time ole' Carl screams, 'Ah, uh huh. Uh huh!' And let me tell you…, that little man gives it to him like he's delivering Christmas presents on Christmas Day and obviously without the damn sleigh.'

The crowd bursts into tears of non-stop laughter, watching and listening.

'Well, to be honest, and I'm not sure because it happened so fast, but I think I heard him ask if he wants more with ole' Carl answering 'Ah, uh huh, uh huh!' about fifteen or more times.'

The crowd bursts into tears of laughter, watching and listening.

'Ok…, so by now, the crowd is screaming for the referee to get ole' Carl out of there because he's limper than a wet noodle.

Now, I'm sitting on the sideline, begging and pleading for the same before their mad little man kills him and I got to go back to the ship and fill out those long ass twenty page mishap reports. Man…, it's gonna (going to) be hell to tell the captain!'

The crowd bursts into more tears of laughter.

'Well, the trainers are not hearing this extraction at all because they have money on the line. So…, here come the last fifteen seconds of the first round, and I feel good because I know that if I can get over there to ole' Carl, he will beg me to stop the fight. I count down the last seconds: five, four. . ., three, three, three. . ., and before I can say two, that little man draws back so hard and deep, bringing a whirlwind with his fast short-range rocket launched fist.'

The crowd bursts into tears of laughter, getting louder.

'Well…, let me tell you…, he plows so far into Carl's gut that I think it went straight through his spine when Carl folds, and there are pork rinds and bright red, Wild Spanish Rose all over that damn canvas.'

The crowd bursts into more tears of laughter, listening.

'And let me tell you…, Ole Carl looks like the star of a Gladiator movie. . ., you know, the part where he's just been thrust through? Carl just stands for seconds, too afraid to fall. Now, that is a darn Navy adventure and whipping for Carl's monkey ass!' Keyonton yells in laughter. "Sweet revenge…, sweet revenge!"

The crowd bursts into tears of laughter, watching and listening.

Keyonton paces, waiting for a minute or so for the crowd to calm down.

'Well, I feel sorry about ole' Carl, and years later, you see, Carl and I go to a Navy football game. You know…, one of those annual games where the Navy whips the snot out of the Army. That's where one of Carl's elementary schoolmates tells me about Carl's misdiagnosis of some disorder as a kid.

As time went on, the professionals figured out that it was not a symptom but habitual. Now, this is no lie…, the guy says that the doctor said that all his parents had to do was whip his ass to stop him from saying it when he was younger, and it would naturally go away.' Keyonton looks down at the time, realizing there is no time for another story or joke, when throwing up the peace sign. "Well, it's been fun, people!" Keyonton yells, bowing, then backing up a few feet and bowing again. He waves then motion the D.J. to crank up a beat and dance his way off stage. He heads to the back, makes his way to the dressing room, and changes, meeting his posse outback and heading to the after-party.

Keyonton arrives at the after-party thirty minutes later, walking over, talking to four women who want him. He reaches for a drink from the bar and sees a woman dressed in all white, unknowingly to him, but intentionally intercepting him.

The knockout, gorgeous Asian chick slowly passes, walking even slower to ensure she has Keyonton's full attention.

Keyonton intentionally waits for the perfect moment and then turns, playfully sliding out in front of her. "Hi, I'm Key," he smoothly says.

"Ok, and? Duh! Everyone here knows you; besides, it's your party!" She giggles.

"Yeah, girl…, I know that!" he says, looking silly. "It's my party, but the silly thing is, I don't know your name. Man. . ., you are the hottest thang here." He briefly turns away and then back with squinty eyes to look sexy when staring into beautiful, slanted eyes.

"It's Titeaundra," she responds.

"Hey, can I get you a drink?" He looks back at the four women, getting mean stares until they turn up their noses. "Oh…, ok…, them too," he nervously says, pointing the bartender to the four women.

The five women rise when Keyonton motions and points for them to take seats in the V.I.P. section on plush lounge chairs.

Keyonton phone rings, and he takes a call from his female cousin, which lasts well over ten minutes, talking about her man until the conversation moves on to her needing money. He soon hangs up, motioning the female server to bring another round while listening to the women talk about pregnancy when growing interested. He eases closer and sits, smiling, and instantly bursts into a burst of silly laughter when the last girl comments on wanting a foreign man so she could have pretty babies.

"Hold up! Rewind that right there, and. . ., play!" He stares at the girl, then the caller I.D., finding his cousin's number again when looking back at the girl. "Girl, look..., I don't know how many of these damn drinks you had, but you need to shut it down because you up in here talking that silly-ass elementary mess," Keyonton says, digging deep in his pocket and throwing a couple of fifties on the table. "What's with this foreign man crap?" he asks, pissed.

The woman acts a little bashful, looking at the others and then slowly back at him.

Keyonton takes another deep sip and then stirs the drink with his index finger.

The four women thirstily stare at his finger as if they want to lick the residue.

"I said, if I get pregnant, I want it to be by a foreign man or any man for that fact, but they have to have a good complexion and good hair."

Keyonton's hands shoot to his mouth, but not fast enough, when a heavy, powerful overspray shoots across the table into the girl's face, slightly knocking her back. He jumps, wipes himself, and seconds later, hands her a handful of his drenched tissues. "Hey, look, I'm sorry," he says, wiping a few wet spots from her arm while she wipes her face. "Where did you get a crazy thought? You know what..., when I first saw you, I thought you were: one..., well-educated, and two..., a little sophisticated. Well, that little comment negates all the above because now you're just beautiful, uneducated, and sophisticated-looking."

Laughter burst out at the table and in the vicinity.

"Yeah, you may end up with a beautiful baby, and I can see you now: 'Look at my pretty baby, look at my pretty baby.' Yeah, she or he might be beautiful or handsome, but they will be starving like hell cause you can't find their daddy, or they might end up dumber than a brick wall, but he/she sho (sure) will be pretty or handsome," he sarcastically says while shaking his head.

"Hmm..., look at that stuff on your head. Hell..., a horse has good hair, and you burn fewer brain cells, not having to track the daddy down for child support because he'll be in the owner's stable but on the real, that's sinful. My point is this..., I mean, you can always steal him from the owner and sell him your support money," Keyonton says in a silly laugh when others join in the laughter. "Do you even know about the epidemic in this country and the States? You got all these damn foreigners getting American women pregnant, then hightailing it back to another city, state, or country without paying child support. If you ask me, it is just a tactic to break down the Social Services system. So what you gone do then..., a pretty baby, and you can't afford to feed it? What are you going to do? I tell you exactly what you're gone (are going to) do: take that pretty baby down to the Department of Social Services and get public assistance while this grease monkey with the pretty, gelled-up hair goes and impregnates more women who have the same silly philosophy. Hell yeah, I think it's a conspiracy to bankrupt Social Services," he says, giggling. "Shoot, I pay enough taxes as-is for your trifling tail to be out here making pretty babies on the system." He causes the other girls to burst into laughter.

"If I was the president, I would create one of those things like ole' Bill's, 'Don't Ask Don't Tell' but mine would be geared toward social services: 'If you ain't got no D.N.A., then don't look for us to pay.' Now that is a motto for your pretty hair and pretty complexion one-night stand, tail. I bet you will try and keep track of who comes in and out of that bed then, won't you? My other policy would create jobs because I would create a baby-daddy tracking agency to track down all deadbeats the next year. The days of men saying they ain't got a job and can't pay will be long over. I'll get him a job in the penal system working for pennies and take every penny he earns. I bet after two trips down a six months stretch; he'll be out cutting grass or selling booty on the corner, to keep from going back in there and hanging curtains for Big Buddha or tossing salads for free," he says in laughter and tears. He gets a good laugh when others converge around him, and he feels the full effects of the drink, not realizing he's got a packed audience.

"Shitttt! What you need to do is get smart. Save the goodies until you get some identification: driver's license, passport, license tags, or something. Moreover, ladies, stop jumping in bed with a man on the first night; that's a straight-up booty call if he never calls you back…, so stop calling it lovemaking afterward when it's not even a booty call, it's a snack pack.

Shucks, have you forgotten all the diseases in the world? Get to know these men and women. Here you are, trusting your life to a piece of latex if that. I mean…, what is a little broken latex rubber amongst perfect strangers? You wake up the next morning thinking you found love, and that cat is sitting there thinking about how he can shake you so you don't burn up his day. Yeah, he'll take you to a nice restaurant for breakfast, so he can feed his brain and figure out what he's going to say or do to shake your trifling tail and be ghost (gone)," he says, taking another sip.

"Next thing you know, you're on the phone telling your girl you found a man. A few days later, he's ducking and dodging you like the plague or as if you're the damn Grim Reaper. Here you are sitting around blowing up his number; if he even gave you the right number, and if not, it's back to the ole drawing board. Now, you're home lonely again, and a few days later, up in the club, shaking your tail, and then home with another dude. You lie in bed crying your heart out about the last dude and then give it up, and he leaves the same way — think cycle, women…, cycle! How will that man respect you if you drop those drawers so easily and don't even know his real name?"

Keyonton takes another sip, finding a dude staring down as if something is on his mind. "How you doing, sir? You look like you got a lot on your mind," he says, expanding his hand outward and pointing to draw attention to the man's big head when looking the man over before he can look up.

"Yeah, maybe…, hey, look…, why do you get off on bashing people in your shows?"

"Now, see! There you go! I wasn't going to say anything along those lines tonight. Bashing, bashing. . ., I'm not bashing, and if anything, I'm word bashing. I'm not the one with the power to say its right or wrong. Equal rights! Well, equal rights mean you have the right to be talked about like others without crying bashing to get the heat off and seem invisible. Look…, I have homeboys I went to school with that I just found out are not as they claim, but they're still friends, and if I care about their well-being, I'm going to tell them the truth, but they're still homies. Yeah, yeah, yeah, they talk crap when I talk to them about. . .," he says, cutting off the word when shaking his head. "Yawl (you all) kills me with this bashing crap!.

"And one more thing before I get off this mic..., let me tell you right now, don't none of yawl come calling me to tell me you want a darn formal apology unless you can show me where it's right, and don't give me that deer-in-the-headlight look. Bashing! In the past, people bashed people just for wearing bifocal glasses, torn clothes, being poor, having congenital disabilities, you name it! Suddenly, you want to call it bashing so you can feel good on your pedestal. It's your life, so have at it! Moreover, let me tell you one thing: I'm a Black, Chinese, equal-opportunity comic, joking on all of you, Brothas (Brothers), and that's what I do! I don't discriminate. Hell! Momma needs a butt lift, and baby needs some of that expensive darn baby formula!"

Some are still in tears, but many draw quiet when Keyonton points to the D.J., who throws on a lovely track.

The dance floor fills quickly, but some folks turn back from the crowded floor.

A few songs play, and then the D.J. clear the floor, introducing the first comedian, who walks out dancing.

"How yawl doing out there?" the comedian screams, looking around and positioning his water bottle on the stool. "Damn Kids! I was almost late tonight, messing around with my badass kids. Shoot. . ., I had my clothes neatly laid out, and their pathetic little tail gone (is going to) hide my shoes, keys, and wallet because I said no to new school clothes. Bad little mothers for no reason," he says, looking around. "How many of you have had kids lately?" He waits for a show of hands. "Well, join the club, but let me ask you this: Do yawl (you all) use those solid plastic bottles or the hollow bottles?" He waits for responses and then bursts into laughter. 'Well, my girl go out and get the hollow bottles, you know, the ones with the plastic bags? Come on now. . ., ok, now some of you men might be clueless on this, but you will get it in a minute. Now, for some reason, my girl does not believe in giving the baby anything cold to drink.

How about the other day, when I got home, I played with my baby girl and girlfriend, then took a nice shower. I come out and stand by the bed drying off and feel something wet at my feet and look down, finding this big ole' thick latex-looking plastic. Woo! Man! I know some of yawl (you all) call it some ole' senseless name like going ham as in hamburger, but damnit, I thought about going hamburger, cheeseburger, and quarter-burger with damn fries and shake on her ass. I mean, at first, I was weak at the knees and so weak that I had to grab the bed to break my fall. I was hurt to my Soul..., people. I was so hurt, that I was speechless, and the main thing that came to mind was..., damn! This damn woman done messed about and hooked up with damn Bigfoot, King Kong, or Godzilalilalila!

I B.S. you not. . ., this latex had to be bigger than an enormous cucumber you've seen, but shriveled up and with a white load still inside that looks like old glue. Now, being the man I am, I'm not going to front, but I cried like a newborn but was not about to let her see me crying like no punk and ask what it was and have to tell her. Shoot, I bow my head like a chump and walk into the kitchen after getting the tears out. Yeah, my soul was torn all the hell up. Whew! When I get in that kitchen, I think I must have drank everything that even looked like it had liquor in it, and trust me; I keep an unusually generous stock of the top shelf at all times.

Meanwhile, I sit there, tore the hell up. I'm distraught beyond the wildest imagination of the word.

Anyway, she wanders in, about, oh say, fifteen minutes later and tries to get fresh, as if she's in the mood for love after being devoured. She runs her fingers through this good grade of hair, which is a total turn-off for me. Man, I tell you, the only thing I could think about was King Kong, Ching Chong, and big old Ding Dong devouring my sweet little flower. I stared her down with red, bloodshot eyes for minutes, and I think she thought it was sexy because she grew more turned on and got friskier.

Now, until this day, I still don't know how a rap radio station that plays nothing but rap all damn day long gonna play an oldie. You know that song. . ., that song, 'We Cried Together?' Yeah, that song comes on...come on, yawl (you all) know that song. And you talking about a damn crying man; I cried like a damn newborn, you hear me?

The next thing I know, we hear the baby crying.

She jumps, rushes to the sink, flings the cabinet door open, and pulls out another bottle and box of disposable sleeves. Hell! You talking about some crying? I was doing some crying and laughing at the same damn time! Hell..., I think I was the happiest man on this Earth seeing those sleeves when recalling the wet foot. For some reason, I knew there was no competition with something as round as that sleeve," he says, laughing. The comedian goes on to other colorful jokes, which bring the audience to their knees.

DAYS PRIOR: Barry's SUV swerves around a curve, with Ken riding shotgun around midday.

Ken grabs hold of the safety strap, slightly rising out of his seat, reaching for his seat belt, and buckling in tight.

Barry reaches for the dash, punching in a few numbers, then looks through his rearview and then ahead, refocusing on traffic at the upcoming stoplight.

On the north side of town, while in his car, Alfred's cell phone rings, and he picks up on the third ring.

Barry and Alfred continue driving, screaming back and forth until Ken leans, turning down the speaker's volume.

On the south side of town, Greg is home packing. He sits stuffing last-minute items in his overstuffed luggage and then attempts to close it on the bed until throwing it to the floor in frustration. He stomps it and then sits on it until finally closing it, but when he stands, there's a loud rip as the luggage bursts at the seams, sending clothes flying everywhere.

Barry's SUV rushes upon another intersection and comes to a screeching halt. He finds a local sandwich business mascot doing crazy and exotic dances while holding a submarine sandwich sign. The young man begins flipping the sign like a skilled professional, adding a few dances and more flips. He flings the sign high, catches it with one hand, and shoves it between his legs as if it is a towel, then works the shiny new sign back and forth as if wiping himself.

The submarine shop owner stands fuming and turning red until the door flies open, and he rushes across the lawn toward the corner. His mouth flies open, and his balled fists go high, screaming and bringing the rolling pin high above his head, swinging it rodeo-style while kicking up a trail of dust when barreling toward the mascot.

Barry and Ken giggle for minutes until the car behind them blows a few times.

"Well, I know that will certainly drop sales, and I know damn well that if I was thinking subs, that thought would have instantly diminished," Barry says, giggling when rechecking traffic before turning and pulling away.

"Yeah, no doubt, but you have to admit, that would have been great if he was on the corner marketing for a tax business because the Republicans sure are putting it to the middle and lower class, huh? Non-party affiliate," Ken says, looking back through the side mirror to find the owner, rushing up behind the young man and cracking him a few good whacks in the head with the rolling pin.

"You can say that again…, what a deceptive plot. The so-called leaders create laws to protect their jobs and themselves from having to go through things they take Americans through, like sequestration. I don't see anything about a sea in the sense of the word, so why not call it what it really is; more like a straight castration. What part of the budget is that? They are no better than big financial institution presidents and C.E.O.s who are in prison for mishandling money and cooking the books. Those companies went through their money and started going through other people's money, and now the government is doing the same exact thing by cutting into America's 401K and mishandling it. One thing is for sure; we definitely need to go back after this mess and review the laws, especially for people in Washington who make a career of it. Cooking darn books is an understatement; I think they have been deep-frying books and doing a great job. We need new ideas and eyes in Washington, not these old heads who are obviously too childish to make grown-folk decisions. Hell…, our so-called leadership is on display before nations," Barry says.

"No doubt, and now they claim they can't come to an agreement. Well, if they can't, then the people need to, which will change the laws for the lawmakers in the future, so that pay cuts and layoffs affect them as well. I bet you they will take decision-making more seriously then. I bet you a hundred bucks right now that when they finally come up with a workaround to this mess, the first thing they'll do is give themselves a raise," Ken says, laughing and shaking his head.

"Man, you crazy? I wouldn't even bet a red cent because I would have to be dumber than Farmer Sam Sausage Head on that bet." Barry laughs hard with blurry eyes.

"They need to be locked in a room, and every night at midnight, lay one off, indefinitely and without pension or severance. I bet after the first; they will get really creative about getting this country on track." Ken looks out the side window at a woman walking up to her car.

Barry's eyes stay watery, with shoulders going up and down in deep laughter until slightly swerving. "I've got one better than that...," Barry says, still in tears. "They need to put them in that room..., on the floor, and hotwire their chairs, and at midnight someone—me..., hint, hint—hits a mechanical switch that causes the lights to go out," he says in a crazy laugh. "Then another switch is hit by you..., hint, hint that sends a surge to a random seat, and when the lights come back on, they carry the unlucky son-of-a-gun out of there. Heck, if they want to act like kids, then let's just put them in an arena and let them play musical chairs for their jobs," Barry says, stopping at the light and bending over the steering wheel in deep laughter.

"Yeah, I wonder what that cat (past president) that was driving the plane with the country onboard, and heading us straight to the ground, is doing now, especially after getting the country into this mess? They need to go back and cut his pay, his security staff, and anything else the American people are still paying toward his retirement. I bet that will send a strong signal quick and in a hurry to future leaders," Ken says.

"Well, we better not talk too much because they're cutting the military back like it ain't nothing..., so tell me..., who does that? Not to mention, we got this foreign clown overseas making and testing nuclear weapons like nobody's business. With the cuts and downsizing, along with other things going on in the world, it will be easy for Mr. Nuke to get his allies to start a bunch of junk now, to spread conflicts, and we won't be good for anything except humanitarian missions, if that! Who is going to fight the wars to come is my question!" Barry says with a more serious face.

"Yeah, no doubt. Well, I guess we won't know the answers until we're lying in bed at night with missiles inbound from oilers and tankers off the coast, hitting our houses. I mean, with budget cuts, who's watching the hen house?" Ken says in deep thought when his hand goes forward, pointing to the next street.

"Well, it should be over soon, for sure," Barry says with a concerned stare.

"I don't know about that because those guys in Washington are long-winded."

"Well, for the players, and I do mean the players and only the players. . ., I'm sure they'll come up with something quick when their mistresses' funds run low. I bet when they can't afford hotels, apartments, penthouses, cars, and luxurious lifestyles for their mistresses because the dollars are under strict scrutiny, there is no doubt they'll agree quick," Barry says.

"Well, let's hope they're not cheap like those guys in that foreign country on escort duty who were too cheap to pay a few dollars for some cheap coo-coo (sex)!" Barry says, laughing.

"Yeah, no doubt..., I heard that place even had twenty-five-cent blow-up doll machines, and those knuckleheads refused even to put in a quarter," Ken says, bursting into a crazy laugh that lasts so long that he almost chokes.

Minutes later, Alfred turns down Greg's street, pulling in front of his house. He blows, jumping out and unloading luggage. He hears loud music, throws up his hands and freezes when noticing a female walking away a few houses down.

Barry blows at Alfred a few times and then slows to almost a complete stop, seeing the beautiful young woman.

Ken's body extends out the window with two fingers coming to his lips to whistle, making a few birdcalls to the female in tight white spandex with the protruding pelvis.

Barry slightly leans over Ken's shoulder, with all thirty-two teeth showing.

They intercept the woman but quickly look past her, finding a mean-looking man on the porch staring back over his shades.

The man turns easing his hand to his waistband, slightly sliding his shirt up when patting the handle of his 9MM and rocking his head back and forth with a continual mean stare.

Their heads quickly turn forward as if never looking.

Barry hits the gas, swerves, and pulls up in front of Alfred's car.

Alfred continues looking until hearing hissing when finding Ken's erratic motions until his hands anxiously display a time-out. Alfred rolls his things over to the SUV, and Barry meets him in the back.

"What is with Ken and the time-out, man?" Alfred asks, looking back once more until Barry notices, snatching him by the collar and turning him into the back of the SUV.

"You gone (are going to) mess around and get us smoked out here! Her man is on the porch packing and waiting for a reason to smoke us…, well, another reason," Barry says giggling when snatching him in an even tighter grip until feeling less resistance.

Barry pops the locks, lifting Alfred's things inside, and walks up to the driver's door. He leans inside, honking a few times, and then stares at the porch and door for minutes.

The three look up, hearing the door slam, and finds Greg with pink luggage.

"Are you serious?" Alfred asks, shaking his head. "I mean, really?"

"What! My zipper busted on mine, so I have nothing else," he says, proudly rolling the luggage down the steps, with wheels clapping with each drop to the next step.

The man with the gun bends over the handrail, still looking down in disbelief toward where they're standing hoping to make eyes contact and cause trouble.

"You are either undeniably bold or just plain stupid. I would have come out with fifteen grocery bags or with my stuff bundled in a sheet on a damn stick first," Barry says, climbing inside and popping the back window's lock from the dash.

"Time," Ken calls, looking at this watch. "We need to see if we can break the record from Alfred's last trip," Ken says, looking at the time on the dash and comparing both.

Greg slams the back window shut and jumps in the backseat.

Barry cranks up, skids wheels, and dashes for the main road then cuts over a few streets, coming upon the expressway in record time.

Alfred slips on shades, whistling a tune from the low-volume radio. He looks out the driver's window, until staring over at Greg's arms, feeling a little uneasy but looks again when taking off his shades, staring at Greg's arms out of the corner of his eye.

Ken looks back and does a double-take, feeling uneasy as he stares, for some reason, so he puts on his shades, lowers the sun visor's mirror, and observes closely.

Alfred cut his eyes over again, but this time to Ken, who looked like he was checking out Greg from head to toe.

Ken leans over, pretending to reach for the radio knob but gets Barry's attention and motions for him to look back.

Barry quickly adjusts the rearview, riding high and continually gazing.

"Man! I've got to get back in that gym. Look at you!" Alfred says, boldly staring at Greg's muscular arms. "Man, you got your swoll (build) on, for real! You buff, buff..., boi!" he says, changing his voice to sound manly and with a semi-tight, balled fist, which he playfully spoke through as if it was a bullhorn.

"Yeah, I been lifting aight. . ., lifting biscuits and meat," Greg so proudly says.

Barry slams on brakes in the middle of the highway, speeding off when hearing horns and tires skid as vehicles swerves past them fast. He looks at Greg through the rearview when Ken looks back, and Alfred slightly tilts his shades down.

"What? Come on, man! You can't be real with that comment..., right? That's so far out in the left field that the pitcher can't see it coming. Please tell me you meant lifting meat and biscuits, right..., please?" Barry continually stares with a serious face.

There is total silence until Greg's eyes wander around, and his mind wanders for the right answer. He keeps a serious face a little longer and then bursts into laughter, which sounds a little female, but in an exceptionally high-pitched voice with several feminine hand motions. "Man, go head (ahead)! You..., you..., you know what I meant," he nervously stutters, curiously looking while laughing a little longer to play it down.

"For a minute there, you were about to scare me, too," Ken says, looking back at Greg and nodding to Barry to let him know he did not buy it.

Everyone joins in on a slow, dry laugh.

Barry grows quiet and looks decidedly curious until staring up at the exit sign. He veers off and comes down onto a country road. "Hey, is anyone going to watch the game next weekend?" Barry sarcastically asks, turning the radio up a little.

"I doubt it! Kim and I split a few weeks ago," Greg says, looking out the window.

"Great. . ., that chick's trifling, especially if you caught sniffing your underwear?"

"What?" Greg asks as if confused.

"Yeah, I remember. . ., you caught Kim sniffing your drawers one night when you came home late from the club?" Barry says, smiling when recalling the conversation.

"Oh, yeah, yeah. . ., what about it?"

"What..., what about it? That's just downright crazy and straight nasty, dude! She would only do that once, and after that, she would be guaranteed to find some ole' intentionally left, tractor-pull skid marks in my drawers," Alfred says, bursting into a crazy laugh.

"She's what, a nurse, right?" Ken asks, looking over his shoulder. "What, L.P.N., C.N., R.N., or what?" He looks out the window and then back for an answer.

"L.P.N., but what does her job have to do with what happened?"

"I see..., so, right now, she's just a Licensed Practical Nut (L.P.N.), then a Certified Nut (C.N.), and later a Registered Nut (R.N.)! Man, if you know like I know, you better drop that bad habit for good and never go back!" Ken says, shaking his head and laughing even harder.

"Yeah, whatever!"

Barry thinks long and hard. "Isn't that the same girl who walks around all day with sex balls inside her private?"

"And?" Greg responds with a mean look. "Whatever floats her boat. Hey, look..., they're just balls!" he says, staring down at the fast-moving asphalt.

"Just balls? Yeah, they have a name for that. . ., nymphomaniac!" Barry says, giggling as the others join in laughter.

"Yeah, whatever!" Greg sarcastically responds again.

Ken stares with a shitty looking grin. "One thing for sure, it ain't the balls you have to worry about, but the many men she'll need when pulling the balls out because they nor you will be able to satisfy her," he says, bursting into laughter with everyone except Greg.

"Man, no wonder she could not hold a decent conversation; she's too busy trying to get hers," Alfred says, causing more laughter.

"Yeah, whatever!" Greg responds a third time.

"What? Come on, Jack! You can come up with something more original. You know, not to challenge your manhood or anything, but that sounds so. . ., well, you knooowwww!" Ken says in a long, very high, comical pitch when cutting his eyes through the rearview.

"For real, for real!" Ken says, slapping the back of his hand in his other hand and acting overly manly. "That whatever thing. . ., definitely woman…, Jack!"

Barry comes to a stoplight, watching traffic slowly float past. He waits for the last car, and enters, coming up on a ramp, veering onto another highway.

Minutes later, it is quiet, and everyone is comfortable.

Greg slips off his shoes. "Woowee…, man, that feels good," Greg whispers, looking over and finding Alfred asleep with his eyes half open and mildly snoring. Greg wiggles his toes and eases them onto the back of the driver's seat headrest.

Ken turns to ask Barry a question and notices movement near Barry's head, and grows anxious, trying to signal Barry with warnings that go unnoticed.

Barry finally yawns, rolling his window all the way up.

Ken motions to Barry again and then stares at Barry, whose eyes remain glued to the road. "What? What is it?" Ken asks, seeing Barry in deep thought and hoping to get Barry to look, but when Ken cuts his eyes back, he's eye-to-eye with Greg, who stares back with a mean look.

"Oh nothing," Barry says. "It's just that I have this sudden urge for butter popcorn," he says, smacking and quickly brightening his dim eyes a few times.

Alfred's head slightly turns, and his eyes open to find Greg's wiggly toes. "Popcorn! Ugh! Damn the urge; that's Greg's funky ass feet!" Alfred screams in laughter when covering his face and continually fanning until getting his window down fast.

"What?" Barry says, leaning forward and looking back to barely find Greg's wiggly toes when the SUV swerves into oncoming traffic.

Ken's mouth drops open, and his finger points to another oncoming car when continually slamming his balled fist into Barry's leg until the SUV veers into its lane.

Greg snatches his feet down, pulls them to his face, and takes a deep sniff, and then slightly frowns before slipping them back into his shoes.

"It's called soap and water!" Ken says, playfully motioning his fingers around in a feminine two snaps and a half circle to get Greg pissed.

Barry changes lanes for a while and then comes up in the left of the two, hugging the yellow line. He looks behind, finding himself way ahead of traffic when slowing down.

"Hey..., you guys coming to my party next month?" Alfred asks, looking over when feeling a light breeze from Ken's window as he rolls it down fast and rises in his seat.

Within seconds, all windows are down, and everyone has their heads hanging out.

"Damn, Ken! You could have given us a warning before lighting that one off!" Barry yells, swerving back into the lane again and cutting his eyes over at Ken's smiling face, frowning.

Minutes later, the SUV is clear of the scent, but the windows remain halfway down.

Barry looks back at Alfred with a strange look. "What party?" he begins to say when a smile comes, seeing Ken leaning out and waving to an SUV full of beautiful women.

Barry's eyes quickly roam through the SUV when Ken, Alfred, and Greg scream at the top of their lungs, furiously waving to the women, who continually blow kisses.

Ken looks forward a quick second, and his mouth drops, and his eyes bulge while slamming his fist down on Barry's leg, gazing at the possible rear-end collision.

Barry's head flies forward, slamming on the brakes, veering right and off the road, and then paralleling the car in front with dust and dirt flying forward and covering all vehicles and intersection.

Several cars stay still until traffic starts to move again.

Ken looks straight ahead, ashamed, but waves to the folks in the car they almost rear-ended, quickly looking away.

Barry pulls onto the road slowly, rushes to catch the other SUV, and comes alongside at the next red light.

Ken stares deep into the SUV until slamming his head into the headrest, disappearing behind the doors side panel when becoming as stiff as a board.

"What? What is it?" Barry asks, surprised.

"Trannies at three o'clock," he says, with his eyes still forward.

Barry leans past Ken, spotting a sharp Adam's apple when the man takes a swig from his tall beer bottle.

Alfred continues to peep and then quickly rolls up the window but leaves it cracked.

Greg comes almost out of the seat, looking over, and deep into the back door's lightly tinted window.

"Hey! Hey, Adam's apple!" Alfred hollers from behind the cracked-open tinted windows. "Hey, Adam's apple!" Alfred calls out again in deeper laughter.

The other SUV's back window lowers halfway and then quickly comes down when one tranny grows pissed, sticking his middle finger up, raising his butt, and grabbing his crotch. "Suck on this big ole' apple, you son of a b…!" he screams with his voice drowning when the tranny in the front passenger seat screams something unclear louder with a tight fist.

Several hands in the SUV go back and forth with loud, slanderous screaming remarks to provoke Barry into pulling over.

The tranny behind the wheel grabs his crotch rising and pissed. His lips move extremely slowly, but his mouth opens as wide as humanly possible.

Greg bursts into deep laughter, keeping his eyes pierced through the tint. "Oh my goodness! I think he just told us to suck his Johnson!" Greg says, dropping forward, then back and forth in laughter until his hand pounds Barry's headrest.

"Look, damn it, Greg…, if anyone is going to be sucking any Johnsons, you will be the only one doing it!" Ken says, giggling.

"Ahh. . ., come on, Ken, how are you gonna (going to) volunteer him for something he would do willingly?" Barry says, adjusting the mirror to look at Greg with a smile.

The tranny speeds off a few miles ahead, abruptly swerving to the side of the road, slamming on brakes, and leaving deep skid marks along the highway.

Four doors fly open, and six pop tall on the side of the road, motioning them over.

The buff tranny, the driver, takes off his coat, brandishing his twenty-two-inch arms.

The skinny tranny reaches halfway his thigh, grasping what looks like a baby python impression in his pants when humping hard.

The driver steps a few feet onto the road, balls his fists and flexes his muscles, and then turns, flexing his womanly-shaped butt cheeks up and down, one cheek at a time as if twerking like a stripper.

Barry's eyes buck, flooring the gas pedal and swerving around a few cars while looking through the rearview, finding then jumping back in and pulling off with a hit trail of smoke. His eyes float to the gas needle, reading one-fourth of a tank when bringing the SUV up to about eighty miles per hour to gain distance.

Thirty minutes later, they are back to acting crazy when pulling up next to any car they see with a hot chick or two inside.

Later, they pull alongside an old man, unintentionally paralleling him for minutes.

The old man finds Alfred in a constant stare, so he stares back with wavering eyebrows playfully going up and down and then gets pissed when Alfred will not break his stare.

Alfred panics, breaking his daze, seeing the car swerve toward the SUV. He quickly straightens up, noticing the man's sporadic mannerisms, until watching him let go of the wheel when throwing up his arm and slapping his other hand in the crease of his arm.

The man loses control, swerving deeper into the SUV.

"Oh shoot, Barry!" Alfred screams, grabbing and guiding the steering wheel, leaning from the door and watching the old man's face fade under the door.

"Hey…, hey…hey! What?"

"Old dude almost lost control of his car!" Ken yells, motioning Barry further left.

The old man hugs the SUV close, fighting to get control until finally swerving away, overcompensating, and slamming into a plastic yellow sand barrier.

Barry slows with his mouth wide open when slowing more.

They all stare back at the old, smoking car until bursting into laughter when seeing the man jump out with a tight fist held high until reaching through the back window, brandishing a sports gaming foam hand with the middle finger raised, waving it.

Barry slows more and pulls up to a stoplight.

Ken looks at the light, watching girls walk past the hood. His windows come down, and he whistles, catching something out of his peripheral vision when looking over, finding two young boys in the back seat, staring back. He looks without making eye contact then stares.

One kid sticks out his tongue, and the other both middle fingers.

Ken stares at the mother and then father, slowly sticking up both tight fists and shooting both middle fingers up fast until driving them round in circles. He begins goose-necking his head until his middle fingers point down.

The kid behind the passenger seat pulls out a straw and shoots a slimy spitball, hitting Ken in the neck.

"What the…!" Ken yells, grasping and rolling the wet ball in his fingers when pulling it closer, still rolling it back and forth until registering what it is when his face grows grim.

Barry looks at the ball, and Ken jerks in a rage, reaching for the door handle.

The door flies open, and Barry's eyes grow wide.

The kids scream, rolling up their windows fast.

Their parents look over their shoulder in excitement, finding Ken's mean face and his door open.

Barry leans hard, catching Ken by the shirttail, snatching him back.

Barry, Alfred, and Greg burst into laughter.

Ken stares at the kids and parents, slipping his foot back in and slamming the door.

The light changes and Barry burns rubber, looking in the rearview to find the car still at the light when looking over at Ken. "What in the hell, man? Were you going to beat those kids down?" Barry asks in disbelief.

"Yeah! Yes, yes, yes, yes, yes, and yes!" he screams, slamming his fist into the dash in rage as if a mad man with bulged eyes. "I was going to try and take their heads off their shoulders had I got my hands on those little bastards!" Ken says, pissed. He searches through the glove compartment for a tissue, tearing a piece of notepaper off and wiping.

"Yeah, and the headlines would have read the same as the rapper of that song had he beat down that chick the time she had her so-called out-of-body experience off this guy's new song. The only difference is the rapper had a reason, but a spitball? Come on, man!" Barry says, laughing.

CHAPTER THREE

Barry reads the next exit sign, then looks down at the gas needle, exiting and coming to the stop sign making a right turn. He looks in the rearview, turning into the lot, slowly looking into the rearview again. He instantly grows pissed, finding a car too close. "Get off my bumper, you freakin' moron!" His eyes stay on the old man' heavy head nodding when he comes so close that he looks as if he's slumped down in the seat behind Greg. Barry rolls forward slowly with eyes still in the rearview. He looks forward fast when tapped on the shoulder, slamming on the brakes when almost running into the back of another car.

The old man hits his brakes and instantly nods, slamming into the SUV when Barry screams, jumping out and running to the old man's window, cursing.

The old man leans from the window, nervously shaking, becoming hysterical, when Barry nervously tries calming him after looking around, finding people with mean stares.

"Ah…, leave em' (him) alone, you stank-butt bully!" an old grey-head woman screams with her fist high.

The old man rattles on about nonsense. "What am I going to do? What? What? My insurance will go through the freakin' roof!" the old man yells with his un-gripped, false teeth continually flapping when speaking.

"What?" Barry screams, losing what little composure he has left. "Driver's license and registration! Driver's license and registration, now!" Barry screams, almost cross-eyed. "And next time, think about insurance before driving…, I mean sleeping and following people too close!"

The old man stares with a mean frown and then leans into the window. "I sure as hell will not! I surely will not give you a cotton-picking thing, you freakin' jerk!" He rises in his seat, fighting for the door handle as if to get out and open a new can of whip ass right then and there, but cracks the door open, and Barry steps back a few feet.

Ken comes around to the back, motioning Barry over. "What the Bill Hick-Up is this all about? Are you going to beat that old man down?" Ken asks, hoping to pay Barry back with the same words Barry used concerning the kids when shaking his head.

Barry climbs back in, looking through the side mirror, finding the old man with the door finally wide open.

The old man's cane slips out, and he stands as Barry slowly drives from the pump, parking closer to the building.

Barry exits, finding the old man with the door handle held tight and his back to where Barry once stood when without warning, the old man leans, taking a heavy, blind swing with all he has, spinning out in a twirl, and dropping down on brittle knees, screaming.

Barry and Ken are the first to see the old man in his height of anger and fall into each other in heavy laughter.

They look away then s back over at him, finding a few people rushing to help the old man up.

Ken rushes inside for the restroom, exiting minutes later to find the others wandering inside the mega grocery store. He walks down and aisle and stands looking over serval items when, out of nowhere, something hits Ken in the back, and he turns, finding a little old woman with her cane slowly withdrawn.

The old woman's other hand instantly shoots forward, with a mean stare, pointing to the top shelf for an item when reaching again with stern eyes.

Ken spreads his arms as if clueless, then reaches, pretending he can't reach it, yet playfully making false attempts until trying again.

The old woman looks at his height and then at his feet, finding them flat. She cuts her eyes at him and waits for him to reach again when shoving her cane forward, and ramming the hook up his butt.

Ken instantly screams, shooting high on his tiptoes, then higher, overreaching with an even higher-pitch voice, when bringing the can down fast and thrusting it toward her.

The old woman looks with a smile, slightly bowing when gracefully walking away.

A few aisles over, a crackhead stands in the grocery area, shoplifting while watching the big-screen television on the other side of the wall. He stops shoplifting, squinting, when seeing two notorious boxers' pictures, both standing side-by-side with a small, unreadable caption below their names.

The crackhead shifts his head to one side and strains to hear while watching the woman reporter with the mic walking around with the poster-type pictures in the background.

An aisle over, a short, older couple talk mildly about a distant relative shot in another state until the conversation grows louder when another woman's kid screams as they pass the old couple. Their conversation slowly drifts into the crackhead's ear while in a daze, thinking the discussion is from the television when they stop talking while reading a few ingredients on the back of a few can before walking off.

A well-dressed, nosy, tall man stares back at the old couple, listening to their conversation before moving further down the aisle.

"Oh, snap! Hey..., can you turn that up? That's my boi..., that my boi!" the male crackhead screams, scratching his face and the edges of his white, powdery lips.

The tall man turns, nosily looking into the male crackhead's face before looking at the screen and walking away.

The young cashier reaches for the remote, and before he can get the volume up, another commercial flash across the screen.

The male crackhead cuts his eyes at the cashier, still stuffing more canned goods in his oversized pockets, then comes to almost a standstill looking down again and grabbing more items. He turns like a ballerina, rising and looking for his female accomplice, his girlfriend, until spotting her near the meat counter. He looks over a few more aisles and then rushes to another empty aisle. He turns the corner, almost bumping into the tall man, who slowly walks toward the crackhead's girlfriend with a curious stare.

The tall man's mouth drops open, finding the female stealing a few steaks when the boyfriend yells out.

"Hey, yo! That's foul! Did you just see that last news clip? Man! The boxer Little Geezie just shot the other boxer, Little Weezie!" he exclaims, scratching his white, foamed lips.

"What..., for real?" his girlfriend responds, slipping a few more quality, cold steaks in her makeshift, pregnant elastic-strap belly when looking over at the inattentive butcher. She keeps her eye on the butcher, and each time he turns from her, she cautiously lifts something else, and when he looks, she smiles and nods, showing off her brown, brown rusty-looking rough teeth.

With one last look, the butcher suspiciously stares at her, too friendly stare when patrolling the meat display, and soon scratching his head. He grows amazed at how fast they had to restock the meat freezer.

Seconds later, the butcher's shop door flies open, and his assistant rushes over. "What's wrong, Jerry? I've seen you pacing back and forth and scratching your head for minutes. You keep on; you gone (are going to) run a path straight through what little frail stuff you have left. It's pitiful enough that you've got that serious cowlick going on there." The assistant giggles lightly, playfully running a finger over the butcher's head when snatching his hand back, giggling when the butcher smacks his hand.

The butcher backs up and looks at him as if crazy as his face frowns and then quickly grows into a big smile. "We gonna (are going to) get a good bonus this month, Ben! Man…, we been pushing meat out the door like nobody's business!"

The tall man's eye grows wider when looking away and then doing a double-take to confirm that the woman just stuffed a roast under her shirt and into her pants.

The woman stops in her tracks, feeling the man's constant stare, when nervously cutting her eyes over at him, then looking straight ahead when freezing. Her head slowly turns and snaps in the man's direction even quicker, trying to catch him off guard but he's swifter to turn away.

The game of cat and mouse goes on for minutes until the man's eyes shoot away, staring at the wall for seconds as if afraid to look again.

An old woman walks up, scrolling the meat case until sidestepping. She closes the tall man, accidentally bumping him, and he refuses to go around, with eyes still straightforward.

"Excuse me…, excuse me," the senile woman says while continually shoving when he flexes in the direction of the female crackhead, springing back into the senile woman stiff as a board.

The senile woman stares at him for seconds until he steps back a few paces when passing and replicating the movement when rolling up on the female crackhead, who stares at her with a mean look.

The crackhead's boyfriend rushes up and notices his girlfriend's cautious stare toward the tall man when he stares back with bulged eyes without blinking. "Nosy gets rosy!" he senselessly blurts out, balling a tight little fist and slowly leaning closer to the man.

"Excuse me?" the tall man says with a frown, expressing confusion.

"You heard me…, I said…, nosseeyyy (nosy) gets rossseeyyy (rosy) !" he says again, but dragging the word out this time when loudly and boldly slapping his fist in his other hand. "You know…, like snitches get stitches?" His bug eyes stare the tall man up and down for seconds until his hand comes to his white, crusty lips when scratching his mouth a few times again.

The tall man stares more sinisterly and then eases up on the crackhead with a serious face and one eyebrow raised. He begins exerting attitude when the crackhead backs up a few inches, nervously cutting his eyes away until looking at the man a few more times.

The crackhead turns, walking over to his girlfriend. "As I said, yeah, it was just on the news, and I'm sure it will come on again this evening around six o'clock. Ain't that some foul crap?" he says, cutting his eyes back at the tall, nosey man and rolling his eyes.

The female crackhead stops in suspense and is in a daze for seconds then a delayed response. "Man, get out of here! I saw that commercial on earlier; you know…, the Italian suit commercial that came out not too long ago. Man, that commercial is dope!" she says, breaking out in a silly laugh when cutting her eyes over at the butcher, his assistant, and then anxiously down the other way at the tall man, who nervously looks away quickly.

"What. . .? So Little Geezie didn't shot (shoot) Little Weezie?" The male crackhead burst into a silly laugh, cutting it short when finding the tall man further away but still cutting his eyes back.

"Hellz (Hell) naw (no), Nut! The commercial says something about Little Geezie now shops at Luigis. . ., you know that high-tail Italian store we hit up for thousands, off 33rd and Broad?" She eases her hand to her lopsided, indented belly, straightening it and then rubbing it to adjust the distinguishable meat shape wrapping. Her eyes wander up and down the meat aisle and then over her shoulder when growing more focused.

The male crackhead goes into deep thought but wanders off, still puzzled, but keeps his eyes on his girlfriend and several stock workers, who seem to be a little too attentive.

A few minutes later, the male crackhead bursts into loud, crazy laughter, finally understanding the commercial when he accidentally bumps into a short man. He quickly apologizes and laughs even harder, staggering. "Hey, Boo-boo! I get it now; it was a commercial! Man! That is crazy as heck, huh?"

The female crackhead looks back, shaking her head until cautiously looking around to find the butchers at the end of the meat case. She watches for minutes until they leave, heading for the back room, and the double door swings freely and then stop. She looks around, then slams a pork shoulder down in her deep pouch when looking around.

Two surveillance cameras zoom in on each crackhead, with the picture blurry before clearing several times.

The security officer and store manager zoom in and out until the picture adjusts.

The crackheads' movements become almost twice as fast as they move around, overly dressed for hot weather. The two come up on the last aisle when their storages are full, nodding almost simultaneously.

The male crackhead's eyes swiftly swept over near the registers, jumping in excitement when finding an empty, register and making eye contact while rushing to the counter. He reaches onto the shelf for a handful of gum, scrolling it over the conveyor.

The cashier activates the conveyor and slightly bends, grabbing the gum. She slowly counts, mysteriously looking up at them from time to time.

Another old, grey-head woman comes up on the crackheads and off to one side, staring at the bloody floor until noticing blood dripping from the cuff of the woman's pant leg. "Excuse me, madam, but I think your water just broke!" she says, pointing with bulged eyes.

The male crackhead backs up, looking around, then looks down, finally seeing the long trail of blood droplets leading around the corner.

Several registers away, a tall, heavy-set woman leans forward, still listening to her husband's nervous, whimpering, and whispering voice. Her eyes soon grow wide and begin feverishly wandering over low-cut shelves and around corners with her face turning a pink blush to fire engine red instantly while growing furious. The tall, heavy-set woman's hand shoots up fast, snatching her husband in the collar, gripping his tie in a tight balled fat fist. She forcefully marches toward the register where the crackheads stand, finding them still looking down at the blood in shock.

The tall, heavy-set woman leans even harder, straining more with her husband's feet slipping and sliding when trying to resist his wife's tow.

The cashier finally nosily and heavily leans forward, looking down at the female crackhead's bloody clothes and then over the red-dotted floor. "Cleanup on register four!" She yells, going back to counting and taking her time but continually looking around to see if there's a manager anywhere in sight.

The crackheads finally register some commotion behind them when hearing squeaky shoes slipping and sliding, then a weak man's voice whining when finally turning slowly and looking around but in the wrong direction.

The old woman's eyes grow big when staring deep into the tall, heavy-set woman's big flaring nostrils and mean face, grabbing the edge of the register in a death grip, dropping down, and vanishing as if never there.

The crackheads soon turn, looking in the other direction when the male crackhead catches a mouthful of fat, cosmetic ring-covered fist, thrusting his body several feet high with shoes still perfectly planted, side-by-side, beside his girlfriend.

His girlfriend's head goes down quick, in shock, instantly registering the slick squeak from the shoes quick jerk and finding his shoes smoking. Her eyes quickly follow the thin trail of dust in shock, looking back fast and finding his body still careening through the air, backward and growing small, yet seemingly in slow motion.

Canned foods, boxes of snacks, bags of flour, and sugar fly through the air, with bags bursting as he continually flies through several pre-staged stocking pallets, creating a thick cloud of white dust.

Other customers on the aisle scream, scrambling when hearing the bags burst and seeing his body coming toward them like a cruise missile.

"You damn right...bitches get stitches!" the heavy-set woman screams with her fat, balled fist still stretched forward while still in a leaning stance. She quickly jerks upward, standing from the dealt devastating, professional boxing-looking blow, balancing. She finally releases her husband's necktie when he staggers off fast, falling back heavily then looking like he's walking sideways when foolishly stumbling into a four-foot stack of canned goods.

Folks quickly converge at the front when distant store security sirens sound off.

The store and security managers run for the front doors, and the old woman's head quickly pops back up, covered in unused but pre-dispensed plastic bags previously stuffed under the register.

The heavy-set woman bends, reaching down, grabbing her husband by the collar, when straddling, reaching down a little further, and pulling him to his feet fast.

The husband staggers more and then leans into the counter when regaining balance with eyes quickly thrown back and staring at the thick cloud of slow settling dust.

The dazed male crackhead stays flat on his back, and seconds later, he eases his head up slowly, shaking off the devastating pain. He sits slowly, suddenly banging the side of his head to get rid of the loud ringing.

Instantly, loud sirens grow louder when the girlfriend breaks out of her daze, moving side to side, wide-legged, and faking out the store and security manager. She backs up quickly, snatching a woman's empty shopping cart as it slightly rolls forward, rushing toward the managers then stopping and backing even faster. Without warning, she lunges forward, screaming with eyes closed, heading toward them in a fast sprint when stopping and toying with them.

The two men scream and sway each time the cart rushes forward and stops.

The sweaty and crazed female crackhead thrust forward one last time, stopping and quickly looking for her mate with eyes wandering until he comes up slowly on his knees. She backs up more, staring at the managers stoned out of her mind with fast back and forth cart jerks to fearfully keep them away.

The store manager leans back, grabbing and holding the door tight with eyes scrolling over the huge crowd of instigating shoppers huddling near the registers. His thumb goes feverishly back and forth, accidentally slipping between the door and metal frame, bumping it, and mildly screaming when snatching it back and sucking quickly to ease the pain. He looks back fast with eyes glued on the cart, which she shoves back and forth as if at the start of a professional Jamaican bobsled race.

The male crackhead finally jumps to his feet.

The female crackhead's eyes turn bloodshot, screaming as loud as she can when taking off in a mad dash.

In excitement, Barry, Ken, Alfred, and Greg stand on the sideline.

The store manager's eyes bulge in fear when screaming again but at an exceptionally high pitch with eyes following the express cart. Out of nowhere, from his peripheral, the store manager watches the male crackhead float in from between a register aisle, coming up behind his girlfriend, who is still in a wide-legged, steady sprint.

The female crackhead's huge, meat-stuffed belly flops up and down, looking as if in slow motion; leaving a long trail of blood from bloody steaks in her wake.

The store manager screams even louder, excitedly dancing on alternating, fast-moving feet.

The male crackhead eyes constantly wink with a hand expressly brushing across his floury face with the other hand tight on the cart.

The store manager screams louder and continues nervously dancing from side to side.

The male crackhead's hand rests on his girlfriend's shoulder when his other goes up, snatching the heavy-set woman's wig while she's still bent over, tying a knot in her stocking.

The tall, heavy-set woman screams, running her fingers over her long plats when towering quickly with a tight, fat, bald fist.

The store manager screams even louder, closing his eyes and pulling his body as far away from the door as possible, cringing.

A loud crash rings throughout the store when the cart bursts through the metal frame, shattering the glass door.

The store manager screams a death cry, falling away, shaking his hands up and down when nervously falling backward and onto the floor, trembling in fear.

The crackheads fly through the crumbled glass in slow motion, slamming onto the hood of the police cruiser as it pulls up to the door.

Without warning hams, steaks, a turkey, and a tray of hamburgers fall from the air, landing on top of the crackheads and the police cruiser.

The store manager springs up, happily dancing and feverishly shaking his huge, red, throbbing thumb with eyes glued on the scary security officer peeking from behind a low-cut shelf with a trembling hand on his gun.

The two officers in the cruiser stare through a smashed windshield in disbelief, leaning to the left, drawing weapons fast.

The store manager holds his finger to his face, staring at his thumb, which looks like a thick, ripe plum. He begins shaking off the pain more and then dives forward, running down aisles. He rushes upon the meat counter, plunging his thumb into the ice, and holds it for minutes while continually high-stepping on alternating feet.

Barry, Ken, Alfred, and Greg stay in tears of laughter, watching the commotion, then hangs around longer until after the arrest before hitting the road.

"There goes our timeline," Ken says, staring at his watch.

An hour later, they make one more stop at a roadside country store.

Barry, Alfred, and Greg use the bathroom while Ken tops off the gas.

Seconds later, Ken eases the gas cap back on, looking around when hearing dry leaves moving about. He stares into total darkness, looks around, then down, and jumps back when seeing movement near his feet.

"Aii!" Ken screams, high-stepping when backing about six feet when the light winds pick up with his second scream echoing around the valley for seconds, then fades into a whisper. He backs up further against the SUV, looking and squinting while bent over, staring at what looks like a skunk on its back with its eyes closed. He fearfully backs into the second pump, nervously reaching for the squeegee, and turns it, slowly inching up until poking at the skunk's face and then its fat, round belly until hearing a giggle that fades off and into the winds quick.

The store's front door flies open with Barry, Alfred, and Greg stepping out, deep in conversation, until freezing in a stare with Barry's arms still spread wide, stopping them.

Greg and Alfred lean on Barry's shoulder, staring to see if it's alive.

Barry's arms stay spread wide, backing them quick. "Ken, have you lost your freakin' mind? In case you have never seen one, that's a damn...!" Barry begins to say when a thick, solid, long watery spray shoots up from the skunk into Ken's face.

Their faces frown when backing further and faster with heels clicking.

Ken's hands shot forward with his face instantly transforming into the look of the worst stench when wiping his eyes and falling back, screaming and springing for the guys with hands wide open.

The three scatter, running around the truck until dodging into an open field. Deep and endless laughter echoes throughout the little valley as they keep their distance, bobbing and weaving to stay away from Ken.

The fun eventually dies, but they can't stop chuckling when moving back over to the SUV, where their faces frown from the skunk's heavy overspray.

The funny-looking old store owner continually stares through the dust-covered window and watches as they continue cutting up. He watches longer, then grows curious when flinging the door open, falling back through the door from the stench, and grabbing his nose. He rushes down the steps quickly, motioning them over to the side of the store, where he rushes off, grabbing the hose. He directs Ken over, and when he's within range, he opens the firefighter-type nozzle on high, flipping Ken back several feet and into the gas pump. He immediately adjusts the nozzle to medium and then low as Ken comes to his feet then soaks him for seconds, shaking his pointy head in disbelief.

The old store owner continually lifts his nose high, smelling the scent that seems to get stronger when frustrated. "Shucks! This hea (here) ain't gone do nothing but make that stench milder," the store owner says, adjusting the nozzle from medium to high, when spraying Ken in the face from time to time, just to get a few giggles, and then bends over in laughter. "He will need to soak in oatmeal or maters (tomatoes) to get that stench off, I reckon!" the old store owner says, easing the water off and pinching his nose tighter. "Silly sucker! What did you think that was a pet?"

Ken shakes his head in a disbelief, walking away, drenched, and stops by the passenger door when all locks loudly click.

"Barry..., grab me a couple of sheets from my bag? I don't want to get your seats wet," Ken says, shaking off the smelly water.

Barry snickers. "Man, you gonna (going to) have to ride on the roof or somewhere else with that funk!" Barry giggles harder, with everyone joining in as if harmonized.

Ken's face frowns harder from the smell, but he soon cracks a smile, shaking his head in disbelief at such a ridiculous comment. "Man, you crazier than a damn bed bug! I'm not riding on a freakin' roof on this dangerous highway. It'll be a cold day in hell, and you'll still be running around with gasoline drawers before that happens, pal!" Ken says with a smirk. "How 'bout this: yawl ride up there, and I'll cover the seat and drive?" he says, dropping his head in a smile mixed with a hard frown until bucking bright eyes in a stupid stare.

"Hellz (Hell) to the nawzie (no)...! Ok..., ok..., riding up there may not be safe for any of us," Barry says, stepping out of Ken's view when using the key to unlock the cargo hatch, and motioning Alfred over.

"Man, hurry up! I'm dripping wet, and it's getting cold!" Ken angrily yells, bending slightly over and shaking off the water like a wet dog.

"Hey, Greg..., how about running inside for some rope? We have to make room so Ken can ride in the cargo area," Barry says, winking to Alfred and giving Greg a sneaky look.

Greg heads for the store, meeting the owner at the top step and walking in behind him.

"Which bag did you say the sheets were in?" Barry sticks his head out, looking alongside the truck where Ken is standing. "Oh, never mind!" Barry looks in Alfred's hand, finding a quilt, then leans toward him, whispering. Barry fumbles around more, peeping toward the store until Greg appears with a bag full of rope. Barry pulls everyone's luggage out and looks into an empty yet neatly sheet-covered cargo area. He nudges Alfred to get him to walk around by Ken, but Alfred tries distancing himself. Barry unravels the sheet, shakes it, and then stretches it wide.

Ken comes up on the back of the truck finding a sheet spread neatly over the floor; when grabbing hold of the cargo's hatch, bouncing once and bouncing again until coming up high on the bumper. He braces his stance, balancing when the quilt drapes over his head.

Barry catches him in a bear hug as he falls back, and they drop to their feet.

Ken leans forward, screaming, stomping, and kicking.

Barry rides rodeo while Ken runs in circles, staring at the ground when he can while rushing toward where he thinks the SUV's parked. His eyes continually stare through a little creased opening when be-lining for the SUV and spinning around, smashing Barry's body into the tailgate a few times.

The store owner bursts through the door, watching them go at it aggressively for a few minutes. He begins laughing so hard that he slips and stumbles down the steps with his feet shuffling fast and remains in a heavy lean, tilting forward when slamming headfirst into the gas pump, bursting the glass face.

Ken breaks out in a crazier scream, continually dancing around to get free.

Greg quickly unravels the rope, throwing an end to Alfred, and pulling it tight.

They rush around in a circle, stretching the rope, separating it between Barry's and Ken's bodies until finally staggering forward. They pull tight, trip Ken, and then rush over, hog-tying Ken while Ken continually fights, screaming while his body grows tenser until bound fully. They leave Ken screaming while falling back against the SUV with frowning faces from the mild transferred stench on their clothing.

Alfred and Greg take deep breaths and, minutes later, come off the SUV, staggering over behind Barry.

With the old man's help, they safely mount Ken on their shoulders and raise him onto the SUV's roof.

The old man stares indecisively. "I don't know…, I just don't trust this quilt. At least if you bind him with rope and leave his hands free, he can grab the bar; if needed because it's safer," the old man says, smiling.

Minutes later, they have Ken strapped, face down, and with ropes tied tighter. They also take a dark-colored sheet, tying four corners to cover him, so he does not draw too much attention, then stands off, sniffing their clothes, but only Barry has to change his shirt.

Forty minutes later, the SUV's headlights dim as they shoot past the Port La Gaigiuan Naval Base sign, a hundred yards from the gate.

Barry rolls down his window, and they frown from the pungent stench.

They mildly hear Ken's muffled screams through his sock-stuffed mouth, so Barry turns up the radio, still hearing boots banging hard until somewhat focused when sounding like Ken's untied.

Ken tugs a few more times until getting a hand free when fighting to untie the other.

The short, bucktooth, bifocal security guard eases up on the SUV when the headlights go to park. He motions for them to slow down, then heavily waves for them to cut off the loud music when the radio dwindles to a dull roar. The guard's face begins to frown from the overwhelming stench as he walks to the front, staring at the license tags until his eyes drift to the decal, then quickly into the extended raised SUV.

Another security guard sits on the other side of another shack, about twenty-five feet away. His head moves to a dope beat blaring from his frail headset. He cautiously looks around from time to time and then sneakily slips a plastic bag from his back pocket. He soon lights, pulling on a fat joint a few times, and blowing it in the bag to contain the odor, then takes a few more quick hits, nervously standing and looking around.

The short bucktooth, bifocals-wearing security guard eases to the driver's window. "Now, sir, you know you can't come through the gate with your music that high; around here, acting like this is a party bus!" The bucktooth guard shakes his head, frowning. "You know…, for the life of me, I can't come to the likings, but what is that awful-tail smell?" He leans to one side, hearing a rumble and then Ken's deep strains and groans. "Back windows down, now…, now!" the security guard screams with a hand on his sidearm, backing until wide-legged and holding the gun in the holster, with it off safety.

The other guard takes another hit with a fat marijuana seed burning at the tip until sounding like a mini-firecracker and stinging his lips with hands flying to his thick, numb, and quickly-swelling lip when dancing around. He rubs his throbbing lip again and then calms down. He slips the smoking paraphernalia into his coat pocket, then start dancing like he's doing the Texas two-step but faster until getting the hot pipe back out. He calm himself then reaches for his face again when his lips blow up like balloons, and half his face goes numb.

Ken's foot bangs even harder as he fights to free his hand.

"Woowee! You got a dead body in deah (there)?" the guard screams with his little feet anxiously dancing while fighting to come up on his tiptoes and peep inside. "It smells just like it did in the academy!" He pulls on the high window seal, with feet slipping and sliding against the door until planting both feet on the side, looking like he's mountain climbing. His head finally comes up over the window seal and thick bifocals when slipping and fighting to climb back up. He comes up a third time, quickly sliding until dropping and running to the back.

The other guard rubs his face more and then turns, staring into the reflective glass of the vacant guard shack. His legs shift back and forth for a second when he jumps, runs around the shack, stops, and starts sniffing his clothes.

Barry leans out the window and sees the short security guard at the back, rising high off the balls of his little feet, peeping in the window, and fading when flat on his feet.

Ken finally slips forward and, out of nowhere, grabs Barry at the throat, choking him with one hand.

Greg and Alfred sit looking around then back until hearing a strangling sound; when looking forward with mouths dropped open, shocked to find Ken hanging halfway off, one leg still secured and the other furiously kicking.

Barry fights with all he has to get Ken's funky, tight hands away and eventually slips free, but Ken strains, moaning when grabbing him again before he slips back inside.

Greg instantly slides to the window and tries to help Barry get free.

The other guard runs around in circles looking for somewhere to hide his stash as his feet shuffle back and forth for seconds.

The short bucktooth, bifocal security guard nervously straightens his glasses, scratching his head and looking back when another SUV pulls up, excitedly blowing.

Barry slips from Ken's grip again, drops down in the seat fast, and then laughs as if he's crazy. He turns to find Alfred and Greg in tears, giggling.

The short bucktooth, bifocals guard waves to the second SUV to get them to stop blowing, but the horn blows longer until the guard turns, finding people pointing. He jumps and peeps around, finding Ken's body half-slumped off with hands dangling when his eyes buck, and he jumps into a stance, wide-legged when drawing his weapon.

"Freeze! I say (said) freeze!" he screams, anxiously licking buttery-looking yellow teeth. He straightens his glasses again, reaching for his walkie-talkie and screaming for backup. He swiftly comes up on the driver's side, uncontrollably training the gun with Barry, Alfred, and

Greg, ducking each time he points the trembling gun at them until looking like they are waving.

Ken's head lifts, spitting out the wet sock, which hits the guard in the face with the guard's hand at his wet face, squirming and going into a whimpering cry when running to one side quickly wiping his face.

The other guard nervously peeps, finding the short guard with his gun drawn. "Oh snap, Son! I got you, Boi! I got you!" he screams, dropping his headset and lunging in slow motion. He sprints fifteen feet, stumbling when tangled with the cord and then tripping over the median. He rolls fast, going under the SUV and coming out on the other side, springing up fast and as if never down when nervously looking around.

The second SUV rocks heavily, and the man in the rear laughs so hard that his hand shoots forward, knocking the turban off the head of the man in the front.

The American men in the front chuckle, sadly shaking their heads.

The second guard rushes around the front, waving his gun through the windshield, screaming, and pointing to his badge while motioning everyone out.

Barry, Alfred, and Greg's faces draw serious when their hands rise high, climbing out with their hands stretched even higher.

"Oh, damn! Is that weed? Is that damn weed I smell! Tell me this ain't weed I smell!" the bifocal guard screams, moonwalking with his gun high over his head. "We gone (are going to) get the security guard of the year award and a bonus now cu, cu, cu cuz!" He stutters, looking at his partner, putting Barry and Alfred on the ground, and motioning Greg down.

Ken loosens the last rope, sliding down the windshield , off to the side slowly and coming around to the front.

Everyone's face frowns, standing with their noses clenched tight.

"Call the chief, now!" the bucktooth guard screams, staring at the other nervous guard, when finding him more nervous, and sniffing his uniform. "Did you hear what I said?" he screams, anxiously staring down at the spread-out bodies when smiling and slowly licking buttery teeth when cautiously cutting his eyes over at his partner again.

Barry looks back, laughing, finding the guard sniffing his clothes again and nervously looking around.

The other SUV floors the engine and backs up, with the driver pulling up in the other empty lane and leaning into the horn a few times when the American men flash their military IDs.

The American in the passenger seat secretly motions to the guard for help, but the officers are too excited to catch on.

"Oh, you think this is funny or something, sir?" the bucktooth officer asks Barry when pushing his glasses up and aiming a trembling gun-toting hand at Barry's head.

The other SUV clears the booth, and the driver speeds off fast.

The four foreign men in the back draw their guns on the two in the front seat again.

"No, sir, but newsbreak Tonto! Your partner over here has been hitting the heavy bag!" Barry says, diming out the guard.

"You mean weed?"

"Gong..., gong!" Barry says with a slow swinging gong hand motions.

The weed head guard lowers his gun with shoulders dropping when his arms cluelessly open with one palm up and the other holding the gun.

The smile vanishes from Barry's face, seeing the other SUV make an immediate left and finding the driver with his lips moving with a fearful look. Barry spots a gun's muzzle, coming to the back of the driver's head with eyes stealthily following until the SUV swerves around a building, heading toward the beach.

"So, let me tell you how this plays out, Kemosabe! My partners and I will get up and get into this SUV. Ole' funk boy over here," he says, nodding at Ken, "well, a skunk sprayed him well, so that's why we had him on top. And him," he says, nodding to Ken again. "Oh, he'll be walking from here. Now, as for that reward, it just went through the gate. Grey SUV..., license DEKT-234, heading down by the beach; two Americans up front with four foreign terrorists in the back with guns." Barry smiles with eyes still on the other SUV's taillights.

Both guard's eyes wander along the winding road leading to the beach.

Barry eases up, and so do the others, watching the guards come up tiptoes, looking further down the embankment until finding the SUV in a slow turn and backing down.

Everyone watches the SUV back in, and the lights flash a few times and then go out.

The guards stand side-by-side, watching the SUV's lights come back on as the SUV maneuvers to another covert spot. The taillights flicker on and off until it pulls up alongside another vehicle, which flashes its lights three times and then turns them off.

The officers stay in awe, watching the deceptive plot unfold. "Call the chief and get him here..., now, now, now!" the bucktooth guard nervously and anxiously screams, moonwalking with joy.

The weed head guard looks down, hearing the doors slam almost simultaneously.

"Remember, guns. . ., massive guns, so you better call the locals in on this one," Barry says with one arm leaning out when starting the engine and motioning for Ken to walk.

Barry keeps the windows shut tight and follows Ken to the main building and parks five minutes later.

Greg runs inside to get information from the medic concerning removing the stench.

Barry and Alfred walk away from Ken and climb the hill's edge, spotting the SUV. Their eyes wander to the gate, spotting several state and local vehicles zooming past the fidgety guards who senselessly bump into each other.

The faint sound of a helicopter grows until seeing blue flashing lights behind a steep hill.

Another blue light flashes at a distance when the second helicopter lights up the field.

Several men spring from the back of both covert vehicles, with the men running until gunfire blazes with tracer rounds from the helicopter. The men draw close to the tree line, and the eight terrorists drop weapons before or after coming to their knees.

Law enforcement puts the men face down, and a few dirty cops take swings on the men or kick them in their butts.

Current day: Back in Port Copan Retaunas, the day after Keyonton's big comedy show and the afternoon.

Keyonton's ten-year-old son, Kelvin, is in his bedroom with the door locked. He and a fourteen-year-old friend sit fumbling through a couple of smut magazines.

"Hey, Kev, I'm going before my dad gets home. I have to put these magazines back before he finds them missing," his friend nervously says. The kid's eyes peep back at the door, listening to the gentle, distant voices of Kelvin's mom and dad.

"Just a few more minutes, Jamie," Kelvin replies, quickly flipping through a few more pictures with his eyes bright and his mouth somewhat open while drooling.

"Kev, come on, man!" Jamie stands patiently, waiting with knees slightly crossed and hopping foot to foot before long. "Shoot, I'm going to the bathroom, so be done when I come back, man."

Kelvin watches the door close, then looks back at the stack of magazines, grabbing one from the bottom and slipping it under his pillow.

Minutes later, Jamie flings the door open, snatching the magazine. He flips through the first four, counting when Kelvin backs into the bookshelf, knocking to make Jamie think someone's at the door.

"Quick, hide them…, that's my dad!" Kevin whispers with eager eyes.

Jamie throws the magazines in his hand under Kelvin's colorful cartoon robe and drops the magazines bag on the bed, covering it fast with sheets then whistling. He drops down for minutes then sits longer until growing suspicious of Kevin's wandering eyes.

"Ok, just a few more minutes. You know how my dad plays pranks to get new material for his stupid standups," Kelvin says with eyes on Jamie but nervously looking away when Jamie begins curiously staring back at him.

"Oh, yeah…," Jamie grabs the brown paper bag. "Ok…, no more waiting; I'm out of here, Jack!" Jamie stuffs the other magazines inside, walking to the door, folding the top down with it under his arm.

"Hey Jamie, I'll be out later." Kelvin peeps back at his parent's room, nodding. "He's cooking ribs for dinner." Kelvin sticks a finger in his mouth, pretending to throw up.

Jamie eases the door shut and hears Kelvin's parents whispering and giggling. He quietly tiptoes downstairs, looking over at the stove and then back upstairs, finding the hall clear. Jamie makes it to the oven, pulling off a long piece of plastic wrap and grabbing the tongs when easing the oven open. He slips out two hot, meaty ribs, wrapping them quickly, then closes the oven and grabs his magazines, dropping the hot ribs in his pant pocket when mistakenly hearing footsteps. He takes two steps, jumps up and down continually, then in circles, trying to get to the hot, burning ribs off his thigh. Jamie quietly dances more, lightly cussing until the ribs hit the floor when moonwalking while bent over, blowing his pocket. He picks up the paper bag, sliding the ribs inside when easing out the front door.

Keyonton has his woman pinned against the wall with both hands high when kissing her several times while the pungent smell of the four-hour, simmering BBQ ribs permeates the house with a slight hint of honey and onions.

Keyonton gets one last, long kiss, releasing her. "Get dressed." He winks, performing a silly and sensual dance, which has her giggling. He rushes into the hallway in excitement, approaching Kelvin's room but slides past the door, playfully backing up slowly as if he's playing a choo-choo game and he's the conductor. Keyonton peeps through the cracked-open door, finding Kelvin with his back to him, quiet and looking down when easing the door open to a certain point. He quickly flings the door open, causing it to slam into the wall.

"Ahh!" Kelvin screams, shooting three feet off the floor and coming down stiff as a board with the magazine held out in front of him.

"Let's eat some ribs, bro! Let's eat some ribs!" Keyonton screams.

Kelvin leans forward, easing the dirty magazine down in his pajamas and underwear.

"Hey! What are you doing?" Keyonton curiously asks when Kevin suspiciously looks over his shoulder at his father a second time but never turns.

"Huh? Oh, nothing," Kevin nervously responds but continues looking forward, afraid to turn around.

Keyonton peeps over his shoulder and then looks down at his empty hands with eyes soon drifting out the window, finding two little girls playing jump rope across the street. "That's my boy…! After those little girls like your daddy when he was your age, maybe a little older, huh?" he says in deep thought. Keyonton takes another step and is inches from finding the thick roll of the magazine bulging out at Kelvin's upper thigh.

"Hey, come on, little man, let's eat some ribs, bro…!" he senselessly screams, putting his hand on little Kelvin's shoulder, trying to turn him, but he doesn't budge. "Ok, a few more looks, then you better come on down before your mom sees you."

"Yeah, yeah..., ok," Kevin nervously and quickly responds, staying still and listening to his father's footsteps fade when waiting longer to ensure his dad isn't being sly or comical. Kevin stays still until he hears whistling, then his dad's shoes hit the hardwood floor when the television comes on, and he hears his dad, but the television's volume goes to a whisper.

Kelvin's hand slips inside his pants, grasping the magazine, and turning when his mother peeps inside, smiling.

Her hands slowly come to her face, transforming into a horrified look to scare him. "Kelvin!" She screams.

Kevin fearfully jumps, turning toward her in fear, and she sees the big bulge in his pants. "Ahh!" he screams, unknowingly pointing to it fast and looking like he is running in place from being so nervous.

Her wide eyes stay pierced on his huge inseam, and her mouth drops open wider. "What in the. . ., ?" she furiously screams, rushing up and grabbing his pajamas and the roll, frantically jerking him. She releases it, senselessly shaking him back and forth for minutes until ripping his pajamas and leaving him in just underwear. She back away with the pajamas still tight in hand, mildly screaming until finally coming to her senses when looking at him until he stares back with eyes wide open and his head slightly shaking.

She quickly unravels the roll. "Where did you get this? Tell me this minute, young man, or you'll be grounded until you're twenty-one!" She flips a few pages, and instantly her mouth drops open, and her hand shamefully comes to her chest, breathing hard and gasping for air.

Kelvin eases onto the bedside, cautiously looking around, and his mind goes haywire. He begins taking deep breaths from the thoughts of the mouthwatering ribs when hearing his dad whistle another tune. He stares at the floor for seconds until his eyes purposely fill with tears, then waits a little longer until the first teardrop rolls down his cheek. "Mom, please..., Mom! You have to promise not to tell, dad," he says, staring at a toy on the floor without blinking to make more tears until finally looking up with crocodile tears.

She eases onto the edge of the bed, frowning, watching Kelvin with his head down while he takes his time to look up at her again. Her face somewhat turns from rage to a comforting smile, and she becomes a concerned mother or at least looks that way to him.

He instantly smiles, then wipes it away quickly when assured that he's won her over.

"Ok, just this one time, tell me the truth, and I promise nothing will happen."

"Well..., well..., well, I took it out of Dad's luggage. I mean..., I walked by and saw it half-open, and I saw the back of the magazine and thought maybe..., just maybe, Dad picked me up a couple of my favorite comics while he was away."

His mother stares longer and then runs her fingers through his curly head. "Ok..., I understand, son. Get dressed and ready to eat," she says, helping him into his robe and gently tightening it.

The volume to the television in the kitchen fades when Keyonton turns the television down entirely and sits listening to hear if they're coming.

Seconds later, Keyonton pushes Kelvin's door open and Liandra throws her hands behind her back, clenching the magazine tightly.

"What! What?" he asks curiously, looking at her, then Kelvin who shamefully looks off with wide eyes.

"What! What?" she responds nervously, easing up and walking toward Key while looking back at Kelvin. "As I said, get dressed," she says, winking.

Kelvin smiles, accidentally throwing up a gang sign which he quickly changes when seeing his dad's face transform instantly into confusion.

Keyonton looks back, and his index finger comes up to ask a question, then quickly comes down when finding a peace sign. He looks curious for seconds and takes a step back. "Yeah, get dressed..., so we can eat some..., ribs, bro!" Keyonton playfully yells.

Kelvin smiles, flipping on his television and then opening his closet door.

Keyonton backs out and rushes back down the hallway toward the kitchen but looks back at his girlfriend, who stares back. He smiles, and his lips part when he inhales.

"I know! Let's eat some ribs, bro!" Liandra responds loudly, smiling when beating him to the punch line.

Barry and the guys have been authorized liberty but spend most of it assisting with check-ins, still leaving the base early.

Within fifteen minutes, Barry, Ken, Greg, and Alfred sit at the bar later, having drinks, when Keyonton's face flashes across the big screen. They anxiously watch and try to figure out what was said when the volume rises, and the bar grows perfectly quiet.

The news reporter details the alleged incident on stage and then switches over, providing live footage. Afterward, they interview people standing around anxiously looking for a couple of busted-looking characters whom the news team is sure to target but stay clear of the professional, well-dressed, or educated-looking people.

Back in Port Copan Retaunas, Keyonton continues dancing around while setting the table. He's jolly and sings until seeing the words 'breaking news' at the bottom of the screen. He dashes for the drawer, pulling out pens, easing into the chair, and turning up the volume, hoping to capture a good joke. "I'm gone (going to) get me some damn jokes now!" He giggles, looking toward the steps when turning the volume up, and listening to the end of one woman's comment, which makes no sense. Next…, there's one last interview with a crackhead rattling on about nothing to do with the story, so the reporter pulls the mic away and cuts back in with more general comments.

The reporter stares off as if she lost reception, then chimes back in. "Ok, folks at home, this may be disturbing, so if you have any young kids that you don't want to see this, then make sure you turn their televisions off."

Keyonton rushes over to the stairs looking up stairs. "Hey, Kelvin, make sure your television is off!" Keyonton screams, quickly looking back at the television when the camera zooms through the large audience with patrons flashing over the screen.

Keyonton's smile grows grim, quickly recalling some duplicate footage.

The camera zooms in on Keyonton's face, showing his mouth wide in laughter, and then zooms to his big hand palming and holding the woman's humongous butt cheek.

"As mentioned earlier, there are allegations, and an active investigation has been launched into this sexual assault case. At this point, the defendant is seeking 1.7 million in damages, so stay tuned because there's more to follow on the late-night news."

Kevin freezes with his eyes bulged, hands to his side, and jaws dropped.

Keyonton turns off the television quick, anxiously removing the knobs and slipping them deep into his pocket. He drops in the chair with his head in both hands, shaking his head, then raise his eyes slowly, standing in a daze, dizzy as the room begins spinning. He feels acutely inferno feverish when standing in a crazy stance, frozen.

Keyonton's hands tremble, and his eyes pierce through the curtains, finding the little nosey old woman across the street at her front door and quickly backing out so fast that her walker looks steady and she's running without it touching the ground.

"Let's eat some ribs, bro!" his girlfriend screams, lunging from the third step to the floor, and floating in, in slow motion.

Keyonton almost jumps out of his skin with eyes peeled over his shoulder.

Her shoes slam into the hardwood, and she rushes over, playfully patting him on the butt when falling into a favorite, comical football stance. "Let's eat some of those ribs, bro!" she screams, shaking like a wet dog. "What! What?" she asks, slowly coming up in a normal stance. "Hey, what's with the television? You know I have to watch my show right after the news while eating," she says, walking over and reaching to find the knob missing. A confused stare grows on her face when she stops, turns, and stares.

Keyonton slides over to the seat. "Honey, you're just getting back, so let's have some quiet family time; just you, me, and junior!" he says with nervous, bright glistening eyes.

The phone rings, and he places his hand over it before she can reach for it, but both lean forward, simultaneously staring at the caller ID.

"Key, that's, mom! She's probably calling to see if we made it home safe."

"Uh, uh, family time, remember," he nervously says with a nervous hand still pressed heavily on the phone.

"Well, at least give me the television," she says, opening the drawer and moving paper around when looking for the pliers. "Have you seen the pliers?"

"Right here." He pulls them from his back pocket. "Family tiiimmeee (time)!" he nervously says in a high pitch with a smile, but not a happy one when easing into his chair.

Kelvin gets it together extra fast, tying his shoes, and bursting through his door, slamming into the adjacent wall, almost knocking himself out when falling. He quickly shakes off the pain, runs for the steps, and launches halfway down the steps as if floating in slow motion. "Hey Mommmmm...!" he screams, still floating in mid-air into the kitchen.

Keyonton stands soaked with water beads on his forehead, and with one glimpse of his son, he sees him as if frozen in time until Kelvin's feet instantly hit the floor, quickly shuffling when trying to regain balance when the doorbell rings. "Heyyyy!" Kelvin begins to say.

Keyonton interrupts. "Heyyyy! Let's eat some ribs, bro!" Keyonton screams, grabbing Kelvin by the back of his collar, quickly guiding him to the door, and flinging it open. "Forget to tell you Jamie's outside," Keyonton nervously screams, shoving Kelvin into the little old nosey woman when the two fall back into the lawn chair, kicking.

Keyonton kicks the walker like a seasoned and professional football player onto the lawn, nervously clawing at the doorbell until ripping it off and slamming the door when backing into Liandra's view. He rushes to the stereo, flipping it off when the announcer mentions the word 'breaking news.'

"Key! We agreed that Kelvin would not go out to play until after dinner," she says, easing into her chair and curiously gazing at his erratic behavior.

"Ahh..., Liandra! He's a growing boy, so there's no need to be too hard on him!"

She stands with her arms crossed, and her eyes finally wander over the lawn, finding the walker lying sideways.

The phone rings, startling Keyonton when he jumps. He rushes over, snatching it from the junction box, when several hard knocks come.

"Can't a man get some family time with his woman?" he screams with both hands clenched tight and near his face.

"Key, you're really starting to freak me out!" She backs into the sink to get a better view of the lawn, spotting Kelvin, helping the little old woman stand up on the walker. "Family time, huh? Uh-huh…, did you just knock little ole' lady Johnson over?"

"What?" He rushes to the end of the table, gazing over the lawn. "Girl, you tripping! Jamie and Kev probably ran her over when they ran out." Keyonton drifts into deep thought, slowly gazing at Liandra, when his mind drifts on the ribs, when easing toward her.

Liandra strangely backs away, cautiously making her way around to the other side of the table.

Keyonton eases the hot pan out of the oven, continually smiling to get her at ease. He quietly opens the refrigerator while looking over his shoulder and accidentally pulling out expired milk that Liandra's mother saved for buttermilk biscuits during her last visit. He opens the freezer door and pulls out the metal tray of ice, twisting and then turning it until the ice breaks. He drops several cubes in his glass, pouring then places the carton back. He fixes their plates and then motions for her to sit when more heavy pounding comes upon the door.

Liandra eases into her chair, gazing over the hearty meal, hearing the upstairs phone ring continuously, then hang up repeatedly and non-stop for minutes.

"Family time…, family time…, family…, time!" he says until it sounds like a broken record. He stands, pouring her a glass of tea, and then leans his chair back on its hind legs. His eyes gaze at the ice-cold glass of milk with thick condensation covering the sides, noticing the milk clinging to the ice. He says Grace, quickly digging into the hot, piping meal and hastily eats, continually staring at her until motioning for her to eat. He slams the last piece of warm rib in his mouth, licks his fingers, and grabs the glass. Keyonton opens wide and downs over half in one gulp, and his lips close with jaws instantly filled when trying to lean forward but jerks forward harder. He jerks again and before the front chair legs hit the floor, he blows chunks of ribs and milk all over the table and floor with force and so strong that it tilts his chair back further, causing him to fall against a low cut cabinet.

Liandra frantically springs from her seat, standing behind her chair, crouching when peeping and cautiously staring. "Key, are you alright?"

The thick, wooden rolling pin drops from the cabinet and rolls across the floor, under the table, and over to the other side.

Keyonton suddenly stands to brace his fall against the cabinet until losing his grip and falling flat on his back. He kicks fast to maneuver and gets his footing back.

Suddenly, another hard bang comes at the door, but this time it's so hard that when he finally is on two feet, he jumps, stumbles, and loses his balance again.

Liandra jumps as well and looks toward the door.

Keyonton motions her not to open it. "Family timmeeee (time)!" he sings in a silly yet high pitch with hands extended to her when tripping. He loses his balance with all fingers slipping down inside the toaster, when with weight, accidentally pressing down when letting out a scream from the heating elements burning and smoking his fingers. His other hand accidentally hits the stove's knob, turning a burner on high as he lifts his fingers fast. Keyonton's hand goes over his head and back against the other cabinet, causing him to lose balance again, slamming against the unstable wall cabinet.

The left frame instantly slips off its support hinge, unleashing the half-bent nail with delicate China rolling off one piece at a time, smashing with Liandra's head repeatedly bowing when counting each dish.

The grease in the skillet from the fried Lumpia the night before heats up fast.

Keyonton staggers a few steps, turning on heels when dancing on the rolling pin, one heel after another. He falls back into another flimsy cabinet and then flat on his back, lying there, staring up at a large bag of flour, rocking a few times, before bursting in his face and spraying all over the floor and quickly rising in a light dust.

More residue rises quickly, filling the room until the plume of dust is at waist level.

Liandra stays in a daze with eyes cut over at him until wandering over to the crooked cabinet and then back at him, finally noticing grease popping and the room quickly filling with smoke.

Keyonton's muffled voice murmurs loud words when repeatedly and expressly fighting for footing.

The bubbly-looking cast-iron skillet starts to pop from the little water and dish detergent Liandra had put in earlier to dissolve the grease.

Suddenly, a burst of fire springs up on the stove, with a plume of smoke.

"Ahh!" they scream, grabbing their heads and screaming even louder.

Keyonton jumps to his feet like a superhero and springs into action.

Liandra stands off in fear, still screaming at the top of her lungs.

Keyonton thinks quickly, grabbing a towel when inching up to the stove, then backs off a few times, screaming like a woman until closing again with the towel draped over his arm. He notices when the fire dies down and rushes up, unknowingly grabbing the bare metal with bare hands with the towel still draped over his arm, lifting when searing heat sets in, sizzling his fingers. "Ahh!" he screams, throwing the skillet forward and high-stepping with grease splashing against the window seal, then curtains, and setting them on fire.

Kelvin sees flaming curtains and runs screaming as if he's lost his mind. He runs back and forth in front of the window, jumping high then fading and reappearing after each pass.

Liandra can't get to the sink fast enough, but with quick thinking, she heads for the bathroom for the foot pail under the sink.

Keyonton leans into the counter with throbbing and severe burns, grabbing the handle with the towel, this time, with fire blazing high. He flings the pan toward the sink, missing when pouring grease over the cabinets, watching the paint melt and drip to the slate.

Liandra lunges water forward, drenching him, then runs to the bathroom again, breathing harder than ever, and returning, taking deep breaths, seeing how everything is under control. She frowns in silence, and Keyonton stays in embarrassment, with them looking over the kitchen with sirens mildly blaring in the background and growing louder.

CHAPTER FOUR

In Port La Gaigiuana, Barry, Ken, Greg, and Alfred catch a cab to a pub.

There's a comedy show on the bar side, so they sit in the dining area, listening to comedy in the background while talking or watching television.

Out of nowhere, an outburst of laughter lasts for some time.

"Hey..., this guy is the best so far; let's check him out," Barry says, standing and digging deep in his pockets for a healthy tip.

They approach the podium, pay ten dollars, and enter the small room of about a hundred people deep in laughter.

The comedian pauses, still laughing. "..., for real..., you know I'm not joking!" He leans, taking sips of water before sitting the bottle back on the stool. "Back in the day, more mothers had morals, didn't they? I mean, as soon as they knew a baby was on the way, they first broke out was the Bible and searched for biblical names, huh? They were clueless, not knowing if their child would be the furthest from the Bible. Do you see the trend? Back in the day, biblical names..., but now people name kids after anything..., like Magic, because they know they'll eventually disappear; Star, as in wishing and hoping they will be a star or Mercedes, and most may never own a Mercedes, license or even have a car..., period."

The crowd sounds off in laughter.

"How 'bout the Kadricas, Malekas, and Gazebras? Now there are some names for ya (you)!"

The crowd laughs louder.

"And people..., please..., please..., please! Start learning to sound out your kids' names, letter by letter, you know, like back in elementary school," he says, sounding out a few words but very slow as if teaching a kid for the first time. "If you name your kid Devillier, it's pronounced as it sounds; don't try to get all fancy talking about it is pronounced Devillea, like its freakin' French or some other language," he says, shaking his head. "Let's see..., LIER..., for plier..., PLIER, do we pliea?"

The crowd sounds off in deeper laughter.

"And if you're a girl, and your family wants a boy, and name you Tommi, then damn it, it's Tommy and not, Taymi. Can we please keep it real?" he frowns, staring into the crowd when they sound off in laughter with a few folks yelling the comedian's name.

"And some done (have) messed around and got these kids' names so damn long they can't even spell them, more or less pronounce them until well into their teens. Some of these names are just too damn long, people! Some are damn sure as hell too long for the short signature lines on checks and applications. Shoot. . ., mess around, and somebody ain't gone get paid because their whole name can't fit on the check or they don't get the job because the name is chopped off the application."

The crowd sounds off in laughter with soft whistles in the background.

"I saw a kid last week signing for a library book. His name was so freakin' long that he had to stop in the middle and shake his hands to get the circulation going again."

The crowd sounds off in laughter with moderate screams.

The comedian looks in the corner several times, distracted by a drunk seriously focused on stacking a house of playing cards. After several more interruptions, the comedian stares at the big man, shaking his head. "Excuse me, sir, but are we bothering you? I mean..., you seem to be so focused..., but look ah hea (here); are you having fun?"

The man ignores the comedian until the bouncer gets his attention when pointing the man to the stage.

The crowd sounds off in laughter, with some pointing to the man.

"Excuse me, sir, are you having fun?" the comedian asks again but louder.

The man slumps forward, taking another sip of strong drink, and his face frowns with eyes wandering over the audience and then back at the cards. "Yes, and what's it to yah (you)?" he sarcastically responds.

The comedian smiles, putting a hand on his hip when heading for the far side of the stage, motioning the lighting man over to the drunkard. "Oh, it's no business of mine, sir, but I'm sure the people sitting around you find you annoyed as all hell. I mean, you're stacking a freakin' deck of cards, like a first grader. . ., no, an idiot, plus, you're drunk and look frustrated. You know..., obviously, you're not too damn good at stacking if you can't get past the first tier. I mean..., I'm here thinking, 'damn..., maybe he needs another profession, maybe...hmmm?'"

The crowd sounds off in a loud laughter, and a few hands playfully slam down on table tops in high spirits.

The comedian walks to the edge, staring deep into the man's face, shaking his head before turning and walking away.

"Up yours, buddy! And, uh, uh, uh. . ., as for your jokes, they're. . ., uh, uh, uh, like what, first grade too, or idiotic?" the huge drunk responds, bursting into a silly and uncontrollable giggle that has folks laughing.

"Oooh. . .," a few folks mumble under their breaths.

The comedian stops, slowly turning and frowning with his teeth clenched when turning back to the man who makes the Hulk look like a little baby.

"Ah..., a resident smart-ass, hey! Before I go any further, would you kindly tell me your name, sir? Your name, please..., come on, you don't have to think about it; just spit it out of that little pea brain, you worthless piece of. . .," the comedian begins to say when the man springs up, falling forward, and then back into the wall before balancing.

"Oooh. . .," the crowd mildly groans with some laughter.

"Joffie Haufenmundau!" he proudly responds, balancing against the wall with one hand.

The crowd sounds off in more laughter.

The man's index finger sharply points to the comedian when staggering. He reaches for his beer, downing half a glass in a swallow before chasing it with the other shot of liquor on his table.

"I see. . ., so, Haufenmundau, huh? Like from deep unda (under)? Like from unda (under) me (my) balls?" the comedian says, mocking his strong Australian accent.

The crowd sounds off in a peal of deep laughter, with one man falling backward from his stool, stumbling.

"Very funny..., very funny! Hey, as they say, mate..., never quit yah (your) day job, hey!" the broad man says in a bold and more drunken Australian accent.

"Quit my day job, hey. . ., Jolly ole' Joffie?" the comedian says, watching the drunk snap his finger to get a server's attention. "Excuse me, lovely lady! Would you be kind as to get this drunken bloat another bloody drink so that he can pisseth (piss) his already pissy-ass mattress when he geteth (gets) home?"

The folks laugh at how well the comedian mocks the man's accent.

"Is that the best you got in that lame brain, mate? Yeah. . ., yeah, I'll be bloody pissing alright, but it won't be on me (my) bloody mattress, but on top of your mother's bloody head," he yells, dropping in his chair in a peal of uncontrollable laughter.

A burst of even louder laughter breaks out in the background when another faded groan of, 'Oooh. . ., then ahs' fades off.

In deep thought, the comedian's slight smile turns into a mean stare when walking in circles. "See, folks, this is what I mean by giving your kids off the wall, useless-ass names. They grow up like ole' baby Hulk over here, and their mind is like a fully wet sponge but can't absorb a thing. Well, except more beer and stupidity," he laughs, continually mocking the man until throwing his head and hands back as if drunkenly slamming back drinks.

More laughter breaks out, and folks look back and forth at what they think will end up being a knock-down-drag-out of words by one of them.

"A sponge?" the drunkard laughs. "You're the one who kaint (can't) absorb a thing because if yah (you) could yah (you) would have noticed that I ignored your silly ass when yah (you) tried to get my 'tention (attention) the first time, mate. I think the most prosperous part of yah. . ., uh, uh, uh. . ., well, the functioning part of yah (your) brain must have rolled down your mama's crack at conception and stayed there!" He laughs harder, throws his head back, bangs it into the wall, and then jumps up with the back of his head in his hand and his mouth torn wide open.

Folks go into tears of laughter.

"Yeah…, you clown…, that would be called pain, but I guess it takes your small pea brain some time to register that, huh?"

Folks go deeper in laughter, and a few stand clapping.

"You know. . .," the comedian goes on to say when pretending to be in deep thought while staring at the man who is , carefully examining his fingertips for blood. "Now that I see how slow your response time is, I'm willing to bet a dime to a dozen that your mama's so dumb; she thinks a diaphragm is something stores use to transfer money," the comedian says, reenacting the man bumping his head and drunkenly grabbing it.

Laughter roars and folks are in tears, with some slapping high-fives with others loudly clapping.

The man looks up with a silly smile. "Yeah? Mate, and yah (your) mama's so dumb; she thinks a clitoris is an instrument in the violin family," he responds, bowing his legs when bowing forward and acting like he's strumming a violin.

Louder laughter breaks out.

"Yeah? Well, your mama's so dumb; she thinks the letters NSF stamped on her returned bank checks stand for never short on funds," the comedian laughs, bending.

More laughter breaks out.

"Well, your mama's so dumb; she thinks the Internet is a person that plays volleyball out in front of the nets," the man says when his enormous hand slams down on the table, retracting it quickly yet continually shaking off the pain for seconds while more loud laughter breaks out.

"Your mama's so dumb; she thinks you and your dad have common sense!" the comedian screams when laughter loudly breaks out.

"Your mama's so dumb; she uses your grand mama's hot, freshly used douchebag to brew family tea," the man giggles when laughter breaks out, and a man in the front row falls to the floor in laughter.

"Well, your mama's so dumb; she bought a computer monitor with no CPU and thought she brought a nine-hundred-dollar flat-screen television for nine dollars at the five-and-dime," the comedian says when laughter breaks out.

"Your mama's so dumb; she thinks a crackhead is two men going to it," the man says when a burst of loud laughter breaks out.

"Well, your mama's so dumb; she scans her rent money, faxes it to the rental office, and sits home weeks later, wondering why she's receiving eviction notices," the comedian says when laughter breaks out.

"And your mama's so dumb; she went to the bank and tried to pass off one-sided, faxed copies of ten dollar bills she printed on tan paper," the man says when even louder laughter breaks out.

"Man, your mama's so dumb; she goes through the drive-thru and orders fourteen McNuggets, thinking she's getting fourteen gold carats," the comedian says when laughter breaks out.

"And your mama's so dumb; she thinks Windows 7 Enterprise is a new Star Trek movie coming out soon," the man says.

Deep laughter breaks out, and the crowd goes out of control.

The comedian walks around laughing while waiting for the crowd to calm down. "And you know what, Mr. Haufenmundau? I love your mama!" The comedian smiles.

The crowd's voices dwindle, and they all look at the comedian, somewhat confused.

"And I love your mama too," the man replies, smiling.

"Give it up to my loving brother Kenny, from Australia, everyone!" the comedian shouts, motioning his brother to stand when clapping.

Music comes on, and several folks stand to their drunken feet, dancing.

The comedian lets the music play for seconds, then has the DJ cut the track while motioning with his hand. He leaves the stage and comes back later with more jokes.

Barry leads the way through a narrow passageway and out into the parking lot when the guys are ready to go. They instantly notice that the streets are dry but feel a few raindrops when flagging down a taxi.

The taxi driver pulls over and rolls down his window, informing them that he can take them if they don't mind riding a few blocks to drop off the man in the front seat.

Barry leans down, stares into the taxi, and then reaches for the door.

On the other side of town, dark and gloomy skies heavily send large drops of rain pounding for over ten minutes before subsiding.

Greg sits in the last row, high as a kite and resting his head on the headrest while staring at the art-painted, colorful, dark sky.

The full moon slowly moves in a northern direction while shining through various openings in thin, blue-tinted clouds.

Further up the road, a young couple takes a shortcut through the woods, coming upon a long, well-lit concrete trail when walking about ten minutes in mild conversation.

The young man pulls out a pack of tobacco chew, filling his gums as the couple make it to the end of the walkway and continue to a more lit area.

"Ahh!" the young girl screams, pushing her friend, being the first to spot a body lying in the tall grass, looking somewhat twisted. She fearfully backs away further, holding her fist tight in her companion's chest, trembling. "Ahh!" she screams even louder in horror.

"Get help!" her male friend screams, rushing over and nervously staring at the man. His feet nervously shuffle, contemplating what to do when looking back, finding her still there when rushing and slightly shoving her off. He runs back, turns the body over, and begins administering CPR.

The girl walks fast, crying, then stops, looking around before taking off slowly and coming up to top speed when approaching the trail's steep incline. She sees a distant porch light and runs faster, screaming at the top of her lungs.

The grim-looking, long, and narrow house grows taller as she reaches the top of the hill. Her feet quickly shuffle up the steep steps and onto the porch when her body slams into the door with frantic knocking hands.

Within seconds, the door flings open.

A messy-haired older woman stands startled, breathing hard while holding her tight fist deep in her chest. She stares at the young girl with glassy buckeyes. "Well? Speak up…, speak up like you got a pair!"

The girl's train of thought leaves quick, thinking hard on the manly comment until gathering her thoughts and taking long, deep breaths. Her hand nervously rides across her chest, and her other hand slowly points down the trail. She shockingly opens her mouth but nothing.

A frail-looking man peeps out from the dim hallway seconds later, nervously rocking for minutes with his left arm well hidden behind the wall. He soon eases out a long shotgun, extending it down the hallway with the shadow of the barrel slowly dancing across the dingy floor. His shadow grows tall against the wall until in full view. "Who the hell do you think you are; up here banging on my damn door this time of the evening…, you done lost your cotton-picking mind!" he says in a mean, deep tone.

The girl's pointy finger shakes uncontrollably when speechlessly pointing down the trail again. "Listen to me! Call an ambulance…, please! There's a body lying in the grass along the jogging trail!" she finally frantically cries out, taking a few more deep breaths.

The old man brings the barrel down quickly with old, dusty brogans shuffling across the dusty floor when vanishing behind the wall.

"You don't say, do you?" the old woman finally responds, curiously staring the girl up and down with one eye slightly squinting as if she just had bitten into a sour pickle or lemon. "Can you tell me what he was ah, wearing?"

"Yeah. . .," the girl says, extending her shaky hands to the woman when trying to explain. "Co, co, co, coveralls, and a…, ba, ba, ba, ball cap," she nervously stutters when trying to recall more while still breathing heavily.

"Aw hellz, Jeb! Pay her no damn mind! It's probably just ole' drunk-ass Wiley down there clowning around; either that or doped up off that dea (there) liquid meth!" She responds, shaking her head when thinking more about the foolishness.

The husband dials 911, and the operator answers, asking about the emergency over three times before the husband says a word, until he finally responds, hanging up. "I'd better get down there in case it ain't ole, foolish Wiley!"

The wife stares deep into the young girl's eyes. "Oh, calm down, child, I got my cell right chea (here)! I reckon we'll just mosey on down the trail and see what's unquestionably going on," she says, still fearfully holding her chest. She hears fast-moving footsteps when looking over her shoulder, finding her husband approaching when turning and staring back into the girl's bulged, teary eyes.

The young girl nervously shivers with tears until the wife pushes the door wide, finally pulling her into her arms, rocking and comforting her.

The wife smiles, and quickly turns grim until slightly shoving her away and staring the girl up and down as if she's crazy.

"They're on the way! Let's get down there and see if there's anything we can do!" the old man says, grabbing their overcoats; flinging his on before helping his wife into hers.

Minutes later, they rush toward the boy, who climbs to his feet when hearing them approaching swiftly.

The male companion nervously stands, backing away slowly and nervously shaking. His face stays pale as if he's seen a ghost. "He's not responding," he finally says with his back still to them while wiping teary eyes when snot slowly trails from his nose onto his top lips, dripping to the bottom lip. He turns his head slowly, spitting tobacco, then turns again, looking back at them in a half-bent-over turn when clearing his throat.

Immediately, the three stand cringing while giving him a disgusted look as he tries his best to break the long, three-foot trail of tobacco mixed with saliva. "Turn your heads!…, I said, turn your heads!" he finally screams in a high mumble, still fighting to break the long string again when finally turning away from them with jerking shoulders.

The three finally look down at Wiley's mouth, finding it smeared in a brown paste from the companion giving CPR with a mouthful of tobacco.

The four grow tensed and are startled, hearing slow and then slower crunching leaves in the thick woods. They quickly turn, shuffling and finding a dark silhouette kneeling and then standing until slowly staggering toward them.

The husband curiously cuts his eyes around at the couple, secretly slipping his hand deep into his pocket and pulling out and lowering his old, rusty-looking pistol to his side with cautious eyes constantly glued between the couple and the dark silhouette.

The manly silhouette continually staggers toward them and then stops. The figure stares, taking more slow steps, then accidentally trips over a tree branch, tumbling down a decline screaming and rolling into a well-lit light post several feet from the five.

A senseless, loud giggle grows as the homeless-looking man springs up fast, as if never down when staggering over in even louder laughter which grows, echoing loud. He laughs so hard that he can barely stand but stays bent over with hands at his knees.

"Who the hell are you?" the woman's husband asks, gripping the steel a little tighter, yet keeping it out of view.

The crackhead waves off the woman's husband as if he doesn't have a care in the world. "Ah, shush! Shut your freakin' pie hole, I say!" The crackhead keeps senselessly giggling while tiptoeing up on ole' Wiley, who's still unresponsive. He looks at Wiley, then back at them, then at Wiley, then at them, then back at Wiley. "Wiley! Wiley! Man, get your silly ass up, you ole' coot! I done (already) tolt (told) you not to be hitting this hea (here) stuff so hard," he giggles, whispering a few words that no one can make out when mumbling to himself and answering his own question a time or two. He reaches deep in his coverall pocket, shaking out a long, clear sandwich bag of what looks like tree roots and dry leaves. "Ah…, Wiley, Wiley, Wiley, Wiley. . ., Ah…, Wiley, Wiley, Wiley, Wiley. . ., Ah…, Wiley, Wiley, Wiley, Wiley. . ., Ah…, Wiley, Wiley, Wiley, Wiley!" the crackhead chants, dancing around Wiley's body as if he's in some ceremonial ritual.

The young man turns his back to them fast with shoulders continually jerking up and down but peeps back from time to time, staring at the five while chuckling. His eyes grow over watery until his body begins jerking so hard that he hardly can see them anymore or can barely stand. He peeps again, and the last time he looks back, he definitely can't see anything from being so weak. He falls to his knees in laughter, sounding like he's crying, with more chanting screamed in the background.

"Ah…, Wiley, Wiley, Wiley, Wiley. . ., Ah…, Wiley, Wiley, Wiley, Wiley. . ., Ah…, Wiley, Wiley, Wiley, Wiley. . ., Ah…, Wiley, Wiley, Wiley, Wiley!" the crackhead chants when continuing in his ridiculous-looking shuffle but this time, backing up with heels clicking like Chuck Barry on the guitar when clucking loud like a chicken for seconds.

The young man screams in laughter for seconds until it finally tapers off when pulling himself together and coming to his feet. He turns bright red, trying not to laugh but giggles harder, hearing him cluck again when his eyes quickly fill with more tears.

His girlfriend finally turns, finding him with his back to them, thinking he's crying when walking over, putting her hand on his shoulder and comforting him. She rubs his back while his shoulders continually go up and down in a burst of deep, quiet laughter.

"I think he's dead, you silly son of a bitch!" the wife finally screams, staring at the crazy man and shaking her head in disbelief. "So were you two out yonder (there) getting high?" She asks, still shaking her head in disbelief until staring over at Wiley.

"Hell! Getting high! Getting high? You're 'bout as crazy as a slew-footed horse."

The husband's eyes buck, expressly raising the gun to the man's head, pulling back on the hammer, and cocking one eyebrow when transforming into something vicious.

The man's hands rise slowly until high and trembling.

The wife's hands rest on the gun's barrel, bringing it down slowly, and at her husband's side.

"Shucks, me and ole' Wiley practically live out yonder below the big ole' oak!" he says, dropping his hands when creeping over and kicking Wiley's lifeless foot. He pulls out a dingy and dirt-crusted glass tube, packing some unknown substance from the bag and lighting it.

"Uh, uh, uh," the wife says as if pained, keeping her eyes pierced to the ground and fighting the feeling when anxiously staring at the substance, then away even faster. She clenches her nose tight until losing it when her head goes back, and a peace comes over her as she inhales the sweetest aroma she knows too well.

Her husband replicates her actions until his hand rests on her shoulder, both trembling from the addiction. He shakes his head, stomping a few times when grasping her collar so tight that he accidentally chokes her and her mouth opens to scream in pain.

Without warming, her elbow stealthily lunges back into his chest, and he bends in a deep cough, catching his breath while she tries catching hers.

"Wiley! Man, get your silly ass up! Look! Look!" The man screams, pointing. "You see how his mouth twists? Ain't nothing wrong with him; that's just what they call in the zone; some call it in the mode, but I call it the death zone," the crackhead says, taking one step forward and two back.

"Man! I think you got more brains than senses," the wife yells, staring at the man's oversized, dingy truck driver's hat, covered in dirty fingerprints and tobacco stains.

"Shit! Ole' Wiley is all right..., ain't you alright ole' boy?" he says, slowly looking around until gazing back at them even slower.

The young couple soon walks up beside the old married couple.

"One damn thing for sure! I'm sick and tired of Wiley always bragging about how much he can handle!" The crackhead kicks Wiley's foot again and staggers a few feet back as if nervous. "I see you ain't handling this, ole' boy!" He quickly points his finger at Wiley, swaying and almost falling on top of him. "I'm sick of youuuu! I'm sick of youuu, ole' boy!" he says in a very girlish high pitch when he staggers back, lighting the pipe again and taking a long deep hit. Instantly, he takes a deep breath, continually coughing with a hand continually slamming into his chest until grabbing kneecaps.

The wife stares at the pipe, shaking her head, then turns away fast, groaning as if she can't stand the looks of it. "Uh, uh, uh," she says, pained with eyes glued to the ground.

Her husband's hand comes up to her shoulder again, shaking his head while fighting the overwhelming addition.

The wife tugs, snatching from her husband's death grip. She walks a few feet away and looks, catching the young man looking back and still giggling at the old fool's ridiculous comments. She walks a few more feet along the paved path leading to a busy street, listening for sirens and hearing them within minutes. The wife rushes back over to her husband and the young couple. "Look…, I don't know what happened, but one thing's for sure…if we don't get a hold of this hea (here) lunatic, they might think we had something to do with Wiley's death," she barely whispers with nervous eyes.

The four look back and find the crackhead leaning over Willey, in a trance when looking at her husband, nodding. "Look…, whatever you do…, just don't look him in the eyes," she whispers. "Just keep your backs to him, and on three, we'll have him cornered."

They do accordingly, spreading out until having him somewhat surrounded.

"Three…, two…, one…" she quickly screams over mild, approaching sirens when they turn quickly to where he was standing, staring at each other until looking down and around for him.

"There! There he is!" the husband screams, pointing the gun in the woods at the fast-moving, staggering, and loud laughing man until hearing echoing laughter.

The wife quickly grabs the end of the barrel, shoving it down when secretly and expressly handing him a neatly rolled bag of drugs from her bra, motioning him home with a quick nod.

The husband snatches the goods, taking off and almost skipping up the trail until sprinting, but in a zigzag pattern until fading around a bush and into the woods.

The sirens grow louder with the ambulance and police car making their way around to the other side of the trail, where chains block off the entrance. Headlights soon shine across the mushy field, and the swamp then veers up, shining onto the three a ways off and in the field.

The three frantically jump up and down, waving as lights stay still, then quickly veer off with the ground growing dim again until sirens grow louder when the police and ambulance come around through a broken, paved side street.

The police car blocks the road, and the ambulance swerves behind the cop car, coming onto the busy road.

The ambulance pulls up near the cutover where emergency response vehicles cross over into oncoming traffic, slowly rocking when slightly pulling onto the sidewalk.

Two officers jump out, waving nosey drivers by as quickly as possible, though some ignore them when stopping and peeking through the cutover with angry cops blowing whistles with fast directing hands.

Paramedics rush through the cutover pushing the stretcher as fast as possible until swinging it to the side when near Wiley. They drop to their knees, and one paramedic quickly half-undresses Wiley and begin checking his vital until performing CPR. The paramedic pops up minutes later with a smiling face thinking he has a weak pulse, motioning his partners to swap places, finding her mouth dropped open in a strange stare, shaking her head 'no' and backing away with a frowned face still glued on his brown smeared mouth.

The male medic turns, not getting a clue. After working on Wiley for minutes with an even weaker pulse, the female paramedic covers him, and the female cop acknowledges the female paramedic's nod when reaching for the walkie-talkie, dispatching a detective.

Two women in plain clothes come up to the crime scene, speaking to an officer.

Two other tall women standing in the back peeping over folks' shoulders until one spots the too-familiar-looking dirty coveralls when her face frowns and her mouth drops open. "Ahh! Wiley, Wiley, Wiley!" she screams, her mouth tearing open even wider with not even one straight or half-white tooth. She screams until thrusting forward, knocking folks aside until near the yellow tape.

The female paramedic turns with eyes glued on the woman crying the hardest. "Can you tell me if he's on any medications? Does he have any allergies?" she asks.

The tallest woman looks back, finding her daughter shaking her head nervously 'no' knowing she's lying. "He's never taken any drug his whole life," she says, quickly cutting her head over to the old woman and young couple standing there, shaking their heads when huddling and whispering.

The wife and couple see an officer in the path and point, motioning the young couple to follow, and they do, walking up to the cop, giving a brief account of what happened.

The tall, crying woman backs up quickly with a hand anxiously patting her daughter's shoulder when two sudden screams from the women echo across the field.

An officer approaches, diverting the screaming women to his cruiser.

One paramedic slips an oxygen mask over Wiley's face, and they grab each side of the stretcher, rushing through the cutover.

The ambulance driver watches with both arms still folded as they quickly return to the ambulance, and when halfway through the cutover, he opens the back doors and secures each side. He jumps back in the cab, quickly responding to the dispatcher.

The two paramedics quickly lift the body on the count of three and then stop the stretcher from moving forward when they hear metal loudly bang against something.

The female paramedic's eyes wander over the floor until staring at the two bottles and unsecured equipment that had fallen due to the sudden sharp turns.

With confirmation, they shake their heads, rolling the stretcher out, but due to the muddy grass, they leave Wiley secured to the stretcher and alongside the street.

One police officer reaches for his walkie-talkie with his head slightly tilted and immediately breaks out in a wide-legged sprint. He shoots past Wiley and knocks the sheet from his face.

The other officer freezes, looking back at the other officer acting like a lunatic when directing a few more cars until traffic begins to clear.

"Hey..., there's another accident up the road!" the running officer screams to the others when rushing into the traffic and up to the directing officer's back.

"Ok, you go ahead! I got things covered. The ambulance is off the road, so certainly, there's no need for two of us to stick around."

Traffic slows almost to a standstill and then quickly clears when the officer directs the last car by and then moves his car so it's not to blocking traffic. "Hey, I'm going up the road to help Trooper Ron. You guys got it from here?" he asks, staring at the back of both paramedics' heads while they lean, lifting the long oxygen bottle.

"We're about wrapped up here and should be out in a jiffy." The female paramedic says, looks back again, and straining to lift the last long bottle, when noticing her partner's smeared mouth and motioning him to clean up while uncontrollably and senselessly giggling. They soon climb in, squaring the ambulance away with one bottle and a few pads left to secure as traffic picks back up.

Most cars swerve out and are at a distance, but others come close at times when passing in the narrow curve, spotting flashing emergency lights at the last minute.

The male paramedic looks at his watch, popping two capsules and putting them up to Wiley's nose just for the hell of it, giggling.

Instantly, Wiley rises off the stretcher so responsive that he almost falls off.

The female paramedic helps him balance, then reach into the ambulance and quickly pulls out a pillow, fluffing it before easing it behind Wiley's head, slightly leaning him back.

The ambulance driver steps out, releasing the tension from his underwear, bunching when grabbing a hand full. He jumps back in, accidentally flooring the engine when reaching for the clipboard to fill out his paperwork.

The paramedics generously try making Wiley comfortable, then restrains him at the chest.

Without warning, the female paramedic snatches Wiley's shoes off, throwing them to the front of the ambulance when the wind instantly shifts, and shoe funk rises, with them expressly grabbing their noses and quickly falling away from the stretcher.

The male paramedic sprints off with his foot, accidentally nudging the stretcher, causing it to roll a few feet and slightly down a small concrete embankment.

The stretcher wobbles more, riding over an indentation, making its way into the street, over another slight hump, and then down a steep decline.

Further up the road, an old bifocal glass-wearing woman enters the road, easing out, then takes off cheerfully smiling and raising a tight fist.

Barry's bloodshot eyes go back over the seat as they shoot past the flashing blue cop lights, spotting an officer directing the last car through the intersection when rushing from the street toward his cruiser.

The taxi driver swerves around the sharp corner, instantly spotting the stretcher. "Oh shi...! Mama Mia! Mama..., these damn crazy people!" the Indian-looking cab driver screams at the top of his lungs.

Barry continues looking back while the others have their eyes closed, and his head flies forward, with the others sitting straight and staring straight down at the driver's arm and through the windshield.

"Dayum!" Barry screams, throwing his hand back and slamming his hand on Ken and Alfred's knees to get their attention.

Wiley lays shaking until curiously opening his eyes and staring at the sky when a lusty smile comes, thinking they've given him a strong dose of morphine when staring at his arm almost cross eyed then easing back. He looks down at one arm again, then the other, and does not see an IV when frowning then quickly growing concerned. He wrestles to get free and manages to get one hand loose, frantically yelling and waving for help.

The stretcher rocks again when a horn blows loudly and fades off fast.

Another car enters the road, barely missing the stretcher, when Wiley's peanut head pops up as he flies under a tree branch, slightly wobbling. His mouth flies wide open, and he continually screams for as long as possible. He frowns more, wiggling to get free when hitting a dip, slinging the stretcher around, and now rolling sideways.

The old bifocal glass-wearing woman slows, continually patting brakes, and the stretcher slams into her bumper with stretcher screws puncturing the plastic and sticking. Her head comes up in the rearview, finding Wiley's fast-waving hand, thinking someone she just passed is waving when happily waving back and gripping the wheel tighter with eyes straight ahead.

The paramedics still have their backs turned until a steady horn continually blows over the ambulance's loud engine, causing them to look back, finding the stretcher gone finally. They rush into the road with eyes peeled down the hill, finding the stretcher riding against the back of a car.

The ambulance driver finally sees the stretcher when pulling away slowly and then cutting across the street in front of the cars to stop traffic.

The two paramedics run past the ambulance at top speed.

The ambulance driver's mouth remains wide open as he steps into the gas, throwing the ambulance into overdrive with two oxygen bottles flying out.

One bottle hits the ground, rolling to the side of the road, and the other lands on the nozzle, breaking it off with gas hissing for seconds until the bottle begins vibrating. A mild, steady mist sprays, then a blast of spray when the bottle takes off like a stealth missile, tearing through the woods and little makeshift cardboard house Wiley and his smoking bud call home as he eases out with a stale face and mouth torn open.

Willey's friend slowly pulls the clear bag from his pocket, staring at it, then throws it high in the air, taking off in a wide-legged stagger until running fast and looking back.

The jet-express bottle goes higher, slamming into a distant tree and vectoring, then tearing through the cruiser's side door at the other accident, exploding while the cop runs back to the cruiser.

The officer tries stopping when sliding several feet with boots smoking black when taking off again. He keeps his eyes on the missile-like object, watching it slam into another tree, then another, until heading back toward him. He veers off, diving into a trench just before the next enormous explosion that comes within seconds, slamming into the side of a camper.

Back on the road, the little old, bifocal glass-wearing woman continues driving cheerfully, still not knowing about the attached stretcher. She presses harder on the gas pedal, barely able to look over the dash when increasing speed.

Folks run out into the street, screaming and waving as the old woman flies past and rushes upon a fork-turn, where the stretcher breaks off when she skids, taking the sharp curve without slowing down.

The taxi slows, and the guys' eyes follow the stretcher for seconds.

A loud horn blows, and a car swerves, almost hitting the taxi.

Another loud horn blows, and another car swerves past.

The taxi finally eases into the road and immediately swerves, hearing another horn when pulling off fast.

Both paramedics give out of breath, veering to the side of the road, dry heaving with eyes glued on the miniature-looking stretcher, still picking up momentum on the straightway, and heading for the driveway at the T-intersection.

A car horn blows with black smoke rising when the car misses the stretcher by inches as it dips, goes airborne, and slams back down hard and fast in the long driveway.

The stretcher's wheel finally levels out, and the stretcher stops abruptly, slamming into a window seal with Wiley's frail body slipping through the straps. He shoots out like a missile when bursting through the large, sparking clean glass dining room window and sliding down the long, food-filled table, lunging dish after dish high until slamming into a wall and down to the floor.

The ambulance driver pulls over near the paramedics, and they jump in the back and then jump out, gagging from the sweaty shoe funk.

The male paramedic beats the side of the ambulance, stopping the driver when coming in view, in the passenger side mirror, reaching onto a trash pile, and grabbing a long stick. He holds his nose tight, fishing for the shoes until they hit the ground, when the two slam door, jumping in the cab with the driver speeding off and fearfully cruising at top speed.

The ambulance pulls up at the house, and the paramedics jump out.

Several people who live in the home or are visiting run out, greeting the rescue team while holding their noses and bailing out.

The three-person ambulatory team burst through the door, falling back out and rolling to the ground, screaming while more guest bailout with noses clenched tight.

Another window soon shatters when an old war veteran dives through, hitting the ground like a gymnast and rolling several times until coming to his feet. "Tadah!" the old vet screams, balancing with arms spread apart and standing like a magician ready for his next trick; when looking down and brushing down rusty-looking retirement medals.

The paramedics look up, finding the driver handing them face masks which they quickly don, rushing inside, finding the man sitting with a turkey leg in hand, half-dazed and blurry-eyed.

"Damn! I think there's a skunk in here," an old perceived blind-looking woman says, reentering the dining area and continually sniffing while quickly steering her cane and moving swiftly for the door.

The female paramedic's eyes wander over the room. She reaches for a velour blanket but instead grabs trash bags, throwing them over his feet and wrapping them in tape.

The other paramedics come alongside quick, expressly wrestling his feet into bags until falling to the floor, frowning when he's almost out of breath.

Ten minutes later, the taxi pulls in front of headquarters, and the van doors slide open.

The driver stands, collects his fare, and then goes about his business.

Barry stands stretching when spotting something moving high in the air, in the background, then off to the side. He comes on his tiptoes, looking down the hill toward the bright lights near the ship's berthing, spotting an ordnance team loading a missile.

Greg yawns, taking a few steps toward the front door of the building.

"Now that is what you call a big boy!" Barry says, admiring the large warhead and long missile.

"Yeah, almost as long and large as this big boy," Ken yells, playfully grabbing his crotch.

"Is that your ego, or were you referring to your imaginary friend you're always bragging about?" Barry responds, chuckling as Alfred and Greg burst into loud laughter.

Ken stares at the back of their heads for seconds, then quietly rushes up on them and draws back a broad, sprung hand when slapping Barry, Alfred, and Greg in the back of the head, almost identical to his favorite scene from The Three Stooges television show.

Ken falls back into a fast run, making his way to the front door, finding it locked. He turns quickly, finds them closing in fast, and waits until the perfect moment, and charges, clothes hanging Alfred and Greg but missing Barry, who's smart and quick enough to duck. He hops around on one leg and makes a quick turn, kicking drunk Barry in the butt before Barry can retreat to his feet.

The three drunks continually chase even drunker Ken around for minutes until he sprints, slipping through a side door.

Ken rushes down the hall, fading into a dark corridor until they walk inside; then sits giggling, watching them pass by, and giggles harder yet quietly.

Alfred and Greg open their room door, undress, and then go down the hall to shower.

Alfred walks back inside twenty minutes later, finding Greg playing with a colorful canister with the symbol of a snake stamped on the side.

"Hey, what you got there, Bud?"

"Huh? Oh, just some new prank toy I've been dying to try out," he says, throwing Alfred the canister while sitting on the edge of his bunk. His eyes drift to the ceiling when a humongous smile begins brewing. "Hey, I have a great idea!" He sits up quickly, smiling, motioning Alfred over, and then whispering.

Their door soon opens with them peeping and listening, then rushing to the front desk, checking the log when noticing that the Commanding Officer (CO) has returned hours earlier. They contemplate his condition until debating when knowing without a doubt that he's drunk out of his mind seeing how they've been told that he drinks like a fish out of water. They rush to his quarters, cracking his door open and easing inside the pitch-black, liquor-scented room mixed with mildly scented sweaty feet when grabbing their noses.

Greg holds his nose tight until he's immune to the funk when sniffing harder. He rushes to the bed, extends his hand to the CO's pajama sleeve, and gently rubs the material until quickly putting the snakehead against the fabric and lightly pulls on it.

The CO's arm slightly moves, and they drop down, listening to his snore decrease.

Greg and Alfred ease to their knees.

Greg's head pops up seconds later with hands struggling to get the Velcro head detached with several tugs before success. He creeps into the bathroom, opening the toilet. He stretches a thin wire contraption over the toilet and then pushes the spring back, setting the delayed urine actuator when easing the lid shut. He backs into the room, easing the door shut when the back of his shirt catches the pointy end of a statue that slams to the floor, crumbling.

The CO jumps, sitting as Greg falls to the floor, low-crawling to the foot of the bed.

Alfred strikes a pose in front of the CO's uniform, hanging like a scarecrow from the suit rack.

The CO looks around for a few more seconds, easing his head down, and before long, he's profoundly snoring until moving and pulling cover from his feet, wiggling toes.

Greg gently sniffs a few times, looking up quickly, finding sweaty feet next to his head when pinching his nose tighter. He slowly slides away, moving over by the door. He eases the door open, and Alfred sees the light pierce into the room but waits until the door is fully open when dashing into the hallway. Greg catches the door with his hand, easing it shut, and then backs out, slamming the door hard, hearing the CO jumps up, screaming in a mumbling, slurred tone.

The CO stares at the door, quietly listening to fast shuffling feet until hearing fading laughter. He listens longer until hearing the main door leading to his office slam shut when looking and listening longer. He eases up, slipping his feet into plush slippers with drunken, bloodshot eyes wandering over the darkroom. He heads for the bathroom, flipping on dim-blue, low level lights and rushing to the toilet with drunken, burning eyes somewhat closed tight. He bends over, feeling for the lid, which he flips back fast. His head drops back, and a solid stream comes, letting out a sigh of relief.

Instantly, urine sprays against the time-released mechanism for a few seconds, activating the spring when the fake snake forcefully springs upward, catching him in the inseam. His eyes instantly burst open from the weight, staring eye to eye with the snake head, trying to make out what it is until focusing on its long body and, finally, its wiggly tail. His mouth falls open, going straight into panic mode. "Aii...! Aii..., Aii!" he continually screams at the top of his lungs; his loud voice echoing through the halls with folks jumping up. His hand flies forward, catching the snake behind the head in a death grip when dancing and then jumping on alternate feet when feeling the snake heavily shifting from his heavy movement. He applies a death grip, choking tighter with one hand while letting off more screams when running. He soon hears his heart beating when throwing the door open, springing from the room so fast that he slams into a concrete wall, then turns and flies down the hallway, still screaming.

Several folks spring for their doors, easing into the hallway, or peeping out, finding the CO strutting past as fast as humanly possible.

His feet continually slap against the shiny floor until slowing near the armory door, banging hard while dancing with a frown.

The armory officer flings the door open, rushing up on him with sleepy eyes staring into the CO's mean and scary face until finally his eyes are drifting down to where he's pointing. The armory officer fearfully falls backward over the watch desk, quickly climbing to his feet with his firearm drawn.

"Shoot it! Shoot it, now!" the CO screams at the top of his drunken voice.

The Armory Officer takes a steady aim from the side as the CO turns with the snake head held away. He inhales deep for a steady aim, smelling the CO's stale, drunken breath when backing up slow, fanning and squinting one eye when retaking a steady aim, and quickly easing closer for a perfect shot. His sleepy eyes finally focus, staring harder until finally recognizing the Velcro head when falling back against the desk breathless, and slipping his gun in the holster with a serious face, until in a burst of deep laughter.

The CO's eyes stay closed tight until finally registering laughter when peeping with one eye open, finding the Armory Officer bent over the desk and falling to the floor in laughter. He squeezes harder, finally peeking down, and staring at the fake snake head when snatching it from the material and pulling it up to his face. "Gotcha!" the CO playfully screams, playing down the prank. "I told the fellas that I would get you!" He smiles, laughing while backing out, and walking down the hall, laughing and showing off the snake, sometime slinging it around. He stares with eyes glued on each person, cautiously trying to figure out the culprit. "It is just one of my silly academy pranks, so you all can go back to sleep now!" He comes to the next room, staring at Greg and Alfred's door, hearing laughter.

Two hours later, Barry eases out of his bunk, staggering down the narrow passageway toward the bathroom. He steps inside, and stops, adjusting his sight to the bright lights, when the door flies open, slamming into his back and forcing him several steps forward.

"Oh, excuse me, I didn't see you." The old XO staggers past Barry with eyes lightly squinting when Barry stares at him then curiously at the outer tags of his boxers. He makes his way to the urinal, closing his eyes tight while fumbling around to find the opening in his backward boxers.

"Out doing a little tailgating tonight, huh, XO?" Barry says, smiling when leaning back, confirming that the boxers are indeed on backward.

"Yeah, the guys and I went out to tie on a few." The XO giggles, still fumbling.

"Notches, huh? Obviously, and you were on the receiving end, obviously, huh?" Barry jokingly chuckles.

The XO finally looks down with drunken, bloodshot-red eyes, embarrassed when finding his boxers on backward when Barry's smart-ass comments finally registers. He leans his head back, shaking out his hair when moving closer to the urinal when Barry walks up. The XO keeps his eyes closed and his head thrown back with both hands slowly feeling around, then easing up high on the stall's dividers.

Barry releases first with a steady aim and stream, smiling when leaning his head from the pressure. He goes longer and soon cuts his eyes over at the XO, finding his colossal academy ring resting high on the stall divider. His eyes rove to his shoulder, then his face, finally finding his eyes shut then the other hand on the other divider. Barry's mouth quickly drops open in shock, hearing a loud snore with a loud stream of piss in the background continually hitting the back of the urinal and quickly fading off with a louder splash against the rim when a strong mist sprays Barry's fast, high stepping feet.

"Whoa! Whoa! Whoa! Whoa! Get a hold of that little monster!" Barry screams, jumping back and trying to stop his own stream but can't when his power-house solid, uncontrollable stream hits the XO smack in the butt, quickly shooting up his back and going straight up to his head, high up the wall and almost to the ceiling.

"Ohh! Aii! Aii!" the XO screams in a faint voice, backing down quickly with his limp wrist dangling about as he runs in circles, shaking his hands in disgust.

Barry rushes back up to the urinal, finishing with eyes constantly over his shoulder, closely shadowing the XO.

The door flies open, and another officer walks in, squinting until his eyes buck, seeing the XO still cringed and lifting and dropping on alternating feet.

"Aii! Aii!" the XO continually moans, reaching upward and pulling the wet shirt away from his body, while still trembling.

"What's up, XO? Night sweats again, hey?" the young officer asks when finally spotting the wet crease in the middle of his back.

"Hell, naw! Ask ole' quick-draw Freddy over there!" he screams, pointing to Barry, who just backed away from the urinal.

"Quick-draw? You're the one who fell asleep and pissed on me!" Barry says, walking over to the sink, grabbing paper towels, wetting them, then wiping off the overspray.

"What? Man, please! I've been pissing with my eyes closed since second grade and never on the floor," he proudly says, slamming the shirt in the sink with hot water on high.

"Oh yeah? Well, maybe that's it because you never bothered to check the floor," Barry says, shaking his head when reaching for more paper towels.

The other officer smiles, shaking his head when coming away from the urinal, looking down at the pissy floor and then the piss around both urinals and up the wall.

"It's called the Doppler Effect…, you asshole!" the XO screams, frowning.

"Oh yeah…, then it's time for a hearing exam, hearing aide to be serviced or checked, because the damn train came, and was on track, but it didn't stay on track long, but must have flanked or jumped the damn tracks, and I do mean fast," Barry yells, looking at the other officer, running his finger around his head, insinuating the XO's crazy as hell.

"I know what the hell a train sounds like coming, you young-ass whisper snapper!"

"Ahh…, and its whippersnapper, with your non-Doppler Effect calculating ass!" Barry says, looking back at the pissed-off XO when reaching for the door handle.

"Whisper, whipper…, who gives a damn, you idiot? You just learn how to hold that little, overcharged Super Soaker like a real man!" he says, frowning then smiling when looking over at the other officer, winking as if he's some hotshot or cool guy.

"Well, try pissing in the light with one eye open from now on; maybe you'll get it right. And if I have not taught you anything tonight about the Doppler Effect, sir, please remember…, always follow the strong signal, and if it fades, then learn to compensate, almost like dead-reckoning. Whatever you do, XO…, keep the damn train on the track and don't collide with a human, like tonight!" Barry says, laughing when walking out.

"Ah, screw you, LT (lieutenant). My two-year-old got more pee control than you!" the XO screams as the door eases shut.

Barry staggers to his room in deep laughter, getting a few more hours of sleep.

The PA system sounds throughout the building at 0500 for early breakfast.

Barry walks into the officer's lounge, finding everyone at attention when snapping to attention.

"At ease!" Alfred shouts.

Everyone sits with eyes pierced on the CO standing at the head of the table.

The CO gazes around until finding his favorite female ensign, who had just entered. He stares into her lovely eyes and then quickly focuses on others, so it's not so obvious when quickly noticing a few heads turning to look back. "I'm sure most of you have introduced yourselves by now, so I would like to take a second to welcome everyone. As you all know, everyone involved in this upcoming mission is here for an intelligence briefing. You will return to your commands and receive official orders next month. All of the intelligence information you receive here is real, but the actual Area of Interest (AOI) you will not know until you report for your mission. The operations plans and orders are under review by Admiral Kensington," the CO says, nodding to an ensign when done.

"Attention on deck!" a female ensign shouts, bringing everyone to attention. "Dis-missed!" the ensign shouts after the CO exits.

Everyone disperses except Barry, Ken, Alfred, and Greg, who stagger into the lounge, taking turns calling family, friends, and loved ones back in the States.

"Ok…, let's get some breakfast," Barry says, being the last on the phone when heading for the other side. He holds the door open, allowing Ken to go through first, and kicks him in the butt, slamming the door and locking it while laughing and making faces through the door's window.

Alfred and Greg rush up, pointing and taunting Ken until he walks away.

The three wait longer then walk out but peep around each corner, acting silly but straighten up when finding the CO and Admiral Kensington approaching at a distance.

A tall, dark figure appears in a dark corridor while the three stand waiting for the CO and admiral to get closer when coming to attention. Greg catches quick movement out of this peripheral vision when turning to Ken, motioning him to knock it off when a high-powered fire hose charges in standby; with the five now coming into view.

"Attenti. . . !" Barry begins to say when the five flow sideways, tumbling all over the halls, bouncing off and sliding to the slippery floor.

Ken holds the nozzle on full blast, washing them through the dim corridor, off the platform, and into the grass. He releases the fully-charged hose, which continually uncontrollably flops around in a loud thrashing that grows louder by the minute.

Barry comes up on the other side of the hall fast, finding Ken's shoes quickly vanishing around the corner. He comes up behind the hose, shaking his head when looking again, finding Ken at the far side of the building with his head thrown back and his heels kicking up grass. He inches up on the fully-charged hose, quickly securing it and then begins re-stowing it.

"Who in the Sam Hill pulled this freaking prank?" the admiral screams, being pulled halfway up by the CO until quickly jumping to his feet, pissed.

Barry rushes back into the hallway, drenched.

Alfred and Greg shrug their shoulders when Barry rushes up with a tight-held smile.

Barry, Alfred, and Greg stare straight ahead with somewhat firm faces.

"Well? Who was it?" the admiral screams, eye-to-eye, moving from one to the other in a sidestep, almost nose-to-nose.

"I'm not sure, sir..., I didn't see anyone," Barry responds with a semi-smile.

"Youuuu! Ohhhh! Wipe that shit-eating grin off your face right now, Sailor!"

Barry tries hard to keep a straight face, and it comes easy, finding the CO's firm, disappointing stare.

The admiral and CO stare the men down in total silence.

"A bunch of damn clowns! Lemme (let me) find out you in on this, and I'll have your asses at half-mast quicker than a cat can lick its ass!" the admiral furiously screams walking away.

The admiral and CO turn the corner, and the three burst into laughter for minutes before breaking off in different directions.

The three head over to eat finding Ken there.

After the meal, Barry cleans up and walks down to the library to look for a book he needs for a project, finding no one there, so he calls out a few times and then slips inside a back room. He fiddles around with a few books until whistling and walking around.

Out of nowhere, a feminine, tanned hand slithers around the edge of the shelf with a long, stocking-covered set of entertaining, tanned legs latching onto the edge of the shelf.

Barry keeps looking until finding a beautiful blonde with curly locks, smiling.

"Umm..., what's up, Goldie?"

The blonde stares with glistening eyes as lust instantly sets in, and she draws closer. Her warm breath rushes against Barry's neck when he pulls her into his arms, kissing her slightly-raised collarbone, right up to her slender, sweetly perfumed neck.

The blonde dips her tongue under his earlobe, taking it inside with a slight nibble.

"Whoa, mama..., you done (already) woke Mr. Johnson ," he says, grabbing her hand when it slithers south for his inseam.

The blonde instantly grows overheated, twitching for minutes until she falls into Barry's arms, with her hands grasping each side of the bookshelves which she holds for seconds, trying to break the slow chill running up and down her spine with all that is in her. "Oh, Barry! I've been yearning for your touch since our last time together. Why didn't you call when you returned to the States as promised?"

Barry goes into deep thoughts, staring into her lovely eyes and toying with her spine while thinking of a genuine lie. "The number..., yeah, it was wrong, but I called, and some old lady cursed me out," he says, staring deeper into her eyes until smiling when the blonde smiles, pulling away when fully turned on.

Barry lures her close, kissing her collarbone and neck right up to her perfect lips, reaching for her hand and pulling her closer.

The blonde grows overheated and can't bear any more pleasure when grabbing his massive arms, pushing him away, and bursting into laughter. "Barry! We'll have plenty of time for this." She blushes with the thought of canceling her trip out of town.

"Can I kiss the twins?" He asks, staring at her heavy rack, which is about to burst out of the low cut top.

"No, you ain't even ready for this..., trust me. I want you on your knees begging this time," the blonde finally says, smacking a jaw full of gum.

"You the one who ain't ready," he says, leaning to one side, smiling, then winking.

"Please. . ., stop playing," she says, growing hotter under her collar.

"Who's playing? I'm strictly business, babe, no-nonsense at all times," he says, looking into her lovely face, which glistens from a thin beam of bright light shining through the blinds when slightly pressing deeper into her when she grows excited.

"Umm. . ., a six-shooter perhaps?"

"Hmm. . ., think again," he says, pressing hard. "What do you say, AK, maybe?"

"Umm. . .," she responds, gripping the edge of the bookshelf, seductively twisting a few times until feeling him lean deeper into her until freezing when he kisses her neck.

"Hey. . ., let's not start something you can't finish." She stares into his eyes, winking. Her eyes rove over his hot body until leaning back against the bookshelf, staring with a big smile. "I missed you so much, but don't think you missed me, even the slightest."

"Of course I did," he replies, looking into her sexy eyes. He goes into a daze, amazed at her radiant beauty and, even more so, her dangerously curved body.

The door opens, causing them to break away and go in opposite directions.

Barry sees another female, so he waits and then eases through a side door. He steps into the hallway, finding Ken approaching. "Hey, have you seen Ensign Smith? I've been looking for her; I got some cookies from her the last time I was here and would like to give her money for them. Let her know if you see her."

"Ok, I'll tell her if I see her," Ken says, walking down another hallway and coming up to the office where Ensign Smith works. He turns, finding Alfred coming out of the break room. "Hey, Alfred, have you seen Ensign Smith? Barry told me he got her cookies when he was last here and wanted to give her some money for it, so let her know if you see her."

Alfred turns, heading down the hall toward his room. He opens the hallway door and takes a few steps inside, finding Greg backing out. "Hey Greg, have you seen Ensign Smith? Ken said Barry told him he got her cookies when he was last here and wanted to give her some money for it, so let her know if you see her."

Greg goes about his business and ends up at the wardroom, where the door flies open with a few female officers walking out. Just before turning the corner, he looks back and finds Ensign Smith with two female officers. He rushes down the hall and up to her. "Hey, Kim. . ., Ensign Jones…, Ensign Stalls."

She and her girlfriend stop, looking back, surprised.

Greg pulls her a few steps away. "Hey, look…, Ken told Alfred, who told me that you and Barry got together the last time he was here. He says you gave him some nooky, and now he wants to give you some money for it."

Ensign Jones' friend stands snickering.

Ensign Jones' face turns cherry red when her hand comes up fast, slapping him so hard that he falls back into the wall and then onto the leather couch, kicking.

"What! What is that for?" he asks, springing up fast and slowly rubbing his stinging face.

"You idiot! The only thing Barry has ever gotten from me is nooky. . ., I mean cookies from my daughter's fundraiser, you idiot!"

Her girlfriends shake their heads and then turn, following her.

Greg stands looking dumbfounded when turning and walking away.

Barry walks outside and then walks off, taking a stroll to the back gate.

"Evening, Lieutenant," the female enlisted security guard says, stepping from the shack. She stares at the insignia on his headgear, saluting when he comes closer.

"How are you?" he asks, and before she can respond, a black car pulls up along the side of the road out of nowhere. The windows roll down, and Barry stares at the two sexy women who stare him up and down.

The woman in the passenger seat asks for directions, but the sentry can't give them to her, so Barry walks through the gate and up to the car door.

Barry kneels, trying to look sexy, by continually licking his lips.

"Yeah, you take this road straight out about five miles, then turn right at the pasture, near the intersection. You drive four more miles until you see a white building with a neon woman on top. If I'm not mistaken, they don't open until 1 p.m., maybe earlier."

"Like noon," the driver senselessly responds, leaning further to show a little more cleavage.

The passenger's soft fingers playfully come to Barry's smiling face, running through his hair until the fingertip slips in his ear, and he flinches, rebalancing without notice when smiling. She runs her finger along the edge of his hat, snatching it when leaning away, giggling hard, and pounding her friend's thigh. "Got it! Go…, go…, go…, go!"

Barry lunges forward with tires squealing as the car burns a trail of black rubber with heavy, quick fading black smoke.

Barry springs up, kicking dirt and dusting off while dancing around in frustration. "Ahh! You slew-footed, good-for-nothing, trifling. . . !" he screams, until embarrassingly looking at the shack for the guard who he doesn't see but hears uncontrollably laughing.

"Sir…, please…, that is the oldest one in the book. I wasn't for sure if those were the two women who have been snatching combination hats," she says, finally appearing from behind a beam.

"What! You knew?" he screams, rushing up, grabbing the wooden shack, and rocking it in a rage, trying to turn it over until finding himself staring down the barrel of a 9MM.

Barry's hands instantly go high. "Hey, hey! I'm sorry…, I'm sorry…, I admit I may have gotten a little out of hand," he says with both hands even higher and trembling while easing from the shack. "Well? Do you accept my apology for freaking out?"

"Just get the hell out of here, sir!" she yells, shaking her head.

Barry walks off; his phone rings twice, and he answers on the next ring.

There is talking in the background until a voice resonates. "Barry, we have documents to destroy and need two-person integrity; where are you?" Alfred asks.

"I'll be right up." Barry enters the room, finding Alfred near the safe.

They enter their security codes into the double-locked combination and, once inside, begin retrieving and validating the documents they must destroy for the month.

CHAPTER FIVE

Minutes later, the Security Manager enters, taking his sweet time validating their signatures.

Barry's gentle posture quickly diminishes with all patience. "Here!" Barry says, finally thrusting the documents into his chest. "We're qualified to conduct destruction and carry it out properly, so no need for senseless, unnecessary or thorough checks from a knucklehead like yourself."

"OK, Lieutenant, you're right, but I have a job to do, and I plan to do it as thorough as I like, even if it means crawling up tight asses with flashlights, a freakin' rubber bodysuit, and combat boots," he meanly responds, repeatedly flicking the ballpoint extractor of his decorative gold pen.

The Security Manager finishes but takes more time than usual just to piss them off until done.

Barry snatches the clipboard, sloppily scribbling in the authorization block, and then shoves the clipboard heavily back into his chest.

The Security Manager turns red and grows fierce. "Let me say this, and may it stick in that thick skull of yours! These security issues are handled by the book and just the way I say they will be, or we can take this up with management!" the Manager screams.

Barry stays quiet and holds back for as long as possible when closer to his face and screaming. "What! Now you look ah, here," Barry says with hands to the security manager's lips, leaning so close that he feels warm breath and spit. "Don't even think about taking these rules and regulations up to the chain because those idiots sure as hell wouldn't know!"

"Ugh! That's it..., I'm out of here!" the Manager screams with bulged eyes when storming out.

Barry walks back outside with eyes pierced upward from the sound of loud engines when two low-flying U.S. Secret Service surveillance aircraft passes overhead. He blocks the sun, following the planes until they vanish over the horizon.

A loud announcement comes for Barry to report to the wardroom, and he rushes through the hallways. He burst through the wardroom door, finding senior officers mumbling when cautiously sitting next to Ken, fumbling around for a pen until Ken passes him one and everyone grows quiet.

The CO soon walks inside, and everyone takes a seat when told. He rushes for the podium, vanishing when reaching for the briefing package. He grabs his low-cut spectacles and comes up, starting over his well-rehearsed briefing, and afterward, other high-ranking officers conduct briefings, contributing to the mission.

Everyone breaks for lunch, then wrap up for the evening an hour early.

A NATO Officer stands smiling and gazing around. "This concludes the briefing, ladies and gentlemen," he says, pointing to his junior assistant.

Barry's eyes wander over cheery smiles, acknowledging several friendly nods until finding Greg fast asleep and lightly snoring.

Ken looks over at Barry, seeing Greg's head dip and come up fast a few times, then settle when leaning back with a tight sprung foot and lunging it forward, kicking Greg in the shin when the table's long axis bottom support beam catches him in the shin with a loud, solid thump that leaves heads turning.

Ken falls back, cringing with eyes crossed until closed tight with tears slowly dripping when looking away for nosey bystanders.

The CO slips into a chair next to Ken to ask a few questions, which he responds to quickly, lowly moaning. He continually looks down, unknowingly wiping his face with the drenched tissue on which his water bottle is sitting.

"Ok..., one more thing! Do you think you can add several intelligence coordinates in the Quantus System simultaneously?"

"Why..., yes, sir," he answers in a very high pitch, frowning when the throbbing goes deeper.

"Well..., what about the telemetry? Do you think that information is right?"

"Oh..., yes..., sir, they have it all on point, sir." He cringes more, fighting off the pain.

The CO goes into deep thought for seconds, then gets up.

Ken looks around, finding Barry with his iPad high and at an angle as if looking for something, until realizing he's filming him when spotting a flashing red light.

The CO walks to the podium. "Great briefing..., we'll start at the same time tomorrow."

Some stay and talk, while others slowly stand and eventually exit.

Ken stays seated, slightly swiveling until wiggling his feet with his head down.

Barry leaves, and Ken scans the room, finding the last person exiting when snatching Alfred at the collar. "Look..., you have to help me get Barry's iPad and erase the pics he took before he does something silly, like post it to the Internet.

Alfred sits giggling and soon gets himself together when standing, walking out, looking back, and then shaking his head.

Barry enters his room, locking his iPad in his locker, then walks back out and down to the lounge, looking for Greg. He does a quick, one-hundred and eighty-degree turn, accidentally ending up face-to-face with the Security Manager.

"Look, I have been meditating on what happened earlier, and I want to let you know that if you ever..., and I do mean..., ever try that crap again, we'll get it popping! Let me tell you..., I have no problem bringing the business, pal!" the Manager says, cracking knuckles.

Barry expressly wipes warm spit splatter from his face, frowning. Out of nowhere, he jumps with wide hands, mushing the Security Manager in the face and then palming his face like a basketball while driving him back into metal lockers.

The Security Manager screams like a girl, fighting to free the one hand grip.

"You listen up..., you funky breath bandit! If you ever get up in my face with your filthy breath spraying and smelling like a bucket of chitterlings, we gone (are going to) be doing more than getting it popping or bringing some damn business, pal! Do you understand me?" Barry screams, slightly raising him against the lockers until his feet barely dangle.

"Uh..., uh..., uh..., ok!" he says nervously.

"Now, get out of my freakin' face, ya stank' breath..., pathetic piece of thrash!" Barry thrusts him to the floor, pushes him down by his butt with his feet when on his knees, and sniffs his hand, instantly smelling the security officer's stinky breath.

Back in Port Copan Retaunas, the television network, lawyers, and Keyonton's lawyer converge for a scheduled meeting.

The network manager, Bill Wilson, is the second to arrive, easing into his chair next to the young woman taking the deposition.

Before long, the room grows quiet, and Bill nods and, shortly after that, begins talking out of his head. He keeps nodding, then starts fidgeting with things on the table to stay awake until clumsily knocking a few things over. Bill fights his sleep with all that is in him and does anything he can think of to stay awake until he looks ridiculous.

Another young woman enters and sits off in the corner, silently giggling to herself, and turns quickly, looking away, every time she sees Bill turning toward her.

The Network Owner soon walks in, and the room fills minutes or so later.

Bill Wilson continues fighting his sleep, knowing it's a losing battle for the marathon meeting, so he stands pacing from one place to another. Before long, he makes it around the long table. Bill stops, thinking he's wide awake and sits again, immediately nodding, and soon stands while the owner reviews the long document about pending allegations.

Bill makes it over to an easel, joyfully sliding slightly behind it. He senselessly tries making the secretary appear and reappear when rocking, then stands still listening to a few things clearly, and nods again until playfully making funny faces at anyone making eye contact. He playfully sticks both thumbs in his ears, quickly working fingers back and forth, stopping from time to time when the Network Owner is quiet.

Liandra fights her laugh for some time, staring at fast-moving fingers and different funny faces, then bursts out in tears, quickly apologizing.

The Network Owner sits looking under-eyed at her for seconds until she looks away then at others when continuing.

Bill rocks back and forth behind the easel again and then stops, listening.

Seconds later, Bill lightly rocks then heavily snores.

Instantly, the easel rocks then heavily fall forward, with Bill Wilson riding it down like a surfer.

The edge of the easel slams into the owner's chair, and he turns red, growing so mad that he grabs the easel, shoving Bill and the easel to one side with it still on his chair.

"Damn it, Bill!" the owner screams, pushing the easel again until kicking it and high stepping when it drives deep in his shins before falling flat. The owner screams, cutting it short in embarrassment when freezing and looking around, finding his secretary and others smiling. His eyes drift over his shoulder for Bill, who is bent over, trying to straighten the legs on the busted easel. He regains in thoughts, turning slowly. "So..., what do you have to say for yourself, Key?" He frowns.

"Yeah, Key!" frail-voice Bill says, looking down quick when the owner stares at him with a frown.

Keyonton eases up slow, embarrassingly standing in his three-thousand-dollar suit with pride quickly kicking in. His chest goes out when staring at folks as if he's the president of the United States or some high dignitary. "First and foremost, sir, I'm a comedian, and making people laugh is my profession. I'm created to do this..., and hands down!" he boldly says, leaning back and popping his collar up like he's some sixties pimp.

The owner face surprisingly transforms, turning red. "What!" he screams, coming unglued. "Is that all you feakin' have to say, son? Well, hell..., everyone in the world has a job, be it working or doing nothing, like ole Bill over here, but I can certify, bonify, and damn sure as hell guarantee you there's none legally described as grabbing asses as a profession or should I say welcoming yourself to unwelcomed bootaaayyyy (booty)!" the owner says in a deep dwindling voice.

"Look, sir..., simple and plain: it's an isolated incident," Keyonton says confidently.

"Isolated? Isolated..., now you listen here, junior! If it were so damn isolated, we would not be sitting here discussing your career, or lack thereof..., now would we? If this thing goes to court and you are found guilty, no network on this planet will touch you with a ten-foot pole with a very long string on it! Now that there is some distance for your trifling ass!" the Network owner says, lighting his cigar. He takes a puff, quickly cutting his eyes over at Keyonton to find his shoulder drooping until coming up fast.

"Another network? Sir, can we get real for one minute..., just one minute? Look at how much money I pulled in from one show alone! We're just gearing up for a grand tour. Even the financial projections for the roadshow are off the charts, and you've made millions already," Keyonton says, proudly sticking his chest out like a sprung trophy hen in a chicken coop.

"True..., I must admit you're right there, and that's exactly what I propose we need to talk about: your shares and royalties. Let's see," the owner says, breaking out an oversized notepad calculator from his suit pocket. "Ok..., we made roughly eight million thus far to include that night, sho (surely you are) right. Now Key..., listen to me and hear me well. They are suing you for one-point-seven million plus any royalties, not including the network's share."

The Network Owner freezes, looking at Keyonton with googly eyes for a few minutes until motioning his security guard to escort Key and Liandra out.

Keyonton stares at the security guard until close when throwing up a hand and motioning the security guard to back off. "Oh, you gone (are going to) throw me out, B? You sucker..., you chump! Look..., I got you this J.O.B., Jack! You were nothing but a damn turd chaser on the first floor, shining shoes and wiping toilet seats down there. Now, I'm not downing your job, man, nor would I down anybody's, but just don't forget where you come from, you little sucker!" six-foot-one Keyonton says to the four-foot, thick black-rimmed eyeglasses-wearing security guard.

Keyonton balls paper he's been scribbling on, attentively looking at everyone who stares back and then looks down or away when finding him outstaring them.

The old woman with quad-focal is the only one who continually stares, not flinching, and can't see his face clearly, so she never looks away but sits higher, hearing and looking around for the paper.

Without warning, Keyonton throws the paper to the table, but it hits the back of the chair, bouncing off and flying at the woman like a towering white basketball through bifocals when she jumps, screams, and falls back, kicking.

Keyonton's face surprisingly changes into fear when his shoulders drop, and he turns, anxiously heading for the door.

The old woman jumps to her feet with a mean look. "Now you look hea (here), sucker! You keep on screwing with me, Key..., and a cat gone (is going to) be eating your supper, chump!" she screams in a high pitch, with her head dipping forward with each word.

Keyonton freezes, taking a slow, deep swallow.

Liandra shoves Key in the back and forward, taking a few steps into the hallway.

They cross the hall and stand waiting on the elevator when Liandra unravels her arm from his, asking him to wait while she goes to the lady's room to freshen up.

Meanwhile, a pro baller outside has just finished his extensive ten-mile ride on his particularly-made ten-speed. He comes up at the top of a very steep hill, stopping and getting ready for his brisk wind cool off. He balances, straddling the bike while looking around and wiping his goggles before putting them back on.

Keyonton peeps around the wall, hearing the bathroom door shut when walking onto the opening elevator, riding to the ground floor.

The athlete takes a deep breath, kicking off fast, and the bike instantly picks up momentum in the bike lane. Within seconds, the busted speedometer clocks fifty, coming up to sixty, then seventy miles per hour. He stops peddling, stands hands-free, enjoying the routine ride, and happens to look off in an open field while passing the park to find a pit bull inbound and kicking up the grass with its hind legs. The athlete flops down, grabbing the handlebars tight when pedaling as fast as humanly possible with eyes steadily on the dog.

The dog stretches out more, going into a full stretch when gaining on the bike until a loud whistle blows, and the dog slows, veering off and returning to his owner.

Keyonton exits, expressly making his way to the front door, heading for the street in a daze. He looks past a towering delivery truck and then up the steep hill, watching cars come down fast, some veering off while others zoom past above forty-five. He waits for the last car and sees a car driving excessively fast when closing his eyes and intentionally stepping into the middle of the street, stopping, hearing wheels squealing and a horn blaring with the driver screaming and calling him a freakin' idiot.

"Out of the road, you trifling, insurance fraud jerk!"

The baller slows, finally looking back, finding the dog running away.

Liandra walks out, looking for Key when finding several folks pointing out the big picture window. She instantly catches sight of him in the street when hearing a woman screaming. Liandra screams and then runs over, continually pushing the elevator button, then frantically and repeatedly runs between the window and elevator. "Key! Get out of the street, babe! Mama's coming, babe! Key! Please..., babe!" she nervously screams.

Everyone near the television conference room and those in the main offices run out, looking at her nervously, finding her pointing out the window.

Keyonton stands there for seconds, hearing more car horns when tensing, then hearing nothing until another horn comes with cars swerving so close that his suit coat blows away from his body. He waits longer and then turns, peeping when finding a car veering off with the horn blowing and fading fast.

The elevator bell rings, and Liandra keeps her eye on him, backing through a crowd.

The baller slows a little but still rolls fast, while looking back at the dog and owner longer.

Keyonton slowly turns, instantly lifted high off the ground when caught at the upper back thigh by handlebars, screaming while quickly rising into the baller's arm and screaming loud.

They both scream louder, looking at each other, and then scream even louder when expressly rolling up on the next steep hill, three times steeper than the first.

The player gathers his thoughts quickly, hitting the brakes when rolling up on the peak with tires squealing and smoking when picking up momentum with the brake assembly snatching away from the weight and crumbling in all directions.

They scream, simultaneously noticing the brakes gone when screaming even louder.

They stealthily roll midway through the steep hill when fast-passing cars ahead come into view near the bright red stop sign.

"Hold on tight!" the athlete nervously screams, cutting the wheel hard, and running through several shrubberies and then a very rocky ground.

Their cries heavily tremble as they expressly cross rougher terrain, taking out a few signs and skyrocketing them high when skimming a fifteen feet high feather tail of water until slamming into a long, shallow pond.

Water continually splashes with the tail feather going higher until, quickly diminishing until there's silence. "Not too bad," the baller says, crawling to his feet with a hand held out and leaning to help Key up. "Trye? Trye Stilts from...," Trye says when interrupted.

"I know damn well who your monkey ass is, and I want five million in damages!" Keyonton yells with a serious face.

A few people approach the water's edge where the 'Alligators - Do not swim or fish' sign stands, heavily bent back and busted all to hell, screaming at the top of their lungs.

"What, dude? Man, I just saved your freakin' life! You try to sue me, and there will be a countersuit. Hell..., if you think that chick raped you, you have not seen Mr. Keyonton Worthington's worst to come. Yeah, I know who you are..., you jive-time booty-feeling turkey! The only reason I landed us here is that for a quick second, I felt you grab my bootayyyy (booty)! Look! Now, you look here..., let me tell you how this is going to play out: You gonna (are going to) give me a handshake, and we gonna call it even..., deal?"

Keyonton stays frozen, still lying in the water with hands supporting his posture.

Trye stays bent halfway over when the people's screams grow louder. He happens to turn, seeing something far off on the bank on tippy-toes running and lunging like a torpedo when pointing and standing fast but speechless with his mouth open.

"A..., a..., a..., a..., alligator!" he stutters, screaming when lunging forward in knee-deep water.

"Yeah, right!" Keyonton yells. "You gone (are going to) pay me my millions, sucker! Hell..., I'll fake blind, cripple, and crazy until you do!" Keyonton screams, still down in the water.

Keyonton looks back at the wobbly bike tire sticking out of the water, then back for Trye when Trye dodges right, and Keyonton sees ten or more people pointing and motioning.

Keyonton turns slowly, finding a large, swollen mass at a distance and cruising fast.

Trye drives forward, growing out of breath, when six feet from the shoreline when Keyonton zooms by in a streak, looking like he's walking on water. Trye gets out quickly, out of breath, and Keyonton slows down fifty yards away on dry land when the eight-footer slams into the barrier and lies there hissing loudly, almost out of breath.

"Wooohooo! That is some impressive footage! I got it all on my phone and just uploaded it to the net!" an old Asian woman screams.

Keyonton hears her loud and clear when balling his fists tight and continually swinging in the air as if shadow boxing until hearing Liandra's fearful, screaming voice.

Back in Port La Gaigiuana, everyone is up early the following morning, preparing for the briefing and four-star admiral's visit and inspection. They make time to call the States, their offices, or their home amid work.

Barry walks into the supply office and sees a couple of enlisted men and women doing chores. He pulls out a requisition form, fills it out, and lays it on the desk. He looks up briefly, finding a Sailor who appears to be drunk, sitting in the cage.

A known prankster, a male enlisted Sailor, walks in, wandering into the cage. He begins messing with the drunk and then does all sorts of crazy things to impress a giggling and attractive girl.

Barry looks off so as not to see the actions, but it's obvious when the room quickly fills.

The drunkard slouches, fanning his head when the prankster sticks twisted tissue in his ear, and the drunk laps himself. His head slowly drifts until it slightly and abruptly falls back. His mouth soon falls open, and a mild, deep snore comes, growing and quickly diminishing as the crowded room grows quiet with soft giggling. Several cell phones pop out, and folks begin recording and uploading to the Internet.

The prankster soon turns, taking his time decorating the drunk, going from balancing an empty can on his forehead to stapling paper together to make a gigantic dunce hat.

The cage lights up with several white flashes and more flashes each time the prankster adds more ridiculous pieces to the dress attire.

The prankster runs out and up to the desk, breaking out a magic marker. He rushes back into the cage, drawing all kinds of designs on the drunkard's face until thoroughly making him over and soon has him looking like he's ready for a circus. He bends over, adding one final touch when pulling a dry mop head from the floor, attaching it to the back of his head like a wig.

The room breaks out in a peal of loud laughter, and the drunkard jerks when the prankster makes a mad dash for the door.

The drunkard jumps forward, grabbing each side of the chair's handles with bloodshot eyes swarming over white teeth, big smiles, and an uproar of laughter. His face grows grim, realizing everyone's pointing at him, finally acknowledging something is wrong when flinging his head with the mops bitter ends slapping his face. He jumps up in a rage, tearing and knocking stuff off his head.

The PA system soon blares for divisions to gather personnel for roll call.

Barry retrieves and signs for additional items on his cleaning gear list, then heads for his room but takes a shortcut through the gym. He finds the drunkard in ranks but acts as if he's unaware of the markings on his face. Barry shakes his head, giggling when pushing the door open, and hearing the duty officer screaming for the drunkard to go and clean the mess off his face. Barry comes up on his hall, bypassing it, and goes to the administration office. He peeps in through the narrow door glass, walking inside. Barry looks around and then walks over to the counter, checking his inbox for the pre-brief sheets; when looking off in the corner, finding a lieutenant commander (L.T.C.) sitting and fussing with one of his junior enlisted personnel. Barry hears the L.T.C. ask the young Sailor to find another Sailor and have him report to the office when wandering about the room, taking a seat, and reading a newspaper.

The Sailor leaves and is gone for about five minutes and then walks back inside.

Barry looks over at the kid, then back at the door and keeps reading but turns as the door shuts to see if the other Sailor has come in. He stares back a few times but doesn't see anyone when his eyes drift to the L.T.C., who springs up, looking over the office for the kid as well.

The Sailor stands with his back to the L.T.C. and turns when the L.T.C. calls out to him and asks if he had told the other Sailor what he said.

Barry eases in a seat, anxiously awaiting a response, but there's total silence until the L.T.C.'s feet shuffle over to the Sailor.

The young man nods, confirming that he had told the other Sailor, and his eyes instantly drift down in deep meditation.

The L.T.C.'s feet shuffle more when making his way to the enormous picture window with eyes wandering up and down the passageway. His hands come up on his hips when turning, looking across the room, asking about the Sailor again then what he said.

The young Sailor stares at the floor for some time, then slowly walks up to the L.T.C., acting as if he's afraid to tell the Sailor's response but yells it out fast. "Sir, he said, screw Lieutenant Commander Smith. He said he's the big dog, and you're just a little puppy,'" the Sailor says with eyes quickly drifting to the floor as if even more nervous.

The L.T.C. stomps up and down, then grabs a handful of hair as if to pull it out.

Over in the galley (food court), a fresh out of boot camp, new seaman reports for his first day as a food service attendant.

The short Filipino Senior Chief Petty Officer walks in, continually pacing until he walks up to the seaman, finding him wandering as if lost. His eyes float across the young kid's nametag. "Hey, boy..., you just reporting for duty?"

"Yes, Chief!"

"Chief?" he angrily responds in a nasty tone, instantly flipping out his collar insignia. "Chief? Huh! Senior Chep (Chief), Senior Chep (Chief), damn it!"

"Oh, Ok..., sorry, Senior Chief."

"You know, truck?"

"Truck?"

"Yeah, you know truck, boy?"

The young Sailor looks around at people eating, talking, smiling, and laughing.

"Naw..., I don't know any truck, Senior! Truck? What kind of truck: garbage, Mac, what..., what?" the boy responds, talking with active hands until they are sticking out near his waist in confusion. He tries acting cool, calm, and collective, noticing a few hot females.

"Go out back and help unload the truck," the senior chief says, pointing to the back door. The senior chief rushes over to another chief and discusses other divisional duties.

A young girl walks up behind the young boy, touching his shoulder, and he looks back, finding the beautiful girl with her hand extended to him.

They shake, introducing themselves, and talk for minutes until the boy looks back at the senior chief when he looks over his shoulder, making eye contact.

The senior chief turns in a whirlwind, getting up in the young man's face and clapping his hands so loud that he scares a few people and causes the young man and girl to jump. "Boy! Truck, truck! Chop, chop!" the senior chief yells, clapping a few more times when veering off and over to check the food temperature on the serving line.

"Boy? Man, please…, boy played on Tarzan and Cheetah quit; if you don't know my name, don't call me shi…!" he whispers under his breath, cutting it short but getting a few people that heard it to laugh when reciting an old saying. He quickly turns back to the girl, nodding. "We'll pick this conversation up later," he says, smiling and heading for the door.

"You, you! Go to the freezer near the truck and tell the petty officer to send plastic pork (fork)," the senior chief shouts to the new Sailor from the other side of the galley.

The young Sailor stops, thinking about what he meant. His mouth drops open, and his head slightly turns, but he turns away, saving himself embarrassment when pushing the door open and walking out. He instantly hears the Petty Officer in Charge (POC) shout, giving directions to his crew, and then stops when noticing movement.

"Hey, you must be the new seaman, huh? I'm Petty Officer Jones…, welcome aboard! We have to unload this truck fast before the meats thaw out."

"Got it, but what do you want me to do?"

"Just stand right here in the rotation and pass to the next guy," he says, looking back at the two people in the cold cooler and then the chilled air mingling with warm air.

Everyone jokes around while unloading as quickly as possible.

Minutes later, the young Sailor stands in deep thought, remembering the pork when turning to ask, but finding the petty officer gone. He flings the chiller's door open, wandering in, finding a stack of funny-looking meat wrapped in plastic. He picks up one pack, squinting to read until finding it stamped lightly with the word 'pork.'

"Booyawh!" he says, walking back and finding the senior chief with his back to him when a smile grows as he approaches, slamming the pork on the counter with his chest stuck out.

The senior chief surprisingly stares at the meat, then back, deep into the Sailor's eyes for seconds. "What?" the red-face senior chief says, extending both hands from his chest as a tough guy. "What the hell did you bring me pork for when I ask for plastic pork (fork)? Plastic pork (fork), not damn pork (fork)! You..., you..., you pucking (fucking) wit (with) me, right? Yeah..., yeah..., you pucking (fucking) wit (with) me, right!"

"Pucking? What's pucking? Damn, Senior, speak damn English!" the boy says, talking and motioning each word with hands as if it's a sign language.

"Ahh..., funny little man, huh? Look! When I tell you to get plastic pork (forks)..., I mean..., pork (forks), pork (forks), damn it!" senior yells, snatching the meat and shoving it heavily into the young man's chest.

The young man turns with a sad face, looking over in the corner, finding the petty officer in a senseless giggle and walking up. "Lighten up, little dude! What he wants are plastic forks. Listen, when senior talks, just replace the F with P, or vice-verse," he says, giggling when walking off but looking back at the Sailor walking away with his head down.

A few doors down, a door flies open, and two Chief Petty Officers walk into the chief's lounge.

"Welcome back, fathead!" the short chief says to the taller chief.

"Hey, man..., you ain't gone believe who I met in Virginia," the tall chief says, placing his U.S. stamped luggage down and reaching for a plate handed to him.

"Who?" the short chief asks.

"A few guys who were Red Tailers."

"What? Red Tailers?"

"Yeah, the black aviators back in the day. I never heard of them either..., I mean..., I heard of the Aviator movie, but I never heard anyone refer to them as Red Tails."

"So, did you get their autograph?"

"Naw (No)..., hellz (hell) naw (no)..., actually, I felt stupid and made a fool of myself. The tallest another one walks up and asked if I had seen the movie 'Red Tails.' When I said 'no,' he gave me this nastiest look. I bet…, man…, I bet you ten dollars he was thinking, 'This damn idiot!' the tall chief says, bursting into an uncontrollable laugh.

"So what happened?"

"Oh, nothing!" The tall chief leans over in a peal of deeper laughter.

"What? Man…, you should have just told him that you were not into history like that; besides, you were a player-player growing up, right?"

"Yeah…, a real Mac Daddy, for sho (sure)!"

"Then my response would've been that I've never heard of the Red Tails but spent all my life chasing some fat tails," the short chief says, bursting into an endless laugh.

Inside the main dining area, a petty officer walks up to the microwave to warm her food and stands behind a seasoned, beefy Sailor while staring at the set long timer.

"Surely this is your first time using a microwave? Man, these are not the cheap microwaves like back home; they're commercial and heats in a fifth of the time," she says, slightly easing to her tiptoes, watching the food expand and contract until the hot link sausage expands two inches. "Obviously, you like eating rocks. Man, that stuff will be so hard, you'll need a sandblaster to break it up." She shakes her head, looking at the five minutes remaining.

"Oh, hush up! You up in here talking all that crazy ying, yang! A darn microwave is a microwave! They cook simultaneously and at the same temperature," the hulk-looking, slow-talking, angry Sailor says, staring at the timer until finally turning and looking back with yellow and green snot running from his nose to his bottom lip. He sniffs hard, retracting the thick, yellow trail from one nostril and then green from the other, smiling.

"Eww!" she shouts, snatching her plate away. She walks to the trashcan, throwing away bacon and eggs over easy and grits when storming toward the door.

"Huh! Gone sit here and tell me about a darn conventional versus commercial," he chuckles. "Huh…, must don't know who she's talking to because I'm from Smack-a-hoe, North Carolina!" he says, looking around and finding the girl storming out. He finally looks through the microwave door, finding the Styrofoam plate curling on both sides but stands for a few more minutes, waiting for the timer to ring.

The senior chief sniffs, looking around, smelling a light hint of something burning when looking at the microwave, seeing a small trail of smoke escaping from the vent fan when sprinting, then diving for the microwave. His hand presses hard on the button, and the door flies open with a plume of smoke billowing out. "Hot damn..., hot damn..., what the hell you doing, hot damn it? You pucking up (fucking up), you pucking up (fucking up) damn it! This hea (here) is industrial, not like your nappy head mamma's cheap microwave!"

The heavyset Sailor grabs the plate on each curled end, looking at the bubbling grits and swollen eggs and then the hard, greasy, sizzling bacon and log-looking sausages. He sets the plate down, easing into a chair. He leans close with eyes swarming over the stocky bubbles of grits and bacon grease pops in his face when he jumps, screaming, and running around like a chicken with its head cut off.

Another Sailor giggles and does it so hard that he's in tears and falling out of his chair. He sits up, still laughing, and when able to stop laughing, he disposes of his milk carton and walks into the hallway, staring at the floor until hearing females giggling.

A girl stands off to one side, whispering to her female friends while making it obvious that she's checking him out.

"Uh..., uh..., uh..., you just don't know," he says, rubbing under his chin as if he's cool.

"Know what?" she asks, smiling when cutting her pretty slanted eyes over at him.

"Huh..., you know I can't say what I want because I ain't even trying to get written up for fraternization or sexual harassment."

"Then keep it to yourself, you wimp! Put up or shut up, punk!" She walks up to him, licking her red, glossy coated lips. "But know this! I'll put something on you that Madame Bouchie can't take off," she says, snickering when seductively walking back over to her posse.

The male Sailor stares at her hourglass shape, following her until at a distance.

"Hey, let me get that number." He motions her back over with his index finger.

"For what? Stay in your pay grade..., sucker," she sarcastically says, stopping and looking back before turning down another corridor.

The male Sailor sprints, catching up midway through the hallway, striking up a conversation leading to him making a more slightly-borderline sexist comments, with the last leading to a question. "What..., you scared I might make you leave your man?"

"Huh. . ., if you ask me, I think you would stalk me if I gave you some of this good-good," the girl says, turning and patting her firm, round bottom.

"Girl, please...there ain't even a stalking bone in my body."

"Yeah, right, the last man told me the same thing, and now he's like a certified crackhead when he sees me. Boy, you step to this, and for sure, you will be singing a few of those ole' folk, field hand songs, like back in the day. . ., ah, swing low, knocking on sweet mommas door, or ain't nothing like her sweet la, la," she says, bursting into a burst of great laughter with her friends joining in but even harder.

"How you going to do that, and I'm a thoroughbred..., a stallion in those sheets?"

"Riiiggghhhttt (right)..., and even if that dream was real, I may start saddle up on a stallion, but trust me, I'll be getting off a war-torn, broken-down mule," the girl yells in laughter when turning and greeting one of her girl's high five.

Her girlfriends laugh deeply, leaning against the wall to balance their weak bodies.

"Girl, please! I've got the strength of ten men."

"Boy, please! I'll have you wanting to play pity-pat like those two sisters in the Color Purple when I'm done with you," she says, turning and playing a quick hand of pity-pat with one girl. She goes on, getting the best of him in-jokes with her girls still deep in laughter.

The male Sailor stares at them with a somewhat serious face, embarrassed when looking away, and then turns, looking back at her. "Maybe you need to stop selling all those wolf tickets and give up that number so we can see what's fact and fiction," he says, striking a pose that leaves him leaning into the wall.

The girls look over his shoulder, spotting the C.O. when turning and walking in the opposite direction.

The male Sailor takes off walking like a seventies-style pimp to catch them. He unknowingly grabs his crotch. "You know what I think?" he yells. "I think you are scared to give up that number because you know I'll be standing up in it..., that's what I think," he says, slinging both arms out as if he's the coolest cat ever.

The girls look back, laugh, vanish around the corner, and take off in a stride.

The young man takes a few steps after them when the C.O. snatches him at the collar and taps him on his shoulder. "Hmm..., and what are you supposed to be standing up in..., may I ask?"

"Oh, sir..., how are you doing, sir?" he nervously laughs, wiping the smirk away even faster. "We were just joking around."

"Well, I didn't hear them say a thing, but you were undoubtedly talking about standing up in it..., whatever it is. So, how about this..., you go stand up in the Master-at-Arms office and put yourself on report! When you come before me sexual harassment, we'll see who will be standing up in something," the C.O. angrily says when his devilish smile fades. He stares at the young man, gently patting his shoulder when walking off.

A tall officer walks into the bathroom and finds Greg at the urinal when walking up to the second stall, looking straight ahead.

Greg begins whistling, curiously cutting his eyes over the edge of the urinal divider, when finding the other officer with his eyes straight ahead. He peeps again, and his eyes widen as he looks away and then quickly looks at the officer, who still has his head forward. Greg stares until his eyes slowly rise, finding the officer staring eye-to-eye with a mean stare.

"Eyes right..., ready..., front!" the officer screams, frowning when heavily shaking his manhood a few times until backing away quickly.

Greg grows embarrassed, meeting the officer at the sink, and striking up a conversation. "Did you see the hockey game last night..., what about dem (them) bears?"

"Bears..., dah? Dude..., are you still here? Man look..., you just stared at my Johnson like a hawk! Do you even for a second think I would want to hold a conversation with you? You're freaking me out, and another thing, no talking on the urinal! That's a bogus protocol, period!" he says, storming out.

Greg runs water over his hands and wet fingers through his hair. He cuts the water off, and there's total silence until hearing someone senselessly giggling and then straining. He stalls and begins messing with a pimple on his nose and then turns to walk out when hearing something blast like distant gunfire, followed by a long air trail.

The man in the stall tries not to laugh with fast hands coming to his mouth. He tries not to burst into laughter when bouncy farts come when jerking in heavy laughter.

Greg instantly goes down to his knees in a silent laugh and tries not to burst out in laughter when stumbling for the door, staring over his shoulder.

Another loud blast comes and sounds like distant gunfire, but more muffled.

"Fire in the hole!" Greg screams, breaking out into the hallway, running.

Several officers for the morning meeting meet in the wardroom. Ten minutes later, all officers are well into the meeting, and they take a break two hours later.

A lieutenant completes his brief, and the C.O. walks up and reaches deep into his shirt pocket, plastering a gold, sticky, smiley face on his presentation. "Well done, LT (lieutenant)." The CO smiles, shaking his hand and leaving the room.

The lieutenant with the sticker walks up to an ensign he despises.

"Look it, Mike! Another smiley face," he says, playfully waving the sticker close to his face. "That's better than having a woman and adding another notch to your belt," the lieutenant says with his chest proudly stuck out.

"Yeah, whatever, Joe! You can bite me, you silly somebitch (son of a bitch)."

"Whoa, whoa! Now don't go getting all sassy just because I have ten smiley faces and you don't have your first. Look, I'm a friendly, reasonable guy, and I'm willing to share," he says playfully, looking around when finding he has an audience.

"Who gives a shit about your candy-ass stickers? I call them brown-nose stickers, anyway, so that is right up your alley."

"Oh really? Well, can I just give you an itty-bitty one…, just one?" he says in baby talk, puckering up and faking a sad face. "I'm sorry I can't give you all ten because I know that would certainly make your day. How about a little one?" he says, looking back at a few who nosily listen and laugh. He quickly peels off a sticker, holding it to his face.

"Screw you! You can take all ten and stick them up in your tight rear end for all I care." He pushes his tight fist in his partially-semi-closed hand to make it look tight, continually portraying a packing motion.

Everyone in the room bursts into laughter, closely looking and listening, but a female lieutenant commander who is in the middle of taking a swig of ice tea, sprays it all over her presentation, when bursting into a silly and crazy bee-sounding laugh.

Several more comical officers fan around their heads, hearing the silly-ass bee laugh, which comes again and again.

Another officer quickly rushes to a side desk, playfully grabbing a can of bug spray, when out of nowhere, a blast of spray floats around the female lieutenant commander's head. However, she's too loud to notice but soon sniffs, finally looking around curiously.

The loud P.A. system sounds off for Mail Call.

Several people rush down the long hallway for the post office and quickly form a single line, most pulling out mail cards while talking.

Greg rushes up, fanning across his sweaty forehead. "Ohh, girl, what you been up to? I have not seen you in what..., like three years?" Greg says.

"Hey, Greg, I didn't know that was you. I saw you earlier, but I thought you were a female in those tight-tail white pants," she says with eyes roving up and down his body.

"Honey child, whatever! Please, don't hate! You're just mad because I'm hot, and you're not!" he says, looking her over until gazing over her backside. "Yeah, you're still as flat as a flitter," he whispers, extending his well-manicured finger to her nappy ponytail, and flipping it up. Greg looks back, noticing Barry and Ken approaching but far off, sinking in his intentionally poked-out butt and quickly cleaning up his playful, feminine posture.

Barry and Ken walk past, speaking almost simultaneously.

Greg's voice changes into a deep manly voice, then fluctuates again.

The female's finger comes to the corner of her lips in thought. "Uh..., uh..., uh..., did you just do the damn flip thingy to convince your friends that you're manly? Now, that's just straight trifling. Look..., either be about or be without it!" she says, snapping her finger.

"Haatteerr (Hater)!" he whispers in his high-pitched, feminine voice, realigning his posture until looking like he's about to burst out of his pants.

Two enlisted Sailors walk up behind Greg, and the one in front quickly gets the other Sailor's attention, pointing to Greg's intentionally poked-out, plump butt.

"Uh…, uh…, uh…," the closest Sailor says, smiling and licking his lips.

The second Sailor's hand slips past his friend, without his friend noticing, smacking Greg's ass and then palming it.

Greg smiles, turns, and then smiles even harder.

"Eww!" the first Sailor yells with eyes widened when staring at Greg's thick, bushy mustache.

Greg frowns back, throwing up his middle finger.

The second Sailor gags, continually spitting on his hand and rubbing them on his pants. He turns to his friend, and both fall back in a turn, running to a head (bathroom).

They shuffle inside, shaking off their hands in disgust.

The second Sailor turns on the faucet, but nothing, so he dips his hands in toilet water.

Greg stares at the door for minutes, pissed, and doesn't take his eyes off it. He son makes it to the front, picking up his division's mail and taking it down to distribute the mail in the berthing's lounge.

The door springs open, and several people watch as he lays the mail down and then back up as they scavenge through it.

"Hey, don't forget this one and this one!" Barry screams, lifting stacks of decorative and well-publicized winning sweepstakes envelopes. "You can't be serious about buying all those magazines just for a chance to win at a predestined grand jackpot, can you?"

"Well, somebody got to win it, so it might as well be me," the youngest guy says.

"Huh? Do you remember your old second-grade buddy we ran into a few years back? Well…, he claims that you were young and clueless back then, but now, I know you are much older now," Barry says, shaking his head in disbelief.

"Duh! So what are you trying to say?"

"Oh nothing, you go figure it out…, Brainiac." Barry snickers with others laughing. "The games are all based on numbers, you knucklehead!" Barry shouts, getting up in the guy's face. "You spend your hard-earned money like a gazillion others, and when the company makes tens of billions, they pay one person tens of millions…you go do the math, Einstein. Aiiii! Ha, ha, ha," Barry laughs, turning to find the guy's running buddy with a handful of sweepstakes as well and trying to hide them when Barry walks over.

The buddy shoves the four identical envelopes into his shirt, walking off fast, but Barry pulls him back by his belt, reaching for the rim of his drawers and stretching them halfway through his back. Barry pulls harder and latches the band over his head, and the buddy's head springs back, with his face toward the ceiling when Barry's feet come up, pushing the guy in the butt and into the lockers.

The guy flies forward, careening into stand-up lockers, hands first, then his body.

The laughter grows louder and then settles to a dull roar.

Barry runs one hand in the guy's shirt, releasing the tension from his drawers with his other hand. "My, my, my, a chip off the old block. See. . ., what you need to do, is stop running with this moron, ole' Snizzle Stick, over here," Barry says, pointing to the first guy. "What? You sure plan on winning big, huh?" Barry snickers even harder.

"You know it, and I'm going to be rich..., you big-head bitch!" the guy yells with a mean stare when snatching a hand full of colorful envelopes, fanning them in Barry's face.

"If you think that, you're as dumb as a box of nails!" Barry giggles walking up from behind.

The guy flops down in a chair, anxiously tearing through the first envelope.

"Here, look at this one..., this sweepstake even wants nineteen dollars and ninety-five cents for processing," Barry says, giggling and gazing over the bold print.

"Duh! And? It costs them money to mail this stuff and process the winnings," he says, looking at Barry as if he's clueless.

"Aiii! Ha, ha, ha, ha, ha," Barry laughs even louder.

"Are you serious with that country-ass laugh?" The guy responds, trying to intimidate him.

"Oh hellz (hell) no! Country?" Barry laughs again. "Ok, I'll buy that, but know this: I would rather be country than be country, stupid, and a loser, so listen up, you bucktooth clown! If you had won two million, would they send you three envelopes to tell you that you're a winner? Not to mention your partner over here has the same note. Ding, ding! Its computer generated; you silly ass yabbit (rabbit)! And riddle me this, you clown: why the hell would they ask you to pay nineteen ninety-five when they can just take it out of winnings?" He reads the other guy's announcement. "What difference is it if it says you both are winners and contains the same winning numbers?"

The Sailor sits, looking foolish, while some stare and laugh but wait for his answer.

"Well…, my mother played, grandmother played, great-grandmother, and great-great-grandmother," he says with pride.

"I see…, so, clown, grand clown, great-grand clown, and the greatest clown of all," Barry says, shaking his head when turning and walking away. He gets three feet from the guy when hearing an unfamiliar sound quickly growing louder and louder.

The Sailor's feet heavily pound upon the shiny tiled floor. "Ahh!" he finally screams, inches from Barry's back and airborne with heels thrusting forward until saddling on Barry's back and going expressly forward on the wildest, bucking ride of his life.

Barry tries everything to unsaddle the guy, but he's too strong.

"I got the strength of ten men!" the guy screams about five times until it's garbled.

Some officers and enlisted try to break them apart, but they're no match for Big Country, or so they call him.

Ken approaches the lounge, hearing the commotion when passing loud generators. He climbs the steps in stealth mode and freezes when reaching the top step. His eyes cast over the yellow warning tape, and the signs dazzle him until growing anxious with eyes quickly scanning over a few warning labels when lunging forward. He climbs toward the door until inches away, grabbing the knob, and finding it locked. "Damn it!" He slips and slides until losing balance when falling headfirst into the concrete wall. His head thumps hard, sounding like a thick, broken branch falling from a tall tree when cracking the cinderblock. He grabs his head in both hands with his mouth falling open and tears flying while quickly looking around to see if anyone saw it. He leans against the wall and then moves his head in a circle, ensuring he didn't break his neck.

A door flies open, and two female petty officers enter the hallway.

Ken instantly stands, taking a few steps when becoming a little lightheaded.

The two women continue talking and slowly approaching until making eye contact and immediately bursting into laughter. They stagger, bumping into each other, and then stagger away in laughter but look back several times, laughing harder at his funny-shaped cone head. They look back one last time and approach another corridor, accidentally bumping their heads when crying in laughter. They finally calm down from the pain, frowning and rubbing their foreheads when continuing out of sight.

Ken feels the throbbing area, finding it swollen when taking off and rushing around the horseshoe-shaped hallway. He swiftly comes upon the other door, and his boots loudly slam against the blue tile floor, abruptly stopping. Ken eases into a cut behind a stacked chair's partition, fading deep in the corner with eyes gazing over several long pieces of yellow caution tape roping off the chairs. He comes alongside the last row, peeping out and snickering. "Attention on deck!" he screams, quietly listening and softly laughing at feet shuffling over inspection-ready tile, leaving deep scuff marks.

The men quickly draw to a whisper, then total silence. Everyone's ears stay receptive, and their eyes wander around for a movement while listening for a follow-up command.

A serious outburst of laughter comes from out of nowhere, followed by a row of heavy, shuffling, stacked chairs tumbling forward when Ken falls into them, riding them down after losing his balance.

Chairs continually shoot across the floor, and everyone breaks their stance, looking over to find Ken still clinging on, inches from the floor, while still fighting to keep from hitting the floor.

An even louder bang comes when his head plows deep into the tall, square trashcan, denting it beyond repair.

Ken balls up in the corner with his face and mouth torn up, but there's no sound.

Several people laugh hard, but a few serious-minded people motion their hands as if they've had enough and walk away.

Barry and Big Country continually stare eye-to-eye with noses flaring until losing eye contact when Big Country's friend playfully shoves him to the door.

"Ahh! Ahh!" Ken screams, causing everyone to jump and look back.

Greg rushes over, extending his hand but he refuses, slowly lifting himself. Tears pour as he fakes a painful walk to make the incident look a little more serious than it is.

"For real, Ken?" Barry says, walking past Ken in the opposite direction. He takes a few steps past a row of chairs stacked near the wall and backs up a few feet, finding a pair of legs extended past the chairs when springing from around the chair, looking into the young male ensign's eyes. "Hey!" he shouts, waving then snapping his fingers a few times to get the young officer's attention. "What kind of good stuff you got there, buddy?" he asks with eyes scrolling over a slew of junk mail and personal mail lying all over the place until fixated on a few colorful flyers partially laced in gold.

"Oh, a bunch of junk mail and stuff," he says, placing the mail on the chair and then sifting through the stack of open envelopes again before placing the colorful flyer on top.

"Yeah, well, that's why they call it bulk mail." Barry smiles. "Wow, what do we have here? Aw…, a family reunion, huh?" Barry lifts the flyer, admiring the cost. "Let me see…, wow! Gold trim and the works, huh? All right now! Whew! Nine-hundred dollars? Let's see…, three hundred a night hotel, one hundred for tee shirt, fifty dollar hats, bowling, horseshoes, tug of war, and three-legged races. Man, somebody's clocking some loot."

"Yeah, my Aunt Tootsie, obviously. She's always planning costly reunions, and eventually, some ole' scam done gone down, and there are always fights over where she spent the money." The ensign says, giggling to himself until teary-eyed.

"So, are you going?"

"Oh…, hellz (hell) naw (no)!" he says, smiling when standing and gathering his mail.

"Well, for sure, the ghetto white flyers, fifty percent cheaper: shirts, hats, and hotel would have cut cost by sixty percent." Barry scratches his head with a curious stare.

Ken finally walks over to the far side of the room and sits.

Back in Port Copan Retaunas, Keyonton attends his second meeting. He sits in the lobby and tries to convince his girlfriend that he will be acquitted, then tries convincing her that the film and pictures are somewhat fake and for publicity. "Look, no matter the outcome, I still want us to get married," he says, sugarcoating his words.

"Married! Hmm..., therefore, you have to get knee-deep in crap to propose? You should have thought about marriage before the trouble because this is so lame, Key. Kelvin is how old now? A good man would marry a woman he knocks up the day he finds out she's pregnant, but noooo..., not you. You're pathetic, and this whole thing with this chick, altered or not, is just downright disgusting and disrespectful, Key!"

Keyonton turns away, squeezing his fists in frustration after playing his ace card and finding it to be a loser. "Anything, babe..., name it, just don't leave, please," he says, falling to her feet and then backward when she kicks her feet out and storms off.

The secretary flings the door open, looking down at him, surprised, until shaking her head and motioning them into the conference room.

Liandra walks up next to Bill Wilson, the Network Manager, who's half asleep, but wakes fast, peeping then staring at her bulging twins, slowly down to her lovely legs.

Bill finally looks past her, finding Keyonton's mean face with eyes drifting to his tight fist, which loudly smacks in his other hand when ole Bill's head drifts to the ceiling with horny eyes still staring and looking away fast, when finding Keyonton looking off.

Bill gets one good, long look until she sits, then turns away, nodding.

The owner drifts in, and the meeting starts as the previous, with the owner drilling Keyonton. "I just don't know, Key, this agreement thing you are saying she agreed to is just not adding up, man! She says the whispering in her ear was all fake, also."

"Fake? No way! We discussed things, and she agreed, sir," Keyonton says, getting up and walking over for a glass of water.

"Well, if you ask my opinion, I think she agreed to the gun plot, but you can look at her face and tell that she definitely didn't sign up to have you grabbing all that ass."

Keyonton's embarrassed eyes drift to Liandra, then quickly away when finding her squinting in disgust. "That's not true..., you were backstage and saw the whole thing, sir!" Keyonton looks back, hearing Bill's loud snore fade to a whisper.

"Look, Key..., I have a job as owner, so don't take this as boisterous, but there are many women here who have asses that I would love to grab," he says, subconsciously clenching his fists so tight that both hands shake. "Well, excuse me, Betty, Liandra, ma'am..., but I just can't do it, Key. Do you know why? Because..., it's not right, son. There's just something disturbingly wrong with all that ass grabbing," he says, walking to the window. He freezes, looking across the field at a woman running in tight white spandex with each timed cheek rising and falling like jelly. His eyes drop to her thick thighs and curved bottom again. "Hot dayum..., good googly moogly! Will you look at...?" he says, cutting off the comment with a dumbfounded look and eyes cutting back when hearing chairs moving fast with feet shuffling.

Several folks rush to the window, finding the woman slowing down, stopping, and bending over when his eyes grow wider.

Their faces frown, staring slowly back at him until he quickly breaks his concentration. "Look at the grass, will you..., it hasn't been cut in weeks. Betty..., right after this meeting, get the lawn company's boss online. So..., where was I?" He turns with a mysterious stare.

Bill drifts into a dream, and a lusty smile comes. He twitches a few times and then leans toward the young woman next to him, coughing a prolonged cough, and the girl's face frowns from his stinking breath, when fanning until it comes again but stronger.

"Daaayyyuu...," she yells, cutting the curse word short when shoving back fast until the back of her chair slams against the wall. She stares with a frown, getting her steno equipment and changing seats.

The owner looks at Bill, regaining his thought, again. "Now..., where was I? Oh yeah..., sexual harassment..., now, ole' Bill over here, well hell..., he blatantly walks around staring at asses all day as if he's the damn invisible man. Now that's what I call blatant sexual harassment, so he'll also be losing his job today. Ain't that right, Bill?"

Bill jumps, hearing his name. "Booty, booty, booty, booty, booty!" Bill yells, looking around. "Brrrr!" he whispers, shaking off the chill from the big-booty women in his dream. He finally awakes and sits listening for seconds while trying to figure out what's happening to make people want to look at him so surprised.

The owner goes silent in deep thought until looking up. "The network can't sustain all the publicity from Ms. Levington's suit; not to mention the other suits people will claim for their kids' therapy, pain, and suffering," he says with horny eyes gazing over at his hot secretary when she walks over for a water bottle. His eyes lock onto her sexy shape and double-jointed hips, still following her as she twists a little more than usual when looking back with gold-digging eyes, finding him locked on like a full-breed pit bull.

Liandra immediately snaps her finger in the Network Owner's dazed face a few times until finally getting his attention, and his eyes drop to the floor quickly.

"Is that a stain on the carpet?" he asks, looking at the spot near her, unable to break his stare until seeing his attorney's face frown when his eyes drift. He swivels and springs forward, rushing over and lightly working his feet across the carpet. "Betty, get someone from janitorial to come and shampoo this carpet after this meeting!"

Liandra rolls her eyes at him and then shakes her head in disbelief.

The owner rushes to his seat with his eyes wandering over the newspaper placed before him by the girl's attorney when throwing it up and falling in his seat. "See?" He quickly leans forward, picking up the paper and slapping it with the back of his other hand when throwing it down. "A kid lawsuit already!" he screams, unbelievably shaking his head.

Seconds later, another secretary sticks her head inside, pointing to the big screen, which activates the unit.

The owner reaches forward fast for the remote, turning up the volume when seeing the words 'more breaking news' flash and then a middle age foreign man standing with his young son held close by his shoulder, seeming to be almost in tears.

The father goes one. 'Since that comedy incident, I just can't stop him from grabbing booty!" the man says in fake tears. "There's nothing but booty on his mind..., booty, booty, booty, booty! I come home and ask him how school was today..., my son, and the response is..., booty! The answer is always booty!" he nervously says, "anything I ask..., anything..., its booty..., booty..., booty!" The father talks more and keeps his nervous, lying eyes on the ground.

The reporter stares in disbelief, hearing a young kid speak when handed a piece of paper from a printer broadcast. 'But sir, do you think this is something that came from that, or is this something he's had problems with for a while?' the news reporter asks, unfolding papers that look official when looking them over. 'It says here, sir..., that your son has had over fourteen sexual harassment charges stemming from pre-K through elementary school alone, not to mention high school.'

'What? I don't know…, I don't know where you get these papers!" the man angrily yells with eyes immediately glued on a fat-booty girl the news team paid to prance by.

"Look, Daddy! There…!" the kid joyfully yells, reaching for her booty when she passes.

The dad over excitedly stares until his hand shoots forward, his other hand snatching his son when both lunge forward,

They rush from the interview, following the girl with both their hands forward for her booty until a police officer intervenes.

Keyonton's mouth drops open. "What? This mess is absurd! This is crazy! Do you expect something like that to go to court for a suit? Be real, sir," Keyonton screams.

"Court for that? Well, not really that Key, but for this, I do!" He quickly flips to another queued-up screen, flipping to Keyonton's stage still shot with his mouth wide open, as if he just hit the jackpot lottery. "Look, we're here for you morally, Key, but right now…, well…, we'll just have to honor what they're asking for; one-point-seven million and royalties," the owner says, looking over at Levington's lawyer out of the corner of his eyes.

"Now, listen, this is just an out-of-court settlement," the girl's attorney finally says with nervous and sweaty hands anxiously rubbing together.

"What? This mess is absurd…, that will wipe me out!" Keyonton yells, looking down when lowering his head further and crying with his head on the table for minutes.

People begin slowly getting up, staring at the puddle of tears rolling from under his sleeve and, seconds later, over one-third then two, then the entire long table, until trickling to the floor.

"Well, anyway…, that is the skinny right now," the Network Owner says, backing further away when he sees tears soaking the floor near his feet.

"Just let me talk to her. I know I can get her to drop all charges or settle for a hell of a lot less." Keyonton finally looks over at her lawyer with a dry, wrinkled, prune-looking face with dark rings around his eyes, looking a hundred years old with a head full of grey hair.

The girl's attorney shakes his head, confirming that he wouldn't be speaking with her.

"Well, her attorney said 'no,' but anyways, you're terminated per the contract for misconduct until after an investigation, the court hearing, settlement, or dissolve."

"Well…, what if there's no hearing or clearance through the investigation?" He nervously gulps water, and his wrinkles fade with hair turning black again.

"Then it's not an issue, but you'll still have to handle other small claims against the network. Look, Mr. Worthington…, have a fantastic day…, Liandra," the owner says, standing and straightening his expensive suit. "Betty, get the janitor up here with a wet and dry vacuum." The owner motions her to the room, taking a few steps away. He looks down at his shoes as Keyonton's tears rise through the soaked carpet with each timed step, motioning for the security guard to bring boxes forward.

The guard eases an oversized box in front of sleeping Bill.

"Bill…, Bill!" the Network Owner screams, causing Bill to jump when awakening.

Bills stares at Keyonton half dazed. "Yeah, Keyonton, the network can't afford this behavior!" the now fired Network Manager says, guiding his hand around the table and finding it empty.

The guard slides the box further in front of Bill, whose eyes wander over it. "What are my things doing in this box? Is this the company's lost and found box now?"

The Network Owner stares in disbelief. "Yeah…, you can consider it that, or should I say, lost and find because you just lost this job, now go out and find a new one!" the owner responds, looking at Bill over his shoulder when walking out with security.

CHAPTER SIX

Greg sits, picking his teeth back at the naval base in Port La Gaigiuana after complaining about getting a piece of meat out my teeth. "Man, I still ain't got that meat out." Greg moves his tongue, until digging back and forth then deeper with a toothpick, frowning.

"Oh really? Well, I just hope it ain't the same biscuits and meat from earlier," Barry says, looking at him and getting a good laugh when the fellas join in.

"Yeah, whatever!" Greg says, anxiously trying with his tongue again. "I thought my breath would smell by now, but that's not the case."

"Yeah? Well, I've meant to talk to you about that." Ken giggles.

Barry leaves the office after some time, heading for the smoking area on the second deck. He walks through double doors, running into another officer deep in meditation. Barry pretends not to stare when looking down at the small waves rolling away from the rocks inside the small brook when leaning over the handrails, spotting something glowing.

The officer looks over, pretending not to see Barry when gazing back into the glistening water. "Are you saved, my brother?" the long-haired, out-of-regulation uniform-wearing officer asks.

"Why? Why do you ask? And before you answer, just wait..., and hear me out. You see, many self-righteous people proclaim they're saved, but they'll curse you out in a heartbeat, then turn around and pray with the same filthy mouths. So, to answer your question, no..., I don't think I'm saved because I just don't know; and most people just don't know, but I'm a believer in Jesus Christ..., I mean..., I try and live my life right and treat people right."

"Ok, good response, but that's not enough to get into Heaven," the frail-looking officer says, cutting his eyes at Barry and then refocusing on the pond.

"Yeah, I know, but I'm taking small steps each day to make it a lifestyle change at becoming not perfect but the best you can be, and I know that can only be by getting more and more into the Word. Most of all, I read the Bible daily…, you know…, a closer walk with the Father; for HE's the only one who knows if we're truly saved…, right? On the other hand, those folks I just mentioned are right in a sense because they're saved, really; either saved from Heaven or saved from Hell, though a lot of the self-proclaimed are saved from Heaven; that's just my personal opinion," Barry says, staring out and over a field.

Barry continues talking, and the conversation dwindles when he turns, piercing eyes toward the water again, trying to make out the gold, now glittery object. He comes up and sees the Chaplain about to pass when leaning further when something lightly touches his back pocket, but he pays it no mind. He looks the pond over longer until feeling the officer a little too fidgety when finally turning, finding the officer thumbing through his wallet, college photo, then a thick wad of big face bills.

Barry stares with fiery eyes for seconds until deeply clearing his throat.

"Oh!" The officer jumps as if about to come out of his skin. "An old habit from my former life, but I've changed." The officer slips a twenty out right before Barry's eyes.

"Now see…, something like that gone (is going to) get you tore the hell out the freakin' frame!" Barry says, snatching his wallet, thoroughly checking when snapping fingers at the officer to express urgency, when realizing things are missing.

The officer stares and then reaches deep down, putting Barry's ID, money, and toothpick in his hand, then hands him ten other things Barry forgot were in the wallet.

The loud PA announcement comes for bulk mail and a few pieces of first-class mail.

Greg tears through a side door out of nowhere, and he's the first in line. He rushes up, looks around, and then looks back at the group of people rushing up.

A Minute later, the lounge door springs open, and several people watch as Greg lays the mail down when they converge, scavenging through it.

Ken sifts through the last few pieces, walking away and finding an upset officer balled up in the corner, whining when he walks over. "Hey…, you alright?"

"Man, damn this..., another child support case; the fourth this year! Hell, they got my damn paycheck broken down to parade rest. Shoot! Any more deductions, and I'll be the first man in the Navy working for free, on S & H stamps and needing to be in a soup line when on liberty."

"Hmm..., well, let me ask you this; have you ever considered condoms, maybe? You know..., the ole pulling out method has never worked with a leaking pipe."

"Man, please, I always wrap it up!"

"Oh really? Then what is the name of your three kids?"

"Well..., there's Cura, Michael, and Daniele," he says in a daze, trying to recall others.

"Hmm..., then if you truly wrap up, you should consider renaming those little monsters Houdini One, Two, and Three!"

The sad officer laughs for a good spell, then quickly drifts back into massive depression when looking down at the court documents again. "Man, this is crazy! They need to start making it mandatory to identify these little rascals. Heck! They got all these kids climbing in wrong bloodlines just because they think the guy's family has money or some other unknown reason."

Another short officer sits off a ways, listening with his back to them until turning and taking steps over to them. "Huh..., speaking of bloodlines, I don't even know who my donor is, but I bet he had a grand ole' time depositing. I told my daughters that they need to start slipping up in those wallets when those slick cats are knocked out and at least get a real name, social or license."

Ken and the first officer look at the short officer with curious eyes before slowly looking off in another direction with bucked eyes and open mouths, staring in disbelief.

"Bullshit..., Bullshit..., Bullshit!" Ken repeats as if coughing in his hand until staring at the ceiling and lightly whistles when cutting his eyes back over at them.

"Is that it?" the other guy asks, quickly cutting his eye over at Ken when slowly looking back at the short officer, waiting to hear more.

"Yeah..., no..., aight (ok), you got me! I also told them to slip a few dollars, but really..., mothers should be careful. For all I know, my Father could have hit the lottery or been wealthy by now. Here I am busted and disgusted because you messed around and put me on this pretty boy just because you thought his family had money, but it turns out that he's a bum, has twenty-one kids, and ain't worked a day; in his entire life."

After work, the four are anxious to paint the town early, so they stop by the ABC Store, loading up. They head to the beach on base, finding it closed, for cleaning, so they take a joyride through the city and to other local cities, sightseeing.

They make time for calling back to the States or home along the way.

Barry stays quiet when getting off his last call while looking at his watch. "Hey, let's grab that new movie, Tainted Obsessions. I heard a few folks mention it last week."

"I'm game," Ken says, looking at his watch and digging in his pocket for the keys.

Due to heavy traffic, it takes them an additional thirty minutes to get there, and they soon climb out, staring at the long marquee list of movies.

"Tainted Obsessions it is, or we can split up," Barry says.

"I'm good with Tainted." Ken reaches in the backseat for the flask and shot glasses.

"Yeah! That's what I'm talking about!" Greg gazes at the booze, giving a high five.

They rush inside and to the counter with eyes gazing over the different show times.

"Popcorn or candy, anyone?" Alfred asks.

They buy snacks and head for the cheerful attendant reaching for tickets.

"Thanks, gentlemen…, welcome to Cinema 54," the ticket attendant smiles.

Barry opens the door, and soft music gently rises like a whisper.

"Evening, ma'am, sir," Barry says, speaking to an older couple when climbing to the highest rows.

A young, sexy female attendant peeps around the corner, moving the trashcan against the wall, when looking up, and waving.

Alfred winks, but his smile quickly diminishes, finding Barry's eyes set on him. He playfully jumps at Barry, causing him to flinch when laughing. "What you looking at, punk?" Alfred whispers, playfully drawing an open hand back. "I ought to pimp-slap you, punk!" he whispers, giggling.

After the hour and a half movie, they search for a back road club they had heard an out-processing officer, one of the admiral's staff members, mention. They park in the vacant lot as told, cut through a long path, and head down a snake-like dirt trail, coming upon the back of an abandoned building and nervously looking around for minutes. They hear a loud commotion when making their way around to the front until they find a lot half-full and hear distant voices and loud, distant engines roaring.

Seconds pass when engines seem to roar closer and fast.

They stay in the middle of the street, cautiously looking around with eyes wandering over the lot, then up and down the adjoining roads, and against the medium-cut long wall.

Out of nowhere, a car swerves into the lot.

A tall, dark-skinned Jamaican man stands from his car. He brushes down his suit, then leans into his car, grabbing a gigantic bottle and concealing it in a brown bag. His hands come to his eyes, blocking the bright sun rays when looking at his watch and rushing to the street. He looks up, finally finding the four in the street. "My friends, my friends. . ., it's not a good ting (thing) to stand in the street!" he yells, pointing at a few rusty and faded signs. He motions them over quickly, gazing back at the low-cut wall and then up the hill in the background, seeing a lot of fast-moving mini-triangular, fluorescent flags viciously waving.

The four hear him unclearly mumble while still in the street, staring at the long-haired Jamaican as if he's on serious drugs by the way he moves, rocks, and jerks.

The engine noise escalates until they're unable to hear him.

The Jamaican points to the signs and then nervously rocks while staring back at the low-cut wall.

The four bring hands to their ears, muffling engine sounds while trying to determine what the man means.

Barry's eyes float along the low-cut brick wall, finally spotting several florescent little flags that zoom by, one after the other.

Without warning, a go-cart shoots out, spins out in a wide turn, and straightens up, racing straight toward them.

The four scream, scattering and holding on to each other while jumping left to right and managing to dodge the first through fifth go-carts.

The tall Jamaican man's body rocks as if about to do a hundred-yard dash. His eyes float by with the fifth go-cart, dashing into the street, stretching out his arm, and rushing the four against the wall.

His expensive, gigantic bottle of cognac slams onto the stone wall, unknowingly bursting and soaking the bag.

"What the hell were you guys tinking (thinking), mon (man)? You could haf (have) killed yoselfs (yourselfs), you no (know)?" the Jamaican screams as more loud engines continually roar past, as he gazes over his shoulder at the street full of go-carts. "You feakin guys are crazy, mon (man)! I yell to you! I say ittiz (it is) not good to stond (stand) in de (the) street, but you look me (at me) like I (I'm) crazy, mon (man)! You see dez (these) signs posted all over for go-cart and danger, yet you ignore dem (them), why?" he asks, frantically staring in a slight, drunken sway.

The stocky Jamaican turns, slamming his fist into the door until exchanging hands with the light bottleneck gripped tightly when instantly dancing up and down, finally noticing liquor dripping. His eyes float to the cinder block wall, finally noticing the big, wet spot. "Damn, mon (man)! You made me bust a damn too (two) tousand (thousand) dollar bottle of the most expensive booze, mon!" he says, stumbling over, throwing the bottle in the trashcan next to the wall, and then shaking off wet hands.

"Hey, man, sorry about your bottle," Alfred says, staring at the big puddle.

The Jamaican looks down at the puddle then his suit. "Damn mon (man)! You mess up a tree (three) tousand (thousand) dollar suit and five-hundred-dollar suede shoes!" he says in a drunken voice, still heavily shaking residue from his hand and quickly wiping his hands on the back of Alfred's shirt when Alfred turns to watch the last go-cart speed past.

Alfred jumps again, drawing back a tight fist in a stance when finally feeling his back wet.

"Hea (hey)…, hea (hey)…, easy deah (there), yong (young) blood!" the Jamaican says, backing with hands high. He eases back into the door, pounding on it with his fist and then the bottom of his foot a few times. "Hea (hey), mon…, you Yankee noodles (doodles) need to figure out some compensation for my losses," he drunkenly says, staring.

"Shiiittt (shit)…!" Barry says, shaking his head in disbelief.

"What?" he says, under-eyed when slightly pulling his jacket back, revealing his 9MM with a squinty, mean-looking stare.

"Oh yeah..., yeah..., the suit, shoes, hat, bottle..., oh yeah!" Barry nervously responds, finally noticing the shiny gold tooth.

The door finally swings open, and the Jamaican motions the four inside. "This is my club, mon (man), so you guys come, have a good time, and we discuss compensation before you leave, ok? We have plenty of blow and women," he says over the loud bass in a nod, winking to the bouncer.

The muscle-bound bouncer smiles at a half-nude female Spanish server with a serving tray of champagne, passing all of them a glass.

Another woman slowly walks past, winking at Ken before running her well-manicured nails under his chin, motioning him to follow her.

Ken takes two steps forward and falls one step back when Barry's hand catches him at the back of his collar.

Barry stares, finally sizing up the tall, stocky Jamaican club owner, perceiving him to be a pimp, drug dealer, or warlord, when finding him heading for the other side of the room.

The Jamaican club owner, turns to them, raising his index finger to his eye, pointing to them a few times until rubbing his fingers together to indicate money, until pointing again and actively moving his trigger finger at his head.

"Ohh shiiiitttt (shit)!" Barry fearfully says with his mouth dropping open when quickly looking away, pretending he had not seen him when looking off to one side and coming up on tiptoes, pretending he's looking for someone.

Still, he doesn't see Barry's facial expression because of the thick curtain of Jamaican Caribumba Weed smoke, which quickly drifts over him as he melts into the back room.

"Oh shit, what?" Ken asks. Finally registering the expression with eyes floating down to another girl's thick, round bottom, laced in a swallowed G-string. "Hot dayum!" Ken says, losing his mind.

Ken, Alfred, and Greg stay in a daze, staring at the most beautiful woman they have seen, who continually walks by, serving gangster-looking wealthy men.

Barry snaps his finger in their faces and then waves to interrupt their concentration. "Did you clowns see the Jamaican dude?" Barry nervously asks, looking over to where the Jamaican was standing, finding a wall of smoke until a few people float through it.

The three look back for minutes, not seeing a thing until finding the Jamaican in a light haze talking with two shady-looking characters.

The Jamaican continually stares and then does the same movement with his index finger and fingers.

"Oh shit!" Alfred moans in fear with fast fading eyes, seeing him this time.

Barry, Ken, and Greg instantly turn a blind eye, pretending they're looking at a few women.

Suddenly, a sharp, heavy knock comes upon the door, breaking Barry's concentration; when he steps back but stays in a location where he can see the bouncer and club owner.

The door slowly eases open and, in intervals, then flings open.

A medium-built Jamaican enters, straining when pulling on the duffle-bag-covered, two-wheel dolly when Barry's eyes lock onto the man and bag. The man rolls past with his gun-toting male friends close in tow.

Barry's eyes buck, seeing the thick bundles of cocaine and weed in partially-open bags.

The men make a hard right turn and head in the opposite direction of where the owner is, then down a heavily-guarded, narrow hallway.

"Somebody set us up!" Barry says, looking at Ken. "By the way, do you remember that kid's name that referred us to this place?"

"No, but he took off already, heading back to the States for some kind of training," Ken says with eyes wandering back over to a girl who looks back, smiling.

"Well..., remind me to get a quick shoe shine out of his tail when I see him," Barry says with a serious face. He goes into deep thought, distracted when Jamaican music rises and over fifty folks hit the dance floor.

The club owner whispers to a female server, who proceeds to the bar and whispers in the bartender's ear until he smiles.

"Here's the plan." Barry slowly walks them over with his eyes glued to the owner.

"The owner eyes seem to be on me only, so Greg, you slip out and warm the truck. I want you out of the seat when you see me coming because you drive like a sissy; besides, it could take about ten minutes tops to get your fat ass to the truck, but face the truck outward."

"From the word go, we roll because one call from either of them, and we're trapped," Ken says, cuttings his eyes over at the owner, quickly looking away when he stares back, not blinking but pounding his hand in his fist and then to this head, stoned and giggling.

The bartender looks around, keeping the four glasses low when spiking the drinks and easing them back onto the decorative tray.

"Great plan, Barry, but only one thing is missing," Alfred says, turning up his drink and nodding an imaginary, distant toast to the bouncer, who stares suspiciously back.

Barry nods as well, seeing the girl approach with additional drinks. "Shh...!"

They reach for the glasses and admire her lovely G-string, pasty-covered top and bottom as she walks away.

Greg downs his while the others slow sip.

"The bouncer..., good point," Barry says, looking at Greg.

"What?" Greg asks when staring back.

"You seem to have this bouncer thing down pretty good. Think you can turn him on like you did the others?" Barry laughs.

"Oh, screw you, dude! You're over here, tripping about something with bouncers!" Greg frowns, looking back at the bouncer. "All I got to do is fake like I have to puke because he ain't my type," Greg says in a girlish voice, laughing.

They slow sip, but Greg downs his, quickly waving for another.

Barry motions them closer to the wall near the door, where they keenly recruit women to indulge in conversation after buying them drinks.

Greg keeps his eye on the bouncer and owner.

The owner turns away, and Greg finds the bouncer with his back slightly turned, counting money when ducking into the narrow entrance. He comes up on the bouncer quickly, breathing heavily and grabbing his chest while pointing to the door.

Barry motions the women to a booth, nodding for Ken to sit, but only when the owner looks back at them.

The bouncer's hand anxiously rushes to his chest, surprised. He grabs Greg's shoulder, shoving him out the door but holding Greg by the collar, not releasing him when he drops to his knees, gagging until feeling the man's grip loosen.

Greg slowly stands, pointing to his throat. "I need my medicine," Greg moans in a whine with a disfigured face when gasping his throat tighter. "Tell my friends I'll be right back," he says, dimming his eyes to look sick. He tries hard to look as if he's out of it but certainly feels sluggish from the drugs, which had kicked in like boosters. Greg sluggishly moves along the wall and leans into it until hearing the door slam loudly.

Barry hears the bouncer's feet shuffle across the lightly sandy slate when easing out. He pretends as if he's going for another drink when the bouncer comes to the inner door, calling out to Barry.

"Hey, your friend is sick; he went for his meds!"

Barry acknowledges and waits for the owner to look before easing back into the booth.

Greg comes up to top speed, and his heart pounds so loud that he hears it. His shoes slam into the pavement as he breaks his speed, making the corner and then running fast on the short strip of pavement until hitting the dirt trail so fast that he leaves a dust trail in his wake.

Barry checks his watch, motioning for Ken, and they sit at the bar. He orders more drinks for everyone, talks to the girls by the door, then sends them away.

A knock comes upon the outer door, and the bouncer pushes it open, holding it wide open for beer delivery.

Greg finally reaches the SUV, almost out of breath and dizzy, when his vision doubles and things heavily blur. He profusely sweats in the scorching heat, climbing in and trying to catch his breath when yawning, and in a split second, he nods off with the door open and head on the steering column.

The owner cut his eyes over at them and then turns, talking to a wealthy-looking man with six model-type women surrounding him.

Barry sees the bouncer bend over the counter and fades back into the narrow hallway, grabbing the bouncer's Taser from his hip and hitting with two full charges.

The deliveryman turns fast from the bouncer's short outburst and screams, seeing the commotion, when bursting through the door with his mouth open, double-timing when running wide-legged.

Barry trains the Taser around fast, finding Ken and Alfred barreling down on him.

The three scream, bursting through the door, and immediately fall back into the wall in a louder scream seeing the gargantuan beer truck toward them when passing close.

The deliveryman bounces up and down while leaning in the passenger seat, pointing and screaming something in his native language.

Immediately, the drugs kick in from adrenaline, causing them to stumble when their speech slurs. Their vision doubles from the heat, and their movement slows with things feeling very sluggish as they push off from the wall with faces torn up when exerting everything to run while staggering into each other. They hit the dirt trail, stumbling over each other's feet while trampling to the dusty ground and squirming around. They quickly appear to be drunkenly staggering as they try taking off again.

The tallest female server comes around the corner, counting a thick stack of loose bills when freezing with eyes widening when her mouth drops open as if in slow motion when falling back screaming a death cry that exceeds the volume of the music.

The owner jumps with eyes staring back at the commotion, quickly pointing to two shady workers who run over.

The two men roll up, pulling out guns, quickly checking to find the bouncer slowly moving. They back down fast, bursting through the door and running into the street and then the parking lot, rushing around and between several vehicles. They soon slow their pace and begin checking inside and around every vehicle until reaching the far end of the lot, about fifty to seventy-five feet away from the building.

An old woman floats into view from alongside the building, bent over and laughing so hard that she barely can stand. She slowly eases two grocery bags down, pointing along the trail in a crazy laugh when falling forward in deep laughter. She steps onto the paved street kneeling on one knee in tears, giggling. She looks back, peeping and pointing to the three whom she thinks are drunk as they endlessly try scaling the low-cut wall.

Barry stains finally making it over, then pulls Ken up, and staggers across another narrow road, finding the truck facing inward and Greg's head slumped over, fast asleep.

Alfred slips out of Ken's grip for the third time, rolling a few feet down the hill but swiftly coming up to his feet, drunkenly staggering back over to Ken.

The Jamaican owner rushes out with his assault rifle high and freezes with the woman's loud laughter finally registering. He looks around for seconds, finding the crazy-sounding woman on her back, kicking in laughter when frowning in confusion. His eyes wander more, finally spotting his men when waving and firing high, on automatic.

The old woman instantly cringes, fearfully rolling to one side of the building, low-crawling back along the side, and peeping from around grocery bags.

The club owner notices the woman's eyes peeled alongside the building and gearing up to laugh when pointing behind the club uncontrollably.

The two men stealthily sprint up, passing the woman and hitting the dirt trail.

The club owner shoots out behind them, looking up the long, winding trail, finding Alfred, releasing Ken's hand and Ken vanishing quickly with Alfred staggering.

The club owner and his goons run fast and get halfway up the trail when the owner stops, almost out of breath. "Duck! Duck!" the owner screams, leaning back and tensing.

The men's heads fearfully float backward, then forward fast, diving when the assault rifle tears through sizeable chunks of cinderblock with the men firing in prone positions.

Ken and Alfred drop quick, low-crawling and staggering to the truck.

Barry pulls Greg into his arms, heavily wrestling him into the backseat when grabbing the door, accidentally slamming Greg's foot when the door retracts.

Louder shots ring out when Ken and Alfred jump inside, slamming the door and looking back when Barry cranks up, backs out fast, skidding wheels.

Barry throws the SUV into drive, and the back door flies open with Greg's body flinging outward when Alfred stealthily grabs him by his belt loop, holding on tight until looking over, finding his finger in the crease of Greg's hairy butt.

"Aii!" Alfred screams, crying and peeping while continually looking and looking away even quicker each time. "Aii. . .!Aii. . .!" he screams with eyes closed, pulling hard to get Greg inside with all his might.

Barry makes the first sharp turn when Alfred shifts Greg's body hard and further inside as Barry brings the SUV up to top speed when the door shuts.

Alfred releases Greg, slowly bringing his fingers to his seriously frowned face with eyes slightly crossed. "Aii. . . !" Alfred screams, staring at his finger while easing his hand out the window and looking at it as if it's a foreign object.

Barry evasively handles the SUV in sharp and narrow turns. He skillfully misses several pedestrians at intervals along the road and by inches, expressly making his way from the top of the mountain down toward the super highway. He makes the last curve before the expressway when Ken points to an over-path ahead, spotting the owner and two men closing in fast as the SUV barrels down toward them. Barry floors the pedal, swaying on the straightway, then fights to remain conscious when finding Ken passed out. He quickly gazes at the speedometer, registering ninety when stepping into it and dropping the needle off the display.

The club owner and one of his goons climb the wall, pointing guns from the underpass.

The heavier set, a burly man, runs to the wall but overcompensates for the narrow ledge, falls forward, and screaming with steel rebar catching his pant leg, leaving him upside down. His arm uncontrollably flops, and he continually screams with the SUV closing faster.

The assault rifle begins tearing up the narrow road while walking the pavement and meeting the SUV. The last round leaves the barrel, landing inches before riddling the SUV's hood when empty.

The other drunk assassin sways, firing until empty and hitting nothing but weeds.

Barry shoots under the overpass with no odometer reading when slowing and entering the main highway, which he travels until exiting onto the expressway. He looks back quickly, finding Alfred passed out with his arm still hanging out of the window, then looks ahead, sweating profusely with the road wobbling a few times and the lines blurring. Barry exits, making several turns until pulling onto a dirt trail and following it until unable to go further. He pulls over quickly with weak eyes, throwing the SUV into park. He turns off the engine when falling back lifelessly, with the faint sounds of a waterfall trickling and birds lightly singing at a distance.

Four hours later, there is movement in the SUV as they begin to come around.

Greg jumps quickly, grabbing his throbbing foot when screaming bloody murder.

Ken's mouth drops open, and his face frowns in pain when his hands go straight to his neck, messaging the cramp out while moaning.

Alfred's mouth drops open, and his face frowns. He eases his hand out to the window to massage it, lifts his numb right arm back inside when his face straightens, then frowns when his arm comes inside. He slowly turns from his hand, looks over to Greg, then back at his hand, wiggling his fingers until easing his fingers to his nose, gagging a few times. "Wooooot! Woooot!" He gags again, waking Barry.

Barry jumps with nervous eyes, snatching the steering wheel and pushing the brakes to the floor with eyes glued on the water until embarrassingly staring back at Alfred's torn-up face and scream that goes higher and longer.

"Hey! Hey! Hey!" Ken finally yells, frowning when finding Alfred staring at his hand like a foreign object, with tears running down his cheeks.

Greg looks over, shaking his head in a confused look.

Alfred grabs the door handle jumping out. He breaks out in one direction in a crazy stride and runs back by, breaking out in another in long strides until running by repeatedly. He stops by the passenger front side on the fourth pass, looking around, and then grows quiet, hearing a loud bird.

The sound of the waterfall soon rises in his ear as a sweet, gentle breeze when his foot rises knee high, sprinting toward a hill.

Barry, Ken, and Greg jump out and walk around the SUV, assessing any damages.

"What happened?" Ken asks, looking over at Barry.

"Man, you will not fathom this in your peanut gourd!" Barry says, glowing. Instantly, Barry dives into a massive lie about how he evaded the precision shots, rifle, grenade launcher, and rocket launchers. His body jerks from side to side when he reenacts his evasive driving with an imaginary steering wheel and heavily swerving body, having their full attention.

Ten minutes later, Alfred's head pops up near the hill with bucked eyes.

Barry spots him first and immediately ends the trail of lies, walking to the back of the SUV to distance himself from any requests for more information. "Hey, Ken, check out that side to see if we hit anything." Barry looks back at Alfred when he takes off, searching before climbing inside. Barry cranks up the music to keep them from asking questions when pulling off and driving to a restaurant where they grab a hearty meal.

The four enter the city hours later, walking the main strip and sticking their heads inside a few establishments, getting a feel for the crowd and atmosphere. They enter the next-to-last nightclub and stand outside, talking for a few minutes.

Barry breaks off and goes up the last few steps, finding a door cracked slightly open, and reaching when a couple of older, classy women walk out.

One woman makes steady eye contact, but the others smile and wink.

Barry flings the door open, asking the attendant if it's alright to look inside.

The attendant confirms its ok, and Barry sticks his head inside, finding several eyes pierced back. He finds a woman standing while the other kneels, straightening her stockings. He peeps around, finding more women against the wall. Barry sees a few men entertaining other women with some acting silly. He counts a few heads, then eases the door shut until there's a hairline crack while still holding it in a tightly-gripped fist.

Barry heads down a narrow passageway, unexpectedly coming up on a young female attendant. "Hey, thanks for letting me peep inside," he says, smiling when walking past her and others in a small line waiting to get in.

Barry walks back into the streets, finding the guys in deep laughter.

"What? Did I miss something?" Barry asks, sliding his shades over his eyes.

"No…, not really…, ole' Greg here was telling us about something he read…, about the government having a device that can hold a person back. You know…, like a laser beam! He says he saw the television demonstration the other day," Ken says, laughing.

"Ok, so what's so funny about that?" Barry asks, looking curious.

"Well, right after that…, Alfred farts and walks off." Ken uncontrollably laughs.

"Ok, really…, that's corny!" Barry shakes his head in disbelief, backing away when smelling something like Limburger cheese, funky feet, and rotten eggs, when stopping in his tracks and backing fast.

Ken and Greg disperse quickly but laugh so hard that they're in tears.

"Man, that is straight-up wrong!" Barry says, moving back even further until giggling harder when cutting his eyes over at Alfred, who is still in the same spot.

Alfred's head playfully hangs over, and his hands rest on his kneecaps, having no clue that a group of old women are coming up from behind.

"Ok, so…, now you got it…, government invention, and Alfred's new invention?" Ken says, anxiously watching the old women making their way up the sidewalk.

Ken grows weak from laughter until dropping to one knee, then the other, crawling along the sidewalk in the opposite direction of the women.

The women go deeper in conversation when the first woman's face transforms into a stale frown until torn up. She jumps back as if shoved, being the first to hear something rip like a weed eater on choke while cranking when Alfred stains with a frown, cutting another one, but longer. The other women freeze, watching both her arms spread wide, hearing heavy sniffing when backing with the others parting ways and curiously marching forward as she swiftly fades to the back.

"Kotomightyno! (Damn)…, Damn! Which one of you nasty hussies cut that one?" she screams, almost shaking her grey wig off when pinching her nose tight, in tears and still falling back.

The other women look back but continue walking until their faces instantly transform when stopping simultaneously and backing fast. They start cussing, fussing, and pointing to one another until one-woman points to Alfred, Ken, Barry, and then Greg, who simultaneously points back to Alfred.

"You should be ashamed, you common buzzard! It smells like something done crawled up your little narrow tail and died with legs still hanging out," the closest woman screams, frowning and almost cross-eyed.

The other women burst into tears, directing so many offensive words toward Alfred, who finally looks back at them with wet cheeks and blurry eyes from laughing so hard.

Barry, Ken, and Greg keep quiet, not wanting to disrespect the women when staggering between cars and walking into the street. They try keeping straight faces until they no longer can when bursting out, screaming in laughter.

"Look! That's certainly not funny! You need to take your friend to a doctor so they can check him out for uh, uh, uh…, monkeypox…, I mean monkey poops!" one woman screams with a mean stare.

"Yeah, and while he's in there, get that dead man out of him!" another woman screams with tears filling her eyes when senselessly shaking her head in laughter.

"Look! I know one thing for sure; he needs to go and change his damn drawers!" the medium-built woman screams, looking over her shoulders and shaking her head.

One woman looks back, finding a group of younger women closing the four. "Hey, you young women may not want to go down there because those guys are not proper; they been popping off farts like nobody's business," the oldest woman yells in a high-pitch voice.

The six young women barely understand and continue until a few nudge each other, finding four pieces of eye candy dead ahead.

Alfred throws his head back, seeing the cuties fading instantly around a corner when taking off in a mad sprint.

"Hello, ladies!" Barry intercepts them, looking over their shoulders, finding one of the older women with her middle finger up. He finds another with her legs straddled, leaning back and grabbing her crotch, and yet another bending over and patting her wide butt.

"Hmm…, I thought there were four of you," one girl says, standing alone when looking around for Alfred.

"Yeah…, right," Barry says, looking around as if surprised while pretending he's looking for Alfred. "Oh, yeah, the lady who mentioned popping something off is his grandmother; I think he ran back to get her gas pills," Barry says, smiling.

"So, where are you ladies off to?" Ken asks.

"Club Royale..., happy hour..., don't you want to come?" a medium-built girl asks.

The tallest girls take a few steps toward the club when Ken cuts her off. "Hey you," he says, smiling and grabbing her hand.

Ken maneuvers her straight and away from the clear curtain of the notorious farts.

Barry looks over the outdoor pub menu where they're standing with eyes wandering over the heavy beverage advertisements. "Hey, double and triple shots of Sekif on me," he says, reaching back and swinging the little, spring-loaded, decorative gate open and holding it for the women.

The tall woman waits for her friends to go in and then steps toward the club when Ken grabs her by the hand again.

"Really..., I'm not a drinker. I'll see you guys at the club; besides, I'm supposed to meet a date there." She smiles, gently pulling away.

"A date? What if I want to be your date? Just one drink, please!" Ken says, enticing her for minutes before letting her hand go when he sees a short, older man step onto the curb almost near where Alfred had farted.

The short man stops and reads a few advertisements for the nightclubs. He wanders a few more feet and reads a few more ads with his hands still folded behind his back.

"I understand, so hey, maybe I can get a dance later?" Ken says, turning from her and then looking again, staring at how she seductively and slowly switches her hips as if she doesn't want to leave.

The old man advances, still looking down and talking to himself, when finally looking up and finding the girl on a collision course.

They simultaneously step to the same side and collide where Alfred's fart had drifted.

The girl's head jerks back fast, frowning, and the man backs up quickly, staring at her with wide eyes and one eyebrow slightly raised when his face begins frowning.

"Excuse me," she says with a slight frown.

The man leans forward, sniffing, then leans further until backing up and staring. "You know? You are an exceedingly beautiful girl, but hooooon! Your coo-coo stanks (stinks)!" he seriously says, grabbing his nose. He backs up fast and hard with his head, accidentally slamming into the steel street post when screaming and rubbing.

Ken bursts into loud laughter.

The girl looks back at Ken in embarrassment and then at the man with a mean face. "What? Are you serious? If anything, you must smell your cheesy-ass mustache," she says, watching the man frown while rubbing the back of his head.

The girl rolls her eyes at the man, shakes her head, and walks off.

Ten minutes pass, and Alfred appears, giggling and heading toward the club until Ken calls him, motioning him over. They sit longer, drink more, and then everyone staggers toward the club. They make their way up the steps, single-filing inside with everyone in tears of laughter from one of Barry's silly jokes.

Ken digs deep in his pockets, treating everyone to the cover charge.

The main door abruptly flies open with a tall bouncer holding the door. He stares at the well-dressed, sexy women and smiles but quickly turns macho when Barry and the guys scroll past.

"What the hell are you looking at?" Greg playfully asks, smiling, patting, and then rubbing the bouncer's muscular arms with eyes heavily glued on the back of Barry, Ken, and Alfred's heads.

"Dumb shit like that'll get you f-d up," the gay bouncer playfully smiles, winking until going into a serious gaze when turning, grabbing a handful of Greg's butt off-guard.

Greg shockingly thrusts forward, accidentally running up on Ken's heels while looking back and smiling in a sexy stare.

Ken looks back, frowning and shoving him back.

The bouncer comes up on his tiptoes, staring at Greg until he fades into the crowd.

Hours pass.

Barry and his friends begin to mingle with others, and the girls do the same.

Barry notices that Greg is disappearing for long spells and returning cheerful, so the last time Greg peels off, Barry heads off, coming up on the other side of the bar. He finds Greg easing into a chair next to a woman with long hair and quickly looking over his shoulder. Barry ducks, resting against the wall when thinking Greg sees him. He eases up on the side of the wall curtains, extending it out a little to cover his face. Barry spots an empty, low-cut table behind a high chair table, making his way over to the seat and picking up a menu. He covers his face with eyes barely over the top, finding Greg deep in conversation until playfully touching her thigh from time to time.

Minutes later, Ken and Alfred, wander around to the other side, spotting Greg when making their way over to him until noticing a fast-waving hand, realizing its Barry. They rush up, easing into chairs, and lean midway into the table when Barry leans forward in deep laughter and begins briefing them on what he's seen thus far. The three slouches with high-held menus, anticipating what's to come when waiting a little longer, but nothing happens.

"Come on, silly..., are you keeping it a hundud (hundred) and fiddy (fifty)?" Ken asks Barry with a doubtful face.

"Look, I'm telling you, this dude may not be as we thought. He's all over this woman!" Barry says, staring with an eager eye.

"I thought for sure he went the other way with something about lifting biscuits and meat but left it alone," Alfred says, bursting into an uncontrollable giggle, and putting them in tears.

"Look! Look!" Ken says with bucked eyes, seeing the long-haired woman laugh and put a hand on Greg's upper thigh, run it to his kneecap, and then deep in his crotch.

The three continually make intermittent eye contact with Greg and the woman until, in deep stares for minutes, speechless.

The gay bouncer walks up seconds later with drinks.

Greg briefly looks back, finally finding the three watching when shooting up from his stool with bulged eyes and feet slamming to the floor.

The person they think is a woman finally turns with runs fingers and thumb over his mustache, lightly pushes his mustache back against his face.

Greg turns, leaning into the bouncer, telling him about his friends, when the drunk bouncer's wide hand draws back without warning and smacks Greg square in the butt, slightly lifting him from the floor. Greg's eyes fly over his shoulder, finding the three with their mouths torn open. He snaps his head forward and points at the low-volume television, which has sports on but finds the news on the broadcast. Greg looks back quickly, foolishly laughing while patting the bouncer on the shoulder. He digs deep in his pockets, stretching out a twenty-dollar bill so Barry, Ken, and Alfred can see it before laying it on the table. He finds the sport on again when whispering to the bouncer again, excitingly cutting his eyes toward the television. Greg points to the screen jumping as if cheering before swiftly walking over to them with a big grin, trying to read into them. "Man, did you guys see that playback?" He asks, laughing until nervously slapping Ken on the back.

Ken's mouth slowly closes, then Barry's, but Alfred's is still open.

Barry closes his mouth, and his hand extends to Alfred's face, pushing the bottom of his chin to close his mouth. "Ah…, yeah…, yeah, we saw the game alright…, didn't we, fellas? It sure as hell wasn't a playback, but more so a brawny hand full of fatback, and right before that was the Dill Pickle Bowl!" Barry blurts out, somewhat in a daze.

"What can I say? He wilds out over sports!" Greg says, trying to get more readings from them.

"Well, the only wilding out I saw then was you excited when he grabbed a handful of buttocks and the other little deal!" Alfred says in a slow, low voice.

"What! Man, yawl is seriously tripping! He did that thing like baseball players. . ., you know…, Uh!" Greg moves his wide hand back, popping it forward. "And dill? I don't know anything about that. Maybe yall (you all) are seeing too much from sitting too far back and drinking too much. I think it's time for that annual eye exam, obviously!"

"Ah, hellz (hell) naw (no)! Man, that dude's hand was not flat like that, it was all curve, and there was no 'Uh'; it was POW, squeeze, and pull! It was more like a beefy hand-baller gripping a basketball, faking a shot, but still got the ball." Ken says, "and well…, well, the other thing was all foul!"

"Yeah…, whateverrr!"

"Hmm. . . !" the three of them sound off almost simultaneously.

"But hey, look…, let's get out of here before we find you in the bathroom with those three guys, butt ball and spread eagle," Barry says, standing.

"What? I know that is a lie because I'm strictly…," Greg says, looking down to find them playfully looking at each other and curiously cutting their eyes around.

"Yeah, and your point? Let's get going, buddy!" Barry says, looking around and waving to a few girls they had come in with.

"And the strictly thing, definitely a woman's line," Ken says, shaking his head.

The four soon end up on the boardwalk. They stop at a little bar halfway into the walk and run into an officer from work hanging out with a few enlisted men.

Barry and the guys sit across from the officer and Sailors, having drinks and watching television until a few commercials appear.

The division officer stands, buying another round for his men, and then heads for the bathroom with his pants sagging.

Barry's face frowns, and his eyes follow the young officer until fading. Barry waits for a few, then heads to the bathroom, intercepting the officer heading to his table. "Hey, you ever think about pulling those pants up? You're an officer and need to carry yourself like one, on and off-duty. Man, pull your pants up! Nobody wants to see your behind!" Barry says in a loud, pissed-off, and authoritative voice. "That's some kiddy shit; even a two-year-old has the common sense to know that you don't wear pants like that! You're what twenty-two or twenty-three?" Barry asks, still meanly staring him down.

"Twenty-four, so step the hell off! What's it to you, anyway?" the officer asks, cutting his eyes over at his guys, who can't see him when gazing back, deep into Barry's eyes.

Barry's hand springs forward, wrapping tightly around his neck when they fade into an adjacent walkway. "Now, you look here, you Jackass! You're right, it means nothing to me, but it looks stupid as hell. I wish the hell your trifling ass would try to step to someone in my family; around here looking like a damn clown." Barry finally releases the heavy breathing officer, looking back, finding two waiters peeping into the corridor.

"Man, go head (ahead) with that bull! I wouldn't step to none of your raggedy peeps (people) anyway," the guy says, brushing his collar down and instantly sticking his chest out when seeing a sexy female server pass.

"Raggedy?" Barry says in a mean tone, snatching the young officer by the throat this time and falling into the wall. "You're the one who dresses like that from playing follow the leader. You are no leader, or you would set a good example for these other young kids in your division.

"Oh man, screw you!"

Hours later, the four end up at a Spanish comedy club where they hear a comedian deep into jokes about the fiscal cliff.

"Yah (you) know…, damn, a fiscal cliff," the Spanish-American comedian says, taking a quick hit from his glass. "Man, that is some bull-shit! That is nothing but Congress punishing people for re-electing a black president. I tell you, it's nothing but modern-day oppression. You see…, what the people in the States need to do is have a law passed for more frequent congressional votes. Shoot! They probably need to go to annual elections for those slick ass cats. They need to vote some of those sorry officials out at the end of the fiscal year, then designate December 31st as the fiscal cliff and a nationally observed holiday with live television while pushing some of them right off the damn cliff and into unemployment."

The four walk into the bar area, sitting at a corner table.

Ken looks over at Alfred. "Hey, before we left to come down, did you get the memo about the upcoming alcohol abuse training? I think they said it will be held in Building 2400 a week after we get back," Ken says, looking at the female server when throwing up a finger for two more beers and then motioning her to get everyone another round.

"Can you assure us that it was not only for management? I think they're in building 2400, but we can do ours online. I'm sure there is a link in the e-mail," Alfred responds.

"Well, I think you both are wrong. I think it said you should report if you feel you have an alcohol problem, and I know for sure that it said; if you did have a problem, you should discuss it with your boss over a few beers," Barry says bursting into laughter.

The rest of them burst into laughter and soon find themselves in tears.

Greg is in deep thought for seconds while staring at his glass of beer when Barry's hand swipes before his eyes a few times. "Earth…, calling to Klingon! Earth…, calling Klingon!" Barry says, bursting into laughter.

A smile comes upon Greg's face when registering the comment. "I forget to tell you guys about the guy in my division…, you know, Mr. Perfect? Well…, the other day, I was in the office, and this guy literally sat there taking his whole keyboard apart. I mean, he popped off each freakin' key, one key at a time, and cleaned that board inside and out. He had that whole thing dismantled and broken down to parade rest."

Barry shakes his head and turns up his beer bottle when asking the server for another. "Man, you 'bout to drive me to drinking! You're his division officer, and you actually watched him doing that silly crap and did nothing? Hmm…, if it were me, I would have put my boot so far up his tail that he would have been smelling the tar in the polish while singing the Star Spangle Banner. Ain't this the same guy you said is the lowest productive person in your division?"

"Well here…, now you see why he's non-productive, and it makes me wonder what other kind of other silly crap you let him and others get away with while you sit there looking at them like a freakin' idiot," Ken says, shaking his head.

Out of nowhere, Alfred bursts into a peal of silly laughter and can't stop laughing as they stare at him, wondering what he's laughing at and if he'll even share.

"Well?" Barry finally says, gazing at his watch until playfully tapping the face.

Alfred's laugh quiets and then bursts into more profound laughter. "Look…, look…, everyone in the command is busting their asses for this upcoming intelligence competition, and Greg's guy is getting away with pure-T murder. This guy obviously has too much time on his damn hands!" Alfred screams in deeper laughter.

Ken and Barry laugh until they are in tears.

Barry laughs so hard that he leans back too far, almost losing his balance when jumping and causing them to laugh even harder.

They get most of the laughter out and then sit ordering another round when Greg picks up the menu.

"Are you planning on eating because we're about to roll out," Barry says, looking at his watch and then the twenty empty bottles when they begin debating on whether they should get a bite first or wait.

"Hey, look, it's not like we'll starve or die if we wait," Barry says, standing and playfully poking his belly out to make it look like he's four months pregnant. "Let's go over to that popular strip club we passed on the way in the other night, you can eat there."

"What strip club?" Ken asks, looking clueless.

"Oh, you wouldn't know, skunk boy," Alfred says, giggling.

The three stand, laughing, but Ken looks off and then back at them, shaking his head when reflecting on the roof ride.

"I don't know why he didn't see that big sign; he had an open view from the roof," Greg says, digging deep in his pocket for a healthy tip.

Barry walks up, throwing the keys to Ken.

They arrive at the strip club about twenty minutes later.

Ken pulls into the parking lot and veers over into the valet when Barry grabs the steering column, steering him toward standard parking.

They fight over the wheel until the SUV stops, blocking the long line.

"Ok, go ahead, but you're paying. Ken's got this one, fellas since he wants to play VIP tonight," Barry says, rolling his eyes when releasing the wheel.

Ken pulls up to the attendant, jumps out, and pops his collar like someone powerful.

The others ease out and stroll over to the door for the bouncers to search them.

Two bouncers check Barry and Ken, one takes Alfred, and the other takes another guy who walks around Greg, who is looking around at the bright lights.

Barry looks back, finding Greg staring off into space and toward the brightly-lit strip.

The bouncer looks at Greg, whistling.

"Oh," Greg says, turning and looking back when taking a few fast steps toward the door, throwing up his hands for the search.

"Hey, he likes slow searches, almost cavity-style," Barry says, clutching the door handle and opening it for the guy behind him with music blaring into the streets.

Ken and Alfred dance at the entrance, and Barry stands at the door, watching cheerful Greg.

Greg continually playfully dances around while the bouncer searches him with the wand. "Don't forget to search my Johnson…, he's always packing," Greg says, smiling when putting his hands on his hips, drunkenly and playfully humping a few times.

The bouncer laughs, grabbing him and motioning him to turn. "Trust me, sir; if there is unquestionably a Mr. Johnson, I would have seen him by now. Maybe he's WIA…, you know, Wounded in Action," the bouncer says, looking at the other bouncer and laughing.

Greg passes Barry and comes up behind Ken and Alfred.

They approach the register, paying, and the girl pulls the door open, greeting them.

Alfred approaches a woman against the wall who is into the beat, dancing. He blows her a kiss, but she backs a little and then playfully spanks him on his butt as he passes.

They step over to where the room expands, looking over the big establishment.

A female server walks up from nowhere, taking their first order.

Barry's eyes wander over the place, following the tops and bottoms of every woman that passes until looking toward the main stage, finding the hottest women in the club thus far. He nudges Ken, who stares as well until his mouth drops open. Barry's hand comes up to Ken's chin, slightly pushing it up. "There…, there," Barry says, pointing to the seat not too far from the packed runway.

A new beat comes, and the men sit around the runway, digging deep in their pockets. Some pull out a wad of singles, but others pull out fives, tens, and even twenties.

Barry sits, staring at the beautiful woman as if mesmerized when digging deep in his pockets. He sits back down with the twenties, an unknowingly few hidden hundreds, and singles tight in his fist, with eyes wandering up and down the long runway for an empty seat.

One guy jumps from his seat on the other side, and Barry jumps up anxiously, tripping over Ken's big feet and fading behind the seat in a slight twist, rolling over to the side of a dance pedestal. He jumps up, embarrassed, frowning, and pointing to Ken when quickly bursting into laughter and playing like Ken intentionally tripped him. He makes his way to the runway and comes upon the other side when another man pulls the chair out, taking the seat while Barry childishly and drunkenly stomps.

Barry stands off to one side, gazing at the woman as she slowly crawls over the stage staring at Barry a few times until winking.

The stripper stops at the man sitting in front of Barry, doing all kinds of erotic dances, making Barry feel momentous.

Barry waits for the guy to put his money in her waistband and then leans forward, flashing a twenty. He slowly pulls her panty band from her soft flesh, rubbing his index finger against her warm flesh until lightly releasing but allowing it to snap back gently.

The stripper winks, playfully flickering her tongue until turning her back to them, twirling her hips until twerking. She leans forward with her breast into the floor, back arched downward when stretching and making her cheeks go up and down for minutes.

The men watch until mesmerized when one cheek bounces, then both look like two basketballs dribbling down a court.

Barry's tight fist comes to his mouth, and his teeth slightly press down on his index knuckle with eyes bulging.

The stripper turns, bringing her bottom high until coming upon elbows, and slowly lowers her bottom until rolling and running hands between her creamy thighs.

Barry's eyes grow even wider when drunkenly turning in circles, then bouncing up and down like a baby just learning how to walk when turning too quickly the last time and accidentally banging his head against the concrete wall.

The last song draws to its end, and the girl begins making her way around the stage, collecting the bills until the song finally ends. She stands, and several men lean forward, pushing the bills in a pile and closer to her, when an intermission song begins playing.

Before long, there are several empty seats at the runway.

The stripper bends over one last time, and the men begin cheering when she turns, smiling when leaning and grabbing her scarf she just had laid down. She throws the bills on the scarf, bundles them, and then walks off the stage, looking around at a few men, then over at Barry, blowing a shy kiss. She sensually twists her hips, strutting her thang to the top of the runway, where she fades behind sheer curtains.

Before long, the empty seats quickly fill again when the next girl stands off to the side, waiting for the DJ to put on her song, and it changes to another when the next girl walks out, starting in on her erotic dance that has more men making their way to the runway.

Barry sits next to Ken, looking around for Alfred and Greg, who are a few seats back with other strippers and a guy.

The female server soon comes by, refreshing their drinks.

"Hey, hey…, the girl that just came off…, who is she? Her name?" Barry anxiously asks in excitement.

"Oh…, you mean Sinnamon?" She looks down at him, placing a napkin down.

"Yeah, yeah..., please send her favorite drink..., it's on me!" Barry shouts over the loud music when leaning and reaching in his pockets.

"Ok..., that'll be fourteen ninety-five." She sexily twirls one long curl that slightly hangs from her pretty face while smacking gum until blowing a few bubbles.

Barry hands her eighteen dollars, smiling and nodding.

"That's it?" she says, with a serious stare. "Well, you can keep that! The gentleman a few seats over gave me a fifty to send the same drink," she says, cutting her eyes over at the man in the nice, Italian-looking suit.

Barry cut his eyes over at the well-suited man who is looking immensely wealthy when leaning to one side again, slipping her sixty dollars when Ken looks off.

The girl smiles, walks away, and goes to the bar, where she orders one drink. She counts off about four hundred plus dollars that she's collected from six different men. She passes the money to the bartender and waits for her personal deposit receipt.

"Girl, you and Sinnamon are making that money tonight, huh?" the male bartender yells over the loud music, smiling.

"Oh, put half of that on Sinnamon's account, and give me her favorite," she says, looking around, cheerfully nodding and smiling at the desperate men.

Sinnamon comes from behind a door and stands in the hallway, where she takes the drink and talks to the female server while identifying the men who sent her drinks.

The waiter walks back out, and Sinnamon follows at a distance and then peels off, making her rounds by her cheerful buyers. She laughs, smiles, and flirts with the different men for a short spell, finally making her way over to Barry. She talks to Barry for seconds, gives him the same treatment, and then walks away. She reappears at the bar, acting more playful and flirtatious with a thug at the head of the bar; her bodyguard, leaving all of them thinking he's her man when hanging all over him.

"You sucker!" Ken says, laughing and watching Sinnamon dance around and in front of the man. "Do you know how many drinks you could have bought for sixty smack-a-roos (dollars)? You could have just brought her the drink when she passed, knucklehead. Man, the more I teach you, the dumber I get!" Ken says, shaking his head in disbelief.

The third song ends, and the next girl comes on stage.

Sinnamon walks closer to the stage and begins cheering extremely loud for her best friend. She comes beside Barry, ignoring him until he turns his chair toward the floor, paying close attention to the girl on stage.

Sinnamon peeps down, playfully running her fingers through Barry's hair, then smiles when he looks up. She claps, whistling when the guys go wild over her friend.

Ken jumps up, rushing up to the stage, grabbing a chair when accidentally bumping into a dwarf who snatches the chair back, thrusts his chest out, and shoulders back.

The dwarf jumps back a few inches, then head butts Ken in his groin, and Ken's hand instantly goes to his inseam, plopping straight down onto brittle knees. A vein expressly rises in his forehead as he crawls a few feet until the dwarf's little feet press hard on his butt, slowly leaning him forward until he falls flat on his belly.

Sinnamon shakes her head, laughing at Ken, and then laughs even harder when falling into the seat next to Barry.

Barry immediately reaches for her hand. "Sinnamon, right? Well, I'm Barry," he says, grasping her soft hand and looking into her beautiful face.

Minutes later, she controls her laugh, supporting her best friend with more call-outs and whistles.

Barry moves closer, motioning for the female server to bring her another drink.

Ken finally gets his strength back, easing down in the seat next to Barry and looking over to find Sinnamon deep in laughter and pointing at him. His face stays slightly frowned when waving her humor off, slightly laying his head back, then jerking a little when feeling the room spinning.

Before long, Sinnamon is tipsy and giggling at Barry's jokes and sense of humor. Her hands begin touching his body when leaning into him, laughing and having fun.

The last song ends for Sinnamon's friend, so she stands, applauding again.

Barry eases back, staring at Sinnamon's delicate, round, firm bottom for minutes until his eyes drift to the ceiling when realizing she's staring back.

Sinnamon turns once more, dancing to the next exciting beat, then turns smiling at Barry when moving the table back, giving him a lap dance.

Barry digs deep in his pockets several times, pulling out a few tens and ones when taking his time, placing the bills in her G-string or on the pedestal.

Ken remains in pain, with his head thrown back and his eyes closed.

The female server runs her routine on the extensive drink buyers, leaving the other dancer her share on her books, and then walks over, singling out her buyers.

The other dancer, Sinnamon's best friend, soon comes out, making her rounds, and then comes up on Sinnamon, who turns and eases into the seat next to Barry. She looks down at Ken for a few seconds and then leans forward, running her soft, warm, feminine hands through his hair, massaging his scalp.

Ken opens his eyes with the slight frown vanishing when smiling and easing over.

"Delightful," she says, reaching for his fully extended hand.

Ken orders another round and then pays for a personal lap dance.

Ten minutes later, the four are sitting together and deep into laughter. From time to time, the women hold out hands for dollars, which they take to the stage and throw out to help motivate men who were hesitant to give money to amateur dancers.

Barry and Ken are now full of the drinks and feeling the full effects.

A dope beat plays, and Barry bounces up and down for a laugh from the girls. He grabs the thick, tall, shooter glass tube and jumps up, screaming at the top of his voice like a lunatic when rapping to the tune and sounds almost as good as the actual rapper.

The women constantly stay in tears of laughter.

Ken leans back, putting his feet up on the furniture, when Delightful, Mr. Canton's fiancé, points to his dull shoes, bursting into laughter. Ken's head jerks forward and he stares at his shoe for a few seconds until he pulls them closer to his face, finding them very dull from perspiration. He leans over to her, whispering, then walks away, heading by the front door near the bar as if to get a drink but watches the three and fade out the front door, running across the street to a shoeshine booth he had seen earlier.

An old man anxiously watching for new customers looks up when Ken screams at him but pretends he doesn't see or hear him. He turns, flipping the open sign to closed, and recaptures Ken from his peripheral view as he waves cars past. Ken staggers upon the old man with his hands feverishly waving. "Sir, please, sir…, please, you have to shine my shoes before you go!" he says, breathing hard.

"No…, no…, no…, I'm close; I have to get home!" the old Asian man says, looking at his watch while trying to keep a straight face.

"Look, I'll pay extra!" Ken says, pulling out a wad of cash with eyes scrolling over the charge sheet. Ken flips through a few twenties, pulling one out for the seven-dollar shine. The man takes the twenty, rubbing his fingers a few times to indicate he wants more and Ken shakes his head 'no,' then 'yes' quickly when finding the man handing the twenty back. Ken pulls out another five, and the man flips the sign back to open.

Minutes later, Ken pats the man's shoulder, staggering back across the busy street.

CHAPTER SEVEN

Greg and Alfred peel off a few more dollars for the women at their table.

"Yeah, boy! That's how we ball…, boooiii (boi)," Alfred screams, digging deep and slowly pulling out rabbit ears.

Seconds later, Greg taps out, laying his last dollar down, checking his wallet, and finding it empty when checking all pockets.

Greg motions for more dollars to contribute to the lap dances.

Alfred springs for the ATM. He swipes his card, and within seconds the prominent warning banner' Non-Sufficient Funds' pops up.

Alfred's face surprisingly transforms, making several unsuccessful attempts until staring at the ATM as if the machine has issues.

Another guy walks up with the same credit card issues, looking back at his partner clueless.

Greg soon proudly walks up with a joyful hand on Alfred's shoulder. "Come on…, man! We been balling like real ballers up in here!" Greg smiles. "What?" he asks, looking at Alfred's pale face. "Hey, man…, let's ball some more, son!"

"Ball?" Alfred says with the longest belch ever, which seems connected to the first. "More like brawling…, because I feel like fighting to get my money back because we broke as all get-up! Man…, I had about eight hundred when I last checked."

"Oh? What? So you didn't mean to give up the three-hundred-dollar bills back-to-back?"

"What? Are you freakin' serious?" He screams, choking Greg and taking him straight to the wall until stumbling when they slam into another wall.

"Screw you, dude! You were the one hollering about balling!" Greg yells, reversing the situation when grabbing and choking Alfred by his collar.

"Yeah, but a hundred bucks? Man, please! We're balling all right…, more like getting broke the hell out! I'm broke…, no dinars…, no loot…, no money…, no moolah!" Alfred drunkenly screams with a stale face.

They drunkenly wrestle in the dark corner for minutes until Alfred's legs quickly jog up and down.

Alfred's eyes get bigger. "Stop! Stop! I have to go drain the ole' snake-a-roo! I have to drain it, now!" Alfred yells, bouncing up and down until grabbing his inseam.

They rush off and fall through the bathroom door, almost on top of each other when continually slipping and sliding over the well-saturated pissy floor.

Ken rushes back inside, looking over at Barry and the girls until stumbling to the bar.

Alfred rushes to the first urinal, still slipping and sliding with his head thrown back.

The room begins to spin when Alfred's left foot slowly rises, then his right when he puts the left down and then does it again until the room becomes somewhat stable.

Greg stares into the first smeared mirror, moving to the last, swaying while checking his hair to look good.

The door flings open, and Tommy, a bodyguard for a mean mob boss, Mr. Thomas Canton, the same man Sinnamon danced for at the bar, walks in, washing his hands. He curious stares at Greg, ignoring him when looking into the mirror, over his well-groomed beard, wetting his hair, and slicking it back.

"Hey, man! Dude! Did you see that hot chick all over Barry?" Alfred asks, looking down and continually shaking himself.

Greg looks back, watching Alfred's jerking elbow until turning to the mirror.

"Hey…, if you shake it more than three times, you're playing with it!" Greg laughs.

"But dude…, did you see her? I think the DJ introduced her as Sinnamon or something like that. Man, I'd like to spank that like there's no tomorrow." Alfred giggles senselessly. He rushes from the urinal, jerking his boots forward and around in a circle, slightly slipping and sliding again.

The bodyguard looks at Alfred through the mirror with a mean stare materializing when looking down and washing his hands.

"Oh yeah? Well, if she's all over Barry, then the chances of that happening are like, what…, slim to none, right?" Greg responds.

"Man…, screw Barry!"

"Oh…, no, thank you, but you can feel free to do it yourself," Greg says, giggling.

Alfred takes baby steps over the slippery floor. "Why don't you tell ole' Sinnamon to come and get on this shroon (mushroom)?" He grabs his crotch, giggling until in a crazier laugh. Alfred staggers to the sink, finally noticing the man's obviously rolling his eyes. He approaches Tommy, watching him lean forward and dip his face into a handful of running water. Alfred finds Greg watching when throwing his shoulders back and chest out as if tough when inching, then jerking from Tommy and veering off when Tommy comes up fast.

"Rolling up on a man's back? Little silly crap like that will get you torn the hell out the frame! And another thing; keep Sinnamon's name out of your filthy mouths before I wash it out with soap. Mr. Canton will not take you talking about her or any of his girls likely for that fact."

Alfred backs away with his chest out again, looking swollen. "Mr. Canton? Dude…, I ain't even trying to hear nothing about no Mr. Canton, Hard Stone, or freakin' Flintstone, and I damn sure as hell ain't trying to hear nothing about Mr. Ching Chong! My boy Barry is about to wax that, so if you ask me, Mr. Canton better worry about Mr. Ding Dong!"

"Oh…, I see…, so, Mr. Funny Man, hey? Real comical…, you jerk!" Tommy says, turning and walking up to Alfred with a tightly balled fist.

The two draw near until toe-to-toe, staring eye-to-eye without an inkling of a blink.

The bodyguard jumps, and Alfred flinches, screaming like a little girl.

Greg rushes forward and comes between them, driving Alfred back.

"Move, Greg! This punk is all up in my business, talking about a damn Mr. Canton!"

"Oh yeah, well, you're going to hear it! And you can thank your boy here for keeping your lights on and not letting you go nighty-night!" Tommy screams, his veins protruding at his neck.

"Oh, hell naw! My lights…, my lights, sucker? Shiiiiittt (Shit)! My lights, chump? Punk, these lights always gone be on…, always and with an exclamation mark!" Alfred screams, backing with bulging eyes. He bucks his eyes more to exert fear when frowning and hardening his lips to look tough.

Greg finally intervenes. "Look, dude, whatever! We come to have a good time and see some towering boobies and big ole booties. Yeah…, we ain't even trying to hear nothing about no, Mr. Canton. He'll Mr. Canton can come and toss my damn salad for all I care!" Greg says, turning and patting his butt while bursting into drunken laughter.

Alfred's head slightly turns from the bodyguard, staring Greg down with raised and concerned eyebrows. "Damn, Greg, ok…, that's just straight gross!"

The bodyguard stares at Alfred with nostrils flaring.

Alfred's eyebrows slowly lower, thinking the guard is gone when rising high, finding him still there when his chest shoots back out. "Hey, look, man…, why are you even still here? Look…, you got some beef with me? What…, you want some of this? Because if so, we can get it poppin', Jack!" Alfred says, growing heated.

"Look, Alfred, just forget about him! Why are you starting something? You know you've been drinking too much to be fighting. Now, I ain't gone let you fight because you too drunk, and you know you too slow when drunk. I just ain't gone let you do it, now! And another thing…," Greg whispers, telling all of Alfred's slow-moving secrets when cutting his words short and eyeing the musclebound bodyguard.

"Naw, man. . ., he up in here sizing me up and everything! He acts like he wants a piece of the damn, ah…, ah…, ah…, RAZOR!" Alfred screams loud and even deeper, making the man think he's all about the business and then some.

"Razor?" Greg curiously responds, holding his smile and about to burst out into crazy laughter. He looks at Alfred as if he's lost his damn mind. "Naw, see. . ., I already told you that I ain't gone let you fight because you're too drunk, and you know when you drunk, you swing too slow, so just come on and let's get out of here!"

Alfred drops back into a fighting stance without warning, with nostrils flaring.

Greg pushes Alfred back, and Alfred hacks up spit just as Greg shoves him back once more, and the thick wad misses Tommy's face by inches with overspray in his face when the wad slams into the wall and slowly oozes down.

Out of nowhere, the door opens, and a drunk staggers to the urinal.

The bodyguard backs up, unbuttoning his vest fast and taking off his cuff links even faster.

"Oh yeah, it's on now!" Alfred screams, bouncing around as if a seasoned boxer. He does fancy legwork and performs impressive moves, feeling good because he knows he's provoked the fight to the point of no return.

The drunk quickly washes his hand, dries them on his jeans, and excitedly backs out but continues peeping until finally closing the door, and nosily peeping once more.

"Is this what you want? Because if you get your butt whipped, I will tell Barry and Ken, detail-for-detail! I already told you, Raaaaazzzooorr (Razor)…, you're too drunk! Ok, you want to fight? Do you want to fight? I said…, do you want to fight? Ok then, I'm going to record it, and if you lose, you'll be on the Internet under loser…, L-O-U-Z-E-R!" Greg shouts, pulling out all stops to prevent Alfred from fighting, but nothing works.

Greg stumbles with his hands in his tight jeans until flipping out a camera and getting in Alfred's face, letting him know he's serious.

Another man stumbles inside, seeing the commotion when backing out quickly.

Alfred looks at Greg, quickly shoving him to one side when slowly looking up, finding Tommy closing in stealth mode, with both big fists clenched tight.

Tommy swings past Alfred's face, only missing because Greg pushes Alfred back fast.

Greg's adrenaline goes high, feeling and hearing wind from the devastating blows when feeling sober. He forcefully moves Alfred's sluggish body about until Tommy starts in on Alfred, taking a couple of headshots and then more devastating body blows. The last blow comes like a missile, lunging Alfred back and staggering him off his feet.

Tommy comes in swiftly again with a deep rib shot that goes straight through Alfred and Greg's bodies, and they fold forward on top of each other before slowly peeling apart, like spirit and flesh separating in a horror movie.

Greg falls back against the wall with his hand on his stomach and his mouth torn wide open when flipping the camera on quickly.

Alfred takes one to the lips, riding high on tiptoes and wobbling out of control. His lips swell, looking like two stacked hotdogs with ketchup running down.

The continual stealth blows keep coming and are so complex that they sound like a mighty hand slapping a pack of freshly wrapped hamburger meat but louder.

Suddenly, two men burst through the door, laughing and looking back over their shoulders hearing a few loud slaps with heads shifting forward fast when stopping and backing out.

Greg stands off looking through the camera phone so long that he grows excited from seeing live, close-up footage. He loses focus on the reality of Alfred getting the snot knocked out of him until the thought finally registers in his drunken mind when he pulls the phone back and recognizes how bloody Alfred's face really is when freezing and screaming like a woman for help.

Alfred staggers, taking baby steps like a ninety-year-old, tiptoeing. He stops and stands so devastated that he unintentionally walks into the guy administering one last blow, landing him on his back and sliding over the pissy floor, TKO'ed (knocked out).

Greg stops screaming instantly, bending over slightly and peeping around the bodyguard to find Alfred's eyes swollen shut and him propped up lightly snoring with a smile.

The bodyguard stands still, trembling until hearing Greg's heart beating when jumping swiftly, grabbing Greg by the collar. He raises him high with eyes drifting to the phone while Greg slides the phone into his pocket.

Greg shakes like a leaf as Tommy slowly lifts him higher, head-butting him, knocking him out, and then easing him down to the pissy floor, still frowning.

Tommy walks around in circles, pissed. He turns, putting on his vest and then his cuff links, looking back at Alfred. Tommy's eyes scroll over the dirty basin until reaching for a bar of wet, dirt-covered soap, shoving it in Alfred's mouth. He steps back, kicking Alfred in the ribs, and then grabs him in the collar.

The door flies open with Tommy's friend walking in.

"Hey Gino, give me a hand with these punks!" he screams over the loud music.

The two lift Alfred and then Greg and hang them in the stalls by the hooks and their belts so that they bend at the waist when leaving them.

Several other men come in and leave, but the next man walks to the stall, pulling the door open while looking back in the mirror, and jumps, screaming when seeing Alfred's lifeless body swaying. He sprints for the door, still screaming when running out into the lounge.

The door opens minutes later, and Ken walks in, stopping when spotting blood over the wall and floor. His eyes stay fixated on the floor until swinging the stall door open, still looking back when Greg's head bumps his back. Ken sprints for the main door but tries to play manly when the door flies fully open, and a fragile-looking man walks in, looking at him as if he's crazy.

"Hey, give me a hand getting him down," Ken says, turning and looking back at the man looking down at his manicured nail.

"Not even, boo-boo," the man responds, opening the other stall and screaming like a little girl while backing against the sink.

"Oh, shit!" Ken screams, looking at who he thinks is Alfred though unsure.

The man stares at Alfred's swollen face and then screams again, running out when Alfred moves his arms and begins kicking like a maniac.

Ken rushes into the main area, finding Sinnamon giving Barry another lap dance when rushing up, snatching Barry up by his collar.

Tommy sits in a dark corner, laughing at Barry and Ken as they frantically scream at each other over the loud music before turning and running for the bathroom.

"Greg and Alfred were mugged!" Ken screams when the DJ pauses between tracks, shoving Barry into the hallway when the music cranks up again.

They burst into the bathroom and take down Greg, who's still out cold, and then Alfred, who is somewhat coherent but sloppily drunk, racing them over to the sinks.

The outside bouncer flings the door open, and in walks a pimp-suit-wearing man who quickly makes his way over to Tommy.

The two exchange a few words, and then Tommy passes him a 9MM, walking out.

Barry and Ken stand watching the two pull themselves together when walking off behind them, trying to piece together what happened.

Greg suddenly raises his head from the cool running water faucet and bursts into a silly, drunken laugh out of nowhere.

"What? What's so funny? Am I missing something?" Barry asks.

"Man, why didn't you steal that clown?" Alfred finally yells after being fed up with Greg's silly and irritating laughter when spitting out blood from his swollen lips and then a side tooth.

"What's so funny, Greg?" Ken finally asks, holding his laughter.

"Why? Because you started that mess, Al! I tried to stop you, but…, noooo! That dude was about to walk out, but…, noooo! The way I see it…, you provoked him into that well-deserved butt-whipping!" Greg says, giggling until slipping his hands to his knees when in a heavy bend.

"Butt whipping? Man, I waxed that clown! The Razor was in full effect, dude! No one can take the Razor because he's invincible!" Alfred screams, with blood and saliva drooling when staggering to his feet, taking a couple of less-than-stellar boxing swings with fancy footwork, when slipping over the pissy floor.

Barry and Ken make eye contact with heads slightly turned and hands over their eyes, holding their laughs but smiling.

"Waxed? Yeah, right…, the only waxing was his knuckles in your face!" Greg laughs.

"Enough!" Barry says. "Obviously, you lose if you end up hanging on a hook in a stall."

"Yeah, right…, obviously, I just slipped on this pissy floor, bumped my head, and passed out. Maybe that's when he got the best of me!" Alfred says, pointing to wet spots and sliding his feet back and forth in heavy saturated, and slippery spots.

"Yeah, right…, the only thing you repeatedly slipped into was his fat-ass fist. Yeah…, I bet you're worried about a damn Mr. Canton now, ain't you?"

"Mr. Canton? Hell…, you must have been worried about him, talking about him tossing your damn salad! Now that was lame crap if I ever heard of lame!" Alfred screams, senselessly giggling.

"Enough of the small talk…, here, let's see if you slipped or not," Greg says, digging deep in his pocket and pulling out his phone with Alfred's nervous eyes glued to it.

Alfred slightly turns as if not interested when anxiously diving for the phone and missing when slipping and sliding in the deepest puddle with urine spraying over his shoes.

Everyone's head turns to Alfred, shaking in disbelief and giggling.

Greg rewinds, passing the phone to Barry and Ken, and then makes his way to their side, hearing the loud commotion replaying.

Alfred comes up slow, shaking his head while leaning into the sink, embarrassed.

"Hey, isn't that the bouncer sitting at the bar earlier?" Barry asks.

"Wow! Whoa! Damn! Man…, that dude handled you like a rag doll!" Ken screams, laughing hard until his hands are on his knees, trying to catch his breath.

"More like a rag mop. You sure that dude didn't knock the piss out of you?" Barry says, turning and staring at dense puddles. "It was probably your piss you were slipping and sliding in."

Ken uses the urinal, backing off quickly when turning and looking at Greg and then Alfred. "Come on…, we'll get you guys a taxi back to the base."

"Taxi? Not I…, the night is still young, so I'm not going back so soon," Greg says.

"What about you, Al…, I mean Razor? At least go back so Doc can see if you need stitches for those balloon lips and maybe check your brain and spine to see if it's still intact," Ken says, smiling.

"Naw, I'm cool, but I think I'll go back and get my other bank card."

"Alright, champ! I mean, Blazer!" Barry says, patting Alfred on the shoulder when doing a few crazy, quiet reenactments behind Alfred's back.

"It's Razor, chump…, and don't you ever forget it, sucker!" Alfred screams, pissed.

Barry reaches for the door, and Ken grabs it, following him out.

Greg stops and gets a few dollars from Barry, walking Alfred out to the road, turning from him then back to him, finding Alfred flagging down a taxi.

"What? What?" Greg asks, bursting into laughter and staring back at Alfred. "Oh man, go on! I erased it already; you know I wasn't going to post it," Greg says, eyeballing the female taxi driver as she pulls up and looks over with a smile.

Alfred climbs inside, and Greg goes back inside the club.

Within the hour, Barry and Ken manage to win over the two strippers they've practically spent their entire evening with, except for their runway time, lap dances with others, or when other men pull them away, lavishing them with hundreds of dollars.

Before long, Barry and Ken are back into laughs with the women until breaking off, meeting in the bathroom, and plotting on getting the girls out for a night on the town.

Barry and Sinnamon retreat to a corner, leaving Ken and Delightful alone, but Barry and Ken stay in eye contact, ensuring they're progressing.

Ken takes the lead, finally leaning in for a sensual kiss, but Delightful stops him with an index finger to his lips, smiling.

She smiles with eyes glued on the attentive bouncer at the bar. . "No..., my boss is watching." She finds the new angry-looking bodyguard staring at her and then Sinnamon.

Barry runs a gentle hand down Sinnamon's spine in no time, causing her to arch her back sensually. Sinnamon eyes roam over her perfect, cupped breasts, down to her thin waist and curvy hips. Barry gazes at her pretty, raised pelvis, forming a perfect, round cup from a different angle as she twitches in a slow turn. He turns up his last sip, leaning forward, and gently pressing against her soft but firm body.

Sinnamon leans and pushes him back harder. "No, no..., my boss is watching," she says, looking over at the bodyguard, sitting with his glasses tilted and eyes swarming.

Barry looks at the man she's talking about with arms sliding from Sinnamon's waist. He pulls her closer when the intense fragrance of her sweet perfume suddenly rushes deep into his nostrils.

Her lovely scent arouses him more until Barry inhales her like a fresh breath of roses, then takes another deep breath. He digs in his pockets, peeling off a twenty as she stands and gives him a fifth lap dance.

Tension grows within him as she moves about sensually and then continually and seductively sways. The faint fragrance of her Egyptian body spray rises in his nostrils, lingering until overpowered by a light hint of a breathtaking, quiet but deadly fart.

"Ooops!" she whispers, grabbing her stomach, rubbing it, and then smiling.

Barry holds back for as long as possible and then bursts into a loud, crazy laugh that seems to echo endlessly. "What the…? Did you just…, you know?" he asks, bursting into a laugh so hard and loud that folks begin looking over at them.

Sinnamon holds her laugh and then falls into him in laughter. "Man, I have been trying to get that bubble out of my gut all night. Whew!"

"Huh…, I think you might need to go and check the string in the G-string," he says, playfully shoving her away and popping her G-string strap.

"So, what are you saying? You don't want this good-good now?" she asks, running her fingers deep between her thighs with fingers vanishing.

Barry puts his fingernails to his teeth, playfully acting as if he's nervously chewing nails, almost cartoonish, to get a whopping laugh out of her, and it works.

"You are so silly! I could spend my whole night laughing at your silly butt," she says, leaning then bending over, mounting both hands on his knees. "Umm, excuse me while I get ready to go back on," she says, turning but not taking her eyes off him.

Barry looks over by the bar, finding the bodyguard with his head turned while talking to a female server, and leans forward to caress her thick, round bottom.

Sinnamon catches him, speedily pulling away and smiling until bursting into laughter when her soft laugh turns into a silly giggle that fades when distancing herself.

Delightful also goes to the back since she follows Sinnamon's on-stage acts.

"So, what's the plan?" Ken asks, dropping down in a seat next to Barry.

"You tell me." Barry winks to a girl on stage, motioning for him over to a vacant seat on the runway when he points to the dressing rooms, playfully waving the girl off.

"Well, Delightful is game with hanging out and said she'll talk to Sinnamon, but first they have to shake this clown in the suit," Ken says, nodding to the new bodyguard.

"Ok, so how do they suppose they do that?"

"Heck, I have no clue, my friend…, no clue." Ken looks up slowly, mesmerized by the same girl on stage with her head between her legs with round, apple-bottom cheeks flapping like wings.

An hour or so later, the girls come off stage doing their routine run for money until walking back over, and standing in front of Barry and Ken, smiling.

Barry turns up his drink, motioning Sinnamon to the plush couch.

The next song comes, and Barry turns to Sinnamon, smiling when breaking out in a dance and acting like he's giving her a lap dance. He does several dances, almost better than some of the stiffer amateur girls, and there is soon a peal of loud laughter when he turns, bowing to his attentive little audience when flopping down in the chair.

The four go into tears of laughter and can't stop laughing for minutes.

Barry is the first to settle down and get serious. "So, what do you girls say to painting the town?" Barry digs in his pocket, paying for another round of overpriced drinks.

"Well, ok, but look…, we'll have to wait for two other girls to come to work first, then sneak out," Sinnamon says, looking toward the bar.

"What?" Barry asks with a fake, concerned face. "Ok…, I have to ask because we've had this Combat Trafficking in Persons (CTIP) training. Are you under any duress? Are you part of a human trafficking ring?" he asks, pretending he's shocked with both hands to his face when peeping and laughing.

"No, silly," Sinnamon says, giggling.

"Hey, look…, since your friend is still here and needs transportation, you guys get a taxi and have it wait near the club's restaurant side. The guy at the bar normally runs out for a smoke when his girlfriend gets here for her set. I'm sure he will have to run out for a lighter," Delightful says, showing them the guy's lighter she took from the bar. "When you see him come out, you know we're coming," Delightful says, winking at Ken.

"Wow! Just like in one of those old special-agent movies…, like spy stuff…, I like…, I like," Barry says, slowly standing and hugging Delightful when Barry hugs Sinnamon.

Ken whispers to Barry and then walks over, giving the SUV keys to Greg.

Greg hangs around for some time, kicking it with a girl and guy until leaving with them and heading over to pick up a comedy DVD they talked about, when leaving the SUV.

Barry and Ken do as asked, and while waiting, Ken sees the shoeshine man shining a man's shoes with several other customers in line. He stares with a mean look, taking a few steps to confront the man but stops when like clockwork, he spots the bouncer, and seconds later, the girls sprinting out.

Within minutes, the four begin barhopping and eventually end up at a huge karaoke club, where the enormous crowd eventually separates the couples.

Barry ends up at Sinnamon's house two hours or so later.

Sinnamon stands at the door, kissing all over him while opening the door.

Barry kisses her longer until she falls through the door, backing into the living room; when she reaches back, easing the door shut when she sees headlights at the corner and looks longer, with excited then nervously shuts the door.

Fast moving headlights turn onto her street, quickly extinguishing with two sets of eyes sitting and watching Sinnamon's house for minutes.

Sinnamon walks over, opening the sliding patio doors. "I have to keep an eye on this patio deck because I found a baby snake in the house last month though I think my ex-husband put it inside intentionally so I would take him back," she says, giggling.

"Snake? Did you say snake?" Barry nervously swallows, gazing over her hot body and growing bold. "A little itty-bitty ole' snake?" he giggles, looking over the penthouse.

"Well, I wouldn't say itty-bitty unless you call this itty-bitty," she says, connecting her thumb and fingers to show the diameter until stretching out arms as wide as possible.

Barry takes an even deeper swallow, then walks onto the patio, staring over the lovely landscaping, into the huge pool, and then nervously around flower pots and shrubbery.

Sinnamon walks off and returns minutes later, handing him a chilled glass of wine. She talks a few with her hands all over him and then fades back into the house.

Barry walks close to the pool, looking back at the immense architectural structure. He stands in amazement and then turns, finding her with a fresh glass of white wine. His mind goes deep into thoughts of the snake until reminiscing about the fun at karaoke. Finally, he refocuses, finding Sinnamon inside and fading off to one side. He walks back in, looks around, then stands still, hearing central air kicking in until blowing across the back of his neck. He takes another sip, fading into deep thoughts about their earlier fun.

Within minutes, Sinnamon comes back out, dressed in Daisy Duke shorts.

Barry's eyes fill with excitement, and he grows aroused.

The aroma of Sinnamon Egyptian Musk grows, breaking his intense concentration when she comes closer, falling into his arms, taking his glass, and walking away.

Barry stares back through the glass patio door and into distant lights in the field, drifting up into the mountains.

Sinnamon stands off in the corner, in a trance, still pouring another drink, when a smile grows with horny eyes roaming over Barry's muscular body.

Barry looks back, finally finding Sinnamon near the bar in a single glimpse.

Sinnamon stares back with a smirk until winking and walking over in a sexy stance, staring at him for seconds. She playfully bats her lovely eyes and then gives him this sultry look, arousing him more. She turns to put on the house alarm, but she's distracted when hearing her bedroom alarm clock chiming. She rushes out, coming back seconds later, and they start in on a conversation about her ex-husband. She laughs and goes into the story about her ex, which leads to the break-up and him possibly putting the snake inside.

Two foreheads lightly press against a breath-fogged windowpane. Their eyes follow their every move until they giggle and silhouettes senselessly bump into each other.

Several minutes later, another set of bright headlights appear a couple of houses down from Sinnamon's house and go out fast.

A manly silhouette steps from the car, walking to the trunk, pulling out a shotgun. The tall, stocky-built body runs up to Sinnamon's house alongside the two giggling clowns getting silent updates.

Sinnamon again excuses herself, changing into something sexier, and returns five minutes later or so with white spandex painted over her dangerously curvy body.

Barry turns in deep thought, finding her, unraveling her long hair and pulling it to one shoulder when easing his empty glass down, becoming mesmerized when standing in a stupor until backing up a foot or so into the couch.

Sinnamon seductively walks over to him with her hips sensually switching.

Dark eyes stare out from the darkest corner under the couch, the head going back and forth slowly while tensing. A shadow continually reaches out at intervals until, on the seventh stretch, sharp teeth instantly sink through Barry's socks and skin.

"Aii...!" Barry screams, shooting four feet high, slamming his head through Sheetrock and crumbling it where the roof is low before extending to a cathedral ceiling when continually high-stepping.

Sinnamon eyes drift down quickly when seeing the little paw retracted and falling back with her hands on her hips, bursting out in a crazy laugh.

Barry finally slows, gasping for air while frantically walking in circles, nervously shaking off his shoulder and hands. "What in the hell was that? Please..., not a snake!" Barry screams with eyes pierced near the couch with nervous shaking hands while backing when finally hearing a long and continual hissing.

The three outside fall backward from the window in a quiet yet hearty laugh and bend in deep laughter, quickly climbing up again with heads coming together.

The cat finally thrusts forward and into view, freezing with its back hunched, hissing. The three-tone, black, brown, and grey cat eases further toward Barry, hissing louder until backing. It hisses louder, staring at Barry, from side to side, seeing Barry fully covered in Sheetrock dust.

Barry freezes, swiveling his neck when brushing his shoulder off. He begins working his neck and rubbing his throbbing head, feeling a knot.

The cat hisses even louder and then roars like a little tiger when lunging in a flash, pouncing for Barry's throat when its claws clench Barry's collar, shredding it.

Barry fights to grab the cat, constantly snatching back from its mouth when it sharply turns to bite while clawing. With one last swipe, he catches the cat by the arms, trying to pry him away.

Sinnamon and the three men fall back in laughter and are in continual tears.

The cat's paws slip from the material, clawing at about ten claws per second until Barry grabs both front legs, going in a fast turn until swinging the cat in circles and switching to holding the hinds legs when letting go.

The cat flies backward toward the kitchen, landing on the counter near the stove, bracing fast, hunching, and hissing until roaring again. The cat backs up fast as if almost transparent, lunging toward the floor, picking up momentum when pouncing again for Barry's throat. Its paw swipes faster until running across Barry's lips a few times.

The three fight back laughter and grow deep into tears of silent laughter.

Barry finally gets a hold of the free paw and swings the cat again.

Sinnamon screams, but with a burst of zealous laughter, finally rushing up. "Storm!" Sinnamon screams, trying not to laugh when grabbing the cat and easing it to the floor.

Barry draws and arm back in fear, flexing when the cat hunches in a stare.

The cat's little head goes back and forth until looking and sounding as if it's uncontrollably laughing when shaking its head and running down the hallway.

Sinnamon rushes to the sink, grabbing a dishrag, not knowing it's soaked in greasy dish detergent water, when quickly wringing it out and rushing up to Barry, passing it.

Barry grabs the rag, running it across his lips. "You should've warned me about the little lion vice the snake," he says, finding bubbles forming on his lips while talking.

"I'm sorry…, I'm so sorry!" she pouts. "That's my ex-husband's little cat, the one he gave me after the snake incident. He can be devilish sometimes around new people, but seriously, he's a sweetheart," she says with soft-batting eyes.

Barry stares at the bubble-filled rag, rushing to the sink, rinsing it until staring at the filthy-looking old greasy dishwater when spitting until grabbing paper towels.

Sinnamon rushes down the hall, closing the door to the room she thinks the cat faded into though it's questionable when fading into the kitchen, pulling out the first aid kit.

Seconds later, she steps to one side, and with one last pull, his lips are bandaged when she kisses his cheek before handing him another cool glass of wine.

The two ease into high chairs at the granite bar and begin talking until there's a moment of silence when she kisses him and grabs his hand, running it over her curves.

Sinnamon eases up, leading him halfway down the dim hallway until pushing him against the wall and taking him into another slow, seductive kiss.

Eyes instantly pierce through the patio window, finding their tightly mingled silhouettes embracing.

Barry's hands begin rubbing all over her hot, curvaceous body.

The suited man's eyes run over Sinnamon's hot body, guided along with Barry's gentle touch when clenching the gun tighter. He turns, finding one guy with his gun in a steady aim through the glass when the suited man snatches the barrel, slowly gliding it down. "No..., I want to see how far she goes." He looks in mean stare.

Sinnamon snatches Barry from the wall, backing him into the bedroom.

Seconds later, eyes peep through the sheer bedroom curtains, the two men on tiptoes while the third, shorter man runs around trying to find something to stand on.

The shortest one soon gazes over at the grass, finding an old ten-speed bike.

Sinnamon pulls away, manipulating the cd player until jazz lightly flows from pristine speakers. She inches up to Barry, pushing him into the plush, king-size bed.

Barry digs into his pocket, pulls out his wallet, and sets it on the dresser.

Sinnamon turns, unzipping her top, allowing the sheer material to drape slightly over her shoulder without exposing her breast. She playfully extends an index finger forward, motioning him closer, loosening his shirt, then belt until easing onto the bed.

Barry removes his shirt, dropping his pants. He grasps the rim of his boxers, playfully extending them outward with playful and excited eyes when going into an erotic dance.

Beady eyes peep out from under the edge of the bed, and the cat springs high, pouncing with claws latching onto Barry's boxers, shredding them while sliding down and furiously grasping for more material.

The three burst into laughter, falling away from the wall and coming back up fast.

"Aii...!" Barry screams, expressly turning in circles about three or four times until the cat drops, and runs into the bathroom, turning and hissing.

The three men burst into laughter, leaning heavily to the wall, trying to balance.

Sinnamon rushes to the door, using her foot to hold the cat back, while shutting the door.

The three men fall back into the window in tears of laughter.

The short man laughs harder, falling off the bike, wobbling until sliding forward and down the sharp, rugged concrete wall, coming up fast, expressly jumping in pain with his mouth torn open, but no sound. Tears continually trail until his face is saturated, finally biting on the knuckle when running off. He runs to the front of the house and then a few houses down, where he eventually sounds off at the top of his lungs.

Barry and Sinnamon freeze when quietly but fearfully, listening until the sound fades until another wolf-like call sounds off from a coyote high out in the hills, almost identical.

"What the hell is that?" Barry jumps when the coyote sounds come and fade into that of a screaming man.

"Who knows? Probably a wolf, coyote, or dog, but whatever it is, its soul sure as hell is hurting." Her concerned eyes stare at his shredded boxers when looking away, hiding her smile until her shoulders jerk up and down with silent laughter growing heavier. She takes a deep breath, thinking of something serious to get the thought off her mind, when quickly pulling herself together and gazing over her shoulder to find Barry with his back turned and head down.

"Are you alright, buddy?" he playfully whispers in baby talk, still looking inside his boxers.

Sinnamon reaches for his shoulder, but he playfully pulls away.

Barry's playful, sad eyes peep over his shoulder at intervals. "You knew that cat was in here! Man, that's not even funny…, not funny!" he repeats, staring down until looking over his shoulder again.

"Really…, I didn't…, I thought he was in the laundry room," she says, easing soft, gentle massaging hands on his shoulders.

Barry dresses but keeps complaining. He reaches for his wallet, and the lights go out, leaving the house pitch-black with Sinnamon screaming and embracing. Barry's hands swipe for his wallet, and then he quiets her, listening when hearing glass crack and fall to the marble floor, and there's silence until more is loudly punched out.

Barry's hand run over the door, cracking it open with a thin beam of light from the hall's skylight fading inside. "Hey…, do you have a gun?" he whispers, looking down at the top of her head.

"No, I'm afraid of guns," she whispers, grasping her collar in fear.

Barry grows tense until in a serious mean stare with his mouth dropping when a vein begins popping in his neck. "Hey, give me the gun…, bullets…, now…, now…, now, hurry!" Barry loudly screams with a neck full of veins listing to his voice echoing.

Sinnamon nervously backs away, looking him up and down, staring at his empty hands, shaking her head and covering her mouth so she doesn't burst into laughter. She fights back her laugh until she uncontrollably bursts into a roar of laughter when rushing back into him and clinging to him, still giggling.

The two ease into the long hallway, and Sinnamon looks back, finding a dark shadow with what looks like a shotgun.

She freezes and, without a word or notion, quietly backs into another room, easing the door shut and locking it.

Barry reaches back for her a few times until turning, finding her gone when piercing eyes through darkness, spotting the long barrel aimed into the hallway though not recognizing what it is. He takes steps back, reaching for the closet door, finding it locked when making a few more quiet advances until easing up on another open door. His eyes glaze over the darkroom, hearing a whiny voice fade in when piercing through the darkness over the gigantic dark room, spotting a man climbing from the window with his back to him, while slowly peeking over his shoulders.

Another dark, tall, manly silhouette turns, standing in another corner with a baseball bat drawn high over his shoulder. He keeps quiet for seconds, then whines like a cat while continually rocking as if ready to hit a home run.

Barry spots the tall figure when his hand slowly rises, spreading wide while beginning to take backward baby steps. "Now, just wait; there must be some mistake..., I'm just visiting my cousin!" Barry nervously yells, thinking it's her crazy ex.

The heavy hitter steps and takes a stealth swing, quickly returning to a batter's stance.

"Now, now..., I'm going to have to ask you to put down," Barry stutters, backing away.

The tall man takes another swift swing and a quick stance to gain a better advantage. "Cousin, huh? Well, if this is all a mistake, then you just freeze and hold it right there until my boy gets in here," the man says in a deep, authoritative, echoing voice.

Barry looks slowly over his shoulder and then quickly back at the man, taking a few unintentional but nervous steps forward with his hands up.

"Come any closer, and it's on, like popcoun (popcorn), kid!" the man screams. "You think you can just come up in hea (here) and take my boy's wife, you, you..., Mr. Big shot, huh? Who do you think you are?"

"Umm..., now that would be an old song from back in the day, but now, look..., there is some kind of a mix-up. I'm family, I tell you..., do you hear me..., family?" Barry nervously says.

"That cat's whipping is nothing compared to what we plan to do," the man loudly says, taking a few steps forward to clear the low-hanging light fixture.

Barry keeps his hands out while backing into the hallway where something catches his eye, causing him to look again when focusing clearly on another dark, short, kid-like silhouette in the doorway of one of the bedrooms with a shiny knife drawn.

"Now, look here..., you just put that down before you get torn out the frame!" Barry confidently says, looking both ways and clearly back down to the two.

Out of nowhere, a powerful feminine scream comes when a door slams shut, and continual scream follows with loud licks like a belt slapping against pure flesh.

The two men burst into a silly giggle hearing Sinnamon screaming with each solid lick, which now sounds more like a leather whip against pure flesh.

Barry makes his way slowly down the long hall. His heart beats faster and he hears it when quickly shaking his head a few times to make the heart-thumping sound disappear.

Another slammed door echoes, and he looks over the first man's shoulder, finding the second in a beam of light, shining possibly from a streetlight.

Barry's head shifts, hearing something thrown against the wall, when catching sight of Sinnamon's limp body sliding down slowly like a wet slab of meat.

Sinnamon fights to stand but staggers as if drunk when falling again.

Barry squints, finding a third body stepping into the hallway, holding a long, shiny object, when a gun registers, and he swiftly turns, sprinting down the long hall in a flash.

The rifle quickly repositions, pointing to the living room, when Barry enters in a blur.

"Fire in the damn hole!" the gun-toting man screams in a thunderous voice, which echoes when the two accomplices fall backward into separate rooms with gun blasts echoing.

Barry hits the floor, chest first, with his arms forward, sliding and rolling, for cover.

Smoke fills the hall, and gun-toting Mr. Canton briefly fades through it, reappearing and taking more slow steps forward. He forcefully advances as if dragging himself until the next step bringing Sinnamon forward, clinging and pleading for him to stop.

Mr. Canton freezes, aiming down the long hall again with buckshot spraying the back of the living room wall, bursting the ninety-inch television screen with the Victorian-style expensive loveseat's ostrich feathers flying and slowly falling to the floor.

Barry swiftly low-crawls behind the leather couch and over near the window.

Mr. Canton loses his balance, hopping while waving the gun with teary eyes.

"Over by the couch!" his best friend screams low-crawling with eyes piercing over his shoulder at Mr. Canton, who struggles to push forward with Sinnamon still clinging onto his boot, crying until stopping and listening.

There is silence, and everyone listens for movement when closing the living room.

Barry quietly low-crawls until rolling over one of the cat's toys, making a strange sound when another shot comes with buckshot spraying over by the couch.

The next barrage of fire misses Barry's exposed foot by inches when he draws it in swiftly.

Barry stays in silent tears, and his vision blurs more when he lightly whines with lips moving in a whisper with eyes piercing up at the ceiling.

A too-familiar sound comes with an empty shell casing bouncing when Barry springs to his feet, running for what he perceives as the garage door when the other tall man sounds off with a steady stream of 9MM rounds.

Mr. Canton fumbles around even quicker for more shells from his leather vest strap.

A loud click rises in Barry's ears when swinging the door open.

The stock realigns, and Sheetrock crumbles as Mr. Canton takes shots along the wall.

Barry slams into the garage door, and the external door bows out and then quickly retracts as Barry's body flies a few feet backward. He grabs the door's handle with adrenaline, pulling a few times but nothing when hearing someone pull on the inner garage's doorknob. Barry's mind shifts, grabbing a long futon pillow, gripping it tight against his body when quickly backing to the wall's far side. His feet shuffle, scrolling across the double-car garage's floor and diving through the large glass window.

Another shot rings out, tearing a massive hole in the Sheetrock while Barry's body is airborne and slamming to the ground. He expressly rolls, bounces, and then swiftly comes to his feet as if never down when increasing in long strides, distancing himself.

"You damn..., you coward! How can you leave a lady in distress?" Mr. Canton screams from the front door with his voice echoing against the valley.

"Screw you!" Barry screams in a hasty response, throwing his head back further and running even faster until the wind makes his narrow head and ears sound aerodynamic.

Sinnamon quietly listens for her ex's footsteps and then cries more until she hears branches breaking with Barry plowing through thick trees and bushes when she goes into quiet laughter.

The men burst into laughter, hearing Barry tearing through a wood fence and stumble over tires, hubcaps, and buckets in a neighbor's backyard. The three rush to the kitchen window, anxiously peeping through the curtains with fast roving eyes.

Mr. Canton gains sight of Barry under a distant lamppost. His boots shuffle, striking out for the back door, firing a few more near precise shots with Barry zigzagging.

Barry finally sees a drop when dropping and rolling out of control until his body stops when springing up and taking off in a stealth run. He finds himself almost out of breath and slows down, taking cover in a thick tree line. He quiets, and his ears become exceedingly receptive while hiding out for about thirty minutes but nervously jumping at the slightest sound of anything, even the wind or insects.

Thirty minutes later, karaoke closes.

Kenneth and Delightful arrive at her house, and she flips the lights on and dim them.

"Help yourself to your favorite," she says, pointing to the bar at the far side of the room. She flips on the television and vanishes down a dim-lit hallway, and seconds later, Ken hears her talking to someone.

Delightful open another door, whispering again to her mother when her two-year-old son turns, yawns, and springs from his grandmother's bed.

The kid staggers into the wall, slipping and falling into the adjacent room when Delightful grabs him, motioning that he's ok. She rubs his forehead and walks toward the living room, stopping midway through the hall. "Now, do you remember what mommy told you about strangers? Well mommy has company, so I need you to stay awake if you don't want anyone to hurt mommy, ok," she says, looking into his sleepy eyes while pulling him into her arms.

The kid nods then lay his head on her shoulder and slightly nods.

Delightful walks into the living room, finding Ken dispensing ice from the chiller.

Ken puts ice in the glasses and sits them on the slate countertop. He looks over his shoulder around the immaculate house and turns again, noticing her there with her son.

"Mr. Ken, this is Donavon," she says, walking up with her heavy son now on her hip.

Ken reaches to shake the kid's hand, and his sleepy eyes buck wide, sticking his tongue out without his mother noticing when placing his head on her shoulder again.

"So…, how old is he?" Ken asks, reaching for the kid's face when his head turns quickly, showing a full rack of sharp, white teeth when Ken's hand draws back fast with his scary smile transforming and quickly subsiding.

"Take a guess…, a terrible two." She looks at Ken, reaching for the remote. She kisses her son, and the kid looks at Ken, licking his tongue out when she looks away.

"I want my daddy!" he moans, half-dazed with eyes dimming when looking at Ken.

Ken pours drinks and hands her a glass which she takes to the head, and he follows.

Delightful eases her son down, but his legs draw in until she leans further, sitting him on the floor. She walks to the gigantic toy chest in the den, coming back with large wooden blocks, casting them over the floor with other toys before walking away.

The kid sits alert, staring at Ken, who sits sneakily looking at his mother's backside with lustful eyes as she walks away. His eyes go from Ken to his mother several times until she vanished then gives him the meanest look, rolling his eyes.

A commercial comes on, and the kid cheerfully comes to life out of nowhere.

"Hey, I'm going to get comfortable," she says, fading into the hallway again.

"You like this toy commercial, huh?" Ken flips the channel a few times again, finding the kid smiling.

The kid cuts his eyes over at Ken, instantly wiping the smile away, and his face transforms into a mean and even meaner look until he looks sinister.

Ken flips the kid a bird (middle finger), takes another sip, when flips the channel in the middle of another toy commercial, and then flips it a few more times. He stops on his favorite late-night comedy show, gazing at the screen when dropping into deep laughter. Ken watches reruns, sometimes blurting out punch lines. He soon looks over, finding the kid with his eyes closed and his head going in circles as if it's going to fall off his shoulders; when the kid's body falls back, jumping up and falling forward.

Ken burst into a peal of crazy, loud laughter, meddlesomely pointing.

The kid's eyes buck, and his face turns fiery red when sitting and staring for seconds, not blinking until his eyes dim, almost when he's falling back again.

Ken eases to the edge of the couch, drawn deeper into the show.

The kid becomes delirious when his eyes cross, and he grows bored each time he becomes coherent, staring at Ken before drifting off.

Ken's laughter grows louder as he gets to the funnier scenes, and each time his loud outburst comes, it scares the kid until one of the deepest outbursts throws him in shock.

The kid's tensed body moves fast with eyes scrambling until his hand grabs a heavy wooden block. He patiently waits, staring at the show, and then moves his lips along with the characters and Ken in anticipation, when springing a heavy block toting hand back, lunging forward with all his strength as Ken's mouth flies open.

The block flies high, descending fast, and lodges into Ken's temple, knocking him against the back of the couch.

Ken stays still for seconds, and the kid slowly peeps over the chair arm, finally seeing Ken's index finger move then other fingers. A little moaning and groaning comes when Ken slowly springs forward. His eyes wander around, finally finding the large, blood-tipped, heavy, wooden, dented block. Ken stands, pulling the block slowly to his face in rage, lightly throwing it up and catching it a few times, then higher the last time, when almost invisibly slinging it at the kid, knocking him back a few feet and in a triple tumble and he's out cold.

Ken eases up, watching for seconds, then rises on the couch's arm, peeping at the kid's frozen body. He watches longer, waiting for a loud outburst or cry but nothing.

The kid finally comes to seconds later, staring at the ceiling, and then finally, he slightly lifts his head, shaking off the pain in a dizzy smile. He sits, looking over his shoulder with his face quickly transforming into horror until smiling. The kid shakes off more pain, and his body flexes like a gymnast when dashing for the kitchen.

Ken bends, looking toward the counter's edge where the kid vanished. He hears many things thrown about, cranked, turned off, and on until there's total silence.

Instantly, he hears tiny feet slapping against the terrazzo floor as the kid draws near fast until the sound fades, then disappears.

Ken tiptoes, easing up on the counter's edge. He kneels, peeps around the counter's corner while slowly advancing, then turns at the next corner and doesn't see the kid. He spots a shadow when a metal bat comes down hard across the top of his head.

Ken cocks his head dizzily, smiling when hearing birds chirping. He quickly rises, and the sound cuts short when dropping like putty and going out again. He comes to within minutes and sits, shaking off the devastating pain while fighting to stand, when the kid gives him another hard whack, forcing him into a roll and stopping in the living room. Ken stays out even longer and then comes to, hearing a loud motor revving. He staggers around the island again, then squints, still dazed and stuck on stupid, only to find the kid with an auto pitcher tight in his hand.

The kid leans forward, aligning the pitcher when running to the back and quickly aligning it toward Ken. He hits the auto button, holding the barrel tight while his eyes anxiously wander, gasping for air in excitement when fiddling for the foot pedal.

Ken's eyes buck and his mind tells him to move, but his body tenses, trying to duck, when balls shoot at fast intervals.

The kid precisely targets hitting each of Ken's anticipated slow and drunken moves.

Ken ducks with the tenth ball, hitting him in the head, and he falls back, quickly coming to his feet.

The kid lunges forward, giving chases until vanishing and reappearing in the other section of the kitchen, sticking out his tongue.

Ken turns quickly, rushing toward the kid, finding hundreds of marbles strewn over the floor when his big feet go wild as he comes into a few moves, making him look like he's doing the robot when the kid hits a musical toy and the song' Dancing machine' blares with Ken dancing for minutes. His momentum slows when he comes to a clear floor, and his hands come up begging for mercy when spotting the kid with a Super Soaker filled with some bubbly solution.

The kid sprays Ken's eyes and then quickly soaks the floor.

Ken takes one precise step and begins dancing with the song Dancing machine on again until he falls flat on his back. He continually tries getting up while watching the kid through burning eyes as the kid rushes, trying to reload the pitcher. Ken low-crawls exceptionally fast until finally slipping out of the slippery solution and coming up on the kid by surprise. His hand drapes over the kid's mouth, sneakily looking around while thinking of what to do next with an evil stare. He rushes to the bar, grabbing the oversized bottle of lemon juice, vigorously shaking it when popping off the top with his mouth when the kid bites down on his hand.

Ken's mouth drops open, and he quietly dances with his mouth wide while grabbing the kid at the collar, finding his mouth wide open and about to scream when filling it and dropping the kid to his feet.

The kid stabilizes, shakes drastically, and then stops and continually shakes for seconds. Before long, he looks like he's in the matrix and doing the robot with added steps. The kid freezes and starts shaking like crazy again when accidentally gulping and downing another swallow vice spitting it out when going through the routine again.

The kid leans forward in slow motion to run, and Ken grabs him by the back of his shirt, stretching the shirt until it looks like he's grown a few feet until releasing him.

The kid stealthily comes up in the hallway, looking back and screaming, hearing his mother's door open when she drifts back into the hallway.

Ken rushes down the hall and sees her when coming upon the kid, grabbing him at the arm, tugging, and then pulling him into his arms as if playing.

Delightful grabs her son, feeling his little heart beating as if it were about to burst. "What did I tell you about playing too rough?" She guides him by his shoulder, walks him into the living room, and stops at the door with eyes bucked wide. "You might as well march your little-self right in there and clean all of it up this minute, young man!"

The kid rushes, cleaning up most of the mess, and then jumps on her lap, reaching for hard-bottom shoes on the table with a big smile when cutting cunning eyes over at Ken.

Delightful leans over, finally giving in, and then sits watching him try and put the shoe on. After a few more tries, Delightful leans forward, helping, then places the other shoe on the table. "No..., on second thought, you're getting ready for bed in a few, mister!" she says, pushing the other shoe away from him.

Ken looks down at the kid's cheery face, which instantly transforms into that of a red scaly devil when doing a double-take.

"Whoa! Look at the time..., look at the time," he says, looking at his watch and tapping the watch face.

"Are you sure you have to leave, sweetie? He'll be asleep soon," she playfully pouts, leaning into Ken, whispering naughty words when backing away, smiling.

Ken thinks of hot sex, when smiling then looks down at the kid, who's fully awake, without a drop of sleep in sight.

The kid's eyes intentionally buck so hard that they appear as if they're about to burst. "Really..., I better get going," he says. "Maybe some other time." Ken looks at the kid again, then stands, pulling out the cabbie's number and then his phone.

Delightful walks him to the door, staring back at the television while smiling at a joke from her favorite comedian.

The kid pulls from his mother, grabs her leg, and then let's go instantly.

Ken says a few words to the cabbie and then stutters when the concrete-feeling shoe drives two good, quick whacks into his shins before Ken can move when the third comes and kind off peels off.

Delightful cuts the last giggle short, finally registering the second thump then light third when seeing the third retracting and sounding like a hammer against wood when snatching him back fast. "That is not nice! Now apologize," she says, looking up at Ken, whose mouth is torn wide open in excruciating pain with tears pouring down like a waterfall.

Greg stands at the couple's apartment door on the other side of town, waiting for his girlfriend to open the door.

Greg and the couple walk into the foyer, where Greg and the girl stand mysteriously staring at each other for minutes.

The boyfriend stands wasted, and by now, he's pissed at his girlfriend, but finally looks at her, and she tries secretly motioning to him to get rid of Greg, but he looks away, swings snacks and movies back and forth in a bag until staring dumbfounded.

Greg turns, looking out the window when the girlfriend steps on her boyfriend's toe, heavily easing onto it until his face frowns.

She smiles, easing off her weight, running a hand over her face when turning, finding Greg watching. "Ugh!" she screams, storming out, and slamming the door. She stands listening and anticipating the door opening when peeping from time to time.

Her boyfriend sways, then take off, staggers upstairs, hugging the toilet bowl for minutes, dry heaving.

Greg eases onto the couch, taking his shoes off, wiggling toes through worn-down socks until the big toe pops out.

The girlfriend waits a few more minutes and then looks back at the door, pissed.

Greg jumps to his feet, grabs the bag, scatters snacks over the table, and then rushes into the kitchen, grabbing a few cups of ice and bowls. He has the perfect, full-scale snack layout within seconds with a woman's touch.

The girlfriend stands a little longer with teary eyes, then looks back at the door, turning away and heading for her car. She climbs inside, crying until her fingers ease to the radio, tuning the dial, then turning down the volume.

A sad song ends, and another comes with a woman singing about how she plans to take another woman's man and the intimate things she wants to do, but the girlfriend pays the words no mind until registering one catchy word when turning up the volume.

She gets a hold of herself, finally catching more distasteful words when reaching for her cell, calling her best friend, and telling her the questionable things that transpired.

Her girlfriend listens more, and then out of nowhere, she asks who's singing in the background, but the girlfriend ignores her, talking more about the dreadful night.

'What! Who does that, girl?" her friend asks when asking about the song again. The girlfriend initially thinks it's a woman singing until realizing it is a high-pitch man's voice and freezes.

She sits in deep thought with her girlfriend's voice falling on deaf ears and sounding like bees when frowning. "Ooh..., gross!" She says out of the blue, flipping the radio off.

The girlfriend grows quiet in deep thought. "Girl, are you crazy..., go fight for your man! He could have him bent over right now with nothing on but a hardhat and combat boots! He could be clocking in for a full night's shift, or even worse, preparing to toss his salad or have his tossed," the girlfriend says disgustingly.

The girlfriend stares at the bedroom window, where the lights instantly go out when her boyfriend closes the bathroom door again, dropping to the floor, dry heaving.

The guy's girlfriend feverishly drops the phone with hands on her chest. She soon hears her girlfriend screaming, but her body goes numb when her mouth drops open, and hands feverishly fight for the handle, breaking out in a crazy run and frantic scream.

Greg turns down the television, hearing the second muffled scream, looking over his shoulder toward the window and staring back at the cozy fireplace while smiling.

The girlfriend's hands frantically bang until quickly looking down for the jiggling noise, realizing she has keys when the door flies open. She stumbles inside, looking upstairs, finding lights fading into the room as her boyfriend walks out of the bathroom.

"Great! I see you got the movie started," she says, panicking until looking up to find her boyfriend at the top step and descending in a heavy stagger with slow steps.

"Yeah, I got it all laid out right here," Greg femininely says, pointing to the spread.

"Yeah, I see..., gummies, drinks, and hotdogs, wow, but where's the popcorn?" she asks when her mouth unknowingly drops open with eyes slightly bulging when finding Greg's wallet at the table's edge, with the big, worn-down, leather, condom-print.

"Popcorn? What popcorn? Do you see any freakin' popcorn?" Greg says sarcastically.

"No…, not even, but you got this room smelling like cheese popcorn!" She frowns with eyes gazing at the condom-printed wallet again when taking deep swallows.

"What?" He looks down and then surprisingly gazes over his frayed sock with his corpulent toe sticking out.

The girlfriend looks at her boyfriend mean and then walks up to Greg, pissed. "Yeah, I know…, don't ask and don't tell, but you make it too obvious to even bother," she says, rocking with her fists balled tight. "Pack it up and roll the hell out, Jack Daddy from the Broke Back Mountain movie!"

Greg looks at her boyfriend, who shrugs his shoulders with clueless dimming eyes.

"She's right, Jack…, I mean, dude…, you better get going, man, before she turns this joint out!" Her boyfriend walks over to the dining room table. "Here, I'll call you a cab." He reaches for the phone near the kitchen wall.

"Uh, uh…, naw…, see…, you brought me here, so take me back to get my truck."

"This will be swell for a fare." The boyfriend reaches in his wallet, pulling out singles before opening the door.

"Jack-Ass!" Greg screams slipping into his shoes and walking out.

CHAPTER EIGHT

Back in the woods and not too far from Sinnamon's house, Barry hears a scream, and then something hits the ground hard, shuffling fast when Barry springs up, coming up to top speed.

Automatic gunfire rings out with the shooter in a standing prone position, engulfed in gun smoke, when more rounds spray the tree Barry just passed.

"Woooweee!" Barry nervously murmurs, running toward the road faster until at a high incline, with no footing, legs flapping fast when airborne and lowering like a plane coming in for a landing. He hits the ground hard and quickly veers to the side of the road, spotting headlights while looking over his shoulder. Barry throws out a hand quick as if thumbing when almost swerving into the path of a quick swerving taxi while keeping an eye glued on the colorful yellow hood. He high-steps, picking up speed until paralleling the now slower-moving taxi when he reaches for the door as the taxi barely passes, keeping his pace until he slips the back door open, breathing heavily.

The foreign, heavyset cabbie looks back, slamming on brakes, flinging Barry past the car, and sending him stumbling before tripping and rolling to the side of the road.

The cabbie shifts to park, jumping from the cab rendering assistance.

Barry springs up, sitting and quickly shaking off the pain of his wrist when looking up, finding the cabbie with a hand extended when grabbing it and quickly coming up. He limps to the back door as the cabbie runs to the driver's side.

The cabbie leans, looking at Barry slowly climbing inside, in severe pain.

"Naval base..., pronto"!" Barry screams with eyes instantly floating out the back window.

Out of nowhere, distant voices rise with profanity when the cabbie climbs inside, looking back at Barry fast waving hand, motioning him to go.

"What's wrong with you..., my friend? You caused me to throw you, so you do not sue, ok? You need help..., I take you to the doctor!" he nervously says. "You know, truck? Wooo..., woo!" he says, motioning an index finger inches from the roof, in circles replicating an ambulance's siren and lights.

"Go! Go! Go!" Barry screams again with fast, wandering eyes frequently over his shoulder.

Profanity grows louder when the cabbie and Barry grow silent, still looking back until seeing gun-toting Mr. Canton lunging high off a low cliff as if floating in slow motion until touching down and running out into the middle of the road.

Mr. Canton screams louder, running toward the taxi with the gun high over his head until slowing and looking back, hearing a high-speed car slamming on brakes. "

"Go! Go! Go!" Barry repeatedly screams with fast, wandering eyes over his shoulder, banging hard on the cabbie's thick arm on the front seat backrest.

Another man lunges high off the same cliff, replicating Mr. Canton's approach when running out into the middle of the road.

The unidentified car floors the gas, kicking up dust in a turn, and heavily weaving until sliding sideways when pulling up beside Mr. Canton, who's still in a standing prone position.

"Go! Go! Go!" Barry repeatedly screams with fast, wandering eyes still over his shoulder when heavily pushing the cabbie by his shoulder, finding him frozen in shock.

Mr. Canton takes a steady aim, blasting through the taxi's 'No Vacancy' roof sign when the cabbie comes out of shock, screaming with Barry screaming even louder.

The cabbie slams the door with knees almost to his chest fast, slamming his fat foot down with tires spinning, and burning deep rubber across the asphalt until swerving. "No! No! Look..., look..., this is not good for me, my friend..., not good!" He quickly looks over his shoulder at Barry and then back at the road, finding the car gaining fast when taking the first sharp curb, trying to shake the car when it closes in even faster.

The chase car comes up on the taxi's bumper, slamming into it a few times when the cabbie's eyes go into the rear mirror, side mirror, and then back to the road and yellow then red dangerously curvy road signs.

The cabbie makes all ten of the sharp curves drenched in sweat with beads of sweat on his face when the road straightens, giving it all that the car has when the chase car comes in close for another ram. The cabbie hangs a hard turn, running into someone's yard, tearing up their fresh sod, neat landscape, and the water fountain with him and Barry screaming.

The chase car swings around fast, making a quick, high squealing doughnut turn in the road, gunning the engine, cutting through another section of the same yard, demolishing the rest of the landscaping with the driver's head going left-to-right, trying to gain his bearings when spotting the cabbie coming out on the other side of the house.

The cabbie and Barry scream, heading toward the road when swerving back into the street, leveling out on the straightaway.

Tires squeal as the chase car turns the corner, sideswiping several parked cars with all heads looking back, finding sparks blazing while sideswiping several more and coming up to top speed when finally veering off.

Several rounds ring out, hitting the taxi's trunk when the cabbie and Barry scream.

The cab veers off the main stretch of a two-lane road, plowing through the woods.

Secondary gunfire accidentally hits the rear bumper of a parked car, piercing the gas tank and causing an explosion with a fireball, leaving the car engulfed in flames until the mushroom cloud.

The chase car veers off into a marshy patch of road, stuck until expressly rocking from the loud groaning engine, flinging mud over other cars.

The cabbie continually tears through several more small trees and bushes then fights the wheel hard until veering, then springing forward from a slight slope, slamming almost perfectly onto the road when heavily swerving. He quickly levels out on the straightway, screaming for joy along with Barry. He anxiously fights for the radio, nervously keying up the mic with eyes bucked wide and his mouth wide open, swerving hard when almost T-boning a vehicle when running a stop sign. "Helpa, Helpa. . . ! Send police quickly…, shots fired, shots fired!

Highway 401, northbound in the damn middle lane!" he senselessly screams.

The dispatcher sits cheerfully polishing her nails while talking on her cell with her boyfriend, who has her heated and in another world with a mouthful of familiar lies.

"Do you hear me, you crazy lady?" he screams with eyes nervously in the rearview. "Helpa, Helpa. . .! Send police quickly..., shots fired, shots fired, police officer down, robbery in progress, 187, 211, 411, 911, domestic violence, hog chitterling, collard greens and ham hocks on sale 10 pounds for three cents..., Highway 401 northbound!" he screams again.

The dispatcher puts her caller on hold. "Now you listen here..., Hauzus! I done (already) told you now! You better learn proper radio codes..., now stop bothering me with this nonsense! Shoot! Always playing like you ain't got no sense!" She turns down the volume with the rest of his cries falling on deaf ears when returning to her call.

Hauzus makes one last turn, unknowingly speeding toward a cop car tucked neatly behind a billboard. His hand quickly flips through channels with eyes gazing into the rearview.

The cop leans forward with beady eyes that instantly buck, with his mouth dropping open in disbelief. His eyes follow the taxi past the hood when breaking his shocking stare, spilling hot coffee and doughnuts between his legs. He swiftly flips on the siren and lights with widening eyes, screaming when his butt begins burning. He humps fast, fighting for the door handle until hard on the lever when the door flies open, and he jumps out, dancing around in low-cut cowboy boots until the heat subsides. He jumps back in quickly, kicking up a cloud of dust when speeding away.

The chase vehicle slings around the steep curve at ninety mph, then spins across the grass on the other side of the street. It swerves back onto the road, slowing when the passenger slams his fist on the driver's knee, seeing blue lights ahead and pulling away. Within minutes, the chase car comes up over another hill, and the passenger points when the driver pulls over. He cuts off the lights and then backs up, turning around.

The siren blares from a distance until the cop floors the pedal, closing in faster and calling out one visible tag number.

The cabbie finally registers the bright blue lights closing when releasing the wheel, joyfully clapping when Barry throws up a victory fist. The cabbie claps harder, swerving and almost losing control when grabbing the steering wheel in a tight grip.

Their eyes stay in the back window, watching blue lights until hearing the elevating siren when the cop's headlights fade below the trunk.

The cop unlatches his shotgun, fiddling a little more before reaching for his radio. He looks up and then down, calling out another single unclear letter from the mud-covered tag again.

The taxi driver's foot anxiously pats the floorboard until his door shoots open, and he anxiously runs to the cruiser so fast that his boot taps spark.

The cop's eyes stay down, and before he can look up, his car sways from side to side from the heavyset cabbie pulling on the passenger door handle until breaking it off.

The officer jumps out with his sidearm drawn and pointing over the roof with the dot from the laser almost aligned in the middle of the man's forehead.

"Hold it right there, red dot or feather!" the racist officer senselessly screams, lifting and dropping each leg a few times to get his drawers un-bunched until grabbing a handful of sticky drawers and tugging.

"Look..., someone...," the cabbie begins to say when cut off.

"No..., now..., you look! I'm the one who's going to be doing all the yapping (talking), so you just shut your chicken pie hole. One more word, and I'll hold you in contempt!"

The cabbie listens to harsh words with a concerned frown that turns into a confused stare thinking of the word 'contempt.'

Barry peeps over the headrest, finding the cop tugging at the seat of his pants when cracking the window. "Doo-doo!" Barry intentionally yells, dropping down fast.

The officer eases toward the hood. "Get on up to the front and spread em' wide, Buddy!" The nervous officer closely watches the cabbie with curious eyes glued on the car when seeing the top of Barry's head slouch again. He walks wide-legged, fast, grabbing another handful of drawers. The officer quickly maneuvers, high-stepping when cuffing the cabbie, and shoves him forward onto the hood, sneakily looking back over his shoulder. "Tell your buddy to show me some hands and ease out of the car on the driver's side, slowly, before I peel your cap!" the officer excitedly screams when backing down.

Barry obeys, coming out slowly and backing as directed until easing next to the cabbie, who now looks different from his frazzled hair after being slung into the hood.

The officer holds the gun on them, quickly exchanging his handgun for his Taser when slamming Barry forward and onto the hood.

Barry and the cabbie nervously stare eye-to-eye when the cabbie's face frowns, whispering obscenity to Barry, who continually shakes his head, pissed.

The heavyset officer leans into Barry's butt, keeping him in place while trying to free the other cuffs at the back of his wide belt loop, gently then heavily grinding while continually attempting to reach again.

A faint, then loud ring rises with the officer slightly backing off but still close, answering his cellphone on the second ring and he's in deep laughter within seconds.

Barry's eyes buck, intimidated from the light grinding when feeling him hard on him again when his face frowns in disgust with eyes bucked when the officer unintentionally humps a few times with his plump belly laying on Barry's butt, keeping them closer.

The cabbie cuts his head back when Barry's head shifts forward a few times. His eyes fill with tears, and his stomach jumps each time he looks at the officer humping in laughter, staying in tears, and can't stop laughing each time he looks.

The officer draws quiet, listening closely to the deep manly voice talking. "Yeah…, yeah, that's me, off Ravey Road!" the officer responds in deep laughter. "Oh? You don't say…, do you?" he responds in a burst of even deeper laughter, fumbling and trying to adjust the phone to his ear when it slides down his sweaty face, accidentally activating the speaker.

The conversation continues with loud laughter when the officer begins swishing his wide butt, balancing when sticking one leg out and holding it there, straining. He rests his foot, then throws out the other leg holding it out, straining until vigorously shaking a leg back and forth as if in a seizure when letting out a long, trembling, obnoxious and endless fart.

Barry and the cabbie's eyes close tight, and their faces transform into frowns from the long lingering and awful smell.

"Yeah, I saw your brother the other night up in JB's with those crazy-tail colors on..., up in there looking like a damn clown!" Mr. Canton says.

The cop throws his head back and bursts into tears of laughter, with his belly shaking faster when humping harder, and fumbling to take the phone off speaker.

"But forget all that," Mr. Canton says. "I'm turning around now and coming back up there for those...,"

Barry and the cabbie hear the manly voice say before the speaker shuts off.

Barry and the cabbie's eyes buck, knowing he's referring to them, when Barry jerks upward fast, head-butting the officer and knocking him back into the taxi's trunk and to the ground when wrestling for the Taser while holding his gun in his holster.

For what seems like minutes, the two wrestle, screaming and hollering until a little old woman pulls up out of nowhere, stopping with keen eyes scrolling over each of them until staring wide-eyed at the two grown men going to it as if they're having sex. She shakes her head in disappointment, staring at the giggling, teary-eyed cabbie and then down at the two again. "Get a freakin' hotel room!" she screams, peeling rubber with a tight fist raised high, leaving them in a thick black cloud of smoke that slowly drips into the light wind.

The two continue wrestling, unable to see one another until the officer's head appears in a clear patch when Barry head-butts him, knocking him out.

Barry staggers upward and then around a bit until falling onto the cop's car and immediately springs up, getting the keys and un-cuffing the cabbie.

The two run around quick, patting themselves down and checking that they had not dropped anything when jumping in the taxi and speeding off.

The cop lay as still as a board until a slow finger move. His shiny padded leather shoes flop slowly from side to side when coming up slow, dizzily shaking when jumping up just before the cab dips down a wide loop under-path, coming up on a busy intersection. "Halta! Halta!" the cop senselessly screams, taking a steady aim at bumper-to-bumper traffic when several double vision shots spark off a metal part of the bridge, missing the shot.

There is total silence in the taxi, but the cabbie continually frowns, staring into the backseat through the rearview from time to time or looking slightly over his shoulder.

Barry sits quietly looking around until his eyes glisten from looking through the window, down from the mountain, finding naval vessels at the seaside of the base.

Twenty minutes pass. "Here, here...! Drop me off in housing," Barry says, hoping to deceive the driver from thinking he's military when the back door flies open. Barry reaches deep in his pockets, peeling off a few hundred, bringing a huge smile back on the cabbie's face.

The cabbie thanks him, cheerfully waving when pulling off. "Good riddance, and I hope never to see you again!" The cabbie shakes his head.

Barry walks toward the gated townhouses, ducking across the street and charging for the main gate, when spotting the taxi's taillights fading around the corner.

Seconds later, the cabbie gets a call about a relative being in the hospital when merging into traffic. The cabbie comes up on the main road speeding, and blue light flashes with the cabbie pulling over, watching a young cop sitting for seconds before approaching.

One of Mr. Canton's hired cops gets information on Barry's drop from the cabbie, releasing him and heading down by the naval base's main gate, patrolling.

Minutes later, the Chief of Police pulls up to one of many of Mr. Canton's hired cops with Mr. Canton riding shotgun, locked and loaded.

The cabbie arrives at the hospital minutes later, finding his family in tears. He stands in the hallway, talking to his father before walking into the room, finding his cousin lying in bed with a fresh, plastic-bag-covered Jheri curl. He finds the cousin's wife and kids sitting against the wall with grease-spotted turbans on their heads while chuckling. He relaxes, and his eyes begin nervously wandering over all the warning signs until noticing the oxygen bottle near his cousin's head with all the warning signs to 'Keep out of reach of grease and oils.' The cabbie grows fidgety, and his eyes grow wide when nervously backing into the hallway in fear of an explosion.

His father eventually eases into the hallway alongside him, trying to get him back in until dragging him when they break out into a brawl for minutes until the cabbie breaks free. He takes deep breaths with wide eyes, still backing down fast when springing down the hall wide-legged. He looks back once, slowing to turn the corner, then rushes to the parking lot, jumping in his taxi. He sits for minutes, staring at the hospital, when suddenly feeling tremors, not knowing it's from a demolition down the street when breaking out into a scream with tears falling when skidding wheels and speeding off.

An hour later, Mr. Canton's driver turns the stretch limousine into the strip club lot. He goes to the other side, stretching out Mr. Canton's long, thin, mink coat.

Mr. Canton puts one arm in, and the man helps him with the other when pointy-toed shoes step onto the curve. He stops when halfway up the sidewalk, wanting to be noticed when stepping off again and initiating his pimp strut.

In Port Copan Retaunas, Keyonton and his lawyer stand outside his attorney's car in a rough neighborhood, cautiously looking around. They stand for minutes until his nervous attorney pulls a slip of paper out, and they step off together. They walk several blocks and then turn the corner, finding a woman with her back to them while backing out of the door of a dilapidated row house.

The woman slowly turns, hearing slow footsteps while looking toward them and walking up to the rusty sidewalk gate.

Keyonton and his attorney shield disguised faces, moving further from the light post, alongside a tree, blocking the light. They peep to see if she's indeed the woman they are looking for when Keyonton squints, barely confirming that she's the one from the show when turning away quickly and looking at the ground.

The woman stands at the gate longer in deep thought, then looks down, counting a handful of coins before heading in the opposite direction.

The attorney stares at a few sheets of paper while Keyonton straightens his fake mustache, rushing up to the door, gently knocking.

"Who is it?" a frail voice soon answers.

"An attorney from Wellington, Jackson, & Chandler, ma'am. I'm looking for a Ms. Levington," the attorney falsely claims when naming Ms. Levington's attorney's firm.

The woman's great-grandmother opens the door, peeping out through coke-bottle glasses, which leaves two spotlight prints on Keyonton's jacket from the 100-watt bulbs burning in the ceiling from behind her.

Keyonton's eyes go over her shoulder, staring at what looks like a nude, big, square-booty girl standing in the back room and about to back out when distracted when his chest heats up fast. He sniffs, smelling smoke, and looks down quick, finding two ashy-looking stained circles in his lightly smoke-smelling coat. "Whoa! Mama!" Keyonton says, shielding the reflective glare with his hand, which he pulls back fast, from the heat and seeing his fingers smoking. He quickly steps to one side, cutting his eyes over at his attorney, who is on tiptoes, still trying to keep an eye on the woman.

"Hot Dayum!" Keyonton says, covering his eyes when finally staring into the old woman's enormous eyeballs that are finally staring back. "I mean..., ah, ah, ah..., excuse me..., I mean Hotdamuline..., I was referring to my prescription that I forgot to take today," Keyonton says in another focused stare. "Well, yes, ma'am, I'm Mr. Jackson with Wellington, Jackson, & Chandler..., I'm looking for Ms. Levington."

"What? Well hell..., you must have just missed her. You had to have seen her because I thought you were her knocking."

"That was her?" Keyonton slightly turns, winking to the attorney.

The nosey old woman looks at him without making complete eye contact. "Well, anyway..., what's this all about? Did you bring the check for the big suit?" she asks, curiously staring with her head in a slow up and down nod when he smiles, instantly flinging the door open and jumping on him and clinging to him like a cat.

Keyonton wrestles with her, trying to loosen her grip, then uses all his strength to push her back inside with her sliding backward in filthy white socks. He shoves her away one last time, and she slides across the room, fading until she slams into the wall. He leans back, proudly brushing his clean threads (clothes) down, then slowly looking up, finding her barreling down on him again.

The old woman leaps when in the middle of the floor, several feet away.

Keyonton's eyes grow wide, snatching the doorknob fast and leaving just a crease in the opening when she slams into it, vibrating the house with a low, painfully whining voice fizzling out, with the breath knocked out of her, leaving her snoring.

"What are we waiting for?" Keyonton says, jumping from the porch.

The attorney takes off running and passing him, but Keyonton catches up at the next corner. He leaps, coming up and standing on a bench, looking over a few heads until spotting the woman when she darts out in front of a couple.

The woman begins happily skipping as if she's a kid until making a few crazy leg moves and jumping in squares as if playing hopscotch.

The two rush up on the woman in stealth mode, dropping back, so they don't spook her when ducking into several corners and alleys while staying well-hidden. They soon take their time, stopping along the way to ensure their disguises remain intact.

The woman stops at one corner and seems fidgety when looking around before vanishing into a dark alley.

Keyonton and the attorney walk past the alley with eyes scrolling in and around, when doubling back fast and checking out the alley.

The attorney rushes up, drifting into the alley first, and they maintain a reasonable distance. He turns the next corner, finding a group of men hanging out when hearing bird calls and seeing the woman a ways off. He looks down fast, fearfully backing up when looking around the corner unnoticed, when motioning Keyonton to hurry.

They ease up on the corner again and peep before stepping deeper into the alley.

"Follow my actions," Keyonton says, pushing off fast and playfully staggering when taking two fake drunken steps forward and one back when heavily swaying.

The men freeze, hearing Keyonton bump into a trashcan when turning slowly, finding the dark silhouette along the dark wall.

Keyonton looks back for his attorney, who is further behind than he thinks, so he slows, looking ahead while waiting for him to catch up.

Without warning, the attorney finally bumps into Keyonton seconds later.

Keyonton turns with a long string of thick saliva drooling, finding the attorney looking down until finally looking up.

"Dayum!" the attorney screams, backing up and quickly taking another look.

Keyonton wipes and advances toward him with saliva still dripping from his dingy gloves when the attorney backs faster, losing his balance and tumbling over a trashcan.

The attorney comes up fast, stumbling again and ramming his head into another trashcan while trying to stand when falling to the ground.

The men cautiously watch, breaking out in a burst of deep, uncontrollable laughter that trickles off when the leader looks at his watch, motioning his crew away.

Keyonton hears a commotion and turns back quickly, cutting his eye over to where the men were standing, finding them with their backs to him, and turning the corner. He wipes his hand on a cardboard box, pulling the attorney up and into him by his collar.

"Aii!" the attorney screams, furiously swinging to keep Keyonton's wet, snot, and saliva-gloved hand back until finally calming down when leaning forward to stand. "Great call!"

Keyonton looks back, finding the attorney backing away fast.

They slightly stagger into one another, then step off, picking up their pace until in a steady jog. The two reach the next intersection, finding the street empty, but the attorney quickly points when spotting movement through the window of an abandoned building.

The attorney turns, squinting when finding the woman, creeping up a set of stairs and vanishing through rusty towering doors. "Here," the attorney whispers, pointing to steps leading to the tall, war-torn doors when they rush inside a foyer.

A squeaky door soon opens with a thick cloud of smoke floating out and over them. "Welcome to the Jungle!" the huge, mean man says, motioning for arms to come up.

Keyonton and the attorney's eyes slowly drop together, stepping forward with slow rising arms when the man advances, patting them down and pointing them to the narrow, worn-down staircase.

The two climb the questionably supported steps with a few missing steps, slowing peeping inside before walking in and around for minutes on the first, second, and third floors. They enter the fourth, walking through half the room, finding the woman sitting on a dirty, spring-busted couch when nervously approaching.

The woman lies there, not flinching but doped up, with her mouth heavily twisted.

The two ease up on the couch, slowly sitting on each side, gazing at her.

"Ms. Levington?" the attorney asks when her head turns slowly, and it takes almost a minute before, she's gazes at him, frowning while zoned out of her mind.

"Shit! Now we're stuck here for thirty minutes to an hour before she comes around," Keyonton says, disgusted when looking at his watch. He waits patiently and rechecks his watch when she moves a little more, with her head slumping over after thirty minutes.

"Ms. Levington?" the attorney asks again with wandering eyes when seeing others float into the room and walk off a distance.

Ms. Levington sits with eyeballs slowly rolling around until staring at the dirty floor, dazed. She lifts her head, but her body stays exceptionally numb. "Whoo, waanaano?" she finally answers in a long, slurred voice, with saliva drooling from the corner of white lips.

"Ma'am..., Mr. Jackson with Thompson, James & Collier," Keyonton says, lying with his head slightly turned and his hat crooked, hiding his face and lopsided mustache.

"Ayn (and)! Youz (You) clownz (clowns) beaaaa (better) haaa (have) mmmm (come) doooow (down) heeea (here) tauuu (to) brrrrriii (bring) miiii(me my) mooony (money)," she says, in a longer slurred speech with even worse twisted lips.

"What did she say?" the attorney whispers with eyes glued on Keyonton with a hand quickly coming up to his mustache, letting him know it's crooked. "We'll never get anywhere with her talking that damn ying-yang," the attorney says, giggling yet pissed.

'She said..., you clowns better have come down here to bring her money,' Keyonton slowly recites.

The attorney does a double-take with a confused stare. "Really? How do you suppose she said that exact thing? I couldn't make out one damn word," the attorney whispers, looking into Ms. Levington's deceased-looking face.

Ms. Levington sniffs, slowly coming back around more, and without warning, she sits then leans, spitting on the dirt-covered floor.

Her drool continually stretches until it slowly hits the floor when she goes side to side, trying to break off the string. Her eyes go to their feet, cutting her head to one side, eye to eye with the attorney, then back at Keyonton when he looks away quickly. Her head flings back to the attorney, eye to eye with him, and focused without blinking. "Torn (turn) yo (your) head..., I said to torn (turn) yo (your) damn haid (head)!" she embarrassingly screams, trying to break the string of saliva with a few more quick headshakes. She cuts her eyes back at Keyonton, finding him still looking away, then at the attorney when he looks away fast. She grabs the string at her nose, pinching and heavily slinging it forward and onto the bare leg of a man passing by who jumps, running off screaming and dragging his leg like he's shot.

The attorney leans, reaching deep in his coat pocket for the altered legal paperwork, which has the signature block cut out with an authentic document on top, a fake one on the bottom, and a duplicate under that document. He stares at the paper for seconds and carefully aligns it by aligning the signature block appropriately. "Look, ma'am, I know you're not in a position to talk right now, but I need you to listen to me. We received your attorney's offer for one-point-seven million. Still, we will offer you an on-the-spot, one-time counteroffer for two thousand right now and one-point-five million in this contract without royalties," the attorney nervously says, looking at a few shady characters when sidetracked and screwing up the plan when mixing words with Keyonton nervously cringing.

"Now..., you and your attorney can fight us on this, but we will drag it out in court for four to five years. With this kind of money, you can build many crack houses and get high every day. I think this is better than what you'll get in court because there was a point when you two were on stage whispering, which is room for reasonable doubt. After all, Mr. Worthington claims you agreed to the whole plot. Look, sign here, and here's two thousand," he says, flashing the thick bundle of the twenties until stuffing it back in his jacket when seeing a few nosey folks stopping in their tracks like statues with glistening eyes.

Ms. Levington sits up, trying to stand when Keyonton's eyes quickly drift down to her bottom, which is flat as a flitter and nothing close to what he saw on stage.

"Mama Mia! I will be, damn! Woman, what happened to your butt? Oh, never mind," Keyonton says with eyes finally drifting to the dirty pipe in her hand. He looks in her other hand, finding another dirty crack pipe filled with dirt. "Stem fast diet, huh?" Keyonton shakes his head. "I don't know why they don't just call it ASS, since that's the first thing to go, and actually, it has nothing to do with the crack." He giggles.

The attorney laughs and becomes nervous, finding more shady characters gathering like zombies with some shyly whispering and pointing to them. His eyes feverishly wander around more when slouching beside Ms. Levington, quickly and nervously explaining the contract so fast that it no longer sounds like English or any other language. He finally takes a deep breath, sweating when pointing out the large sums, confirming she'll get 1.5 million later and two thousand on the spot.

Ms. Levington crossed eyes slowly follow his fingers until stale when staring at the dollar signs when a languid smile comes. "I got that sucker, didn't I? I bet he'll never touch another fake butt as big as mine was that night," she says, slurring when giggling.

Keyonton gathers a tight fist until eye to eye with the attorney's disapproving head.

Ms. Levington staggers to stand but drops down, reaching for the pen; the attorney is still holding out but misses several times until in a stale stare and concentrating before the last try. "Yeah!" she screams, smiling with hands over her head, cheering herself up.

Keyonton nervously looks around, quickly quieting her.

A loud noise rises outside when a two-ton truck moves a half-filled dumpster to another side of the building to clean debris from the roof.

The attorney guides Ms. Levington's hand to where he wants her to sign and rushes her scribbling. "Good enough," the attorney says, slipping her two thousand and folding the actual agreement for fifty thousand and the on-the-spot dollars she has signed, quickly slipping it in an envelope and passing it to her.

Keyonton and the attorney spring up simultaneously, walking fast. They rush for the stairs, looking back into the zombie-filled room and the woman slowly fading into the thick smoke, both feeling a light buzz. He turns, accidentally bumping into a tall, stoned-out man's chest, and his fake mustache sticks to the wool sweater when they stop and surprisingly stares at the mustache.

The man's hands slowly come up with curious eyes, pulling the mustache off when looking at Keyonton with his face transforming into a bright smile.

The attorney looks back at the group of men in the corner, noticing one patting the other man in the chest with the back of his hand when a posse of about ten slowly lunges forward.

"Keyonton Worthington! Well, I'll be damn! If it isn't the Mac Daddy of Bootilicious…, the Mayor of Buttyconomus! The President of Bootyfeelingopolis!" the man jokingly screams, leaning forward to hug Key, who shakes his hand fast instead and quickly pulls away.

The attorney's eyes drift back over his shoulder, quickly finding the posse approaching faster with more crackheads whispering and falling in ranks.

Ms. Levington's head immediately springs forward, and her eyes buck when looking over her shoulder at Keyonton with squinty eyes and raised eyebrows. She opens the envelope, scrolling over the fake agreement with the fifty-thousand stamped in bold, then the thick wad of the twenties when her mouth slowly opens. "Two thousand in cash for anyone who catches them and gets those papers!" she screams clearly and faster than the attorney when explaining things. She tries standing but jerking forward then falling back on the couch, screaming the amount again.

Keyonton and his attorney burst through the door with feet quickly shuffling down the steps. They fly through a door, slamming the third-floor door and lodging metal in the lock.

Another crackhead runs past Ms. Levington, grabbing a handful of twenties and running for the window, diving out headfirst expecting the cushioned dumpster he had seen before, when his body slamming into the soft grass seconds later and almost invisible from sinking so deep into the soft mud, where the truck had just removed the cardboard-filled trashcan.

A mild gust of wind comes from nowhere when the sunken crackhead's limp hands slowly open, blowing twenties over the grounds with screams heard when people rush out of the woodwork, chasing money down so quick that it's as if it was never there.

Keyonton and his attorney rush down to the second floor.

The attorney flings the door open, and the doorman looks up, hearing all the commotion. He slams the door, pushing a broken chair to it, and they run through the second level, looking out windows until finally spotting the dumpster below another window.

The second-floor door falls from top to bottom, and the mob spots Key in the window, lunging forward with worn down shoes fading when rushing up, finding Key landing inches from the attorney.

Keyonton and the attorney come eye to eye, screaming when double-timing and climbing out, quickly making their way out of the alley.

Back over at the naval base, the cop's car sits parked outside the gate.

Another car pulls up, and Tommy climbs in the backseat of the cop's car, pointing to Alfred when he sloppily strolls out of the main gate.

The cop pulls out his phone, calling for a decoy and hired taxi driver.

Ten minutes later, Alfred stands, swaying for seconds, and his hand anxiously comes up when seeing the taxi speed up out of nowhere.

The taxi door shuts, and the driver pulls away with his vacant light still lit.

The cop car follows and then veers off down another road.

Another taxi immediately drops Ken off, and he stands, unknowingly catching sight of Alfred's taxi's taillights vanishing over the hill.

Greg pulls up to the main gate in the SUV about ten minutes later.

The cabbie drives the route toward the main strip, and it seems like Alfred is familiar with the area. He asks Alfred a few questions to see if he knows how to get to the strip club Alfred inquired about, but when the driver looks back, he finds Alfred with his mouth open and his head thrown back, mildly snoring. The driver slows then turns, coming up to high speeds along a country road until turning and stopping on a dark street. He jumps out, swinging the door open, calling out to Alfred several times.

Alfred's drunken, bloodshot, red eyes finally peep open and close until expressly springing open, staring down double barrels and into the face of a masked man.

The cabbie motions Alfred out, immediately putting him face-down.

Alfred's hands nervously shake. "Ok…, Ok…, just be cool, ok!" he says, nervously shaking. "Anything…, anything you want, money…, I have," he says with a trembling voice.

The cabbie slams the back door with his foot. "Keep your face down and count to a hundred. I'm going to turn around, and I better not find you out of the count, buster!" the driver says, easing inside and backing up quickly until skidding wheels and vanishing into the darkness with the sound of crickets rising.

Alfred continues sluggishly counting and listening to the engine vanish until a soft wind whistle amongst pure silence. He eases to his knees, backing up quickly when hearing a dog bark from afar. His feet hit the ground fast, hearing the deep barks draw closer and at an even faster pace when the slight sound of a long chain rises with a slight sound of a baby's rattler dangling on the end of the chain.

Alfred backs into a dark corner, taking deep breaths and listening for the fast-moving chain again and rattler when Alfred's deep, loud bark comes, one deeper than the dog's.

The dog stops with a thick trail of dust rising when his legs lock but in a charging stance when the cloud of dust rises higher from his trail, covering the dog. The dog sniffs, slowly advancing and looking around until taking little steps to where he last saw Alfred.

Alfred makes another deep bark, listens to the slow-moving chain and rattler when letting out another deep, loud bark, and then follows through with a dog's long whine.

The dog stops again, taking steps and repeatedly stopping until at the corner when Alfred finally sees the towering, monstrous shadow projected across the dim-lit pavement.

Alfred freezes, slowly backing up into a corner with his heart beating fast, trying to slow his breathing, but he's too nervous. His eyes quickly gaze over the ground, finding a long chain and pipe not too far from the wall. His eyes remain on the slow-growing shadow when taking baby steps, and being extra quiet.

The dog stops and growls a few times, with glowing eyes piercing into pure darkness. He advances a few paces, then looks behind him into the partially-lit field and barn house ahead then back into darkness again. His head inches forward, taking deep sniffs in the air, cautiously looking around and listening.

Alfred takes one too many steps, brushing against a trashcan, knocking the lid to the ground, and causing a commotion, and the shadow slowly rises, taking off in stealth mode.

The dog's long nails scrape the ground when heavily veering and slowing when eye-to-eye with Alfred while he's bent forward, clenching the chain, which he slowly brings high over his head and in a stealthily swing.

The dog's head leans back and then goes in circles with eyes timing the chain at high speeds, then slower speeds when Alfred brings it down a few notches when growing weak. The dog waits on the momentum to slow to almost all stop when easing in and jumping over the long chain a few times as it passes until backing out.

Out of nowhere, Alfred lets off a long, tiring scream, and the dog backs up when the chain sends sparks flying. He attempts to keep the dog a ways off several times, but he's too tired and can barely swing. Alfred makes one more attempt when stepping toward the dog this time, and it works until the chain sparks, and the dog jumps at it a few times again, barking. Alfred uses all his strength, swinging again but accidentally hits a beam, offsetting the motion when he binds his legs and falls back in a scream at the top of his murderous voice.

The chain semi-locks around both ankles, and he fights to free himself as the dog's growl grows deeper.

Alfred stays still but mumbles a fearful cry. He closes his eyes until hearing the chain jiggle and feeling a slight tug. He looks up, finding the pit bull with the chain in his mouth as if smiling and winking.

Alfred quickly sits up, trying to calm the dog and loosen the chain, when the dog takes off with brute strength, pulling Alfred across the edge of the pavement and through a field of shrubs and cactus with the rattler loudly rattling. Alfred screams at the top of his lungs, when bouncing up and down over the grassy surface while sitting as he tries freeing his legs until falling back, weak.

The dog reaches the end of the long, dusty trail, coming alongside a barn, and running even faster. The dog shoots past the barn's side door when Alfred's weight drops, and legs lift when a sharp ax severs the thin chain against the concrete, with the rattler sound fading.

"Get! Get on in the house!" the owner screams. The tall and mean-looking farmer dressed in coveralls stands with a long wheat straw sticking from his brown, stained teeth. "Here, let me give you a hand," he says, extending a wide-callused hand forward.

"Hey, thanks for saving my life…, I'm Alfred," he says, looking back with eyes wandering down at the thick dirt trail and then left, spotting the large but small-looking building he was drug from: way out in the field.

"Bidda Bing! Bidda Boom, Sam I am," the man senselessly screams before Alfred can turn, drawing back a tight fist and holding it cocked high for seconds, waiting.

"So…," Alfred begins to say, finding something coming hard and fast in his peripheral view when the man delivers the robust, impacted business (fist).

The man strikes Alfred so fast that it looks like Alfred does a few backward cartwheels, landing on his feet and still standing for seconds before falling back.

Laughter bursts out from a distance when two more of Mr. Canton's men approach, quickly converging on Alfred, whose head slightly rises, going in a few circles, cross-eyed until dropping back.

"Call the boss and tell him we've got one of those clowns," the shortest man yells, grabbing Alfred by both feet when leaning forward and slowly pulling him as if he's pulling a wheelbarrow from behind.

The man who knocked Alfred out holds his watch to the street-type light. "Naw, the boss ain't up this time of the morning. We'll just keep him here on ice in the barn and let ole' Duke and the others watch over him while we get some more shuteye."

They drag Alfred into the barn, tying him to a post, and then chain vicious junkyard dogs at the three entrances.

Around 5 a.m., at Mr. Canton's ex-wife Sinnamon's house, liquor, wine, and champagne bottles lie over the bedroom floor, and there are light moans and grumbles with a few loud farts popping off.

Mr. Canton lays face down, squirming and rocking back and forth with his hands high above his head, and before he's whining, begging and pleading for someone in his dreams not to shoot him.

Sinnamon tosses and turns to get comfortable when curling in a fetal position, then toss more to get comfortable until it's repetitious. Her stomach loudly growls, and then she moans when something fires off, this time like a shotgun. She grabs her butt, and Mr. Canton shoves her fast, drunkenly springing up, holding his leg, screaming.

"Someone shot me! Someone shot me!"

Sinnamon grips the mattress's edge until rocking one last time when hitting the floor, holding her butt. She jumps up quickly, backing against the wall when Mr. Canton rushes up next to her.

They nervously run around screaming in fear.

"What, what! Who's shooting? Who's shooting?" he screams, limping with his hand still on his upper thigh.

"What? What? Shooting? Why did you hit me on my butt?" she pouts.

"Ouch! Ouch!" he screams, holding his upper thigh tighter.

"What? What is it?" she asks with a concerned stare, seeing him limping and pointing at the curtain lightly swaying to-and-fro from an open window and a light wind.

"Somebody shot me!" he screams, backing up and pulling Sinnamon close to the wall when they freeze, looking and listening until his face frowns.

They jump when the oxygen sensor sounds off, thinking it's the house alarm.

"Woowee!" he screams, almost out of breath, covering his nose and pointing to the oxygen sensor.

She moves from the wall, nervously looking back at his leg. "I thought you said somebody shot you, but I don't see any blood."

He balls his wide fist up tight to her face. "Shot me! Shot me! Somebody should've shot you…, shot you in your tail with your stankin' self!" He shoves her away, causing her to stumble into another wall and stagger toward the bathroom with a mean stare while looking over his shoulder. He closes the door, and she hears the shower's water running shortly after that, easing into the vanity and removing makeup. He opens the door, and steam rolls out when walking out wrapped in a towel.

Sinnamon accidentally bumps into him. "Oh, damn!" he screams. "Woman, you almost scared the hell out of me…, up in here looking like a damn raccoon! Hell…, what happened to you?"

"You son of a bitch! You know what happened exactly," she says, frowning.

"Ok, my little sugar lump, you know I didn't mean that. I was just high off that crap; the boys had me snorting. You know…, soaring like!" he says, raising arms as if he's an eagle when prancing around and then turning into a plane with both arms gliding when playfully looking like he's leveling out slowly to make a safe landing. He looks back, finding her shaking her head, and feels embarrassed when cutting his eyes back with a frown. He messes around longer and then looks at his watch, rushing to put on his shirt.

Sinnamon jumps when out of nowhere comes this ridiculous ringtone.

Mr. Canton hurries over to his double-knit pants, digging deep in the pockets. "Yeah, yeah, yeah!" he says, dropping down on the edge of the bed in deep thought.

"Morning, boss! We got a little gift for you. . ., one of those knuckleheads seen with the girls," the deep country voice proclaims.

"You don't say, do (ya) you? Great…, that's just great!" he says, standing and turning his back to her. He eases over near the bedroom door. "String him up over at the boat warehouse, and I'll be there shortly, but find the damn others, pronto!"

Mr. Canton hangs up, sitting in deep thought, and then stands, dressing. He steps into the hallway, running into his eighteen-year-old son, who he reaches out to pat on the head when the kid jumps at him like a vicious pit bull.

"What punk! Get your hands off me…, you flaming faggot!"

Sinnamon rushes out, sneakily smiling at her son, who turns, walking back into his room, slamming the door.

Mr. Canton turns with his chest stuck out. "See…, you need to teach him some damn manners before he messes around and makes me drop a hot ball (bullet) in his young ass. All I did was try to playfully pat him on the head."

"What? Ugh…, how are you going to tell me how to raise a child that you've never even talked to, man? Suddenly, you walk around here trying to pat him on his head as if he's a damn little kid or a pet dog. Hell…, the boy just turned eighteen and didn't have a damn father figure because you always interfered and ran men off before marriage." She shakes her head.

"Oh yeah…, well, this last clown was nothing but a booty call and the furthest thing from a date. Until you find a real man who will respect you, I'm the only man getting that bootaaaayyy (booty)!" He giggles lighting a cigar. He takes a few puffs, looks at the floor then stares at his son's door with eyes gazing over the 'Do not enter' signs.

He grabs the knob, turns it, and walks in, finding him at the window with his back to Mr. Canton.

"Look, boi! You're going to show me some respect around here…, you got it! Do you hear me?" He yells with one eyebrow slightly raised.

The son says nothing, but his hand slips forward and into his waistband. His body twitches, and so does his eye when blinking with fingers moving fast as if he's a real gunslinger in a live showdown.

"I said…," Mr. Canton starts to say when snatching his son's shoulder to one side.

The kid spins out and around quickly, brandishing a 9MM, and pointing it at Thomas Canton's face.

"Tireek! Tireek!" Sinnamon screams, backing fast while being forced backward by Mr. Canton's hard body.

Mr. Canton stumbles back with excited wide eyes and keeps backing her so hard and fast that the two fall into the wall, cracking Sheetrock.

The two stand slumped back and until covered in mild Sheetrock dust, screaming.

Tireek inches up with a frown, slowly cocking his head, looking at the gun and then his hand. His mind scatters, trying to figure out if his head or hand is to turn sideways, so he alters both until it feels right, then nods with a devilish smile and crazy eyes.

Mr. Canton keeps backing Sinnamon against the caved-in wall while she fights to get unpinned until stopping with a confused look when his cigar falls to the floor. "Tireek? I thought you said his name was Davion," Thomas Canton mysteriously asks, looking off to one side. He attempts to reposition, still looking over his shoulder to see if he can see her face, but she continually inches further out of his sight. Mr. Canton quickly turns forward, finding the gun between his eyes when his hands go even higher, and tears fall faster when he accidentally shifting forward from Sinnamon moving behind him so much.

Sinnamon finally slips out after one hard shove and dives to the floor. She rolls over and walks backward on her hands and feet to get further away.

The barrel touches Thomas' forehead, and he begins begging even harder until it sounds like he's speaking a foreign language.

"On your knees, you little shit! You come around here tearing up somebody's damn house like a little kid and like you don't have any damn sense! I wish I were home when you and your goons came up in here! Me and my homies would have smoked all you busted-ass chumps! And another thing, you don't get another chance to put your hands on my mother! Now, on your knees, sucker, and don't let me have to tell you twice!"

"Now listen, Tiree!"

"No, you listen and get it right; it's Tireek, you idiot!" the young man yells, guiding the gun down with Thomas lowering to his knees. "And let's get this straight, my father lives in East Orange," he says, cutting his head like an original gangster (OG).

Mr. Canton cut his fierce eyes over to Sinnamon, who nervously sits with her legs crossed.

Sinnamon nervously rocks and then eases to her feet, getting out of his sight, and then eases onto the floor, sitting and rocking again.

A drip of water leaks, trickling from Mr. Canton's forehead, around his nose, through his mustache, and over his lips when his eyes refocus, licking again with eyes excitedly wandering around in circles when licking a third time. He smiles, and a mean but mild frown grows, turning into pure evil.

Tireek finally notices he has the wrong gun when quickly patting his pockets down and then looking back, finding the real gun on the dresser under a tablet, and the cartridge on the bed, slightly extended from under the pillow. "Oh, shit!" he whispers with keen eyes when swinging and hitting Mr. Canton in the temple with the toy gun, knocking him to one side and onto his face.

The mother nervously screams low when crawling into her room, locking the door.

The son dives to the floor and kicks until slamming the door shut. He springs up, running to the window, trying to open it.

Mr. Canton swiftly climbs up, leaning back and brandishing his gun from his back when dropkicking the door, leveling it from top to bottom with fast scrolling eyes until finding expensive, two-hundred dollar sneakers dropping below the window. He instantly hears the boy moan in pain from the long drop when rushing to the window, rubbing his aching face when carelessly pointing his gun around in the yard and firing off a few un-aimed shots.

Tireek springs up, pressed hard against the wall with his eyes nervously pierced upward at the smoking barrel when a few hot shells bounce off his head.

Mr. Canton runs out, coming up on the mother's bedroom door, finding it locked when taking a step back, balancing when kicking it in. He searches, finding the screen torn out when rushing to the window, not seeing her pressed against the wall, under the pot holder.

She and Tireek quietly cry, keeping fearful yet continual eye contact. Their hands tremble as they inch toward each other until their fingers intertwine.

Mr. Canton stands in the window for seconds, looking for anything moving, and then fires on auto, just for the hell of it. He sees the tall weeds move when firing a few shots, barely missing a cat that runs out in a flash, staring in the window and at the two pressed against the wall before scattering from the next few shots.

Mr. Canton pulls out his phone, calls his dirty-cop friend, and receives a callback minutes later. He briefly explains what happened but leads the cop into believing that the two tried robbing him. "Now, I want you to find them and bring them directly to me! I'll handle that punk kid myself! Hell, he's not even my damn son! She's gone pay me every freakin' red cent..., trust me. I don't care if I have to put her on hoes (whores) row! How a hoe (whore) gone try and play a damn pimp?" he angrily screams with his loud voice fading from the window as he makes his way into the hallway.

The cop sits and still has him on speaker while sitting longer, making faces until he talks with his hands and replicates Mr. Canton's screaming as he continues. Minutes later, he rests his head on the headrest, checking his watch from time to time until raising and lowering his hat over his eyes, kicking up dusty cowboy boots.

Mr. Canton's voice lowers when slowly walking down the long hallway, listening.

Sinnamon listens longer and when his voice fades off, she motions Tireek to run as they join hands, running off behind a neighbor's house deep into the woods, which thickens.

Ten minutes pass, and Mr. Canton rattles on for about three more minutes.

"Did you get all that?" he asks, not getting a response when pressing the phone closer, hearing light snoring. He pulls the phone away, looks at it then hangs up. He takes a few steps past the boy's room and then walks in, getting the real gun and clip, shoving it in the back of his waistband.

Over at Mr. Canton's warehouse, the lead bodyguard, Jeb, who's Mr. Canton's right-hand man; two-hundred-and-thirty pounds, six feet tall, and pot-bellied, sits, thinking of something creative to do with Alfred. He thinks long and hard, trying to find some way to impress the boss and keep his questionable ranking when calling a meeting.

Five of the ten men show up within the hour.

Jeb paces with his hands behind his back. "The boss depends on us to round up all these misfits, so I want to use the guy we have to catch the rest of those clowns."

"What does Buck think?" Buck's best friend asks, knowing Buck is gunning for Jeb's position.

"Buck! Buck! Damn a Buck! Ah, Buck this and damn Buck that, you gone (are going to) keep on messing with me and get Bucked up! Damn it! I'm in charge of this hea (here) outfit until the boss says so!"

"Oh, I'm sorry, but if I'm not mistaken, your job is based on merits which you haven't been producing lately, so you need this catch, huh?" the tall, skinny man sarcastically says.

"Look here..., you darn fish-eyed weasel! Either you get to steppin' by doing your job and getting the boss his due catch, or you'll be back on the next circus caravan coming through next month. Did you forget the record you were about to break picking up the most animal poop before I agreed to bring you and Buck onboard?"

The young man grows quiet, shyly easing into his seat with his head down, shamefully and with eyes wandering.

"Now, get the hell out there and beat down those streets. I want them as in yesterday, so chop..., chop; chop..., chop...!" Jeb yells, clapping ashy hands so hard that a thin layer of dust flies off them when the men quickly disperse as if never there. Jeb eases into his chair, thinking when pulling out a pencil, and scribbling on blank paper.

The door eases opens minutes later, and Buck walks in, looking cautious. "Perfect timing, huh?" Buck says, removing his clip from his weapon. He walks over by Jeb, staring at the drawing when frowning as he slightly turns it sideways, bursting into a silly giggle. "What the hell are you doing, now? Mr. C is not paying you to draw stick figures or play hangman on his dime, you freakin' idiot! You're getting what..., a hundred thousand or so a year, and you're in here acting like you're in Romper Room? You need to pull your head out of your two biscuits and start paying attention around here!" Buck screams in rage.

Jeb trembles, slowly balling the paper up when quickly deflecting to other hot issues.

The two continue talking until going into other pressing issues, including illegal actions on pending collections, casino corruption, and a few drug transactions, before sitting around for hours, deciding on what to do with Alfred.

Jeb grows anxious when picking up the phone, calling the house attached to the barn where Alfred is held with someone picking up on the third ring. "Hey, have you guys fed our visitor?" he asks, waiting for a response.

"Yeah, he's as full as a damn tick in a blood bank. Hell, I would rather clothe him than feed him. Boy, let me tell you; he went to work on Hattie's flapjacks, biscuits, molasses, and fried fatback skins," the short guy says, turning up a cold beer and crunching on BBQ meat skins.

"Yeah…, well, you just ensure he's strong and coherent when he gets what's coming to him from the boss. By the way, go ahead and move him to the boat warehouse," Jeb says, flipping open a knife and cleaning dirt from under his nails.

"Well, alright, boss! We'll move him within the hour." The man hangs up, rushing across the yard and into the barn. "Hey, I just got word to move our little visitor to the boat warehouse, so get your things because we have an hour or so ride ahead of us," the short guy says, curiously cutting his eyes over at Alfred's head, covered with a pointy and too familiar looking sheet-like cloth.

"Well, I'd better get going," the tall man says, walking away.

Jeb pulls out another pen from his desk-mounted holder when three knocks come upon the door, with it opening swiftly.

The youngest, bravest goon walks in. "So what are we doing with the guy we caught?" he asks, reaching in the refrigerator for an ice-cold beer and popping the top. "So, has the boss approved how to handle this clown?" He lays his gun down as accustomed to seeing Buck do and then sits, dropping boots on the desk when riding the chair on hind legs.

Buck stares down at the young man. "What? What..., you a lead now? You walk up in here talking like you're boss! You up in here giving damn orders and requesting information like you're a boss or a lead!" he says, staring under-eyed.

The young man's phone rings, and he drops forward with the chair's legs slamming into the floor with dust slightly rising. He motions Buck to be quiet, pressing his phone closer and sitting for minutes, listening to his woman rant for minutes until ending the call.

Buck shakes his head in disbelief and walks around in circles, quiet yet steaming.

"Sorry, but where were we?" the young man asks, riding on hind legs again.

Buck walks over as if to pass him, snatching the young man up by the collar, leaning him and the chair back and into the sofa. He grabs the beer with one hand, pouring it over his face until almost drowning him in muffled screams.

The chair slides down and off to the side from being too far down when Buck lets it go, and the young kid slams onto his back, quickly scrambling to his knees.

Buck walks away, pissed. "The nerve of you little punks coming up in hea (here) with no respect! Damn it! I'm going to be respected, always!" he says, slamming his tightly-balled fist in his hand. "Look, I don't expect you to have common sense, but you better learn something before I have to teach you a little some'n-some'n (something)."

Fifty yards from the boat warehouse, a big, black-and-silver chromed-out SUV pulls up to the gate, followed by an eighteen-wheeler.

The guard briefly speaks to the SUV driver, motioning the eighteen-wheeler to another road leading to another warehouse not too far from the boat warehouse.

Several men walk out onto the dock as the eighteen-wheeler driver takes his time turning around and backing up to the loading dock.

Four forklifts uniformly roll out alongside each other, parking and waiting for the doors to open and the gap floor plates to be down, then the truck wheels are chocked.

The man in charge of unloading pulls his weapon out, motioning other men to come out with loaded AK-47s to guard the pier. He cautiously looks around and then raises his hand. "To reiterate, we're going into no-movement phase, men…, that means the only thing that moves is the forklifts, so if anything else moves, it's guns-free!" he says, drawing quiet with wandering eyes. "Red lights!" he screams, looking back at the guy in the control room through the infra-red camera.

Immediately, all bodies on the dock look like mannequins.

Red lights begin flashing when the forklifts crank up, and two drivers go in side-by-side and then back out with a full load of max-trailer height marijuana towers.

The other two forklifts follow the same actions until in full rotation.

The main gate opens and closes for two hours, allowing over seventeen eighteen-wheelers through.

The last truck unloads when another SUV pulls up with Alfred in the back; sitting in the middle seat with the hood still over his head.

The electronic gate opens, and the driver veers, heading down a different road.

The man on the dock, in charge of the off-load, sees his brother roll by, waving from a distance, but he doesn't wave back because of the dock's no-movement policy.

Back at the naval base, around 7 a.m., Barry and Kenneth walk down the hallway, finding the Commanding Officer (CO) and a tall, beautiful ensign in deep conversation.

The CO continues talking to her until complimenting her on her outstanding work, which leaves her bashfully blushing.

"Oh, think (thank) you so much, sir, think (thank) you," she says, trying to sound more proper than proper, causing Barry to smile and shake his head.

The ensign steps to one side, finally hearing Barry and Ken walk up the narrow hallway.

The two pass them, and she intentionally opens her hand, allowing papers to fall so the CO can get a good look at her sexy body.

"Silly me! Excuse me, sir, I'm so clumsy at times," she says, turning her backside to him and bending as far as she can with his eyes over her body before looking away. Her hand caresses the crease of her upper thigh just below her cheek, firmly holding it to make her bottom a little thicker than usual when he looks away again.

Barry looks back with eager eyes motioning to Ken, who looks back and smiles. "Oh, think (thank) you so much, sir, think (thank) you!" Barry jokingly repeats with blinking eyelids. "Think what? She needs to get the hell out of here talking about 'think you,' Barry says, pissed at her flirtatious attitude. "That is just stupid as all get-up!"

"Oh man, you know what she meant? She meant…, thank you!"

"Well, why didn't she say that?" Barry says, looking back again, shaking his head.

Barry and Ken look again, almost simultaneously, and stop in their tracks, finding her standing with her back to them; her long legs and round bottom stretched in her tighter-than-regulation skirt.

"Daayyuummm!" Barry says, playfully sticking most of his balled fist's knuckles in his mouth when pretending to be biting down.

Barry and Ken step off, continuing straight but slow to almost a standstill with heads over their shoulder, still advancing.

The CO briefly looks back, and they step off faster, instantly slamming into the T-sectioned wall, busted, when grabbing their heads in laughter and scurrying off.

The CO quickly looks down at her hips when she picks up another paper she intentionally drops while giggling.

Barry and Ken head to the lounge and then go down for breakfast, where they meet Greg. They hang around, waiting for Alfred, then swing by the room, checking on him.

Barry runs to the front, checking the log, and finds that he had logged in and then back out not too long before Greg and Ken returned. He proceeds down the hall and up to Ken and Greg. "Hey, can you believe Alfred checked back out? I wonder if he ran into that gang of misfits and something went wrong," Barry says.

"What the gang…, oh, you mean at the Jamaican joint?" Ken curiously asks.

"Oh, never mind, but look…, we have to cover for him until he gets here. Shit…, he's briefing this afternoon after lunch." Barry goes into deep thought when staring at the administration office closure sign. He breaks from them, sneaking into the storeroom, grabbing Leave Requests Forms.

They rush to Barry's room, quickly doctoring up the papers, and then dash into the empty wardroom, where they immediately execute their plan.

Barry patiently waits for the CO to sit when rushing up to him. "Sir, I forgot that Ensign Boltan has a leave of absence today, and I thought his command forwarded his request but received a call stating they forgot. Anyway, here it is, for your approval and signature…, my deepest apology, sir!" he says, shoving the request before him to glance over when he slowly eases it away.

The CO's eyes follow the slow-moving fraudulent papers when his fist comes down without warning, pressing hard upon it, so Barry can't budge it.

Ken immediately notices what's happening when he intentionally leans toward the microphone, pushing a glass of water over the request. "My apologies, sir," he says, staring at the CO's red face when quickly cleaning up the mess until using the request to suck up the water. He looks over at the admiral who just walked up, shaking his head from watching the whole plot unfold from the door.

"Ok, ok!" the CO says with his head in his hand. He tries calming down in the senior foreign officers' presence as they begin single filing back inside. "Not a problem," he whispers, but you damn sure as hell better have a backup plan for briefing his part after lunch," the CO whispers even lower in a mean stare and tone.

"Oh, oh…, not a problem, sir…, not a problem," Barry whispers, swallowing hard and nervously running an index finger around the inside of his collar when feeling hot and a little dizzy. "Ensign Nelton will brief," Barry says, looking over at Ken, whose eye buck wider.

"Very well!"

Barry, Ken, and Greg step into the hallway with five minutes to spare before the start of the briefing. They come up with many short-range plans, but none aligns with the secret briefing that Alfred has been bragging about to the CO for months.

Ken looks over Barry's shoulder, staring at a hot female who had just stopped and put a handful of new Military Strategy magazines in a rack.

"Hey, I got an idea," Ken says, rushing over and grabbing a magazine.

They enter the conference room, scrambling to take their seats.

The brief begins, and Ken is the second to brief; and after he's done, he winks at Barry and then walks out and comes back minutes later, finding Barry in his seat as planned, so he takes a seat in the back, working on his strategy. Ken flips open his leather portfolio briefing case and then the magazine, thumbing through several pages when trying to create something original to dazzle them. He pulls out a red marker, marks up various pages, and begins writing numbers and reference comments where needed. He then flips through pages, practicing a few dry runs until closing the case and passing it to Greg so he can make copies.

Greg sits longer and then exits, with the sneaky admiral walking out seconds later.

The admiral sees Greg entering the library, so he eases up on the door before it closes. He turns the corner, finding Greg at the copier, so he rushes up to the duty librarian, informing her that they're playing a trick on Greg and he needs her to intercept him for five minutes or so, and she does.

She shoots up, overtaking Greg when adjusting her short skirt, then unbuttons a few buttons, and lowering her bra.

Greg soon hears heels and looks back, finding the woman approaching with playful, sexy, swaying hips.

"Excuse me, but can you help me get this box from the top shelf in the backroom," she says, intentionally showing a little more cleavage.

Greg motions her to wait, then turns anxiously, waiting for the last copy to print.

"You can set your things there," she says, pointing to the desk. "They will be fine," she says, erotically guiding Greg closer with a well-manicured index finger.

The two fade into the storage room with the door closing behind them, and she has him wait for her to get the key to the locked upper storage room.

Greg stands anxiously looking around until impatiently looking at his watch when listening, then easing into a seat.

The admiral quietly runs around, looking for something to add to the copies. He quietly flips through drawers, then more drawers finding scissors, markers, and clipping when grabbing Greg's documents and sprinting off to a distant table. He begins making crazy notations on the copies until drawing funny pictures, some comical and some sexual. He makes one last remark, then glues a bunch of pre-cut clipping to the documents. He smiles, easing back over, placing the document on the desk, then turns, replacing the items when shutting the drawer, vanishing behind bookshelves, and exiting through the back door.

Greg comes out ten minutes later, bidding her a farewell with wandering eyes. He finds the file safe when picking it up. He heads back to the conference room, finding the door closing after the admiral re-enters, not knowing of his presence. Greg eases into the chair next to Ken, cautiously looking around before passing the folder.

Ken boringly flips open the folder, and his eyes grow wide, instantly recognizing they're more convoluted and less defined. He begins flipping through more pages so fast that he misses a few pictures but sees one in the back of a fat-headed man with his middle finger sticking up. A smile comes, and Ken slips the pages into his leather case, sitting it on the floor. He looks up with eyes wandering around until dead set on the admiral, who is staring with a devilish smile. Ken drifts into a deep meditation, then leans over, asking Greg if the files have been out of his sight.

Greg curiously hesitates for a second, then responds, 'no.'

Ken slowly eases back into his seat, watching the admiral repeatedly, and continually catches him looking at the leather case when going into defensive mode.

A foreign officer completes his briefing, and the admiral's finger scrolls down the briefing sheet to Alfred. "Why don't we have Mr. Boltan's ballistic missile briefing right after our next break?" the admiral says, looking over at Ken's drooping disposition.

Barry, Greg, and Ken rush out into the smoking area during the break, taking a seat when Ken slams his leather bag on the stone table and drops down on the bench.

"That bastard got us!" Ken jumps to his feet, snatching Greg in his collar and taking him straight to the wall. "How could he have gotten to my files?"

Greg looks left to right and then up at the sky, remaining quiet but nervous.

The external door flies open, and Ken immediately eases Greg down, brushing his uniform back down as if nothing happened when they stare and gather around the table again.

"Look, ok..., I may have lost sight but not long enough for the admiral to do anything with it."

Ken pulls out the files, scattering them side-by-side. "Yeah..., you're right, not long enough for him to do anything, but everything dam thing!" Ken yells.

Their eyes wander over the documents until they burst into a peal of deep laughter, gazing over funny and sexual pictures as they thumb through until laughing and pointing in more resounding laughter.

Ken's smile is the first to fade, still looking at them smiling. "We're screwed!" Ken shouts in rage.

"No…, not really," Barry says with a hand coming to his lips in deep thought when walking away and coming back seconds later with the same edition of the magazine.

Barry stares in deep thought. "Here…, get back to setting up what you're going to say. We'll go back in and leave these defective copies ripped and in the seats, plus leave the old, marked-up magazine hanging out. If I'm correct, the admiral will be so pissed that he'll steal the magazine just to make us look like idiots, but you will brief with the new magazine," Barry says, smiling.

"Great idea! I read enough from the first magazine to fill in the gaps." Ken looks back quickly, finding the admiral's sharp, peanut head peeping out of his office window. He does a double take, no longer sees the admiral but finds his blinds slowly closing.

Barry goes on to tell them the rest of the plan then stops and looks at his watch, realizing Ken might not have enough time for a review. He steps off, pulling out his cell while walking inside, and coming out seconds later.

Back in Port Copan Retaunas, Erica's cousin, an electronics genius, eases onto the side of his bed, still writing the number and time Barry had given him. The young man soon sits up, tying his sneakers before rushing out of the house. He stops halfway down the step, quickly patting down pockets, then turns, rushing to the door, finding it closing until it clicks when running around back, trying a few windows. He goes to the other side, finds a window out of view, and tries breaking it until staring at the window's fine print, which warns that the window is bulletproof. He panics, walking in circles and talking to himself until going crazy when stomping around the yard for minutes.

An old woman on the next level up peeps out, hearing his muffled voice, then continues peeping over her shoulder when well-hidden, with her back to the wall, until walking away and shaking her head.

Barry stands tapping his watch's face while waiting for two more minutes to pass. He backs up from the bench. "It's show time, gents," he says, smiling.

Ken makes the copies, and the three enter the briefing room and do as planned, then walk back into the hallway while everyone enters, standing around talking.

The three re-enter, finding the magazine gone, as suggested when their eyes wander over at the admiral, finding him with a shit-eating grin.

The following foreign officer to brief accidentally stands, then apologizes for standing when motioned by the admiral to sit when pointing to Ken.

Ken slowly stands, looking at Barry, shrugging his shoulders while sticking out his hand in a questioning gesture, buying more time. Ken begins perspiring so severely that by the time he reaches the podium, his shirt is wet from his neck down to his chest.

"Good afternoon, gentlemen," Ken nervously says, still stalling for Barry's clown-proof plan to go into effect. "How are you gentlemen enjoying this lovely weather? The beaches, the sun, the trees, the flowers and…," he begins to say when the admiral deeply clears his throat. Ken slowly flips his leather case open and jumps when the building alarm sounds and the announcement comes for a bomb threat.

The admiral stares at the CO, slamming his pencil to the table and crumbling it in pure rage with all eyes on him.

Everyone scrambles out, running into the parking lot, where they fall into formation for a headcount and then march from the building to the dispersing area.

Barry, Ken, and Greg rush off, huddling in Ken's room, looking over the documents and cramming Ken's mind with things to make the briefing seem real.

Thirty minutes later, an announcement comes for reassembling for the briefing.

The admiral is the last to walk in, finding Ken at the podium with much confidence.

After the briefing, most senior foreign officer compliments Ken on a job well done, and then they go into several more classified briefings before lunch.

Near the end of the lunch, the financial support officer enters the conference room with the CO's new, seven-thousand-dollar laptop, and the CO signs, thanking her before she walks out.

After lunch, they watch a few film presentations, courtesy of the foreign officers, and end the conference hours earlier than planned.

The CO holds several from his staff back and watches the admiral escort the foreign officers and dignitaries out. "Ok..., OPS, before we get out of here this evening, bring me up to speed on the Contingency of Operations Plan (COOP)," the CO says, easing back in his chair.

The Operations Officer (OPS) gives a long speech about how the Contingency of Operations Plans (COOP) would unfold and then presents several scenarios.

The CO fires off a few questions with OPS stuttering as he plays 'Stump the Chump.'

"Furthermore," the CO goes on to say, "what if a tree falls through the building this very minute? What would we do?"

Greg slowly raises his hand.

"Yes, Ensign!"

"Chains and saws," Greg blurts out.

The CO's face turns cherry red when rolling his eyes and looking back at OPS, who is clueless. "OPS, and no others..., and I mean OPS only! I need to know..., what would we do?"

Barry slowly raises his hand.

"Yes, Lieutenant?"

"Well, sir, we have enough people in this outfit just to move the tree by hand; I mean..., that is why we stay so top-heavy with staff, right?"

The PA system keys up, and an announcement comes for securing water for two hours to work on the city's water supply.

"Oh, great!" Barry says, throwing his notebook high up in the air with it landing on the table. "Perfect timing, right? Just like on the infamous cruise ship," he says, rolling his eyes.

"Well, at least we have water," Greg says. "I mean..., we can just walk away if we're not happy, unlike on a ship."

Ken looks at Barry, then Greg. "While we're on contingency plans and speaking of cruise ships, damn, a simple boat drill! The Coast Guard should make it regulation for these cruise ships to have approved Contingency Plans (CP). Heck! They steam off the coast; they could have easily flown in a hundred portable shitters (toilets). With hull technicians assigned to the ship, they could have rigged a continual flow of waste over the side..., they could have had an air-conditioning unit flown out, redirected it, and connected it to the main air supply to feed the rooms. And for food, that would have been the easiest; they could have dropped coolers, generators, and fresh food daily by helicopter," Ken says, boldly smiling from his clever thinking.

"No doubt, or worst case, pull another cruise vessel alongside and take them off the same day. At least there would be no gestures of all those lawsuits," Barry finally says, smiling.

"My point! Pay me now or pay me later. They need a contingency plan," Greg says, watching the CO lean forward to stand with the laptop.

"Yah think?" the CO screams, shooting straight up with the laptop, in pure anger and unintentionally slamming it down on the table and breaking it into pieces with plastic flying in every direction. His face immediately transforms into total disbelief with wide eyes when jumping one good stomp in rage." You, you, you, and you! Get the hell out of here! What the hell is wrong with you people? OPS…, with his worthless-ass Contingency of Operations Plans (COOP)! Your, your, and your cruise ship contingency thoughts! Oh yeah…, there will be a contingency plan, alright, but I will not use it for getting the tree out of this damn building, but for getting my steel-toed boot removed surgically from your asses!" he screams, jumping up and down a few more times when losing it.

The CO stares at OPS for seconds, taking a few steps toward him with an index finger forward and at eye level with bulging eyes when he leans forward quickly.

OPS eyes bulge when leaning forward in a fall and running around the table.

Barry, Ken, and Greg sprint for the door when the CO heads around the long table, barreling down upon them with the four breaking out into the hallway in screams, causing those walking by to rush off as well, with everyone soon bursting into laughter with padded leather boots squeaking and scuffing the shiny floor.

The crowd comes up to top speed heading for the main door, but the trio sprint out through a side door in great laughter.

CHAPTER NINE

Upon the commencement of the liberty call, the three rush, dressing into their civilian attire. They arrive at the strip club an hour later and park out back, illegally entering through the back door when a stripper rushes out, accidentally leaving the door ajar from a fallen broom handle. They quickly make their way down the smoke-filled hallway, peeping into several rooms, sometimes getting their heads bitten off by obnoxious nude strippers.

Barry turns the corner, backing up fast and forcing Ken and Greg against the wall when spotting Tommy. He gazes quick, finding another door half cracked open when pushing it open with a twenty-dollar bill tight in hand. "Hey, beautiful," Barry says with charm. "We're looking for Sinnamon and Delightful," he says, playfully popping the bill apart a few times to keep her undivided attention.

Ken and Greg stare, stuck on stupid, admiring the young stripper's natural beauty.

The stripper reaches forward, but Barry playfully snatches the money back a few times.

Barry magically displays another twenty. "I tell you what..., a favor for a favor. Look..., I need you to get rid of the bouncer outside their rooms for thirty minutes. We're friends of Sinnamon and Delightful and want to surprise them."

"You mean, Tommy?" She sexily twirls a long curl over one eye. "Oh, that's easy, but forty will cost you a hundred because I'll miss my next lineup." She twirls another curl, dangling it.

Ken and Greg's mouths finally part in amazement at her beauty.

"Okay..., but no less than thirty," he says, reaching for his wallet.

The beautiful stripper exits and comes back in a flash. "Alright..., it's set but no more than thirty because I have to be on stage," she says, holding her hand out.

Barry hands her the crisp hundred, and the three stands at the corner seconds later, peeping at the girl and bouncer when slowly backing back into the bathroom. They continue peeping, almost stacked on top of each other, until shutting the door shuts when seeing them heading toward them and then to her room.

The bathroom door cracks open, then flies open with them, rushing to Sinnamon's room, which is empty, and then across to Delightful's room, where they peep inside, finding the women talking about them with their backs turned while putting on makeup.

The three quietly enter, with Barry bringing up the rear, easing, then slamming the door, causing them to jump and turn.

Sinnamon turns with eyes scrolling until deadest on Barry. "Well, well, well; if it ain't Mr. Leave-me-in-damn-distress!" Sinnamon says, frowning. She walks up to Barry with a fake smile, puckering up, and without warning, drives a knee deep into his inseam.

Barry drops halfway down, and she slaps him, then slaps him again when he's to his knees. "It's because of you that I have these rings around my damn eyes," she says, grabbing his collar in a tight-fisted grip with one eye heavily made up and the other ringed.

"Well, thank goodness for makeup," he says, with a vein protruding at his forehead. "Besides, if I'm not mistaken, you're the one who locked the door and left me to defend myself."

Delightful keeps looking at Ken while slowly approaching.

Ken flinches, eyeing Barry when she eases into him, running fingers through his hair to turn him on.

"Oh..., umm!" Sinnamon says with a deceitful smile. "Ugh..., just like a man to have some made-up, lame excuse!" Sinnamon smiles, helping Barry up when stealthily punching him in the gut, leaving him bent over.

Barry spends minutes calming her with an extended hand, keeping her back while pleading for forgiveness with reasoning concerning the numbers of men and the guns when looking at his watch two to three times.

"You, you...!" Sinnamon points to him in deep rage. "Why do you keep looking at your watch? You're making me very nervous." She rushes him with his collar in her fist.

"Look, our friend is missing, and I think the bouncer may have something to do with it." Barry peeps at his watch again. "About fifteen minutes before your bodyguard returns," he says, looking at his watch again. "Make that twelve."

"You mean Tommy? What have you done to Tommy?" Delightful asks, pouting.

"Look! Tommy's fine, but you have to help us." Ken cracks the door, peeping out.

"Ha! Good for your friend! Look at my eye…, you…, you!" Sinnamon shoves Barry off, reaching for a cigarette with her back to him, thinking about Thomas, her, and her son.

Barry looks at his watch. "Okay, then don't help…, but there will be blood on your hands if he gets killed," Barry says, turning and walking toward Ken.

"Wait…, wait a minute! I think I might know where your friend is, but you'll have to come back after our shifts…, say, three hours, and then get rid of Tommy again," Sinnamon says, easing into her vanity chair puffing.

Barry walks up to thank and hug her, and she greets him with a long kiss, but Greg is left having to pull him and Ken away from the woman while looking at his watch.

They walk out, passing the stripper's door, finding Tommy backing out, and duck into an adjacent hall. They move faster, bursting through the back door, fleeing into the streets, and coming up on the crowded main stretch.

Barry is deep in thought for seconds. "Gentlemen, I think it's time we look less like tourists," he says, pointing to a thrift store across the street.

The three enter and take their time trying on things before putting outfits together and then shades. They walk onto the street and stand profiling when Ken nudges Barry, who nudges Greg when freezing, seeing Tommy step out with hands shielding his eyes until reaching for his v-cut collar for shades and sliding them on.

Tommy stares at the thrift store for seconds and then points, actually pointing behind them to a friend, the manager who is silently waving until screaming Tommy's name.

Barry whispers, for them to play mannequins, and they pose, watching Tommy fast approaching.

Tommy cuts through Barry and Greg sideways with his foot catching Greg by the leg, clipping Greg, and he falls with Greg, spinning without flinching until he's lying on one elbow.

Greg rocks back and forth, firmly keeping his composure while settling.

Tommy jumps up, quickly and proudly, brushing down his clothes and then looks back at Greg, who is so stiff that he continues slightly rocking back and forth until stable.

Tommy takes one step back and lifts Greg with Greg's back to him, and Greg rocks until Tommy's friend grabs his arm, smiling and heavily pulling on the stogie. "Hey…, hey…, forget about it!" his friend happily says when Tommy walks off and into the store.

The manager leads the way, switching like a woman until flicking his wrist, motioning to the young man in the back.

Barry and Ken spring up, staggering and shuffling across the light sandy stones until at top speed, dodging into the traffic with horns blowing and almost causing an accident.

"Jerry…, look…, who put the mannequins out by the street? That is a brilliant idea for promoting business. You deserve a bonus!" the manager screams over the little shop.

"I di…, n't…!" he begins to say when cutting it short.

The boss points to the door. "Go…, get those mannequins up," he says, pointing.

The cowbell on the door rings and an old woman rushes up, looking hysterical when slamming the door. She rushes into the middle of the store, trembling like a leaf when pointing to the door. "Your…, mannequins! Your mannequins!" she screams. "The mannequins came to life and just flew down the street," she says, rushing to the window, pointing. Her eyes pierce through the glass in the direction the three had runoff.

"What? Are you smoking dope? Mannequins can't fly or run! What are you stoned out on, old lady?" the manager asks, rushing off and to the window, looking out.

Tommy's mind flashes back to Greg's familiar-looking hair, grabbing his gun, running into the street, and then quickly hiding the gun. He looks up and down the street, then runs to the other side, but they're nowhere in sight. Tommy runs halfway down the street until finally spotting three mannequins at another shop when swiftly closing in on them. He checks his surroundings when a kid rushes past, making a mannequin's sleeves flop around.

Tommy takes off at top speed, coming up on the side of the mannequins in a scream when lunging for one. His feet go higher than his upper body, tackling the mannequins with immense force, crumbling the chalk-based mannequins into pieces.

Barry, Ken, and Greg stand a block away, quietly watching, laughing, and continually falling into each other, trying to catch their breaths.

The short, female foreign store owner runs out with a broom handle, whacking Tommy on the head while he backs up, then low-crawls until coming up fast and running with a limp. He crosses the street, dodging cars, and then stands, looking around before pulling out his phone, requesting more men in the area for surveillance. Tommy stays a little longer and heads off in another direction away from the guys.

Barry waves down a taxi, leaving the downtown area, and they ride for ten minutes when Barry stops the driver when coming upon a restaurant on the side of the road.

They eat and afterward go out back, hanging out in a makeshift park.

Barry sits on a concrete slab, and Greg eases onto another, looking at Ken.

"Hey, Ken," Greg says, finally reclining and gritting his teeth in thought when a tear falls. "What if they kill Alfred?" he says, feeling weak and sick.

"Well, you should get your mind off that." Ken moves by Greg, patting his shoulder.

"Get my mind off of it?" Greg slowly blinks until turning his head into the wind to secretly dry tears. Greg becomes delusional, and his mind expressly drifts when calling into question whether Alfred will pull through the whole ordeal.

Barry continually looks up and down both sides of the walkway. "Guys, we still have about an hour before we return for the girls. We had better hurry and get back in the vicinity in case they decide to move the girls," Barry mutters, vigilantly looking around and then back down when growing fixated on a running stream of water making its way under the concrete pillars. "Let's go!" Barry says, breaking his concentration and snatching Greg up when tensing to support his off-balanced weight. He braces against Greg and almost stumbles into Ken, who leans into Greg with brute force again to stabilize them.

They creep to the edge of the street and, within minutes, get another taxi.

The driver pulls up at the city's edge, collecting his fare and receiving a healthy tip.

The three wander into a pub, purchasing drinks. They walk onto the back patio, where they sit near the wall with visibility of the club's back door.

There is total silence until Greg immediately begins talking about Alfred again. "I wonder where he could be," Greg says, deep in thought.

"Well, if he were up your butt with little boots on, with bells on them, and hanging out, you'd know," Ken sarcastically says, trying to get Greg's mind off Alfred, and it works when one joke leads to more jokes until everyone is somewhat in good spirits.

Barry and Ken head to the bathroom, but Greg remains in mild conversation with a guy who walks up, asking for directions.

Greg grows bored, thinking he's talked long enough after some time when looking at his watch and then back at the bathroom door.

The door flies open, and Barry walks out, looking back before the door closes. "Fire in the hole!" he screams over the loud music, hearing someone pass gas loud.

"Man! Whatever we ate at that restaurant is not agreeing with my system. I have a serious case of bubble guts, for real." Barry rubs his stomach a little more and then throws up his hand for the female server to bring another round of stiff drinks and beers.

Over at Mr. Canton's warehouse, Jeb thinks long and hard about what to do with Alfred while scribbling on the last sheet he pulls from the new, two-hundred-page art book when a humongous smile grows on his well-concentrated face. He rushes out of the office and to the two men guarding Alfred. "I got it! String him up the same way we had ole' Jeff Loberstein, but put him, head down and feet up."

The two men giggle and then run off, wrestling through a tackle box for more rope.

Alfred kicks and moans with a rubber ball in his mouth attached to the leather strap.

They lift the hood, and one man stands face-to-face, untying Alfred's legs.

"Boy, it looks like someone whipped you with an ugly stick!" the bucktooth man says, smiling.

Alfred whispers something exceptionally low a few times and then gets quiet, then whispers something again and then gets quiet.

"What's that you say..., boy? Sound off like you got a pair!" the man with buckteeth says, leaning forward when Alfred expressly head-butts him.

The man falls backward in excruciating pain, holding his bloody mouth.

Alfred screams, striking out in a fast sprint as if a proud turkey with hands still tied in front, determined to get free.

The bucktooth man's screams grow loud, echoing in and around the warehouse when the other guard strikes out from the restroom in a fast limp.

Jeb and the other man circle Alfred quickly, playfully pushing him around when Jeb grabs hold of the rope, spinning him around until Alfred's dizzy.

Alfred continues high-stepping and side-stepping until tripping, stumbling, and rolling fast. He lay whining for a while, then comes up slow, sitting in tears until his hand rises to the throbbing area on his forehead with fingers rubbing sharp objects. He jumps, moaning in tears, then touches it again, screaming with nervous jerking hands.

Jeb and the other man come close until fearfully staring at the two yellowish pieces of ivory circled mingled in blood when fearfully drawing even closer and slower.

The bucktooth man finally comes to, flinches, then frowns in deep pain, "Ahh...!" the bucktooth man abruptly screams out of nowhere when springing up and running to the side wall in a flash, toward the mirror. His mouth drops open with eyes roving over his bloody gum, reaching forward, then falling back, turning and charging like a crazed lunatic when brandishing the wide, super-thin snow shovel.

Jeb and the other man jerk back, dashing out of the way at the last minute when Alfred looks up, catching the brunt of the wide, very thin aluminum shovel to the face.

The man pulls and works the shovel back and forth a few times and then stumbles backward when it lightens.

Alfred's upper body slams flat onto the concrete, and he's out cold.

The three men standoff, staring at the shovel with leaning heads until making out the spade shape perfectly sculptured after Alfred's face.

Jeb directs the tall man to check Alfred's pulse and strings him upside down.

Thirty minutes later, Alfred comes to, swinging his body slightly upright and secured by his belt.

They bind his hands with rope when he's fully coherent.

Alfred's eyes grow wide, nervously wandering when leaning and trying to see what they've jury-rigged when tears begin to fall.

The bucktooth man walks up pissed, holding something in his heavy, callused hands. "Dees (these) teefes (teeth) right hea (here) cost me a lot of mony (money)," he says in a country, broken English when walking away with Alfred's eyes following.

Alfred slowly looks over at the other two goons standing off to the side with their hands deep in their pockets, giggling and whispering.

The bucktooth man presses a button on the wall, and a loud saw-like tool starts slowly, then comes up to top speed, fast.

Alfred squirms to look above and finally sees a thick saw blade spinning and shooting out what looks like small chips of wood until spotting something red as it slowly drips a few times. The third drip lands on Alfred's lips, and he smells the taste of old, rotten-smelling blood when it sinks into his lips when he spits.

The bucktooth man runs over to another controller, a metal-looking box hanging from a long wired cord extending from the ceiling for a moving winch. He maneuvers Alfred up and down and then back and forth several times. He raises him high and tries to align him with the saw blade, and the trendy square-shaped door underneath that Alfred has not noticed. The bucktooth man acts like a craved maniac when running to another wall switch, activating it to make the door on the floor slowly retract.

One of the other men walks over to what looks like a refrigerator, pulling out a red, bloody block of meat that looks like frozen human intestines. He drops the block in a bucket with wheels and then rolls it over by the door on the floor.

A strip of bloody meat dangles from the side of the bucket, thawing quickly until forming into a teardrop that drips onto the concrete when another drip, then another comes.

Alfred's mind and eyes go haywire. "Please, stop! Please, I beg you!" he screams in a deathly cry. "Let me down! Let me down! Please, I'll do anything," he screams, crying.

The warehouse grows quiet for seconds until the men burst into a silly, uncontrollable giggle.

The dark shade wearing, tall man limps over with the hand controller. "Let you down, you say, huh, boy? Let you down?" he screams. "Now, let's see here, either you wanna go upsi-daisy or downsi-daisy?" he says, toying with Alfred when playfully raising and dropping him quickly.

Alfred looks up at the spinning blade and then down at the calm water, which comes to life after another drop of blood drips through the metal grading near the door.

"So, which will it be, boy? Hurry up! I ain't got forever!" the shaded man screams, toying with him. He looks up at the blade and then down at the wavy water when playfully maneuvering Alfred and centering him over the hole in the floor.

Alfred trembles, crying until his tears are larger than those of a fat rat eating an onion.

"So, which will it be, boy? I know, I know…, too many choices, hey!" he says, bending and giggling when accidentally hitting the button with Alfred vanishing through the door, deep into the water until slowly pulled to the surface.

Alfred gurgles, submerged, screaming in a muffle. "Ahh!" Alfred screams with an echoing voice breaking the water's edge with all that's in him.

The phone rings, and the bucktooth man runs over to answer.

The boss hears Alfred's scream when inquiring about what is happening.

The man tells him, and Mr. Canton directs him to take him down and strap him to the chair on the east side of the warehouse, away from the boats.

Alfred closes his eyes tight, and his heart drops, suddenly hearing deep water swishing around and feeling thick waves of water splash on his face.

The tall man presses the button with all his strength and button sticks, with the winch quickly retracting Alfred when flying upward, with the sound of the blade growing louder with Alfred screaming.

The man smiles at his friends, losing focus when bending over in deep laughter.

"Ahh!" Alfred continually screams at the top of his loud voice.

"Hey! Hey!" the bucktooth man screams, slamming the phone down and pointing.

Jeb snatches the controller, stopping the winch when Alfred's feet are inches from the high-pitch, spinning blade.

Without warning, there's a loud splash when a ten-foot shark lunges from the water three or four feet from Alfred's head out of nowhere.

The men jump and fall into each other with frightened faces, watching the shark expressly fall back through the hole and vanish fast.

The three stay in shock until one burst into laughter, with the others joining in and falling into each other again.

The bucktooth man finally catches his breath after laughing hard and giggling. "The boss wants him down now and in the chair when he gets here!" he screams.

Jeb goes into deep thoughts. "One of you get me a five-gallon bucket of gas from the West End. Yeah, we gonna (are going to) BBQ this hea (here) fellow first and then feed his body to the sharks!" Jeb shouts excitedly.

The guys arrive at the strip club back in town, and Barry goes in alone.

Barry quickly makes his way through the hall, ducking behind a rack of showgirl clothing, when spotting Tommy outside the girls' rooms. He begins climbing through the center of the rack and slowly walking until advancing down the hall at intervals whenever the hall is empty. Within no time, Barry notices the rack is growing skimpy from the girls grabbing things when making it to a corridor where he finds a refrigerator box stashed when leaping from the clothes behind the box. His eyes wander, finding a worker's box cutter near the counter; when peeking around, finding two men putting kitchen appliances together. He cuts a quick hole in the box, climbs inside, cuts holes on each side at eye level, and then quickly makes handgrips. He puts most of the box-formed foam on his head, balancing it, and the smaller foam he kicks to one side. He places his fingers in the hand slots, continually making his way to the girl's room. He freezes, reaching the corner, and inching into the hallway each time Tommy turns, looking at a passing stripper.

Barry spots Sinnamon and Delightful when they run into the hallway with about five other girls and vanish into their rooms.

Tommy stands guard at the girls' rooms, looking down both corridors. He checks his shirt pocket and then pats his thigh for his phone when the DJ calls for him over the microphone, advising of a visitor.

Ken rushes back out front, and runs alongside the building, still looking toward the side of the building when jumping back into the SUV with Greg.

Tommy rushes through the beaded curtain, looking over at the DJ, who throws his hands up, motioning him to the front door.

Barry waits for one girl to clear the hallway and then rushes toward the girls' rooms, dropping the box at Sinnamon's door to block the main entrance when knocking.

Sinnamon peeps out, seconds later, barely hearing his muffled voice over loud music when shutting the door, with the knock coming again. She opens the door, and this time Barry opens the bottom hatch, low-crawling into her room with Sinnamon screams and backing fast until realizing its Barry when he pops up.

"Look! We have to move now before Tommy thinks something is up and before your ex-husband comes by and picks you two up," Barry says nervously.

"Yes darling, now..., now..., take me now, please because Tommy's been acting strange. He's guarding us closer than ever, and I think my ex-husband plans to kill my son and me!"

"Okay, look! You go to Delightful's room, and when you hear the DJ page Tommy again, check that he's gone, then head for the back door. Ken and Greg are in the SUV." Barry says, peeking before stepping out, dropping down, and backing into the box.

Tommy rushes back into the hallway and stops, gazing over the colossal box when his hand comes up, heavily slamming the upper part against the wall, startling Barry and causing him to stupidly stumble. Tommy looks down the hall and sees the kitchen installers. "Hey! How did this box get here? It's in my freakin' way!"

One man throws up his hands, motioning that he has no clue.

"Well, get down here now, and get it out of the freakin' hallway, you moron!"

The man waves him off and then walks away.

Barry stares at Tommy, inches away when his eyes go to the kitchen, spotting the man rolling out a refrigerator dolly.

The installer rushes up to the box, strapping it in, and then leans it back with one hand, quickly catching it with two as the high, top-heavy box slams into Tommy's head.

"Hey, hey, hey! Watch it..., watch it, you idiot!" Tommy screams, heavily shoving the box straight up and into the wall when rubbing his head.

The man strains, rolling the box down the hall near the wall, closing Barry's escape route.

Barry pulls the blade out, quickly carving another door, when the box leans unusually fast, and his weight shifts backward, sloppily throwing him again.

The installer drops it upright again, with it heavily wobbling.

Ken rushes back to the DJ booth and confronts the DJ. "Hey, look, man, I been out there all this time, and Tommy didn't come out!"

"Well, you go down the hall and talk to him!" the DJ yells over the loud music, pointing with one hand and keeping the earphones to his ear.

"I can't..., Hell..., I'm not even supposed to be in this joint (place)! If my PO finds out I'm in here; my ass is grass for sho (sure), man! Do you hear me, grass! As in weed wacker..., puff-puff..., Poppi," Ken senselessly says, faking a sad and scary expression.

The two installers lean the box back again, throwing Barry backward when moving it a few more feet from a door and dropping the box upright.

Tommy continually guards Sinnamon's room thinking they're inside.

The girls keep their ears glued hard to the door.

Tommy nervously paces back and forth until his phone rings once when backing from Sinnamon's door, thinking the girls can no longer hear him when looking at the door.

"Tommy! The boss wants you to bring the girls out when I pull up. And hey, Tommy, between you..., the boss, and me..., he is very pissed. He found out that both his women had been unfaithful, so he plans to do them tonight. Don't miss the party, Tommy! And hey, Tommy? Don't screw this up like the last time..., hey!" the roughest mobster-looking limousine driver says when the music stops with the DJ mumbling in the background.

"Yeah, okay, okay..., I got it! The boss plans to kill both the girls tonight. I got this, and I'll be waiting for you," he drunkenly repeats.

The girls overhear Tommy when scarily dancing on toes with mouths dropping open with excited eyes and hands expressly going to pained hearts.

Tommy hangs up quickly, dialing and relaying the message to another bodyguard, and then looks down both corridors until the DJ pages him again and advises him of a visitor.

Sinnamon and Delightful hear his heels clicking when peeping and locking both room doors. They run as fast as possible, turning the corner and knocking over another stripper sifting through the clothes rack.

The two installers take the box out beside the dumpster, unbuckle it, and boldly push it over. They check the open end, finding Styrofoam, plastic, and paper, so they stomp the side until one guy falls off and almost sprains his ankle. "Come on, that's enough," the taller man yells, giggling.

Ken runs along the back of the building, jumping into the SUV.

Greg sits balled into a knot of laughter after seeing the man stumbling.

"Damn, I'm beginning to worry! I hope everything is alright," Ken says, gazing over at the men walking to the back door when it bursts open, and the girls run out.

Ken cranks up, speeding over near the door with faint high beams on the wall and the box when cutting the wheel hard. He looks into the girls' frightened faces, stepping on the gas and then stopping when seeing a car's headlights shoot into the alley.

The fast-moving car swerves around the SUV and then exits.

"Stop!" the women scream. "Barry's in the box!"

The box rocks back and forth, with Barry, quickly backing out, wobbling, then staggering over and climbing through the back door.

The girls look back, finding Mr. Canton's limousine driver passing the front and looking straight ahead on the main road.

The SUV lights dim, and the limousine driver looks in the alley, seeing the SUV's taillights go out just before he pulls up in front of the club. The SUV's bright taillights brighten when they stop and then dim when the SUV quickly speeds away.

Tommy sees the limousine pulling into the circle and motions to the driver that he will be right out. He rushes inside, giving the DJ a ridiculous look with hands thrown up to let him know there's no one out there. Tommy floats into the hallway and knocks on Delightful's first but gets no answer when trying the lock, backing up and drop-licking the door. He looks around, anxiously pulling his gun out when dropkicking Sinnamon's door. Tommy runs feverishly through the halls, popping into different rooms and asking for the girls. He quickly comes out of the last room, gaining sight of the girl near the clothes rack when he rushes up to her with a gun to her head, and she nervously points to the back door.

Tommy bursts through the door, searching in and around cars before stopping and staring at the box, kicking it. He jumps up and down, firing twice into the box when rushing back inside. He looks around more in the other dressing rooms and then looks up, finding the limousine driver, staring at him and shaking his head in disappointment.

"The girls, Tommy! The girls?" he says in a deep, frightening voice with a fake smile, instantly turning sinister. "The boss gives you a remarkably straightforward task, and what do you do? You screw it up, not once, but two times, hey? Tisk…, tisk!" he says, snapping his thick fingers. "I wouldn't be surprised if the boss puts your head on the chopping block for this screw-up!" He jumps at Tommy with a backhand, causing Tommy to slam back into the wall, then aggressively points Tommy to the front door.

The two exit, climbing in the limousine, and the driver calls Jeb, providing an update, which Jeb relays to Mr. Canton, who is mad as hell.

Thirty minutes pass. "Pull over here!" Barry says, jumping out as the SUV stops with the lights going out.

Everyone gets out and they begin converging in a semicircle.

Barry pulls out his phone, punching in a few numbers on the highly decorative application, which creates various eye-catching designs and then displays the time, which is not visible initially but finally displayed in crystals. His phone chirps a few times, and he looks down at the displayed time, which reads one-and-a-half hours.

"What's that?" Greg curiously asks, amazed.

"A Guardian Angel application." Barry smiles in amazement. "Okay, girls, show us to a nice restaurant..., my treat," Barry says, smiling when everyone looks at him strangely.

"Uh..., we have Alfred to rescue, remember!" Ken says sarcastically.

"Yeah..., and our lives are at stake also; my ex-husband plans to kill us!" Sinnamon fearfully interjects.

"Right..., he may be pissed, but not going to kill you," Barry responds with a smile.

"Newsbreak! Ah..., Yeeeessss! He plans to kill us because we overheard Tommy mention it during a call," Delightful nervously says in a trembling voice.

"Wow! We're just one big ole' happy family here! Six heads on the chopping block at one time. This guy sure is a winner! Anyways..., how did you two end up with this psychopathic jerk? Never mind..., because it will only lead to me asking how you two became best friends," Barry says sarcastically.

"Ohh..., you arrogant...!" Sinnamon screams, taking a swing at his face when he catches her tight fist in mid-stride.

"Dinner, anyone?" Barry says, slowly lowering her tight fist when extending his hand for the truck keys, which Ken releases to him.

They leave the suburbs, ride into the country, and eat at an exquisite restaurant.

Barry is the first to finish, so he walks out onto the patio, fiddling with the drinking straw in his mouth until chewing the tip a little longer.

A couple of them smoke afterward, then load up after seeing Barry rechecking his phone.

Barry drives past the same roadside restaurant with the watery spot as before, passing it and pulling over twenty miles down the road. He veers off and through a deserted-looking road that opens into a big field, where he stares off into the darkness. He wiggles the straw with his tongue as if anxious, then pulls out his phone, jumping out, and followed by the others.

They gather around the phone, which Barry activates when passing it to Ken and then directing him on how to hold the application when it's activated.

Barry pulls the straw out, tapping on the application's face when the phone counts down to the last minute.

A song with the same magnitude as one of Beethoven's famous hits rises with crystal-clear ZHS quality surround sound, which leaves them amazed.

Everyone's eyes glisten as they watch the five dispersed crystals quickly form together.

Immediately, three different bright laser lights appear high in the sky, far off, and vanish into pure darkness.

Without warning, tracker rounds shoot out, and X marks their location, high overhead when their heads fall back, and their eyes lock onto the double and then the third line, which confirms the triangulation.

"Wow, it's beautiful," Sinnamon says looking at what looks like fireworks when an even brighter light appears but twinkles like a little star about ten times and then steadies.

The light sounds of aircraft rotors come but quickly fade when a single light flashes bright once, temporarily blinding them when covering their eyes quickly and staggering around, bumping into one another.

"Wow, Barry! Awesome application, dude! Remind me to pick one up," Ken says sarcastically. "What in the hell does all this mean? What, Barry, you freakin moron?" Ken screams, looking out at the white spots along with the others.

Barry's boots stomp hard, causing everyone to look down when their eyes focus a little, feeling the mild trembling when the ground shakes and various thick cracks form across the ground.

"Whoa!" Greg and Sinnamon say, almost simultaneously, when turning and finding a two-and-a-half-ton black military truck. Dropping when inches from the ground.

"Taudauh!" Barry yells, pointing and continually clapping.

Delightful takes one step toward the truck, and a circle of eight lights begins slowly rising and shining in unison when over twenty-five men slowly fade in from pure darkness, like precision Soldiers.

A tall man with a gold admiral's insignia approaches from the darkness with a pointer stick under his arm. "Afternoon, ladies and officers. Admiral Warrington III…, at ease, men," he says. "Excuse me," he says, nodding to the women and motioning to Barry when walking off with him.

The lead Soldier's hand makes a few strange movements, and the men commence setting up tents deep in the woods.

Minutes later, Barry comes up to Ken, Greg, and the girls. "Hey, look, take the girls in the tent over there so they can provide the team intelligence on Mr. Canton's assets. Ladies, any phones or electronic devices?" he asks, extending his hand.

The women shake their heads 'no.' "My ex never let us carry phones because he thinks we are good candidates for sabotaging his operations or something," Sinnamon says, smiling.

"You guys meet me in the command center in thirty minutes," Barry says, turning to find a young Soldier with a lot of electronic gear draped over his shoulders.

"Malik, this is..., hey, sorry, but I didn't catch your real names," Barry says, looking at Sinnamon and then Delightful.

"Vanishea," Sinnamon says, extending her hand to have it kissed by Malik.

"I'm Joy," Delightful says, extending her hand to have it kissed as well.

"And this is Warrant Officer Kenneth Nelton, and Ensign Greg Washington," Barry says, pointing to them. "Just make sure you don't kiss their hands, especially this one," Barry says, pointing to Greg and then playfully shoving him in the chest. "Malik is Erica's cousin, and the admiral is her father. Oh yeah..., Malik is the one who placed the bomb threat during the briefing."

"Gee! Thanks a bunch..., for a minute there, I thought you would leave us hanging," Ken says, smiling when walking by and patting his shoulder.

"Yeah, my bust! I locked myself out of the house, when heading for the phone booth."

Ken looks back, finding Barry and Greg bursting into laughter.

Barry walks off with Malik, and they meet up with the admiral, who had just walked into the command and control tent.

Soldiers continually work diligently setting up the command and control and an intelligence center and have the entire operations up within two hours tops. Afterward, they back up the trucks and begin unloading non-lethal weapons.

At 2200, they have the women in the tent, lying out of all Mr. Canton's assets.

Several men are dispatched on motorcycles to set up external surveillance cameras in all locations, including the strip club.

Now, those intelligence men return at midnight, and the admiral has the Operations Officer activate the ninety-six-inch plasma screens with over twenty different cameras energizing simultaneously.

Everyone stands amazed, staring into Mr. Canton's enterprise, linked to Spanish government operatives, with coordinates and locations still undisclosed.

"Please leave me be...," the admiral says, easing into his chair, staring at the screen, and looking sleepy when closing his eyes.

Ken's eyes drift to the gold-plated warrior joy-stick type glove, nudging Barry on the way out.

The admiral constantly studies the men's movement for over an hour and then calls everyone back inside for an initial briefing. "As you know, I can't allow my Reservist Soldiers inside the Area of Responsibility (AOR) with live weapons because if something happens, I'm solely responsible. The three of you will have to go, and since Mr. Canton plans on killing the girls, I recommend you leave them here, protected," the admiral says, concerned.

"With no speculation on my part, your friend is in this warehouse," the admiral says, pointing and circling the building in the far right corner of the screen with a laser pointer. This building is the least guarded, but that can change in an instance. Now, this place," he says, staring at another place for seconds when moving the laser over. "This building is heavily guarded, more than likely for illegal interests, but it's so close to your friend that they can call in reinforcements without delay. So..., whatever you do, avoid this loading dock at all costs because it is motion guided with tactics that I've put in place.

"I'll stage a couple of men in the water here and sharpshooters here, who can pick up on anything moving inside the open bay," he says, strategically planning while pointing out those positions. "Now, I can take down anything outside when needed, so hear me and hear me well..., what I'm telling you, men, is that there are no outside threats..., whatsoever. If you feel threatened while outside, the signal is for you to throw up your hands; it is just as simple as that. I will evaluate the threat and immediately eliminate it if it's indeed a threat. The weapons of choice are non-lethal injections," the admiral says, turning and pulling out a few trajectories that look like AK47 shells. "They enter the body instantly and stop upon the first detection of max body heat. They release a chemical that slows the heart rate and puts the brain to sleep for up to two, sometimes three hours, depending on the person's size, and then dissolve in the body, causing hemorrhoids before being discharged as green slime. Just for the record..., my target kill rate is 99.99% to date, and the .01 percent is someone else's targeting error, so you're in good hands, gentlemen!" The admiral looks at his watch and then back at the screens.

"There..., that's Thomas!" Sinnamon blurts out, watching him enter the nightclub in his normal pimp walk.

"You all can go about your business. We start the operation in one hour, so synchronize your watches with the clock on the monitor," the admiral says, pointing at the screen's digital counter.

Everyone disperses, and the women turn in for the night but can't sleep, so they lie in their bunks, watching television.

Barry, Ken, and Greg slip into their bulletproof gear and receive detailed directions on the real weapons they are allowed to use only to preserve life or limb.

The admiral comes out to bid them farewell and watches as they and others operate their Bluetooth headsets and conduct radio checks with the Communications Officer.

Over near Mr. Canton's warehouses, everyone is in position at 0300.

Barry's SUV comes up on the main road when cutting off the lights, turning down a long, winding road and heading deep in the woods.

The canvas flap to the command and control tent flies open at the camp.

"Sir, one of the women, wishes to speak," Malik says.

"Very well, but just this one time," the admiral says, staring deep in the mirror when adjusting medals on his dress uniform.

Sinnamon cautiously enters. "Sir, I just thought about something I overheard a long time ago. The woods surrounding the warehouse have cameras that scan with infrared beams for early detection," Sinnamon says.

"Great..., thanks for sharing," the admiral says, dropping in his seat, taking a deep breath before turning to his Intelligence Officer, who is typing a message to Big Brother, who is circling high overhead in stealth mode.

Minutes later, Big Brother responds, passing a code when the screens light up with sweeping red leaders popping up and overlapping one another around Mr. Canton's warehouse and boathouse for seconds until the last one shows.

"Lima One…, stand by to hold your position in three…, two…, one," the admiral says, watching Barry bring the SUV to a screeching halt with dust rising high and floating overhead. "Please be advised that the back of the buildings have sweeping infrared sensors, but you can drive about 100 more meters and walk due to tight sensor spacing."

"Roger, Alpha One," Barry responds, patiently waiting for the following command before moving forward. Barry looks off, then proceeds, taking ten minutes to safely maneuver until within 100 yards, where they park and jump out. Barry pulls the men together for silent prayer and then proceeds.

The team continues, making all of their tactical advancements based on the admiral's commands. Before long, they are deeper in the woods and closing in on their intended target while being provided real-time updates.

The three come upon a fork in the road and rush off to one side when seeing headlights shine down the road and then veer off quickly. They stay down for minutes and then look up to find a small convoy of eighteen-wheelers veering off as well.

Barry reaches deep in his coat pocket, pulls out a thin light pen then kneels, shining light on his thigh-mounted, plastic-sleeved map.

Ken and Greg gather for detailed instructions on their internal plan of attack.

"Here, this is where we'll enter and come up on the back of the guard and take him by surprise. Alpha One will take him out if need be, but I'll give the signal," Barry says, easing the light back into his pocket.

The three advance from the dark woods with non-lethal handguns drawn, finding a huge guard at the gate talking sweetly to someone on the phone when inching up on him.

They halt their movement at Barry's hand command and then come up on him in stealth mode, quickly surrounding him.

Barry's gloved index finger comes up to his lips, whispering. "Shhh! Now…, if you want to see that sweet little thang again, I suggest you don't even think about doing anything stupid. Now we need you to put down the phone and lie on the ground!"

"What? You punks! Damn, a gun…, come at me like real men!" the muscle-bound, stoned-out guard yells, with thick veins in his neck, constantly sniffing as if he had just done a long line of cocaine. "Hold on, babe…, let me call you back. I got a few punks who've come out for a fresh can of ass-whipping," he says. He softly kisses the mouthpiece, pocketing the phone with eyes wandering over each of them while slowly dropping into an even slower karate stance that leaves him looking like a low-riding praying Mantis. "What a good night to die…, suckers!"

The three look at each other as if clueless with fast-moving eyes.

"Did you choose this night?" Barry asks Ken with a confused look.

"No, I didn't choose this night. Did you choose this night?" he asks Barry while hunching his shoulders.

"Did you choose this night?" Ken asks Greg with an even more confused look.

"No, I didn't choose this night. Did you choose this night?" he asks Barry while hunching his shoulders.

Barry, Ken, and Greg stand looking around at each other a little longer until hunching their shoulders simultaneously and in a round-robin fashion yet speechless.

"Enough of this senseless bull!" the guard screams, fed up and slowly coming out of the stance with eyes glued on Barry until looking at them one at a time, while watching them spread out. "Hmm…, three to one…, my kind of odds," the guard says, smiling and looking even more frightening.

Barry nods, motioning for Ken and Greg to drop their weapons.

Out of nowhere, the guard jumps, making them flinch when bouncing around with fancy footwork and then swinging and kicking. He does some kind of silly move, looking like a ritual dance when getting the best of Ken and Greg, using hands and feet and it works, leaving them dizzily staggering in pain.

Barry soon takes the brunt of a devastating blow to the gut, dropping and springing back up when the guard maneuvers back over to Ken. Barry wobbles then come up, waving high above his head, but the admiral and other officers sit playing spades, though the admiral has an eagle's eye on the situation.

Barry takes a few more stealth jabs to the gut. "Any time now!" Barry finally transmits. "Alpha One, any time now!" Barry speaks through the mouthpiece this time when taking a few more blunt punches to the abdomen when losing his balance and frozen in place like an eagle landing. He stumbles and then anxiously waves high over his head again, watching Ken and Greg takes more punishment.

The three continually groan and roll around in pain.

The guard stumbles from the two in a trot, head-butting then dropkicking Barry when coming around into a crazy-looking stance.

"You can't take me! You can't take me! I'm Bruno! Nobody can handle big Bruno! You busted chumps come up in here thinking you can take ole' Bruno, like talking 'bout (about) it!" he screams, breathing harder. He looks around, then over at his gun when stepping off, walking toward the gun, and pulling out his cell.

The guys don't move from being busted up pretty bad, but Ken is the first to groan the loudest and flinch.

Bruno takes another step, pushing the phone closer to his ear on the first ring with a big smile on his sweat-covered face. He leans forward, and his hand comes to his knees when bending to catch his breath.

Back at the camp, the threat warning on that screen goes from green to yellow the closer Bruno gets to his weapon.

The third ring comes when the guard has the gun at his head, wiping sweat from his eyes, with the back of his hand, and on the fourth, his girl answers.

"Babe! Babe! Three to one…, three to one…! Hell, they can't handle Bruno!" he screams, turning to train the gun around in a stare. He aims, lowering the gun at Barry's body and jerks back fast several times, stumbling backward a few feet and then a few more feet when landing flat on his back when three stealth rounds pierce his body.

His girlfriend calls out for him and then continually calls out until screaming for seconds before hanging up and redialing.

Greg's fingers twitch a few times, then his feet finally move, and then Ken finally moves.

The two sluggishly look around, finding Bruno on his back when jumping up. They rush over, nervously shaking him and jumps back each time his body rocks.

Ken rushes to Barry. "Barry! Barry!" Ken slaps him in the face with a few good whacks.

Barry finally comes to and sits exhausted, looking around.

"What! What happened?" Ken asks, pointing back at the big man.

Barry's eyes slowly drift to the bottom of Bruno's thirteen, maybe fourteen, shoes.

At the command center, the admiral and his staff stand anxiously watching in total silence when mumbling voices come, betting big dollars in tight hands with heavy anticipation while waiting for Barry's response.

"Oh, it was nothing…, almost like the Rocky movie. You know…, when the two fighters hit each other simultaneously and fall out?" Barry confidently responds, heavily massaging his chin and then belly.

The admiral and his staff burst into a peal of great laughter, bumping and falling into one another from laughing so hard then single filing by, throwing handfuls of dollars on the admiral's desk for his winning bet.

"Way to go, man…, way to go!" Greg says, taking a few steps over by the big guy.

"Greg…, no! You and Ken head behind the building while I will move him."

"You sure?" Ken asks. "He's a pretty big boy."

"Oh yeah…, I got him."

The three pick up their weapons, and Barry motions them to go on.

Ken and Greg walk off with nervous eyes peeling back at Bruno until Ken pushes Greg in the back, and they take off, vanishing around the building even faster.

Barry leans down for his big feet and tries to drag him but can't even budge him after several attempts.

The admiral and his staff patiently watch Barry until in deep laughter and tears again.

Barry drops down in another stance when trying to roll him, which doesn't work.

Laughter in the command and control room continues with eyes glued on the screen until laughter brews out of control.

Barry's eyes scan around until glued steadfast on the tip of a hayfork in a bale of hay. He rushes for it, quickly covering the guard's body and jumping when the man's stomach bubbles. He picks up another load of hay when a loud and obnoxious fart comes, then trickles off like a flutter with Barry looking behind him, then down, finding the big green stain in the seat of Bruno's pants. Barry turns and looks back when the funk hits him square in the nose, staggering until wobbling from the lethal funk. He runs off a few feet, almost blowing chunks until turning upwind, then turns to gag, puking for seconds until dry heaving. Barry staggers further away and then eases back up with his nose pinched, completely covering him with one hand handling the fork. He turns, wiping sweat when grabbing the guard's weapon and jumping, thinking his foot moved. He comes up on the other side of the building fast, catching up with Ken and Greg, kneeling at the front entrance when coming alongside, out of breath.

"Dayum!" Barry says, silently and secretly swinging and stomping when spotting the second big guard, who looks a lot bigger than Bruno but calms down quickly, seeing Ken's head about to turn back to him. "Okay, we stand on the count of three..., one, two, three," Barry says with them standing. They take small steps, each looking like they're drifting backward than forward, when creeping up on the weighty man who turns, reaching for his weapon and dropping from the admiral's stealth targeting acquisition.

The three grab the man fast, wrestling him near the end of the fence, where they shove him off hard, rolling the big guy down a steep embankment.

Barry quickly turns, getting his bearing, directing them to the front door.

The three come up on the building slowly and jump, seeing two bodies fall to the ground from the roof. They stand scanning the perimeter when rushing over, quickly dragging the bodies behind a row of low-cut bushes. They fling the last man over the other body, and when he lands, there is a loud fart, which has them giggling and fighting to regain their composure.

"Hold your positions," Barry says with eyes wandering over the grounds and off at a distance from where the admiral says possible reinforcement could come.

The three rushes to the front entrance, entering the building to find three men with their backs to them when firing silent rounds, taking them out, and then simultaneously looking at their watches.

"Okay, we've got to be out of here in an hour, tops," Barry roars over the loud machinery at that end of the boat dock.

"Lima One, this is Alpha One; the eagle has landed! I repeat…, this is Alpha One; the eagle has landed!" the admiral says, seeing Mr. Canton's limousine creeping through an unmapped and undisclosed, grassy-covered road.

Mr. Canton's door flies open, and his shiny shoes shuffle out, with him toting his shiny AK-47.

The driver quickly turns off the engine, jumping out with a mean stare.

"Get back in the damn car and get me those damn girls! I plan to finish this tonight, and I don't want any witnesses! I'm sure the girls have speculated on telling them where their friend is by now, so they should be here any minute," Mr. Canton shouts.

"But boss, something's not right! Security…," the driver begins to say when Mr. Canton stares at him with a mean look that he knows not to question.

The driver jumps back quickly, speeding off and hitting the payment indentation, turning the wheel so hard that the hubcap flies off the front tire, scaring Mr. Canton, who dives into the grass, low crawling.

Mr. Canton quickly looks back through scrubs, spotting the hubcap rolling when jumping to his feet, brushing his suit down. He rushes inside, still looking back, and turns, clobbered with the butt of one of his own men's rifles, which Barry skillfully handles.

"The eagle is down!" Barry says in a proud voice. "I say again; the eagle is down!"

"Roger, Alpha One copies," a feminine voice responds as told by the admiral.

They bind and gag Mr. Canton in a swivel chair.

Barry climbs on top of one of the mammoth boats, quickly making his way to the bow. He peeps around for seconds, then down, finding Alfred bound to a chair with a five-gallon gasoline can inches away. Barry makes his way back to Ken and Greg. "Hey…, they have Alfred tied in a chair and plan on burning his body, so we have to move fast," Barry says excitedly, with eyes scrolling over the warehouse's interior.

The three listen for minutes when Barry grabs the chair, rolling Mr. Canton out and directly in front of Alfred, at the opposite end of the titanic boat warehouse. They remain well hidden behind a partition and quickly create the same fire preparation scenario as Alfred's, except for using water and gas. They douse Mr. Canton in water and save the gas for creating a line from Mr. Canton in the direction of Alfred, then quickly huddle.

Greg vanishes and Ken stands by Mr. Canton with the water in the gas container while Mr. Canton's coming back around.

Barry starts the water line that extends eight feet in front of Mr. Canton's chair.

The three peep, seeing three men near Alfred; the tall man with his weapon held tight and the others with empty hands.

Barry peeps from the barrier, spotting the tall man easing his gun in the back of his trousers, leaning and dousing gas over Alfred, who jerks, choking and gasping for air. Barry whistles, pouring gas from the waterline when walking toward the men and Alfred.

They freeze, hearing a mild scream over a loud engine when the bucktooth man squints, feverishly pointing to the Barry.

"What the hell!" the tall man yells, reaching for his gun.

Barry rolls back the partition with all his strength and keeps pouring the gas line with Mr. Canton's too-familiar attire and shoes finally fully visible.

The bucktooth man grabs the gas can, rushing to pour more over Alfred but stops when finally noticing Mr. Canton. "Da (they) get (got) Boss Contoon (Canton)!"

"Drop it," the tall man yells, brandishing the gun and expressly falling to the floor when one of the snipers in the rib boat in the pond takes him out, with a loud, endless sounding fart following.

Jeb squats fast, grabbing the gun while keeping it down by his side.

The bucktooth man takes off running and dives over the friendly teams camouflaged men's heads, landing in the water. He quickly frog-paddles to the side, exiting, and runs to his SUV, grabbing his twelve gauge pump when taken out by the admiral, bursting a few loud farts.

"Drop it!" Ken yells. "Your boss is sitting here, you freakin' idiot!"

Ken removes the gag from Mr. Canton's mouth.

"Fry his ass..., boy! This hea (here) ain't nothing but water, boys!" Mr. Canton shouts excitedly.

Ken snatches up the real gas can, holding it over Mr. Canton's head. "Ask your boss if this is real, Jack!" Ken shouts, tilting the can hard and dousing him with Mr. Canton's feet shuffling back and forth when gasping for air.

Jeb finally hears Mr. Canton gagging and gasping for air and looks confused yet watches Barry still pouring a wider trail. He eases the gun in front of his waistband, quickly striking a match and holding it when turning and looking when hearing shoes squeaking across the floor.

The match falls, and before it reaches Alfred, Greg tackles the chair advancing forward, lightning fast with squeaky shoes.

A loud blast comes, blowing everyone back, but Greg stumbles, still sliding the chair about fifteen feet away from the gas-soaked floor, then further until the gas trail at the chair's footing dries and fades with flames diminishing fast.

Ken springs up, dragging Mr. Canton's chair back about ten feet from the gas puddle as fire stretches from where Alfred's chair was once sitting to several feet from where Mr. Canton once sat.

Greg quickly unties Alfred, and they joyfully embrace.

Everyone soon hears louder engines roaring when several two-and-a-half tons burst through the warehouse doors, swerving around the partition and several boats up front with the first sliding one hundred and eighty degrees before stopping.

The four quickly load up, and the three trucks barrel out, taking a few direct rounds from the over-armored plant where the eighteen-wheelers are parked.

Other vehicles from the warehouse give chase, but the admiral is determined to maintain his 99.99 percent kill rate, and he does.

The two-and-a-half-ton barrels down the back of the warehouse and drops Barry and Ken off near the SUV.

An hour or so later, everyone returns to the makeshift base, where Barry debriefs the admiral and his staff alone.

The admiral stands shaking Barry, and his men's hands, then turn, guiding Barry off to the side, smiling and playfully mocking Bruno with his chest stuck out.

Barry stops and looks with a curious stare. "Hey, sir..., do you care to enlighten me on my waving, and you not shooting?"

"Why, of course..., I said I had you covered if there was a threat. The way I see it, the big man put his gun down first. You know..., I can't stand to shoot an unarmed man. Regardless, your response to how you took the big fella down made me a lot of money," he says, pointing to the large stack of money on his desk while giggling.

Barry looks with a curious stare again. "And that awesome fart that was breathtaking…, woo…, you did not warn about that funk, but you did say it takes hours, and that was no hour," Barry says, shaking his head in disbelief?"

"Okay…, three shots work almost instantly, especially with all that adrenaline he used when kicking your butts."

Barry smiles, turning and walking to the other tent, where he meets up with the girls, Ken, Alfred, and Greg, and pulls Sinnamon off to the side, talking.

The word soon comes from the messenger that the admiral agrees to let the women stay until he receives word from the Spanish Government that Mr. Canton and his men are no longer a threat.

The admiral walks around and sits, waiting for the last footage with coordinates to load to the Spanish authorities.

Out of nowhere, and like clockwork, several helicopters and ground assets storm Mr. Canton's storage, warehouses, and boat warehouse. More heavy artillery continues en-route to his property a few hours later from other supporting bases.

An even larger helicopter lands on the well-hidden, deserted helicopter pad outback with several government agents jumping out.

Other helicopters simultaneously land until over eighty troops, and Spanish law enforcement officials are boots on the grounds.

Infrared alarms sound, detecting troops activating the alarms, alerting Mr. Canton's men who are deep inside of their presence and causing them to run from both buildings shooting.

Spanish Law enforcement and criminals exchange fire for over an hour, taking out several men from both sides. Spanish law enforcement wounds or apprehends most of the criminals but takes Mr. Canton into custody without a fight.

Several men hide in places created especially for raid prevention but are found and captured with the help of search-and-rescue dogs, but several off-shift men manage to evade the law.

"Man, this is quite an impressive setup," the most senior Spanish officer present says, taking his time to access the entire building and operations. He gazes over bales of marijuana stacked to the top of the fifty-foot ceiling.

"This should bring the government hundreds of billions, huh?" a female DEA agent says, staring at huge bundles of what looks like cocaine before walking on the dock and looking over the facility's exterior.

An hour later, the admiral receives word that the operation is a success, so he arranges for the women's transport to their homes.

The four load up in the SUV and return to the naval base, escorted by a DEA agent.

Around 6 a.m., the chief chef opens the chow line, so the four eat breakfast together, listening to Alfred chat endlessly about the new Navy adventure.

Around 11 a.m., the base admiral's order comes for everyone to wrap up and prepare to head home.

Most men and women rush through the halls or parking lot, loading their vehicles.

The restrooms are full of men who wait for vacant shower stalls, urinals, or sinks.

The Operations Officer staggers in hungover and rushes to the shortest urinal line.

"Man..., how are you going to drive home? You are humming with alcohol, got bloodshot eyes, and definitely got your sway on, like crazy," Barry says in a continual stare with his eyes gazing up and down his limp and continuously swaying body.

"Hell junior..., I plan to sleep it off because I'm not about to break a zero-tolerance policy by drinking and driving," he says, running his fingers through his greasy hair.

The CO approaches the men's room, stopping to talk to a junior officer.

"Hey! Good plan, OPS, and oh, by the way. . ., did you get ole' Captain Swizzle Stick the answers he wants to his revised Contingency of Operations Plans (COOP)?" Barry yells, standing in the bathroom, laughing loudly.

An officer steps away from the urinal, and OPS rushes up on his tiptoes, trying to hold his pee while dancing on both feet and fighting to get his zipper down.

"Oh shit, the infamous Contingency of Operations Plans (COOP)! Wooo! I almost forgot," he says, shaking his manhood when about to release his bladder.

The CO eases closer to the bathroom, and his head cocks, getting an ear full while frowning and turning red. He turns, motioning the junior officer to silence, when stepping closer and quieter when slipping into the bathroom, where some freeze with bulging eyes or exit but others quietly back out of the way in excitement.

Barry walks up to the urinal beside OPS.

"You better sober up and get that Contingency of Operations Plans (COOP) together before you leave, OPS! That silly-ass CO is liable to get Greg's chainsaw, cut that damn tree down, and the whole damn building just to see if your plan works," Barry yells in a crazy and uncontrollable laughter.

"Well, he can take his Contingency of Operations Plans (COOP) and shove it where darkness always prevails, for all I care!" OPS loudly and proudly replies, senselessly giggling. "You know, Barry..., they say that every beer burns about two brain cells, and liquor six. Hmm..., so what do you think happens to those little brain cells? Ooops!" OPS says, releasing a stronger stream of pee. "Well, there goes his Contingency of Operations Plans," OPS yells, bursting into an uncontrollable laugh with heavy jumping shoulders.

The CO eases up slowly, snatching them by their shoulders, and vigorously shakes them until they're pissing on each other's legs.

"Hey, hey, hey!" they scream, almost simultaneously.

"Let's see what kind of Contingency of Operations Plans (COOP) you come up with now, smelling like piss-ants while driving home!" the CO screams in silly laughter when releasing the and standing back gazing in a mean stare. "Piss ant!"

An hour later, Barry, Ken, Alfred, and Greg load the SUV and return to the administration officer, having their orders stamped.

CHAPTER TEN

There is an hour delay for everyone because the C.O. and admiral have not returned from the exchange (department store), but when they arrive, they release everyone after a lengthy farewell speech.

The four misfits walk out, and Barry throws the keys to Ken. "You drive the first two hours, and I'll take the rest." They head down the main stretch leading out of town and are an hour into the drive when stopping for dinner and then getting back on the road.

"Shit! We have to turn around; I forget my Rolex..., shit..., shit..., shit..., shit!" Barry says, slamming his hand on the dash and stomping.

Ken makes a quick sharp turn, skidding wheels across lightly sanded gravel when stepping into the gas. "Man! We're not going to make the comedy club tonight, and if so, we're going to be late. I can hear Jenn's mouth now," Ken says, shaking his head.

"It shouldn't be too late, but without a minute to spare," Barry says, looking at the dashboard clock.

Fifty minutes later, the S.U.V. shoots past the main stretch, stopping for a red light.

A smoke-fogged, strange car pulls up at the adjacent street with condensed pot trails billowing out of the slightly cracked-open window.

The passenger pulls out his cell, dialing. "Hey, boss, is the ten tousand (thousand) per head still open on the fowe (four) dudes from the club the udda (other) day?" the short, Jamaican man asks, dropping and leaning toward the driver in a relaxed lean.

"You bet yo (your) sweet as (ass) it tis (is), mon (man)!" the Jamaican club owner says, spitting out a chicken bone fast when sneakily nodding to three men at the table. "Where are they? Bring them to me..., no, no..., where are you?" he asks.

"We be (are) down by the beach, mon (man), heading down the scratch (stretch), mon (man), and down by de (the) bess (base), mon (man)," he says, rocking to the low, bass thumping Jamaican music.

Ken proceeds through the intersection when the light changes and the unidentified car waits for the light and then follows at a distance.

"Don't lose dem (them)," the front seat passenger says, rocking more to the thumping music when it goes higher until turning the heads of those passing and within range.

The unidentified car pulls over by the naval base gate and parks with all eyes on the S.U.V. as it vanishes around tall barracks-like buildings.

Greg grows fidgety and begins bouncing until grabbing his crotch. "Where is your watch? I'll get it because I have to go now," he says, quickly slinging the door open and running around to the passenger side.

"It's in the nightstand." Barry gets out and climbs back inside, seeing how fast Greg is running.

The Command Center's admiral exits his tent, walking along a short stretch of the winding road until veering off in the woods. He looks down in deep thought and then returns to where his aviator backpack lies against a tree. He reaches down, strapping into it, then secures it around his legs, chest, and waist. He paces for minutes, then looks down at a piece of handheld electronic equipment. He drifts into a daze until breaking his concentration while staring at the phone application counter and his watch.

The sun soon sets and immediately, three lights appear from a distance over the horizon until breaking off to 12 lights.

The field lights up with swaying, bright, white lights with four helicopters hovering overhead for over twenty minutes while the Sailors pack out and neatly stack their gear.

The admiral reaches for his firearm at his side, bringing up a flare gun. He shoots one flare straight up, causing the helicopters to vector off, come into formation and then make their approach and land slowly.

Two junior officers jump from the front helicopter, giving orders.

The ground team lead quickly manages the on-load and then walk a few feet away, smoking cigars with other pilots. Their eyes stay glued on the four helicopters, three fully manned by now, and the fourth they run to when motioned by the lead pilot. They run in full stride and instantly stop, sliding a few feet in the dirt, creating a plume of dust, which rises high when spotting the admiral.

The admiral walks up to the fourth helicopter, and the pilot climbs out with the admiral climbing into the main seat.

The pilot runs off, waving when rushing to another helicopter and squeezing inside.

The two other junior officers look at each other nervously when stepping off slowly and sadly dragging their feet. They continue advancing but slower, with eyes pierced on the other helicopters as they lift off simultaneously.

The taller junior officer kicks up more dirt when looking at the playful admiral, frowning.

"Man up, boys!" the admiral screams, smiling and laughing while twisting his long, waxed mustache before slicking his hair back and putting on his headset. The admiral looks back, checking that the doors shut when lifting off slow, rising high and straight up. He soon advances, closely following in a tight formation for minutes until they reach a high cruise altitude when the admiral keys up the transmitter, transmitting and without warning he banks hard, dipping nose first and so hard that it looks like the helicopter is heading straight for the water.

The two officer's eyes buck, and they scream while the admiral keeps a stern face, still biting down hard on his Cuban cigar.

The water closes fast, and the admiral pulls up at the last minute, with a light mist of trailing overspray, sporadically banking left and right a few times while heading further out to sea.

The two men continue screaming, eye to eye, with wide eyes until the helicopter finally levels out and begins slowing.

The admiral smiles hard, making a few more crazy and dangerous maneuvers, which leaves even him with raised eyebrows and an exceedingly concerned stare.

For minutes, the two officers continue screaming in terror with tears flowing with each deadly maneuver.

The admiral makes a quick, sharp circle, then a slight roll, causing the helicopter to spin out of control when the two officers scream even louder in terror with more tears.

The engine sputters a few times and then blows out a thick plume of black smoke.

The two officers' eyes buck, screaming louder as the helicopter fills with thicker smoke. Their voices go higher, embracing and holding on to each other for dear life, continually begging the admiral to stop the dangerous maneuvers, but he only laughs and begins leveling the helicopter out.

The admiral stays in uncontrollable tears of laughter while remaining level then decreases speed with the helicopter losing control while lighting his cigar until quickly grabbing the controls and steadying again. "Hey!" the admiral screams, looking back over his shoulder with wide, exciting eyes. "Do you remember that training film and the maneuver they said never to perform because it could cause a stall out? Well..., here goes!" he screams over the loud engine, biting down on his cigar when going into a nosedive and performing the most dangerous and highly, un-recommended flip, which stalls the engine with the dash flashing red, then blinking out, until the engine finally comes back online with white flicking lights. He levels out again, looking back and trying to calm them with challenging, manly talk. "Suck it up! Suck it up! Suck up!" he screams, almost choking from laughing so hard. His smile turns into a firm stare when doing another unauthorized maneuver that looks like sudden death when the officers reach for the plastic bags, dispensing and pulling when puking.

Back on land, the Jamaican goons patiently wait and provide updated information to the Jamaican club owner when another two-man team of Jamaicans dispatches from the club. The other cars speed through the city, heading for the main stretch leading to the naval base.

The Jamaican club owner anxiously looks ahead until going in deep thought when calling the driver near the base then the others, instructing them to meet at Dead Man's Bluff, an hour outside of town.

Back on base, Barry grows impatient until anxiously patting his feet while staring at the building, and so does Ken.

"What is taking him so long?" Ken asks, looking at the dashboard clock.

"What?" Alfred says. "Oh..., you think he had to do a number one? Uh uh..., the knock-knees fast sprint is indubitably a number two, dude. You might as well hold your horses because he'll be a minute." Alfred cuts his eyes down by the berthed ships and then the gate.

"I think I might have packed my wallet." Ken feels his back pocket and then jumps out.

Barry gets out as well to get something and then climbs back inside.

The three sit talking, and before long, they find Greg running out fast.

Barry eyes him until reaching for his watch through the window, staring at it to find that it's precisely 5 p.m. when looking at the dash, comparing times.

Greg slams the door, and out of nowhere comes the loud sound of a hard slap, then continuous hard slapping, and then harder slaps when Ken and Barry look back, finding Greg's left hand beating hard and fast on the back of the seat with the right pointing out the window.

Alfred turns, staring at Greg's open mouth, then turns, looking in the direction his finger again. "Go! Go! Go! Go! Go!" Alfred finally screams.

Everyone's heads turn toward the building.

Ken's eyes bulge fighting to get the keys in the ignition.

"Aii...! Aii...! Aii...! they all scream with a mixture of death defying cries, at the top of their lungs, sounding like a bunch of girls, watching the C.O. and Admiral closing in fast with a long charged fire hose.

The four go to deeper screams with eyes wide with Barry's hand slamming into Ken's knee.

The truck rocks hard until Ken steps into the gas several times in park, until finally throwing it into drive and flooring it. The windows slowly rise, and a flood of water shoots forward, soaking them while the S.U.V. skids, swerves, and speeds out of control through the parking lot until Ken gains control.

"Damn!" Barry screams, wiping his face and slicking back his wet hair.

The Jamaicans spot the high-speed S.U.V. coming through the gate, and the passenger reports their movement, motioning the driver to pull away and tail them as they pass.

The admiral conducts a couple more evasive maneuvers back in the air and then comes close along the long stretch of the open road. He begins checking the land surveillance radar on the instruments and then thinks deeply about the excessively high-speed movement of four land targets on the radar, which seem to be racing toward what looks like the same point based on motion indicators leads. He cautiously makes more maneuvers manipulating the controls on the screen until placing the camera in infrared mode and registering the types of guns and weapons on board the vehicles when maneuvering closer. He comes even closer until noticing Barry's S.U.V., when dropping back and confirming personalized tags.

Barry's application flashes and sounds off. "This is Alpha One…, Alpha, standing by for repayment, over!"

Barry turns down the radio, hearing the low transmission. "Sir, what are you up to?" Barry asks, chuckling.

"Oh, nothing…, but hey, do you remember when you asked why I didn't take out that target…, the big dude who beat…," the admiral says in a broken transmission.

Barry screams in laughter, cutting his eyes around. "Hey, hey, hey!" Barry screams, quickly fumbling to come off the speaker. "Hello! Yeah, but what does that have to do with anything?" Barry expressly cuts his eyes around to see if the others made out the admiral's last comment eluding to Bruno's beat down.

"Oh, nothing…, it's just that you have a bogey on your six o'clock, with a full load: A.K.s and M-60s, over." The admiral checks a few gauges, tapping the instrument's faces.

"Nobody turns around!" Barry screams with eyes floating in the side view mirror.

Ken lifts high, instantly catching sight of a car's dim headlights at a distance.

"Based on my surveillance, there are possibly two more bogeys at your one o'clock and two o'clock, but I'm going to swing ahead and check it out…, Alpha One, out!" The admiral nods for the least-junior officer to come up front when slightly banking over the ocean and hugging the coastline tight.

Ken increases speed, and the car falls in behind them and then drops back a little.

"This is Alpha One Alpha with confirmation of two more bogeys, fully loaded with the same armor, plus handguns over." The admiral flies higher until going into a cloud and out of sight. He vectors, coming up behind the last car, but at a distance to align the helicopter high over the highway, then advances fast, passing them undetected.

Barry eyes float upward, spotting the helicopter's bright red taillight, almost invisible to the naked eye just before it fades. "Roger, sir, what do you propose?" Barry presses his phone tighter to his ear, gazing at bright white car lights through the side mirror again.

"Continue your present heading. I see an open land field ahead where you may be able to maneuver, but you should be ready for a crazy ride. I want you to act calm because if you respond too early, they may set up a roadblock." The admiral rechecks coordinates.

Twenty quiet minutes pass.

"This is Alpha One Alpha, no movement in or outside the cars ahead, so you're good! You're passing the first bogey in three, two, one!" the admiral says when the four look off, spotting the other car and finding the car's park lights activated with heads slouched.

Ken slightly lifts, spotting the second car pulling out and dropping back.

Ten more minutes pass.

"This is Alpha One Alpha; there's no movement in the car or outside, so you're good! You're passing the bogey in three, two, one!" the admiral says when Barry and the guys cut their eyes to the right, finding the last parked car with the lights off.

Ken slightly lifts, spotting the last car's lights come on when pulling out and dropping back. His eyes stay on the headlights through the side mirror, accidentally swerving across the yellow lines a few times, with Barry finally noticing.

"Ken, keep your eyes on the road, and I'll cover surveillance." Barry yells, adjusting the side mirror, spotting the last car flashing its headlights three times.

The third car pulls up close on the second and the second on the first when the third with the Jamaican club owner cut out of formation then dips in fast when coming in a curve with a fast approaching car, heavily blowing.

The Jamaican club owner cuts out of formation two or three more times, cussing at increased traffic until coming in view of miles of the highway ahead when dipping out, flooring it, and taking the lead with the four men inside anxiously locking and loading.

Barry's hand begins nervously tapping on the dash. "Come on…, come on…, come on!" Barry nervously whispers in anticipation of the admiral's following command when the helicopter strikes out ahead and vanishes, but Barry still sees the flashing bleak taillight that quickly vanishes.

Minutes pass in silence, so Barry switches back to speaker.

"This is Alpha One-Alpha! Maintain speed, watch solid yellow lines on the passenger side, and then cut through the broken lines. I repeat; watch solid yellow lines on the passenger side and cut through the broken lines. I will call the non-delayed, non-questionable maneuvers after your turn…, over!"

"Roger, sir," Barry nervously says, watching the lines closely, then as far ahead as humanly possible. "What that means is immediately execute, and he will be our eyes," Barry says, looking over and into Ken's bucked eyes.

Ken's eyes stay pierced on the lines, and so does Alfred's and Greg's, slowly until they are excitedly leaning forward when coming up on Plank Walk Road when spotting the rear car coming fast as if to ram them.

The admiral keys up the mic, and all their eyes buck but stay glued to the pavement striping. "Three…, two…, one!" the admiral screams.

"Here, here, here!" Barry screams, being the first to see the line as they close in fast.

Ken cuts the wheel hard, flying through the wide, rocky driveway, which turns into a coca plant field.

"Damn mon (man)! Damn!" The Jamaican owner screams, seeing the S.U.V. make the sharp, sudden turn, with lights immediately vanishing.

Everyone in the S.U.V. screams at the top of their healthy lungs, expressly plowing through larger coca leaves.

The first gang member's car slows then quickly turns, barely making the turn, but a second turn too early, flipping over in the deep trench.

Everyone's vision in the S.U.V. becomes blind by large coca leaves that continually beat heavily upon the hood, sides, and windshield.

Alfred and Greg's heads come slightly out the window until they jump back when slapped in the face with thicker leaves, which instantly turn their faces dark brown and spooky looking when opening bright white eyes.

Barry quickly focuses on the tall oak tree at a distance, safely navigating Ken while awaiting further instructions.

The two Jamaican chase cars blindly run over the coca field, cutting down miles of beautiful plants.

"This is Alpha One Alpha! Remain twenty feet to the right of the oak when you pass, and come up to max speed," he says anxiously.

The other two cars increase speed seeing taillights but lose sight when Ken flips off the light switch, going dark while navigating by the bright moonlight.

The S.U.V. continues barreling through at seventy miles per hour, up to eighty and ninety, with the tree appearing to grow tall and fast in a decline then incline.

The rear Jamaican car keeps straight, then veers off, coming upon a very steep hill when airborne and flying through the air, hitting low-hanging tree branches until slamming to the ground in a nosedive, breaking up the frame.

Barry's eyes stay full of excitement when noticing another main road. "Here…, here, here…, hug the tree by twenty feet! You have to make this sharp turn here…, here…, here!" Barry anxiously screams, pointing as the S.U.V. comes about so fast that the tires ride inches from the edge of the three-hundred-foot steep and rocky waterfall.

The last car continues, closing in on a moonlight reflection of the S.U.V. in a low cut area before the S.U.V. fades in taller leaves, when automatic shots rings out.

The Jamaican in the front seat leans out quick to aim and his faces instantly turn brown and spooky with bright white eyes when dropping down, eye to eye with the screaming driver when both start screaming.

The car goes faster until, at more than ninety miles per hour, when coming upon a slight hill, shooting ten feet upward in the air. The four Jamaicans continuously scream while the car descends fast and into the five-foot-deep reservoir.

"This is Alpha One Alpha, come twenty degrees, right…, now, now, now!" the admiral screams, watching the S.U.V. continually scale the edge of a deep canyon wall by feet.

The tires begin heavily wobbling over small stones and the edges of boulder.

Ken holds the trembling wheel tight with eyes piercing through tall weeds until he straightens the wheel as the dirt road comes into view. He immediately increases speed, coming up on the main road where he stops, looking back when easing onto the road, and making a quick turn. He drives about fifty feet and slows down while the four sit in fear, staring at heavy yellow gear and construction equipment so far down in the canyon that the gear looks like half-inch toys.

The Jamaican club owner comes to, shaking the others when climbing out pissy, drunk, and pissed off. He looks around over the low-cut field, spotting the S.U.V. as it makes its way up to the steep secondary highway.

In the air, the admiral keys up his headset. "This is Alpha One Alpha, debt-free and returning to base. You take good care, son," the admiral says, banking hard. He vectors away, rising high and fast as if piloting a supersonic jet and the two officers' eyes lock, instantly screaming.

The officers begin uselessly begging and pleading for their lives again.

The admiral reaches the highest yet safest altitude and begins flying normally for a while, then jerks the helicopter to one side when filling his smoke-generated pipe and pulling on it hard a few times, blowing hard until the men slightly fade unbuckling in fear of an emergency evacuation.

The two officers stay in tears, barely hugging tightly until nervously staring at the admiral for seconds as he slows, putting the helicopter in a hover while waiting for them to calm down. He pulls his phone out, quickly punching in a few numbers until a ringtone chime when advancing forward and at a moderate pace then hovering again. He cuts his eyes over at the two and rises higher, then higher, still in a hover, when expressly pointing out the passenger side window.

The two pilot's eyes instantly go to where he is pointing until squinting for seconds.

"Are those missiles down there?" The admiral says, quietly peeping when secretly unbuckling.

The men find something twinkling and soon keep their eyes on the tiny land lights, which look like specks, until their eyes drift over at the big, bright, beautiful moon with which they seem parallel.

"I don't see anything; maybe we're too high! Why not take your time and go closer, sir?" the officer in the back calmly yells over the high-pitched rotary blades.

"There! There!" the admiral screams, rechecking his application, with one crystal floating to the center of the screen. "Slide the freakin' door back and look, you moron!"

The door clicks, slowly rolling open, and a brisk wind blows inside.

The two officers sit bent over, looking for seconds, when a stronger wind blows, when the admiral's door flies open. All of a sudden, the helicopter banks hard, heading downward, nose-first.

The copilot's eyes shoot toward the admiral's seat, finding his hands releasing the door as the word 'Sortie' loudly roars and quickly fades.

The two pilot's eyes buck with hair standing straight up as they fight to get to the seat and controls while continually thrown around.

The admiral freefalls until doing some fancy move looking like moon walking then doing the robot dance when repositioning and going head first when his arms come to his side, falling like a human missile. He stares down into the clouds, fading into them for minutes until the ground barely comes into view. He begins making more fancy moves until seeing the ground clearer when pulling at the release with the parachute finally deploying.

Near the ground, the admiral floats along the two-lane highway, constantly adjusting and compensating his movement until gliding into the front seat of a convertible, which slows as his feet hit the headrest then slam to the floor.

High above, the pilots continue in deep screams and chaos while the helicopter plummets to earth like a flashing red meteor.

One officer fall into the second seat headfirst to the floor, continually trying to sit up until he's finally successful. He quickly straps in, and finally gets control with the helicopter barely skimming the water; when the pilot vectors, and they feverishly scream, eye-to eye until bursting into crazy laughs, giving high fives.

The admiral's wife slows, pulling over and stopping when joyfully clapping and watching him retrieve the parachute and remove his goggles.

The admiral leans, embracing and kissing her until she eases back in a smile, watching him wrap up his gear, growing overly excited and straining when laughing until slipping a loud, long fart.

The admiral freezes, looking over the dark field. "Hmm..., that's strange! I didn't know they had reindeer out here!" He says, looking deeper into the field until squinting, then looking back at her with a serious stare.

His wife goes into silent tears of laughter, quickly straightening her face each time he curiously looks back at her.

In Port Copan Retaunas, Jenn swings by, picking up four tickets for the comedy show, and then picks up Erica from her home.

They go out for a lovely dinner and then bar but arrive at the show late because the drawbridge locks in the open position. Jenn and Erica arrive about half an hour later, finding the place packed, but an usher helps them find their seats up front.

The show is in intermission, so there are quite a few empty seats, with the concession stand lines continually growing.

Jenn and Erica ease into the plush seats, unwinding, then look up, finding a handsome server smiling when calling him over for drink refills.

The jazz music fades in minutes later, and the mellow volume rises.

More people pour in from the concession, and voices rise to a dull roar until the place is almost packed and loud.

The jazz soon fades, and a dope beat rises.

The crowd screams in a continual yet crazy uproar and a third of the people ease from their seats, dancing or begin moving to the beat in their seats.

The track fades into a new beat, and more people jump up, dancing.

A few folks hold their liquor glasses high with cheerful laughter.

The beat soon fades into another unheard-of beat, which sounds even tighter when cheers and whistles grow louder when even more, people stand, dancing.

"Alright now..., yawl (you all) is working it, out there!" the D.J. yells, pointing to an old woman dancing fast, when going to the ground, then coming back up even faster.

The old woman blows a kiss while patting her butt and screaming the D.J.'s name.

"Yawl (you all) ready to get this show back on the road?" the producer screams, suddenly appearing from behind towering, plush, blue curtains. Without warning, he breaks out in some crazy dance and then into another dance, making the crowd go wild. He instantly flicks his wrist, and the music stops. "Welcome back, folks! Now..., coming to the stage next is Jeff Tallento, so I'll present the main attraction without further delay!"

The crowd cheers louder, and people whistle and clap harder.

The D.J. cranks the volume to another familiar beat that Jeff has preselected.

"Up next, a fellow out of Greene County, North Carolina, by way of Shreveport, Louisiana!" he says with the microphone close to his mouth when pointing to the slow—rising curtain. "Give it up for Jeff Tallentooooo!" he screams, dragging Jeff's name out like a professional bowing announcer.

The crowd grows even louder until screams quickly taper off to a moderate roar.

The producer turns, walking a few feet when hugging the comedian and passing the microphone with the audience cheering louder.

"Good evening, Port Copan Retaunas!" Jeff yells, turning and waving to the D.J.

Instantly, a new beat blares from the huge, floor model quality speakers.

Most folks hold their drinks high or put them down and dance while Jeff watches, pointing and cracking up.

Jenn and Erica dance for minutes until falling back in their seats, laughing so hard that they can hardly sit up straight while tears are continually dripping.

The music plays until Jeff signals, bursting into a ridiculous laugh when motioning for everyone to settle down.

Erica continually turns, looking for Barry, and then waits until Jenn turns away to check her phone.

"Man, I see some beautiful people out there!" Jeff says, looking at the same old woman with the cane who was patting her butt, continually patting her butt again as if she's a horse jockey. Jeff points to her, giggling like crazy when motioning to the camera and light men over while the woman is still in her own little world, not realizing the spotlight is on her.

Seconds later, someone next to the old lady gets her attention, pointing her to Jeff, and the old woman finally gets notions when turning, sticking up a middle finger until walking back to her seat, flopping down, pissed.

Jeff shakes his head in disbelief. "Damn, speaking of straight gangster, somebody better check and make sure she ain't packing!" Jeff says, giggling. "Hey..., you alright, little mama?" He bends, giggling when the camera zooms in on the old woman, and bringing her onto the big screen when the other camera switches back on him.

People stay in tears, watching the old woman's soon playful gestures.

Jeff bursts out in a loud laugh each time the woman smiles, waving him off, and then leans forward in a drunken laugh. He comes back on his heels, making a full turn, and then heads back to the front edge of the stage, smiling.

The people sound off with loud applauses.

Erica soon turns, looking for Barry, and then secretly rechecks her phone with attentive eyes on Jenn.

Jeff motions the audience to take their seats, pacing a few more times and eagerly looking over the females in the front rows, but Jenn and Erica look away when he looks at them, fearing he may call them up.

Folks burst out in laughter, and more of the crowd goes wild.

Erica turns again, looking for Barry, then secretly rechecks her phone with attentive eyes on Jenn.

Another drunk woman jumps up, dancing until into a crazy, sexual-looking dance when freezing and licking fingers, touching her breast, her private, and her butt.

Jeff points to the woman, and she bursts into a crazy laugh, shaking her head and breaking out in another weird dance, adding more moves to her sexual steps that elude to sex.

The woman's husband soon jumps up, hysterically pacing and continually hitting himself in the chest as if he's going to snatch her up. He stops as if in deep thought, talking to himself when slowly turning, then returning to his seat.

Jeff points to him as well, bursting into a silly laugh. "Oh yeah..., Yawl (you all) see that? He thought long and hard on whether he wanted to step to her or not, huh? Well, let me tell you..., he knows two things: he's either gone (going to) get beat down or she gone (going to) try and break him off with those moves when they in bed tonight!" Jeff playfully says.

The crowd cheers, screaming almost twice as loud as the first time, and a few folks laugh so hard that they lean into one another.

The woman's face transforms from a smile to a serious stare and then a fake smile when staring at Jeff, winking when the husband springs up, swinging at the air a few times.

Jeff bends in tears. "See, it's a proven point that some men can't handle their liquor! If you can't handle it, then mix it with a little water, or you women need to do it when your man ain't watching, so he's not out here in public acting like a clown!" he says, pointing to the man settling down and finding his wife staggering over.

Folks burst into a burst of great laughter.

"Ok, Port Copan Retaunas! Are yawl (you all) ready for some fun out there?"

Yells echo throughout the building.

Jeff motions the D.J. to hit a beat, to get people in the mood, again then breaks out in another crazy dance and the crowd grows louder and crazier than ever.

Erica turns again, looking for Barry, and then rechecks her phone when Jenn's not watching.

"Uh, uh, uh!" Jenn says, finally catching her. "Girl, why do you worry about Barry's sorry ass? Both of them know what time to be here."

"Sorry?" she says, rolling her eyes. You may call your man sorry, but not my babe!" Erica says with attitude.

"Alright! Let's get this thang started right!" Jeff yells, dancing to the mellow music.

"We love you, Jeff!" two women scream.

"Aw! See…, I love you too," country talking Jeff says, pretending to be wiping tears when putting a hand over his eyebrows, blocking the bright stage lights. Jeff pierces his eyes through a semi-smoke-filled room, finding two women waving when waving back. "Pretty little thangs too, but sixteen gets you thirty…, years, that is," he says, laughing. He walks around more, smiling, and then looks at a couple. "Hey, are you two married?"

"Why, yes…, we are," the wife proudly says, looking over at her husband, who slowly raises a hand, taking another sip from his tall glass of cold beer.

"Ok, that question was for you too, sir," Jeff says, laughing. "Look at him…, mad at the damn world for no reason, and she's happy as a lark. So let me guess, he works, and you're the lovely housewife, right?"

The wife smiles, excitedly clapping her hands.

The husband stares at Jeff with a serious face, bashfully nodding for him to move on.

"Wooo! He just gave me the serious, 'I'm going to get up from here and kick your ass if you don't move on to someone else head nod,' Jeff says, laughing. "Alright..., alright, sir, I'm not going to harp on you long because you might be a postal worker for all I know. Ssshhhiiittt (shit)..., all of a sudden, I'm at my next damn show, and you be all up in the rafters, hanging from the lights or some damn where hiding with a gun and scope, chanting, 'Let's see who's the damn funny man now,' and then pop off a couple. You see, security is tight here, but not enough for me to chance messing around with a psychopath," he says, noticing the man's government identification lanyard hanging from his neck.

The crowd bursts into laughter.

"Sir, I see your badge, so I know you're a hardworking man, so I ain't even hating. I know it's hard being on a single income, and those creditors won't give you a break, even with all of the sea-castration or however they pronounce it going on," he says, bursting into tears when the crowd bursts into deeper laughter. "I just hope you and every other hard worker out there can make it during these hard times. The only thing I can say to any of you is if you want it like in the past, and before all this nonsense, go back to the drawing board and bring that good ole' religion back into your homes, schools, and many churches.

Look at history, and you'll see this country's mistakes. The American economy didn't go south until we let our so-called world leaders push prayer out of the school and anywhere else they could find it. The lead advocate for that movement was consumed by the devil and is where now..., and left here how? It was not a pretty sight; I can tell yah (you)! Sounds like the same evil spirit that crept into Jezebel.

Now the world is in an uproar, and the simple solution is to turn back to that ooolllllddd (old)-time religion," he playfully says. "Times are going to get tight, people. If you think creditors were bad back then, you just wait. Shucks..., I get nervous every time a bill comes to my house. Creditors now a day send those damn T.A.B.s to your house. And for those who don't know what a T.A.B. is, it stands for - Thick-Ass Bills."

The crowd bursts into laughter.

"Damn, bills be so thick that I don't know whether I should use it for a coaster, paper to balance out an uneven chair, paperweight, to roll it and smoke it, or what?"

The crowd bursts into laughter.

"Man, soon as that T.A.B. comes…, let me tell you…, I sit that thing on the counter, walk around it a few times, stare at it, and watch it for days," he giggles.

The crowd bursts into a deeper laughter.

"Sometimes it's so big that I really do use it for a paperweight."

The crowd bursts into laughter.

"Come on now, you know good and damn well that when that bill is that thick, they done (have) added some illegal money to it…, and if you ask me, I think they charge by the weight," he says. "Check it the next time you get one…, I bet they got some crazy tax on the weight under some fancy tax name or code. Shucks, got me fussing and cussing at my family before I even open the damn thing!"

The crowd bursts into a burst of great laughter, watching closely and listening.

"With the high bills that we have to pay for anything these days, I'm surprised that optometrists even charge for eye dilations because your eyes dilate on their damn own when you get that T.A.B."

The crowd bursts into laughter.

"Don't get me started! An let me tell you about these alarms companies…, yeah, the ones listed on the Better Business Bureau (B.B.B.) site and plenty of complaint sites and are still in business. Ah…, wwwhhhaaatttt (what)!" he drags the word out for fun. "I'm just saying…, you might want to start checking these people because they're thirsty for money since the pandemic have a lot of folks giving up their luxury. I had to cancel my last carrier two times, and they're still sending me bills, talking about I can't cancel. Well…, biiaaattcchhh (bitch)…, I just did! And let me tell you what burns my tail…, the alarm system goes off, and they give me a call back…, for what? The damn intruder up in your crib (house) tearing your teeth out of your damn head, bludgeoning you to death, and all you get is a vox mail, telling you that your alarm has been activated. Anyway, you call them back, and they say…, oh, you did not pick up…, what the…! I'm just saying…, you pay for quality, then make sure you get damn quality!" He laughs.

The crowd bursts into laughter.

"Then you have the medicine, people! I mean…, come on, people, who in the hell put this team of people together? Have you seen the fine print on medicine bottles these days? Daaaayyyummm (Damn)! You need a damn telescope to read the fine print! To read that mess, you need to be better than 20-20."

The crowd screams in laughter.

"Obviously, they're in bed with big government in an effort to run up medical costs."

The crowd bursts into laughter.

"And have you seen this other stuff on the market they advertise? What do they call it…, uh, uh, uh, clinical trial size or some test or something released without government approval or prematurely released. Shitttt! You can't win for losing," he says in laughter. "Stuff on the television one week as being the best thing since sliced bread, and the next week it's recalled with a thousand and one side effects" He shakes his head and smiles.

The crowd bursts into laughter.

"Check this" 'Now, I was at granny's the other day. Now, mind you, she's already gone through ten levels of thickness, so yeah…, she has the real McCoy in coke-bottle glasses.'

The crowd bursts into crazy laughter, watching and listening.

'I'm talking about the level of thickness that when we take her outside, we have to keep her moving because if we don't, she will start a damn forest fire in a heartbeat from staring at the ground too long,' he says, giggling.

The crowd bursts into loud laughter, watching closely and listening.

"Yeah, ten levels, and she still can't read that fine print. These medicine people are gone (going to) mess around and kill a few people with the fine print because someone is going to take too much or too little," he says, smiling when walking to the far side.

'Well, let me get back to Granny…; so we're sitting there talking, and I noticed that she keeps leaning to one side, cutting one; and look, I'm not talking about just one, but several of those silent and deadly monsters, and back to back, too,' he says, giggling when laughter breaks out. "Come on now; it's Granny, so you want to be nice, so I sit there, sucking it up. I mean…, I'm holding my breath for as long as I can, breathing in slow, with tears running and I'm damn near going deaf."

The crowd bursts into a peal of loud laughter, watching and listening.

'Well, that wasn't enough because Granny cuts more and then has the nerve to ask if I could go in the kitchen and cut off the eggs boiling on the stove.'

Folks burst into laughter.

"Come on, people, I don't know why we don't just call people on things when they happen and call a spade a what?…, a spade!" he says, laughing. 'Now you know as well as I know that there was not a damn egg on that stove, or I would have smelled eggs in the hallway, but as I said, it's Granny, so you got to play along.'

The crowd screams in laughter.

'Well, anyway, I come back into the living room and fall back into the hallway, and I mean literally, folks,' he says, wiping tears.

The crowd bursts into a burst of loud laughter, watching and listening.

'Well, I peep back at her, and I know for sho (sure) that I saw her shoulders going up and down for a second. Well, anyway, I turned and slammed my feet to the floor so she could hear me when I ran toward the bathroom. Aight…, aight (alright)…, to be honest, I went in the room and messed around for a few minutes and then came back out like I was in the bathroom because for sho (sure), it was going take a long time for ventilation,' he says, giggling.

The crowd bursts into a peal of loud laughter, watching and listening.

'Well, anyway, I walk out about twenty minutes later, and she's over there nodding, so I try to sneak out, but she sits up and starts talking about a pill bottle that she can't read. Well, anyways, I reach for the bottle and try reading a few of the words, and before long, I get a serious migraine, but manage to read through it and then ask about her symptoms.'

The crowd bursts into a peal of loud laughter, watching his facial expression.

'She looks at me with a deeply concerned look, and I'll never forget when she says…, well, I've been sitting here farting without any warning or symptoms. I had the lady next door, ah, ah, ah…, Mrs.

Suzie, read the directions, and when she got down to the symptoms, I sat up and got really interested,' Jeff says that his granny said, smiling.

'Well, let me tell you...,' Jeff says, in a snicker. 'Now, when I read it, these pills carried everything you can think of in reference to side effects; I mean red eyes, night sweats, vomiting, nausea, chills, cramps, sore throat, swollen throat, runny nose, heart problems, liver problems, kidney problems, and even death," he says when laughter roars. "Now, let me tell you..., you had to have been there to see the real expression when she rose up and looked at me. She stared into my eyes and said, 'Well, I'll be damn, I'll be better off cutting these (hea) here farts because they can't be that bad. Hell..., you talked right through them, and you only shed a few tears.' He bursts into great laughter.

The crowd bursts into a burst of loud laughter, watching and listening.

Jeff goes on to other jokes until half an hour is left in the show.

Next, the producer brings another comedian out who is boring as all get up, so Jenn and Erica leave.

Erica and Jenn drive by a club on the way home, finding the parking lot packed, so Jenn talks Erica into stopping in for a few, just to cheer her up.

As soon as Jenn gets inside, she pulls the first handsome man she sees to the dance floor, turning and backing into him, then keeps right on backing into him, getting him so excited.

The man instantly goes cheerful but acts strange, though he does have fun grinding on her. He keeps his eyes pierced on the door and over his shoulder, and he's all smiles when pushing up on Jenn and even more so and feeling her backing deeper into him.

Jenn grasps his thighs, sending chills up his spine from time to time, until finally doing a spin out and turn, backing into him, then backs up further when looking back, finding him fading backward with his girlfriend still dragging him until he's off the dance floor, double-timing backwards and floating through double doors.

Another handsome-looking man walks up from behind Erica, sizing her up, and then stares at her curvy bottom. He grows mesmerized until his head remains cocked to one side for seconds until finally looking up and into her mean face.

Erica's backhand flies forward fast, slapping him silly and staggering him before he can straighten his head when knocking him into a few people.

The man continually spins, tripping forward with hands accidentally landing on the stockiest man's sister's towering chest.

Another man in the circle grabs him by his collar, shoving him to another friend, then another, until shoving him into a semicircle and setting him up for the biggest man, who is the woman's boyfriend.

The beefy dude draws back with all he has, bringing the business: a full, powerhouse uppercut when the man shoots up like a missile with the bottom of his worn-out shoes fading. He careens high then slams onto the marble floor, sliding across the dance floor with people walking away or some high-stepping and surprised.

Barry looks at the time and then calls Erica, dialing the wrong number.

Back in Port Copan Retaunas, Jenn and Erica sit, talking to two mature and older gentlemen, and before long, they're on the dance floor until after the third song.

Barry calls Erica a few times before they reach their seats, with Erica's phone barely ringing.

Erica stares at the caller I.D. "I have to take this." She throws up an index finger, walking away. "Hello! Hello, Barry?" she answers excitedly.

"Erica! Erica! Look..., we got off to a late start, but we're heading home now. I'll call when...," Barry says through interference and strange incoming ringtones.

Erica rushes into the lobby, making several unsuccessful attempts to reach him.

Barry attempts several times, but they're fifty miles from the nearest cell tower and heading away from the last tower.

Along the way, they make a few stops, and after the last stop, they have a flat when crossing over into Port Copan Retaunas' city limits around 2:23 a.m.

Barry arrives home forty-five minutes later, totally exhausted and sleepy. He drops his gear at the door, walks into his man cave, and indulges in a stiff drink. Barry eases onto the sofa, drifting deep in thought about all the things they had endured, and before he knows it, he pours another and then another. He takes one last shot, cutting off the downstairs lights, and slowly creeps upstairs in hopes of surprising Erica.

Erica remains in a deep, tipsy sleep but jumps, hearing keys accidentally fall onto the hardwood floor outside the bedroom door.

Mild, mellow jazz in the background drifts deep in her ear when she glimpses over at the indigo digital clock, reading 3:41 a.m., noticing flashes from the voice recorder.

Erica eases up groggy, realizing she's fallen into a deep sleep and missed calls. She sits, yawning, looking back at the door, and finding a shadow moving under the door. Erica rolls over, leaning toward the nightstand and reaching for the gun. Her arms stretch further until her body begins sliding forward over the satin sheet, silently falling headfirst to the floor with her mouth wide open but in total silence while quickly kicking the covers back.

Barry freezes, slowly looking back when hearing her bumbling over the floor.

Erica stands still, looking at the door again. She low-crawls to the nightstand yet still looks back, finding the decorative door handle turning downward slowly. She stands quick, accidentally spinning around on her silky gown when nervously falling to the floor but managing to keep quiet. Erica rises, sliding one hand into the drawer. She comes down in a prone position with the weapon trained, watching the shadow rocking.

Barry leans, attempting to pick up the house keys several more times, stumbling a few times while still bent over.

Erica slowly moves about the room, repositioning closer, then takes a standing prone stance when turning the gun on its side, finally realizing it's not loaded. She quickly turns back. 'Shoot…, no bullets!' She shakes her head, whispering in disgust.

Suddenly, keys jiggle when Barry steps forward twice and back in the dim hallway.

Erica rolls over by the couch, backing up yet continually peeping until the door opens slowly with mild squeaks until fully extended.

Barry's shadow heavily sways, slowly extending across the dim floor with eyes scrolling over the bed, then toward the bathroom.

"Freeze! Don't move!" Erica screams in a deep, manly, demanding, and authoritative voice. "Over near the light!" she screams, slowly easing over by the nightlight. "Well…, well…, well…, what do we have here?"

"Erica?" Barry responds, sluggishly flipping the light on and bursting into a peal of drunken laughter.

"Barry!" She drops the gun on the chair, cheerfully rushing into his arms.

"Why didn't you say something? I could have killed you!" She trembles.

Barry embraces her tighter, kissing her non-stop until his eyes roll over to the chair, finally noticing the gun does not have a clip. "Killed me, huh? With what? Your killer-sexy looks? Umm…," he says, looking into her lovely face.

"Well, get that mind of yours spinning because you better get to explaining, young man," she says, pulling away and walking over to put the gun away.

"Tomorrow, babe…, I'm whipped." He unbuttons his shirt.

Erica watches him undress and then slips out of her gown, laying it on the couch.

"How was the comedy tonight?"

"Oh, just hilarious." She smiles. "Jeff was good, but his new protégé was whack!"

Barry giggles, shaking his head then freezes, staring at her extremely hard when thinking to himself that she had to be the finest woman he's ever known.

Erica finally sits, rummaging through the nightstand until closing the drawer.

They climb into bed almost simultaneously, with Barry lying back on pillows.

"Is this what you want?" she asks, playfully moving his hand toward her firm breast.

"Babe…, I can barely keep my eyes open. That drive is the longest ever, not to mention the frequent stops and the flat, but hey, do you mind a rain check? How about getting me a drink?"

"Sure, I'll get it, but first, you tell me right now why you stood me up," she says, easing up and then back onto the bed, staring back at Barry mischievously when he looks into her intentionally dimmed eyes which make her look even sexier.

"Sweetie, in the morning…, please…" He slightly nods. "Oh yeah, and if you check the phone, you'll see I called and left several messages."

"Are you sure you don't want to play around for a bit? I mean…, your average time is like, what…, a minute, if that, right? I know you have a minute left in Little Barry, right?" she playfully says, still pissed. "I mean…, you do owe me since you stood me up. Sure, you can tell me about the adventure in the morning, but right now, I need you to be a true Sailor of two, if you know what I mean," she says, giggling and gently pulling his hand to wake him.

Barry hears her voice fade in when easing up, holding his hand out for the drink.

Erica playfully guides his slow opening and closing hand up then further up to her chest. "Barry!" she screams, hearing him snore as if shifting gears in a car.

Barry slowly sits with a straight face, smiling until his eyes dim and then open, finding her beside the bed when looking around for the drink and then looking back at her.

Erica turns, playfully spreading her bowlegs with one coming to the edge of the bed.

Barry grows more conscious quickly and can't help but notice her beautiful curves in the sheer, sexy material when her perfume slowly rises with eyes running over her smooth, butter-pecan, tanned complexion.

Erica slowly turns, and he sees her pretty, tan cheeks protruding from the bottom of the faint red ruffle, satin thong.

Barry instantly becomes amazed, admiring her overall beauty, which she leaves with nothing to the imagination until his drunken eyes cross and slowly close.

"Well…, well…, are you going to give me that minute, or do you plan to stand me up in bed tonight as well?" she says, not making eye contact when grabbing his hand and guiding it below her waist, deep between her soft, creamy thighs.

"Whoa, mama! Easy, babe! I'm telling ya…, I'm too tired, and my A-game is way off." He slowly withdraws, slightly covering his face with both hands in laughter.

Erica giggles for seconds. "Honey, you're straight tripping," she says, finally realizing how drunk he is when reaching for her gown and slipping into it.

Barry waves her off again and then looks down, embarrassed.

"Yeah, let me get you that drink," she says, pissed when walking out and into the guest room, where she flips on the light. She rushes into the bathroom, looking through several bottles in the medicine cabinet, pulling out a few, then a few more, until mischievously smiling. 'Yeah…, thanks, pops,' she whispers, quickly twisting the cap and pouring out three pills.

She makes her way to the kitchen, crushing the pills, and then pours Barry's drink, gently stirring the powder until it vanishes when easing into a chair in deep thought. She springs up fast, reaching into the kitchen cabinet, pulling out a bottle of Say-Alert-Always pills, crushing them as well, and putting them in the glass, gently stirring. She finds Barry in a deep snore when coming alongside the bed. "Here, babes. Mama is sorry for pressuring you, sweetie." She smiles, watching him reach for the drink.

"Yeah…, now this will help me sleep better, for sho (sure)." He downs the drink with some of the residue trickling down the side of his mouth when easing back, and before she knows it, he's sound asleep again.

Erica slips out of the silky gown, turns on the television, and watches it for about an hour but continually keeps shaking the bed until hearing his snore fade. She feels when he begins tossing and turning, so she eases up, cutting off the lights. She slips in the covers, laying on her side in all smiles, then gets up, taking off the sexy nighty. Erica slips into her big ole' period panties and flannel pajamas, climbs in bed, shaking the mattress a few more minutes, and then rolls over, finding Barry lying there with the side of his head flat on the pillow; eyes wide open, as if in a trance. His butt stays high in the air from lying on two pillows, looking like a corpse.

"Barry!" she calls out, waving a hand before his eyes. She nervously leans into him, checking his breathing, which is normal, when sliding out and getting her camera. Erica senselessly giggles until it becomes uncontrollable when taking all kinds of kinky pictures until the 32 M.B. stick is almost full. She snaps one more good shot, then covers him but leaves him on his side, and he begins slightly moving until she continually rocks the bed and eventually rocks herself to sleep.

Six hours later, Erica awakens to the bed, still rocking. She looks back in a double take and finds Barry lying on his side, moving back and forth, fast and non-stop.

Barry's eyes stay stale, but he seems to be staring at her.

Erica lies there longer, giggling until she can't take the rocking when jumping up and running for the medicine cabinet. Her eyes feverishly wander over a few bottles when reading a few more bottles until searching and reading up on the pills on the Internet. Erica exits and walks into the bedroom minutes later with a homemade counteractive concoction and sits him up, but she can't stop him from humping. She manages to get most of the medication down when he jerks a few times, moans, and instantly snores.

Later, Erica comes downstairs in tears, easing into the desk, wasting several expensive ink cartridges printing all of the hilarious shots. She finishes and eases into the couch, watching the news, which reports temperatures in the high seventies with rain. A little later, she hears happy feet running back and forth.

Barry runs longer and then cheerfully skips downstairs, intensely motivated when climbing on the couch, cuddling and kissing her. He turns to the television for seconds until about to explode when diving into the drive back, the flat, and the Jamaican encounter, leaving out anything associated with the women.

Erica tells him about her night but intentionally leaves out the nightclub and the two gentlemen.

The conversation quickly dwindles to small talk when Barry grabs the remote, flipping through a few stations, and then a few more when a grill commercial comes on.

Barry looks down at his watch. "The day is still young. Let me make a few calls and get some folks over for a B.B.Q.," he says, looking for confirmation.

Later, around 1 p.m., or so, folks begin floating in and out of the house and Barry's ex-shipmate, a D.J., shows up around 2 p.m.

Erica pulls out the menu, distributing it to various couples.

Barry and Erica are the last to leave, heading to the closest Naval base commissary to buy steaks, shrimp and meats before stopping at the base mini-mart for cases of beer and several bottles of top-shelf liquor.

Jenn stays and bakes until taking the second batch of cookies from the oven and turning, grabbing her chest when startled by a stranger eating cookies from the first batch.

"Yeah, just help your damn self! No..., no..., no..., don't even bother with asking," she says, turning her back to him when closing the oven.

"So..., where's Barry?"

"Forget that..., who the hell are you, Mr. Rude?"

"Naw..., not even, just a friend of Barry."

"Then your name must be Dick! Then again, it can't be that because Barry doesn't have any friends who are dicks," she sarcastically says when bursting into laughter.

"It's Gray..., just tell him Gray stopped by," Tommy, the drug lord's bouncer says in his heavy accent, quickly making up a fake name.

Jenn turns, mixing more cookie batter, then turns in deep thought with her mouth slowly dropping open. "Well, if you were such a friend, you'd know how to get in touch with him, now wouldn't you?" she asks with eyes still drifting back and then nervously around, not finding or hearing him. She walks out and into the living room and then looks upstairs, attentively listening. Her eyes wander nervously into the yard, then the street, finding a car pulling away when hearing another car's tires squealing lightly, not recognizing it's the neighbor's car.

Hours later, the party is in full effect.

Some folks retreat inside when it gets dark, while others remain on the dim-lit patio deck.

Around 7 p.m., an enlisted Sailor from the ship speeds down the road, heavily intoxicated. He passes a cop car sitting on a side street with parking lights on.

The officer's eyes stay peeled on the car when the cruiser's engine turns over, slowly pulling out and following the car for minutes.

The drunk blows through a red light, making a sharp right onto Barry's street, where he speeds up and pulls up in front of Barry's house.

Everyone is on the back porch or inside, playing cards, Dominos, or just hanging out.

The drunkard jumps out quickly, leaning in for his smokes and staring at the dark porch when cheerful voices rise from the back deck.

Bright, blue lights energize when the cop gives him a quarter turn on the siren with blue flashing lights lighting up the street when brakes squeal as the cruiser comes to a slow roll until skidding and speeding up fast.

The drunkard's excited eyes go over his shoulder when he quickly staggers up the steep steps.

The cruiser abruptly stops, and a cop jumps out of the passenger side, expressly dashing across the lawn. "Excuse me, sir…, I need to talk to you!" the cop yells, cautiously easing onto the first step.

The Sailor quickly turns with hands flying behind his back, furiously ringing the doorbell. He listens, soon hearing faint voices screaming for him to go around, but turns, continually laying into the buzzer.

The officer calls out to him again, easing up the steps when the Sailor's head flies over his shoulder with eyes widened as the cop slowly advances.

The Sailor suddenly feels the knob jiggle when turning, finding a female from his division peeping out.

"Sir, I just need you to come out here so we can talk," the cop says with one hand forward and the other over his gun.

"Man, I don't think so…, I ain't lost nothing out there, so I ain't going nowhere," the drunkard says, leaning deeper into the door when the cop sprints forward fast, reaching and grabbing his arm.

The drunkard screams, churning hard on the doorknob, which clicks when he spins, falling toward the dark living room.

The girl jumps, dashing for the kitchen but keeps being nosy, looking over her shoulder until the door fades into darkness.

The cop tugs on the drunk's arm until the drunk leans heavily inside with his body shaking against the door.

The cop in the car sees the commotion and quickly reaches for his radio.

The Sailor's head swivels around to the door, and he jerks heavier, filling his lungs deep when letting out the deepest convincing bark, like that of a big pit bull with deep, forceful, and continual barks with his body jerking more. The Sailor shakes the door, and his body jerks hard when the cop screams, jumping back, releasing him, and high stepping until at the edge of the porch in a high leap.

The cop hang-glides for seconds, as if in slow motion, while still screaming with his head thrown back until his boots slam into a patch of dirt, creating a high plume of dust when at top speed, sprinting for the cruiser.

Simultaneously, a huge commotion breaks out inside, especially in the kitchen, when card players scramble for the back door, finally registering the last heavy bark that shakes the house.

The group breaks chairs, dishes, and the screen door off its hinges, stomping over the deck and causing others to scramble into the yard, screaming.

The officer keeps screaming while high-stepping and not breaking his stride nor looking back with the other officer sitting with blurry eyes full of tears of laughter.

The fast-moving officer springs up high with feet coming up on the cruiser's hood, leaping on the hood, then cab, unable to stop when hitting the trunk, and stumbling to the ground walking lopsided in a circle until limping on a sprained ankle. He flips around, heavily wobbling in pain when leaping forward and jumping up, scrambling to get back on the trunk when the Sailor cracks the door, peeking and barking a few more times, but louder.

The other officer hee-haws non-stop for minutes until sounding like some strange animal with eyes glued on the trunk through the rearview until finally getting control of his laughter which instantly turns to a frown. He instantly turns, hearing the metal bending with each footstep, when jumping out with his shotgun drawn. He aims forward, covering the front of the house with slow eyes scrolling over the hood of his brand new car, dented, all to hell. "Maaaannnn (Man)..., get your scary tail off my trunk! Out here embarrassing me like this! Damn! Look what you've done! Messed around and dented up my brand new car's hood, roof, and trunk..., I'll be damn!"

The scary officer looks down then around, slowly easing off and rushing to the passenger side door, jumping inside trembling with eyes glued at and around the house.

The other officer climbs in quick, pissed. "Are you alright? Do you need a doctor?"

"Damn! He made me break my damn ankle!"

"Yeah, I better get you checked out, and we'll take care of this punk some other time," he says, writing the Sailor's tags down.

The drunk Sailor continues peeping and senselessly giggling for minutes. His eyes stay pierced on the cop car's bright headlights until the blue lights go off and the bright headlights fade off the yard while the cops back down fast, until spinning wheels.

One of Barry's other drunken male enlisted friends rushes down the hall for the bathroom door, finding it locked. He stumbles down the patio steps and rushes between two houses, where it's pitch dark, stumbling next to Barry's neighbor's house, where dim lights shine from a window when his feet begin dancing while fighting to get his zipper down.

Barry and Erica sneak away and head upstairs for a quickie.

Barry's neighbor, an older woman, peeks out the window being nosey, hearing the joyful voices then strolls over from the refrigerator to the sink, staring back at herself in the reflective window, playfully winking a few times. Her hand goes to her head, adjusting one big roller when checking the stiffness of the mud on her face. She looks back winking again and then takes another swig of her orange juice.

Barry's friend's feet settle when almost relieved. He throws his head back with his eyes closed and then slowly opens them.

Barry's neighbor sees a glare when her eyes buck, standing eye-to-eye with the man with both screaming simultaneously. She ducks, frantically running around the kitchen until dropping and pulling the phone from the table by the cord, and scrambles for it. Her little pink bunny rabbit slippers kick until one ear wears off. Her hand runs across the numbers, nervously punching and hanging up several times before correctly dialing 911 to report the Peeping Tom.

The guy finally peeps up seconds later, taking off fast but slow with baby steps limited by his pants sagging but manages to increase speed when pulling them up.

Barry and Erica stop kissing and caressing, hearing a loud car door slam.

Barry quickly turns the stereo down and sits until hearing the guy's tires squeal.

Barry and Erica rush to the window with eyes wandering over the street and down near the corner, finding bright taillights fading around the last house.

Erica walks away, and Barry continues peeping a little longer until finally turning to find Erica with her back to the mirror but in a daze.

Barry approaches and she gazes into his eyes, then stares deeper until she subconsciously loosens her belt buckle. His eyes scroll over her curvaceous body until taking a few steps back, staring into her lovely eyes, and admiring her perfect, somewhat made-up face.

Erica freezes and then seductively takes a few steps forward, taking her time and playfully swaying her hips harder with each step until senselessly giggling.

Barry's eyes roam over her blonde, silky curls and sandy black streaks.

Erica does some silly head move leaving her hair dangling about her face until slightly shaking her head and playfully smiling.

Barry looks her over, shaking his head, knowing she's a knockout and bombshell.

Erica soon breaks her concentration, smiling in a playful mood while pretending to be a supermodel. Her fingers run through her long, soft hair, bringing a handful over her shoulders yet holding it pinned up when blowing kisses and winking.

Without them noticing, the closet door slowly cracks open a few centimeters.

Tommy peeps out, mesmerized, and can't take his eyes off Erica's hot body when staring at the most beautiful woman he's ever seen. He stares for so long that he daydreams of being in the strip club, and she's the stripper dancing before him.

Erica performs a few more erotic moves, taking her out of Tommy's view, but he's still in a semi-daze when leaning too far forward, stumbling, gripping, and pulling down a handful of clothes.

Tommy clumsily tears through the thin wood grating of the closet door, falling to the floor but jumps up quickly, pulling out his gun.

Erica screams, backing deep into Barry and forcing Barry against the wall.

Barry's eyes bulge, fighting with all he has to reach for the drawer and his gun but can't get free from Erica's grip.

Tommy points the gun at them in a slight, alternating fashion.

Erica's eyes dim with eyebrows going up. "I got you, Barry! I told you, Jenn and I just handled these eight freakin' guys," she says, reaching down to her side and continually patting her waistband while looking for her purse.

Tommy's eyes quickly rove over her hot body and fast patting hands.

"Ok, now worry," she says, feeling Barry move away and toward the dresser.

"Enough of this foolishness! You, get over here!" Tommy waves the gun at Erica, who drops to the floor, leaving Barry standing and in the clear.

Barry stares at the top of her head, then looks up, and his hands come slowly up high over his head. He takes a few steps in Tommy's direction, and Tommy points and then takes several more steps back.

Erica slowly stands out of Tommy's line of fire, fixing her hair and slowly caressing her hourglass-shaped body to straighten her clothes. She softly grasps her bra's shoulder strap, gently tugging at it a few times to look pretty again.

Tommy and Barry look at her simultaneously, with eyes roving over her pretty, unblemished, soft skin.

Erica takes a few more minutes fixing herself up and then leans forward, grasping the dresser's edge, and turning to one side, realizing she has their undivided attention. She seductively sticks out one double-jointed, perfectly-curved hip and then the other mesmerizing them more.

Barry grows excited, feeling a heat wave when becoming fully erect from the pill residue. His trousers slowly stretch so far that they hear the jean material lightly yawning while everyone looks down simultaneously. The button on his trousers squeals louder until the button shoots forward, ricocheting off the walls when they duck a few times until it breaks the window, sounding a car alarm. Barry pulls his shirt out of his pants, covering himself quickly.

"Can you hear that?" Erica asks when a low tune from the D.J.'s boom box cranks back up. Her sexy body unconsciously begins snaking in a wanton Egyptian-style dance, hearing the sexy, Egyptian-style beat go higher.

Tommy's hands begin sweating, and he keeps wiping them on his pants.

Erica's hand eases deep between her thighs, and she clenches her hand tight between her thighs until her head gently eases backward and her eyes close tightly. Her glossy, well-manicured fingernails sensually work their way down to the rim of her panties when she begins stroking gently along the elastic band until slightly pulling the band from her soft flesh. She allows the elastic band to snap back against her tender flesh a few times, gently teasing them until they're in a daze with the continual foreplay driving Tommy and Barry wild.

Erica's mind feverishly wonders to what to do next when taking one last tug with the glossy index finger slipping inside the band. Her body slightly turns, and she backs against the dresser. "Umm…, umm…, umm…!" she barely whispers.

Out of nowhere, a sudden crack of thunder roars, and severe flashes of lightning startle them when the lights briefly go out and then come back on for a few minutes.

Tommy's head begins spinning when Barry and Erica continually change places each time the lights go out, but he always expressly aims at Barry repeatedly each time.

The two continually change places until the next time the lights come on, with Erica nowhere to be found, but Barry is at the end of the gun, leaning with his hand in the drawer, gripping his gun.

"Mess around and start slipping if you want, and you can say goodbye to your girl here and now!" Tommy says in a low but convincing tone when waving the gun around and anxiously looking for Erica.

Barry eases the gun down with both empty hands coming back up slowly.

Tommy peeps around, slightly bending around the dresser's edge. He turns, backing quickly to find Erica's shoes sticking out from behind the door. "Look! Enough of this silly nonsense! Get over here!" He snatches her by the collar, pulling her deep into him.

Erica winks at Barry, nervously jumping back when coming up with a quick blast of the pepper spray but accidentally spraying herself and falling into Tommy, screaming.

Tommy backs away fast, swiping his eyes when shoving her into Barry and pointing the gun at Barry, who she pushes away from when running around the room like a chicken with its head cut off.

Barry closes his eyes tightly, and his belly begins jumping until he laughs so hard inside that he thinks he'll bust his gut.

Louder thunderous thrashes come, slightly vibrating the house when everyone outside scatters inside, causing even more loud commotion.

Erica's feet continually shuffle with hands sliding over the wall, fighting to find the bathroom door.

Barry tenses, no longer able to hold in his laugh when turning from the gun, bursting out laughing but making it sound like he's crying when his eyes fill with more tears when continually looking back over his shoulder at Erica.

Erica rips the sheer curtains back fast, screaming when fighting for the nozzle with fast-blinking eyes.

"On your knees!" Tommy screams, giggling at Barry's face changing into deeper laughter when seeing Erica frantically trying to get the water running.

Tommy holds the gun on Barry with eyes wandering over to the dresser when lifting a pair of Erica's panties and pulling them to his face before hesitantly setting them aside when finding a stack of pictures. He stares at them for seconds then curiously lifts the bundle, flipping the first one over when a loud, thunderous, crazy laugh comes from out of nowhere. Tommy immediately goes into tears, pressing his back against the wall until high-stepping in a peel of teary-eyed laughter.

Barry stops laughing, looks over at him, and becomes more curious.

"You are a real freak, dude!" Tommy giggles harder.

Erica's stomach begins uncontrollably jiggling when cutting her blinking eyes back, finding the pictures in Tommy's hand. She tries holding her laugh when bursting into great laughter but tries to make it sound like a cry.

The soothing sound of rain comes, instantly picking up its momentum.

Barry sits in the corner, distracted when turning his head left to right, trying not to burst into a loud cry of laughter when seeing Erica's feet and thinking back on her running around like she's crazy.

Erica soon gets ahold of herself and sits with a frown, and her head cocked, trying to make out if Barry is actually laughing or crying. She soon gets the water on and takes a deep breath of relief as water soothes her burning eyes and her vision slowly returns. She slowly rises, looking around for something to use as a weapon. Her eyes drift over various bottles of medicine used in making her concoction for Barry while giggling. She makes eye contact with Barry, noticing him rubbing his abs continually until slightly bending a few times.

A minute later, she eases into the room, looking over at Barry, finding his shoulder still jumping when slamming the door hard and walking over near him.

Barry feels her presence and keeps an eye on her through the reflection of the stainless steel coat rack, sadly faking and falling into her when she touches his shoulder. He pretends to be upset, holding her close around her legs yet giggling when pretending to cry.

"You..., on your feet! There is no more time for this! We have unfinished business and a long ride ahead of us!" Tommy says, pointing the gun at the back of Barry's head when motioning Erica out front. He grabs Barry by the back of his collar, directing him to move slowly down the steps but pulls back tight on Barry's collar when feeling him moving too fast. Tommy notices that Barry is fidgety and rubbing his belly at times when slightly bending forward, hearing channeling sounds and frowning from silent but deadly trailing farts.

Erica frowns from the hint of gas being expelled when distracted, hearing folks in the kitchen and hallway when she begins loudly begging and pleading.

The two different officers arrive for the Peeping Tom call. "Quick, hit the lights; we don't want to spook him," the cop riding shotgun says as they come up on the corner. They jump out and speak with the caller, then float around houses, then near Barry's back door, with eyes wandering at the over party-goers, carefully canvassing the area, and don't find any of the reported descriptions of the man.

One officer walks off the woman's porch again, catching movement in Barry's house through a window when spotting Tommy's handgun. He stops, carefully watching them turn, when finding his partner looking back at him. He motions for his partner to come back, and the officers converge near the car, devising a quick plan.

The short officer looks back at the house a few times and then reaches for his radio, calling in the incident and requesting backup.

The cops move toward the front porch, slowly creeping up the steps.

The tall officer reaches up, unscrewing the 100-watt bulb, and his mouth flies open, instantly dancing around fast in a soft, up-and-down motion but quietly bouncing until looking down at his partner, who is shaking his head and passing him a handkerchief.

The cop's heads come up slow, peeping through sheer curtains, seeing Erica when the three reach the bottom step, where Barry turns around, slowly facing the door.

Two girls scream, seeing Erica backing into the kitchen and pointing down the hallway.

Everyone peeps, screaming in fear, but a few males and one female drunk peep and then walk down the hallway until the living room is full of spectators.

"Ok, everyone! You can just go on back to your little party. Ole' lover boy here, and I have some unfinished business!" Tommy completely turns Barry, backing up to the door. "Just keep backing up, or there will be pea brains all over this living room."

Barry thinks long and hard until looking up, finding Ken, Greg, and Alfred, and making eye contact when Barry slightly bends forward as if in pain a few times.

Greg's drunken face lights up, finding Barry's pants bulging at the inseam.

Alfred drops his beer, and his tight fist slams into his other hand when his face grows stale.

"Hey, look! I think ole' Barry is sweet on that dude!" Drunken Greg yells out.

"Look, punk! You got some unfinished business with the RAZOR!" Alfred shouts out when Tommy jumps at him, jerks, and Alfred falls back into the crowd, staggering through the long hallway, taking folks out as if he's running for a long touchdown.

"How did you find me?" Barry whispers, looking over his shoulder.

Ken and Greg fight their drunken way through the open path, through the crowd that Alfred made, rushing for the back door.

"Your tags, numb nuts…, from the warehouse cameras?" he says, shaking his head.

They back onto the porch, and without delay, the short cop hits Tommy in the head with the Billy club, leaving him staggers around in a circle while the short officer lunges onto his arm like a pit bull, fighting to keep the gun pointing outward.

The two begin going round and round, and each time the gun points into the house, everyone ducks until it is almost like a wave effect at a game or pep rally.

The tall cop waits for his partner to make one last spin when coming down hard on both their hands with his nightstick, knocking the gun to the floor; when everyone hits the floor, even the tall cop.

The two keep running in circles shaking off the sting while screaming until Tommy leaps, diving into the flowerbed, accidentally head-butting a large memorial stone with Barry's grandmother's name engraved on it.

The short cop quickly stands, dancing around a few more times, still trying to shake off the pain, when the tall officer shuffles down the steps, grabbing stumbling Tommy by his collar and pulling him to his feet.

Barry turns, finding Erica in tears when smiling and motioning to his stomach when the gas pains mellow out.

Erica stares at him a little longer. "Barry, what the hell is this about? What did he mean by lover boy? Did you have sex with someone while you were gone?"

"What…, sex?" he says, pretending to be looking down for something.

"Yes…, S.E.X.…, sex! What part of sex are you not feeling?"

"What…, sex, with a perfect stranger?"

"Exactly! People have sex all the time and for no apparent reason," she says, staring at him until frowning with beady, confrontational eyes.

"You must be tripping for real because I don't sleep around," he says boldly and confidently.

"Sleep around? Is that your best response? And who said anything about sleeping? Man, don't play with me!"

"Well, that's just foul, isn't it?" He tries looking serious.

"Yeah, tore up from the floor up," she says.

Barry grabs her, playfully pulling her in his arms. "So, why are we having this conversation? For what? Because some guy gets the wrong house and uses a basic slang term…, player?" He puts his arms around her. "But hey, the little mace thingy? A real classic, babe," he says, laughing.

"Yeah? And so were the pictures," she says in a loud outburst when jerking away and running from him toward the stairs.

Ken throws Barry a cold one when he looks up, and everyone staggers through the hallways down through the kitchen, converging on the back porch, where the D.J. comes up with an unheard-of dope beat.

Barry goes into some crazy dance and then freezes, doing a robot-looking dance when bouncing. He makes eye contact with D.J., who looks back from time to time until looking back the last time, finding Barry bent slightly over and rubbing his stomach until rocking again when the D.J. switches to Barry's favorite song.

Suddenly, Barry motions for some to move the tables, and everyone starts in on a country line dance that leaves Barry high stepping until the last time the chorus comes with a leg thrown high when the beat halts and a loud, long and obnoxious fart comes with a delayed outburst of laughter then overwhelming funk.

Folks immediately grab their noses, scrambling from the door, and the oxygen sensor sounds off within seconds, leaving others running off.

Hope you enjoyed it!
Best wishes!
Azreay'l

www.ingramcontent.com/pod-product-compliance
Lightning Source LLC
LaVergne TN
LVHW091703070526
838199LV00050B/2262